Lecture Notes in Computer Science

Lecture Notes in Computer Science

Lecture Notes in Computer Science

Edited by G. Goos and J. Hartmanis

441

T. Ito   R.H. Halstead, Jr. (Eds.)

Parallel Lisp: Languages and Systems

US/Japan Workshop on Parallel Lisp
Sendai, Japan, June 5–8, 1989
Proceedings

Foreword by J. McCarthy

Springer-Verlag
Berlin Heidelberg New York London Paris Tokyo Hong Kong

Editors

Takayasu Ito
Department of Information Engineering
Faculty of Engineering, Tohoku University
Sendai, 980, Japan

Robert H. Halstead, Jr.
Cambridge Research Lab
Digital Equipment Corporation
1 Kendall Square, Building 700
Cambridge, MA 02139, USA

CR Subject Classification (1987): C.1.2, C.4, D.1.3, D.3–4

ISBN 3-540-52782-6 Springer-Verlag Berlin Heidelberg New York
ISBN 0-387-52782-6 Springer-Verlag New York Berlin Heidelberg

© Springer-Verlag Berlin Heidelberg 1990
Printed in Germany

Printing and binding: Druckhaus Beltz, Hemsbach/Bergstr.
2145/3140-543210 – Printed on acid-free paper

Foreword

Since computers were first invented, it has been known that serial computation has limits that can be far exceeded by using parallel computation. Even very early computers used parallelism in carrying out arithmetic operations, and improved hardware has expanded this kind of parallelism.

The first project to build a parallel computer was probably Illiac 4 proposed by the early 1960s. It was over-elaborate, the cellular automaton influenced design made it almost immune to programming, and by the time it was working, it had been over-run by the Cray I, and other ordinary serial computers with added vector facilities and pipelining.

Parallel computing poses a harsh dilemma for the system designer. The largest number of arithmetic operations per second is obtained by designs that offer very limited communication among the processors. If the problem fits such a design, it can run very fast, but for many kinds of problem, effective parallelism cannot be obtained without good communication. Designs offering the best communication, e.g. fully shared full-speed memory, cannot compute as fast as other designs and don't scale easily to very large numbers of processors. Ingenuity sometimes provides unexpected solutions, but sometimes it seems that no amount of ingenuity will substitute for shared memory.

The largest numerical computations are those involving partial differential equations. When these are replaced by difference equations in the most obvious ways, they seem to lend themselves to regular arrays of processors. However, as soon as shock waves require concentrating the computation on dynamically selected parts of space, and radiation propagates influences at the speed of light, the most obvious grids waste computation.

The idea of queue-based multiprocessing arose in the early 1960s, but support was not offered for actually implementing it. The idea is that processes can dynamically generate subprocesses that can be done in parallel, and these subtasks are put in a queue structure from which processors take tasks when they become free. On the one hand, queue based multiprocessing seems to require a shared memory, which is expensive. On the other hand, it offers straightforward ways of programming almost any kind of problem using techniques that aren't far from those used in programming for serial computers. Moreover, the programs produced don't depend on the number of processors, which can even change dynamically. The languages needed are just the usual serial languages augmented by a few constructions for declaring parallelism.

Queue-based multiprocessing is particularly well suited for symbolic computation, where the same recursive process may involve data structures of similar structure but of enormously varied size, and where the data structures are dynamically determined. Lisp can be made into a parallel language in a variety of ways without distorting its character. Moreover, many Lisp programs written for serial machines can be made to take advantage of parallelism of this kind. Putting Lisp programs on parallel machines based on the idea of a cellular automaton is problematical, and if a solution is found for a particular program, it is likely to be strongly configuration dependent.

Projects to build parallel Lisp systems in the form of compilers and interpreters for existing or announced shared memory multiprocessors began in the middle 1980s and have proceeded uneventfully. It seems to be a straightforward task whenever the necessary resources can be assembled and maintained. The initial proposals for parallel constructs were similar to each other. In fact my original idea in proposing the workshop reported in these papers was that it would be a standardization conference, and on the basis of some experience with the parallel constructs, a proposal could be made for the incorporation of parallelism into Common Lisp. Unfortunately, it seems that the field of parallel Lisp is not quite ready for standardization. I hope standardization will be pursued in a future meeting.

The present workshop is about the first in which extensive experience in actually implementing and using the parallel constructs is extensively reported. The approaches taken are adequately introduced in the Preface.

It seems to me that both queue-based multi-processing and systems with weaker communication are destined to survive and will be suitable for different kinds of application. Queue-based multi-procesing will provide general and straightforward facilities of all kinds of work, but some kinds of program will compute faster on more specialized systems.

John McCarthy

Preface

Lisp has been the most popular programming language for artificial intelligence and symbolic computing. Since the early 1980's, parallel Lisp languages and parallel execution of Lisp programs have been studied extensively in response to the needs of AI applications and progress in parallel architecture. Early parallel Lisp projects resulted in parallelized Lisp interpreters and data-flow models for parallel execution of Lisp programs. More recently, parallel Lisp systems that can execute realistic applications with "industrial-strength" performance have been developed.

Inspired by two parallel Lisp languages, Qlisp and Multilisp, parallel Lisp languages have been proposed and developed by several research groups in the United States and Japan. The U.S./Japan Workshop on Parallel Lisp, held at Tohoku University in Sendai from June 5–8, 1989, brought together many of these researchers to discuss the techniques and conceptual models underlying their research projects. Significant advances in several areas were reported, notably in high-performance parallel Lisp implementation techniques and language constructs for speculative computing. The future construct emerged as the most popular approach for introducing parallelism into Lisp programs, and several advances in defining future to be compatible with other constructs, such as continuations, were presented.

Workshop participants submitted papers describing their research projects, which were distributed at the workshop. Based on the presentations and discussions at the workshop, participants revised their manuscripts and contributed them to this book. This book is organized into two parts. Part I focuses on parallel Lisp languages and programming models and Part II focuses on parallel Lisp systems and architectures. Contributions in this book are of two kinds: full papers and extended abstracts. Many participants contributed full papers describing the research they presented at the workshop; some participants contributed extended abstracts, because the work had already been published elsewhere or for other reasons. Generally, all the contributions concern how to make parallel computation more practical in Lisp through new approaches to language semantics, system design, or implementation techniques. This preface gives a summary of the workshop activities and the content of the papers included in this book.

The first paper in Part I is by Robert Halstead. It gives an overview of current language design and implementation ideas for parallel Lisp systems, based on his experience with the Multilisp language (an extended version of Scheme) and its implementations. The paper presents three criteria for judging Scheme extensions for parallel computing: compatibility with sequential Scheme, invariance of the result when future is introduced into side-effect-free Scheme programs, and modularity. These criteria are used to evaluate proposed mechanisms for continuations, speculative computing, and exception handling. The paper also discusses several other directions for further research in improving the Multilisp language and its implementations. These research topics include data types to facilitate data-parallel computing; techniques to reduce scheduling costs and enhance locality; garbage collection; and tools to assist in the development of parallel programs.

The next paper is by Takayasu Ito and Manabu Matsui. It introduces the parallel Lisp language PaiLisp and its definition in terms of the kernel language PaiLisp-Kernel. It shows how futures, Qlisp's exclusive `qlambda` closures, and many other concepts can be defined in terms of a small set of kernel constructs. The paper also introduces a novel interpretation of continuations in a parallel language, in which invoking a continuation alters the flow of control in the task that originally captured the continuation, instead of in the invoking task.

A presentation at the workshop by Morry Katz described another way to define continuations in a parallel language. This work is represented in this book by an extended abstract by Katz and Daniel Weise and is also discussed in Halstead's paper. The full paper appears in the 1990 ACM Conference on Lisp and Functional Programming.

A paper by Randy Osborne presents an interesting model for speculative computation called the *sponsor model* and gives performance results from an implementation of this model in Multilisp. The sponsor model is a modular framework for providing more control over scheduling than is provided by standard parallel Lisp systems. This control is useful in many applications, especially those that involve search. The sponsor model can also be useful in system contexts where resources must be shared among users, or wherever a user needs control over groups of subtasks.

James Miller and Barbara Epstein write about copying garbage-collection algorithms for parallel Lisp implementations, discussing the issues crucial to achieving good performance. Their parallel garbage-collection algorithm supports speculative computation with the help of a *weak pair* construct and garbage-collection of irrelevant tasks. Their approach to speculative computation via implicit reclamation of irrelevant tasks contrasts with Osborne's sponsor model, in which irrelevant tasks are identified explicitly by program commands.

Ron Goldman, Richard Gabriel, and Carol Sexton give an overview of the Qlisp language, a parallel version of Common Lisp with "industrial-strength" performance. In addition to futures, Qlisp supports *propositional parameters* to help limit excessive process creation and a `qlambda` construct for monitor-like mutual exclusion. Qlisp also includes `kill-process` and `catch/throw` constructs for killing processes, which is useful for some forms of speculative computation. To reduce the need for programmers to address synchronization problems explicitly, the paper introduces two new mechanisms: *heavyweight futures* and *partially, multiply invoked functions*.

At the workshop, Joseph Weening presented an analytical model of the performance of *dynamic partitioning*—a technique for reducing the frequency of process creation by avoiding it when the number of available processes exceeds the number of processors. Joseph D. Pehoushek reported on a Qlisp implementation using dynamic partitioning and other methods for reducing process creation costs. Pehoushek and Weening have contributed a combined paper to this book, presenting both their experimental and analytical results; experimentally, dynamic partitioning gives performance improvements of up to a factor of 2 in the Qlisp implementation.

Robert Kessler and Mark Swanson describe Concurrent Scheme, a language for parallel programming on a distributed-memory architecture. The central and novel concept of Concurrent Scheme is the *domain*, which is an entity containing mutable data. At most one thread of execution can be active in each domain at any time. A domain thus enforces mutual exclusion on accesses to its contents in a manner similar to Qlisp's qlambda or Hoare's monitors. Though threads cannot execute concurrently in the same domain, threads can execute concurrently in separate domains. Concurrent Scheme has been prototyped on the Bolt, Beranek, and Newman GP1000 multiprocessor, but is ultimately targeted for the Hewlett-Packard Mayfly architecture.

W. Ludwell Harrison gave a workshop presentation describing techniques used in Parcel, a system for interprocedural analysis and restructuring of sequential Scheme programs for parallel execution. Good speedups have been achieved by applying his parallelizing compiler to several programs, including the Boyer benchmark. A detailed paper about his methods appears in *Lisp and Symbolic Computation 2:3/4* (1989, pp. 179–396). Zahira Ammarguellat presented her work on *control-flow normalization*— simplifying the control flow of Scheme programs to facilitate parallelizing transformations. A joint paper in this book by Harrison and Ammarguellat gives an overview and thoughtful critique of Parcel's design. It then outlines the design principles of Miprac, a successor to Parcel that extends Parcel's techniques and applies them to a broad range of procedural languages from FORTRAN to Scheme.

A presentation at the workshop by Akinori Yonezawa discussed reflection in the object-oriented concurrent language ABCL/R. More detail on this subject appears in a collection of papers edited by Yonezawa—*ABCL: An Object-Oriented Concurrent System* (MIT Press, 1990). A brief summary also appears as an extended abstract in this book.

In his presentation, Etsuya Shibayama discussed optimistic and pessimistic synchronization policies in the context of the "car washing problem." A short article in this book by Shibayama and Yonezawa gives the highlights; fuller details appear in Yonezawa's book, *ABCL: An Object-Oriented Concurrent System*.

Mario Tokoro presented *MD-based computing*, which introduces notions of "distance" and "mass" and proposes an approach that models objects as being under the influence of a computational "gravitational field." He summarizes these ideas in an article in this book.

Part II of the book, focusing on parallel Lisp systems and architectures, begins with a paper by Ikuo Takeuchi based on practical experience with TAO, a Lisp dialect that fuses the procedural, object-oriented, and logic-programming paradigms into one language. TAO runs on the ELIS Lisp machine and is in production use by many users. The paper discusses TAO's approaches to process management, sharing Lisp programs among processes and users, name-space problems associated with symbol packages, concurrent primitives, and concurrent program debugging. Most of the key primitives of TAO are implemented in ELIS microcode, leading to good performance, even in interpreted mode—even a TCP/IP network system was run under the interpreter!

A short article by Ken-ichiro Murakami describes the MacELIS multiprocessor, designed to be compatible with single-processor TAO/ELIS systems. Interprocessor communication is supported by an *in-core pseudo-network*, which uses standard network protocols to transmit messages through a shared memory.

An extended abstract by David Kranz, Robert Halstead, and Eric Mohr describes Mul-T, a parallel Lisp system with "industrial-strength" performance. Mul-T uses an optimizing compiler to generate code for an Encore Multimax multiprocessor and offers real speed-ups over good sequential implementations. Additional information about Mul-T appears in the ACM SIGPLAN '89 Conference on Programming Language Design and Implementation and in the paper by Halstead in this book.

Dan Pierson outlines the issues in integrating parallel Lisp systems with modern operating systems. He discusses the application of services provided by the Mach and Unix operating systems to the problems of process management, scheduling, and exception handling in a Qlisp-based parallel Lisp system.

Hideya Iwasaki gives a brief description of mUtilisp, a parallel dialect of Utilisp (University of Tokyo Interactive Lisp). mUtilisp programs are composed of processes that communicate by message-passing; shared objects are not supported. An implementation of mUtilisp that simulates parallelism by time-slicing is available.

A paper by Taiichi Yuasa and Takafumi Kawana describes an experimental parallel computer (the PM1) and the PMLisp language. The PM1 is built around an 8-bit microprocessor (the Z-80) and a butterfly network for interprocessor communication. It is a first prototype of a massively parallel "P-machine." PMLisp is a Scheme-like language with explicit constructs for interprocessor communication. Examples are given showing how to express a shortest-path algorithm and models of various network topologies in PMLisp.

Hiroshi Yasui, Toshikazu Sakaguchi, Kohichi Kudo, and Nobuyuki Hironishi write a short article about the EVLIS machine, a multiprocessor composed of EVAL II processors. *Regulation lists* are introduced as a mechanism for controlling the execution of parallel processes and the performance of the "List-Tarai-4" benchmark (using regulation lists) on EVLIS is analyzed. A multi-port memory system for EVLIS is also proposed as a way of increasing performance.

At the workshop, Norihisa Suzuki described the architecture of the TOP-1 multiprocessor and an ongoing project on parallel Common Lisp based on futures. A novel feature of this Lisp is that it supports the use of futures for expressions that return multiple values. Plans for the installation of a real-time garbage collector were also presented. In this book, Suzuki writes about the architecture of TOP-1 and describes parallel processing research projects that have been performed on it.

Eiichi Goto was invited to the workshop to present his work on high-speed computer architectures based on Josephson-junction computing and cyclic pipeline architectures. Such architectures should complement techniques for using parallelism to achieve high-performance symbolic computing. He gave an interesting talk based on his published article in *IEEE Transactions on Computers* (June 1989).

In addition to the formal presentations, the workshop included three discussion sessions in which the participants exchanged views on applications, benchmarks, architectures for parallel Lisp, and the relationships between parallel Lisp and parallel logic programming. The first two discussion sessions were devoted to informal discussion of language design, performance, scheduling, and architecture for parallel Lisp.

Kazunori Ueda began the final discussion session by giving an overview of the GHC guarded-Horn-clause language for parallel logic programming, developed at the Institute for New Generation Computer Technologies (ICOT). He also explained the relationship between GHC and KL1, an extension of GHC also developed at ICOT, and discussed the need for meta-level operations (reflection) in future logic-programming languages. Akikazu Takeuchi then commented on the close relationship between futures and logic variables in parallel logic languages.

Discussion then turned to the question of applications for parallel symbolic computing. Hiroshi Okuno discussed his experience in parallelizing two large AI systems—the production-system language OPS-5, and the truth-maintenance system ATMS: these programs are of the scale that should be available as benchmark programs. W. Ludwell Harrison commented on the value of the "real" programs in the set of FORTRAN benchmarks that have been collected at the University of Illinois and suggested that a similar collection of Lisp benchmarks should be created. Among the benchmarks proposed by various workshop participants were sorting, the Gabriel Lisp benchmark set, the Japan Lisp benchmark set, a symbolic algebra system such as REDUCE, N-body simulations, fast Fourier transforms, robotics, animation, and graphics. At the close of the workshop, all agreed that a standard set of realistic benchmarks for parallel symbolic computing would be very valuable in advancing parallel symbolic computing toward practical utility and making it easier to compare the merits of different approaches.

Workshop participants had several opportunities for informal discussion while absorbing Japanese culture and technology through a series of events outside of the formal agenda: two receptions, a Japanese banquet, and a day of "extracurricular activities" organized by the workshop's hosts. The day of activities included a tour of the "super-clean room" for VLSI fabrication at Tohoku University (a "Class 0.0001" clean room where the level of dust is so low as to be unmeasurable), the Golden Temple at Hiraizumi, the temples and gardens at Mohtsu-ji, picturesque Matsushima Bay, and another delicious Japanese banquet at Taritsu-an Restaurant overlooking Matsushima Bay.

The papers in this book describe advances in language design and system architecture for parallel Lisp, but few of them discuss theory or applications of realistic size. In the theoretical domain, we would like to see more work done on the semantics of parallel Lisp languages. Specifically, a sound semantic understanding of combining futures (for parallelism) and continuations (for control) would be valuable. Incorporating speculative computation into such a semantic theory is another important challenge.

Experiments with several small- and medium-sized parallel Lisp applications have been conducted (see, for example, Section 3 of Halstead's paper), but it will be very important to have experience with realistic, large-scale applications too. We hope that the availability of parallel Lisp systems with "industrial-strength" performance will enable and encourage the development of such parallel Lisp applications. It is through experience with such applications that we will learn how to make parallel Lisp systems that are effective for programming in the large as well as in the small. This in turn is a vital step to making parallel Lisp a valuable, general-purpose computing technology for a wide range of users.

The idea of holding a U.S./Japan workshop on parallel Lisp was first suggested to one of us (Ito) by John McCarthy in January, 1987. Halstead was recruited as a co-organizer later that year. Dick Gabriel was later recruited to help, and did most of the organizing work on the U.S. side; unfortunately, he was unable to attend the workshop itself. We also regret the absence from the workshop of other parallel Lisp researchers who were unable to attend, and hope to see all parallel Lisp researchers united at a future workshop.

The proposal to publish this book as part of the *Lecture Notes in Computer Science* series was made to Juris Hartmanis (and accepted) in the fall of 1989. We thank him and all of the above people for their vital role in bringing about the workshop and the publication of this book. We also thank Hans Wossner of Springer-Verlag for his assistance in this book's publication. Finally, we thank all those who helped organize, and participated in, the workshop for their invaluable contributions.

Takayasu Ito
Robert H. Halstead, Jr.
Cambridge, Massachusetts
March, 1990

Table of Contents

PART II : Parallel Lisp Systems and Architectures

PART I

Parallel Lisp

Languages and Programming Models

New Ideas in Parallel Lisp:
Language Design, Implementation, and Programming Tools

Robert H. Halstead, Jr.
Digital Equipment Corporation, Cambridge Research Lab
One Kendall Square, Bldg. 700, Cambridge, Mass. 02139
halstead@crl.dec.com

Abstract

A Lisp-based approach is attractive for parallel computing since Lisp languages and systems assume significant clerical burdens, such as storage management. Parallel Lisps thus enable programmers to focus on the new problems introduced by using concurrency. Parallel Lisps now exist that can execute realistic applications with "industrial-strength" performance, but there are applications whose requirements they do not handle elegantly. Recent work has contributed new, elegant ideas in the areas of speculative computation, continuations, exception handling, aggregate data structures, and scheduling. Using these ideas, it should be possible to build "second generation" parallel Lisp systems that are as powerful and elegantly structured as sequential Lisp systems.

This paper surveys these recent ideas and explores how they could fit together in the parallel Lisp systems of the future, examining issues at three levels: language design, implementation techniques, and programming tools. The discussion is based on the Multilisp programming language, which is Scheme (a Lisp dialect) extended with the **future** construct. The paper outlines three criteria for judging Scheme extensions for parallel computing: compatibility with sequential Scheme, invariance of the result when **future** is introduced into side-effect-free Scheme programs, and modularity. Proposed language mechanisms, such as support for first-class continuations, are evaluated against these criteria.

In the area of implementation techniques, results of experiments with lazy task creation, unfair scheduling, and parallel garbage collection are surveyed; some areas that need more investigation, such as scheduler implementation for speculative computing, and interaction between user-level and operating-system schedulers, are identified. Finally, past work in tools to help with the development of Multilisp programs is surveyed, and needs for additional tools are discussed.

1. Introduction

The goals of this paper are to inform readers about the most important current design and implementation ideas for parallel Lisp systems and to stimulate work in combining these ideas into versatile, integrated, efficient, and useful parallel programming systems. Parallel Lisps now exist that can execute realistic applications with "industrial-strength" performance [61], but the requirements of some applications are not handled elegantly. Recent work has contributed new, elegant ideas in the areas of speculative computation, continuations, exception handling, aggregate data structures, and scheduling. Using these ideas, it should be possible to build "second generation" parallel Lisp systems that are as powerful and elegantly structured as their sequential counterparts.

Parallel programming introduces new problems beyond those experienced in developing sequential programs: timing races must be guarded against, sequential bottlenecks must be avoided, and so on. The value of a good program development environment is thus even greater when developing parallel programs than in the sequential case. Lisp systems have long been known for their strong program development environments. In addition to the interactivity and debugging tools for which Lisp systems are known, the Lisp programming language and its Scheme dialect [1, 82, 85] provide run-time services, such as garbage collection and generic operations on tagged data, that relieve clerical burdens faced by programmers when using many other programming languages. As a result, Lisp programmers can spend more of their time focusing on higher-level issues.

A Lisp-like approach is thus attractive for parallel programming. This attractiveness was perhaps first noted by Friedman and Wise [25] and subsequently by several others [69, 88]. As shared-memory parallel architectures came into their own, new parallel Lisp systems were built [27, 34], and eventually implementations with high levels of performance appeared [29, 61]. During this process, the future construct [11, 34, 56] came into wide use and many things were learned about the theory and practice of algorithms for basic parallel Lisp functions such as garbage collection [34, 73, 75] and scheduling [34, 61].

This paper surveys recent ideas in these and other areas and explores how they could fit together in the parallel Lisp systems of the future, focusing on multiple instruction stream, multiple data stream (MIMD) shared-memory parallel architectures. Parallel Lisps for both distributed-memory MIMD architectures [54] and single instruction stream, single data stream (SIMD) architectures such as the Connection Machine [86] are certainly possible as well. However, achieving good performance on either SIMD or distributed-memory MIMD architectures seems likely to require more tuning to the particular characteristics of the architecture than in the shared-memory MIMD case. Knowing how to implement a parallel Lisp efficiently and elegantly on a shared-memory MIMD machine thus seems like a prerequisite for being able to do so on any other kind of parallel machine. Moreover, developments in the field of coherent-cache design seem likely to enable the construction of large, high-performance, shared-memory MIMD multiprocessors [2], making this an important architecture to be able to exploit effectively.

1.1 Overview of the Paper

Section 2 reviews important parallel Lisp designs and systems. Section 3 discusses the role of application programs in parallel Lisp research. Section 4 introduces **future** and the other basic capabilities of Multilisp. Section 5 sets forth some language-design criteria for **future**-based parallel Lisps and then discusses the application of these criteria to speculative computing, continuations, exception handling, and aggregate data objects. There are several synergies among the approaches explored. Section 6 discusses several requirements for efficient implementation and some ways of satisfying those requirements. Among the topics explored are run-time granularity enhancement, scheduling, task management, and garbage collection. Section 7 briefly discusses tools to help programmers write, debug, and tune parallel Lisp programs. Section 8 offers some final words.

2. Parallel Lisp Languages and Systems

Multilisp [34, 37, 38] is an extended version of Scheme that pioneered the use of the **future** construct in a parallel Lisp; Multilisp serves as the framework for discussion of parallel Lisp issues in this paper. The term "Multilisp" can be used to name both a programming language (Scheme plus **future**) and a system that supports programming in that language. Several systems supporting the Multilisp language have been built; moreover, the Multilisp language itself has evolved over time and several experimental versions have added or redefined language features. Consequently, the term "Multilisp" can be confusing, especially in a paper such as this one that surveys several language-design and implementation-level ideas that can be applied to Multilisp. In this paper, "Multilisp" refers to the programming language; when an extended or modified version of Multilisp is meant, context will so indicate. Systems that implement Multilisp are referred to by their names, indicated below.

Three implementations of Multilisp were built at M.I.T. The first, Concert Multilisp [34, 39], ran on Concert [4, 36], a 32-processor multiprocessor built at M.I.T., and has been ported to an Encore Multimax multiprocessor [21] and several other machines. It was built "from scratch" around an interpreter for MCODE, a low-level byte-code language [34, 39].

The second, MultiScheme [73, 74], was derived from the M.I.T. C-Scheme system and is based on an interpreter for the latter's byte-code, known as SCode. It runs on a BBN Butterfly multiprocessor [18]. Butterfly Lisp [3], implemented by BBN, also for the Butterfly, is closely related to MultiScheme.

The third, Mul-T [61, 62], runs on the Encore Multimax. Mul-T is based on the Yale T system [59, 60, 81] and compiles directly to the machine language of the Multimax's NS32000-series processors. Due to its compiler, Mul-T's performance is much greater than that of the other Multilisp implementations and rivals that of high-quality compiled implementations of sequential Lisps [61, 62].

Parallel Lisp systems have also been developed by other research groups: Qlisp [27, 28, 29, 30], implemented for the Alliant FX-8; and a parallel version of Portable Standard Lisp [89], for the Butterfly multiprocessor. Parallel Portable Standard Lisp, like Multilisp, MultiScheme, and Mul-T, rely primarily on future as a concurrency mechanism. Qlisp supports futures but also provides several other concurrency constructs.

There are also Lisps for parallel machines that do not fit the shared-memory MIMD model. Connection Machine Lisp [86] is aimed at a SIMD architecture, though it has ideas that are useful in a MIMD architecture as well—see Section 5.5. Concurrent Scheme [54] is aimed at a distributed-memory MIMD architecture.

Another family of approaches to parallel execution of Lisp programs rely on opportunities for concurrency that are identified mechanically, rather than specified by the programmer. One way to do this is through aggressive compile-time data-flow analysis and restructuring of programs to expose concurrently executable subcomputations [42, 63]. Another is to augment Scheme with a language in which the programmer can specify the *effects* that expressions may have, allowing conflicts between potentially concurrent subcomputations to be checked for in a way very similar to the checking of types in conventional typed programming languages [67].

Yet another approach is to rely on run-time mechanisms to detect available concurrency. The ParaTran system [49, 50] executes ordinary Lisp programs, which are allowed to include side effects, on a parallel machine, without requiring the programmer to specify any concurrency explicitly. Instead, ParaTran's run-time mechanisms automatically sense conflicts over shared variables that would lead to incorrect results. Computations that threaten to cause such conflicts are aborted (and re-executed). ParaTran's overall goals and approach resemble those of Knight's Liquid machine [55] but ParaTran's detailed approach is quite different. Although ParaTran and Liquid will both operate correctly and are capable of generating concurrency, their performance on realistic programs remains untested.

While this paper does not discuss approaches in which the programmer is not required to specify concurrency explicitly, we note that many of the same problems discussed below also arise in some form in the implicit-concurrency approaches and similar solutions will be applicable.

Concert Multilisp was phased out of use when Mul-T became available and the Concert multiprocessor was decommissioned, but Concert Multilisp is still usable as an experimental vehicle on other multiprocessors. Mul-T is operational and heavily used for developing new programs as well as for measuring properties of existing ones. MultiScheme and Qlisp also continue to be used (and developed) by other research groups.

3. Applications

Work with application programs is a vital part of any programming language design effort. Experience with applications provides the necessary evaluation of proposed language constructs and implementation techniques. Only after a number of applications have been built successfully can the designers of a language or system have confidence that they have designed a useful tool. Accordingly, Concert Multilisp and Mul-T have been used to experiment with a library of representative parallel programs.

A major focus of our effort is general-purpose symbolic computing. Several application programs in this domain have been studied, including sorting [34, 37, 38, 40, 61], simulation of logic circuits [13, 14], event-based simulation [68], speech recognition algorithms [64, 76], semantic net retrieval [8], a subset of Prolog not including "cut" [84], a kernel of EMYCIN [58] (developed at MCC), the Boyer benchmark from the Gabriel benchmark set [26], polynomial manipulation, traveling salesman [79], parallel parsing of Lisp expressions, compilers [61], and a parallel version of the Rete algorithm [24] used in production systems.

It is important for many of the benchmarks to be sizable programs, because the ultimate use of high-performance parallel architectures will be for large problems, which often have qualitatively different properties from small ones (for example, small programs are apt to show more locality of reference and put few demands on a garbage collector). While several of the programs listed above are of moderate size (at least several pages of code), there is a great need for more experience with large-scale problems. We can hope that the availability of "industrial strength" parallel Lisp implementations such as Mul-T [61, 76] and Qlisp [29], with good performance and usable user interfaces, will encourage more experimentation with parallel programming for large applications.

4. Multilisp Semantics

Concurrency can be introduced into a Multilisp program using the future construct; unless concurrency is explicitly introduced, Multilisp programs execute sequentially. The form (future X) immediately returns a *future* for the value of X and creates a task to concurrently evaluate X, allowing concurrency between the *computation* of a value and the *use* of that value. When the evaluation of X yields a value, that value replaces the future; we say that the future *resolves* to the value. Any task that needs to know a future's value will be suspended until the future resolves.

We refer to the task evaluating X as the *child* task and to the task evaluating (future X) as the *parent* task. However, unlike many parallel computing paradigms, future does not force the child task to finish before the parent: it is entirely possible for the parent task to resolve *its* future before the child task resolves its future.

We say that a task T *touches* a future when it performs an operation that will cause T to be suspended if the future has not yet resolved. Most operations, such as arithmetic, comparison, and type checking, touch their operands: any operation that is *strict* in an operand touches that operand. (Multilisp also includes a "strict identity" primitive procedure touch that simply touches its one operand and then returns it.) However, simple transmission of a value from one place to another, for example, by assignment, passing as a parameter to a procedure, returning as a result from a procedure, or building the value into a data structure, do *not* touch the value. Thus, many things can be done with a future without waiting for its value. **future** induces some patterns reminiscent of those found in graph-reduction architectures based on "lazy evaluation" [43, 53, 91], yet in other ways **future** creates a style of computation much like that found in data flow architectures [6, 19, 33].

Multilisp also includes a lazy-evaluation construct called **delay**. The form (**delay** X) returns a future for the value of X, just as (**future** X) does, except that evaluation of X in (**delay** X) is guaranteed not to begin until the future is touched.

future provides "producer-consumer" or "data-flow" synchronization. This is the most frequently used kind of synchronization in most Multilisp programs, which tend to have few side effects on shared variables. When exclusive access to shared mutable objects is needed, though, some mutual-exclusion synchronization construct must be used. Multilisp provides low-level atomic operations such as compare-and-swap, with higher-level synchronization constructs such as semaphores built on them, which can be used in such situations [34].

As one might expect, the typical implementation of a future is as a special "place-holder" data type containing a slot for the future's eventual value and a flag indicating whether that slot is full. Strict operations have generic implementations: if they find a placeholder as an operand rather than a value of the expected type, they check to see if the placeholder's value slot is full, using the value found if there is one, and suspending execution otherwise. (A placeholder also has a slot used to point to a queue of waiting, suspended tasks.) Even after a future has resolved, this layer of indirection makes it somewhat more expensive to access the future's value than if **future** had not been used. To prevent this from becoming a long-term cost (and also to economize on memory use) the Multilisp garbage collector "splices out" references to resolved futures, replacing them with references to their values; thus, all evidence that **future** was used in computing a particular value will eventually disappear. (Similar comments apply to **delay**.) There is no semantic reason why this splicing must be performed only by the garbage collector. It could be performed any time a reference to a resolved future is found, but among existing Multilisp implementations, only MultiScheme splices out resolved futures in any place other than the garbage collector [74].

future is actually a composite operation that can be expressed in terms of the simpler primitives **make-future**, **fork**, **determine!**, and **quit**. (**make-future**) returns a newly created, unresolved future. (**quit**) never returns; instead, it terminates execution of the invoking task. (**fork** X) simply creates a new task to evaluate the expression X, without making any provision for capturing X's value or synchronizing X with its parent computation. **determine!** is a function that can be applied to a future f and a value v and resolves f to v. (The name **determine!** has historical origins.)

An expression (**future** X) can be rewritten as in Figure 1, where f is a variable name chosen so as not to conflict with any free variables of X. Note that this implementation records the future to be resolved as part of the continuation for the evaluation

```
(let ((f (make-future)))
  (fork (begin
          (determine! f X)
          (quit))))
  f)
```

Figure 1: Implementation of (future X) in terms of lower-level Multilisp primitives

```
(let ((f (make-future)))
  (fork (begin
          (set-task-future! (the-current-task) f)
          (let ((value X))
            (determine! (task-future (the-current-task)) value))
          (quit))))
  f)
```

Figure 2: Implementation of (future X) in MultiScheme

of the expression X; an alternative approach, used in the MultiScheme system, is to save the future as an attribute of the newly forked task, as suggested by the version in Figure 2 [73, 75]. The semantic difference between these two implementations is subtle and shows up only when, due to the use of some mechanism such as continuations [82], execution of X is suspended and another task resumes it. The Multilisp implementation will always resolve the same future to X's value, no matter which task actually performs the determine! operation. In MultiScheme, the future that is resolved depends on which task finishes the evaluation of X. The significance of this difference is discussed in Section 5.3.3.

While exposing the lower-level primitive components of future, such as make-future and determine!, undeniably has benefits, it has several costs as well. Using the lower-level primitives creates new opportunities for programming errors such as multiple attempts to resolve the same future. Moreover, future induces a simple and useful correspondence between each future and the task responsible for resolving it. When the lower-level primitives are used, establishing such a correspondence may require detailed analysis of the program; indeed, it is no longer guaranteed that there is a task responsible for resolving every future. Finally, certain important optimizations take advantage of the particular combination of operations in future; such optimizations are not, in general, applicable to isolated use of the lower-level primitives—see Sections 5.3.4 and 6.1.

With determine! it is possible to attempt to resolve a future more than once, something that is impossible just using future (unless continuations are explicitly invoked—see Section 5.3.3). Such an attempt is an error, as is any attempt to "resolve" a value that is not a future. (This "resolve-once" behavior of futures resembles that of variables in single-assignment languages such as SISAL [71] or of *I-structures* in Id [7].) Although it is an error to attempt to resolve a future more than once, the splicing out of resolved futures (as by the garbage collector) makes it very difficult to reliably detect this error [51]. Consider a program fragment such as the following:

```
(let ((f (make-future)))
  (determine! f (future X))
      .  .  .
  (determine! f V)
      .  .  .  )
```

This program is clearly incorrect, but suppose the future originally bound to f is spliced out after the first **determine!** operation and before the expression X has yielded a value. Then f will again be bound to an unresolved future, but it will be the future for X, not the future to which f was originally bound. If the second **determine!** operation then occurs before X yields a value, the future intended for the value of X will instead resolve to the value of V, which will probably confound the operation of the program eventually but will not generate any report identifying the erroneous operation. This problem could be solved, for example, by creating a special "determiner" function with each future, and refusing to splice out the reference to the future from its determiner function, but we do not pursue the topic here. We note simply that, while it is an error to attempt to resolve a future more than once, current Multilisp implementations do not reliably detect that error.

5. Language-Design Issues

The preceding section detailed the basic handling of futures and concurrency in Multilisp. While simply adding these constructs opens up a great deal of power to express parallel algorithms, some pieces of the puzzle do not fit in easily. This section discusses some of the more difficult (and in some cases still unresolved) Multilisp language-design issues. All of these issues can be viewed as questions regarding the design of extensions to the basic Multilisp language. In some cases the question is how to include features, such as continuations and exception handling, that exist in sequential languages but pose significant new semantic challenges in a parallel language. In other cases the questions concern issues not confronted by sequential programming languages, such as control over scheduling of subcomputations within a program.

5.1 Language-Design Criteria

When considering Multilisp features that have a sequential Scheme analog, three criteria are applicable:

- A sequential Scheme program should yield the same answer when run in Multilisp as in a standard sequential Scheme implementation.

- If we derive a Multilisp program P' by wrapping future around any subexpression or subexpressions of a side-effect-free Scheme program P—where "wrapping" future around an expression X means replacing X with (future X)—then P and P' should yield the same answer. (Clearly, this equivalence will not hold, in general, for programs with side effects, since wanton insertion of future can create timing races and nondeterministic behavior in such programs.)

- Modularity should be respected: in using a module, it should not be necessary to know whether the module is implemented internally in a sequential or parallel way; similarly, in implementing a module, it should not be necessary to know whether the module is invoked concurrently with other operations.

The final criterion applies even if a construct has no sequential analog.

5.2 Scheduling and Speculative Computing

A program does not always use all the values it computes. In sequential programming, an unused value is often computed because it would be more expensive to decide whether or not the value will eventually be required than just to compute it, but if a value is expensive enough to compute, then it is profitable to delay computing it until it is demanded (note that Multilisp's delay operator is an ideal mechanism for this). In parallel programming, however, the issue is murkier. Starting a computation as early as possible gives it the best chance to execute before computations that require its value; waiting to start a computation until its value is known to be needed reduces concurrency. On the other hand, computing an unused value uses up machine resources that might be devoted to more important matters. Deciding when to start a computation in a parallel system, then, is generally a calculated gamble, balancing the likelihood of the resulting value's being required against the extent to which the computation will take resources away from other computations.

A computation producing a value that is certain (or virtually certain) to be required may be termed a *mandatory computation*, and should begin as soon as the necessary inputs are available. As the cost of a computation increases and the likelihood of its value's being needed decreases, the computation becomes increasingly *speculative*. Programs that search tend to be especially rich in speculative computations, although other kinds of programs (*e.g.*, straight numerical calculations) often are not. Generally, we would like to execute speculative computations as early as possible, subject to the constraint that they not interfere with the progress of any computations closer to the mandatory end of the scale. Moreover, if it becomes clear that a speculative computation's value will not be required (the computation has become *irrelevant*), we would like to expend the smallest possible amount of resources on that computation from that point on.

The basic Multilisp language is oriented toward mandatory computation and contains no constructs designed to facilitate speculative computing; however, Multilisp extensions to support speculative computing have been investigated by Osborne [79, 80].

5.2.1 Fairness of Scheduling

Multilisp semantics make only an extremely weak guarantee of fairness in scheduling: tasks may be starved out arbitrarily by other tasks, provided only that processors are not allowed to remain idle while executable tasks remain unscheduled. Thus, aside from the obvious guarantees that a task will not begin to execute until it has been created (or, in the case of delay, its value has been demanded), and will not continue past a touch until the touched future has resolved, the only guarantee about scheduling is that a task will not be arbitrarily discriminated against when there is no other task to execute. "Busy-waiting" control structures are thus dangerous in Multilisp programs—busy-waiting tasks can starve out other tasks that could make progress. To ensure that a Multilisp program makes progress, it is important to ensure that all blocked tasks are blocked in a way that is visible to the scheduler, such as explicitly waiting on a future or semaphore. This aspect of Multilisp's semantics becomes important when considering what scheduler designs are legal (see Section 6.2), and also comes into play in considering certain optimization strategies that attempt to reduce overhead by "inlining" child tasks into their parents (see Section 6.1).

The weakness of Multilisp's scheduling guarantees may seem surprising when compared with the specifications of other schedulers, such as those for operating systems or real-time control. It is acceptable for Multilisp's scheduling semantics to be weaker because the only design goal for the basic Multilisp language is to execute mandatory parallel computations quickly. This definition of Multilisp's mission does not include goals that other schedulers must meet, such as apportioning a computer system's resources fairly among multiple users or juggling tasks of differing priorities. (Multilisp extensions for speculative computing must specify scheduler behavior in more detail, but that is the subject of subsequent sections.) It is desirable to keep the specification of Multilisp's scheduler as weak as possible to allow more latitude for optimizations such as those discussed in Sections 6.1 and 6.2.

5.2.2 Speculative Computing

Speculative computing is based on the premise that the total time to completion of a computation can be reduced by performing selected subcomputations before they are known to be required. Osborne [79, 80] has classified the opportunities for speculative computing into several categories, including

- *Multiple-approach* speculative computing, in which several alternative procedures for solving a problem may be pursued concurrently. Zero or more of the procedures may succeed, but once one does, the problem is solved. A typical example is the "parallel OR" construct (por E_1 E_2 ... E_n). As soon as any one of the disjunct expressions E_i returns a true value, the por expression yields that true value and the values of any other disjuncts E_j that have not yet finished computing are not required. The "parallel AND" operator pand is a dual of por. A principal concern in many instances of multiple-approach speculative computing is the quick termination of tasks that have become irrelevant due to the successful completion of another task.

- *Order-based* speculative computing, which may be viewed as a specialization of multiple-approach speculative computing. In order-based speculative computing, a heuristic priority ordering on the approaches is known, such that success is likely to come sooner if approaches are tried approximately in priority order. Branch-and-bound algorithms for problems such as the traveling salesman problem are typical examples of order-based speculative computing. A principal concern in many instances of order-based speculative computing is the scheduling of speculative tasks according to a program-specified priority order.

- *Precomputing*, which focuses on computing specific values, such as the next element of a sequence, that are not yet certain to be required. The standard operating-system technique of reading blocks of an input file ahead of those that a user program has currently requested is an example of precomputing. When programming using *streams* [1], precomputing can be applied to calculating values of stream elements beyond those that have been demanded.

Clearly these categories overlap; speculative computing often exhibits a mixture of their attributes.

The examples listed above apply to the compute-intensive portion of a computation, but issues closely related to speculative computing arise in other contexts also. For example, computer systems typically define an "interrupt character" (such as control-C) that a user can type to abort or suspend the execution of a program. The interrupt character can be viewed as notification from the user that the program's results are not (or may not be) required; accordingly, a good mechanism for aborting irrelevant computations in multiple-approach speculative computing would be a good mechanism for handling interrupts from the user as well. (See Section 5.4.)

Another analogy, with order-based speculative computing, comes from the sharing of computational resources among users ("timesharing") or among jobs requested by a single user. Computer systems typically use priorities in scheduling such jobs. While the priorities generally reflect organizational policies concerning the importance of competing uses of a computing facility, rather than heuristics for performing a single computation efficiently, their use is quite similar. Although interrupts and timesharing both have quite serviceable implementations for sequential programs and machines, extending them to parallel programs and machines introduces new challenges, and placing them in the general framework of speculative computing may yield useful solutions.

5.2.3 Control of Speculative Computations

It is awkward, though sometimes possible, to program the scheduling of speculative computations explicitly. An explicit priority queue can be used to schedule the processing of nodes in a branch-and-bound algorithm, or disjuncts of a parallel-OR expression can periodically make explicit checks to see if they have become irrelevant, but a general and elegant framework is preferable [79, 80].

Modularity is a major challenge for such a framework: a subcomputation may be performed by one task or many, and it should be possible to declare a subcomputation as speculative without knowing such details. This implies that a "task ID" referring only to a single task is, in general, an inadequate "handle" on a subcomputation for speculative computing purposes. A better approach builds on *sponsors* [57, 79, 80], which are viewed as sources of "computational energy" for subcomputations. In this view, every task has zero or more sponsors at a given time. Each sponsor may sponsor zero or more tasks, so in general the sponsor-to-task association is a many-to-many mapping.

Sponsors supply *attributes* to the tasks they sponsor. Attributes, abstractly, give a task a claim on processing resources. For order-based speculative computing, a suitable kind of attribute would be a scheduling priority; for precomputing, a more relevant attribute might be a "voucher" for a specified amount of computation that is to be devoted to the task [79]. Current experiments [79, 80] have focused exclusively on priority attributes; the best way to define and use a more general attribute set remains an open question.

Intuitively, sponsors are the needed "handles" on speculative subcomputations. Just as subcomputations may themselves consist of smaller subcomputations, it is natural for sponsors to form a network in which sponsors can sponsor (supply attributes to) other sponsors as well as elementary tasks. In simple cases, such sponsor networks form tree-shaped hierarchies mirroring the parent-child relationships induced by **future**, but more complex relationships are possible. For example, a task A may touch a future whose value is being computed by a task B that is not A's child. If that happens, it is appropriate for A (or, more rigorously, A's sponsor) to begin to sponsor B (in addition to whatever other sponsors B may already have): if this is not done, and B lacks sufficient attributes to execute, A may fail to make progress even though it has a high level of sponsorship. This is a special case of the general principle of *attribute transitivity*: if the subcomputation A is blocked from making progress until the subcomputation (or set of subcomputations) B reaches a certain point, then A should sponsor (*i.e.*, contribute its attributes to) B until B's lack of progress no longer impedes A from proceeding. Attribute transitivity can lead to arbitrary, non-tree-shaped sponsor networks.

Just as the attribute level of a task (or set of tasks) may increase at arbitrary moments as a result of attribute transitivity, the attribute level may decrease when sponsorship is removed. Sponsorship added to a task B because a task A has touched B's result will generally not be removed until task B completes, but there are many other situations in which a task may lose sponsorship before it completes. For example, the parallel-OR computation (por X Y) would initially sponsor both X and Y, but if one of the disjuncts returns a true value, sponsorship of the other disjunct will be removed. Other examples can arise in the presence of side effects: if task B holds a lock required by task A, A can sponsor B just until B releases the lock, after which A's sponsorship of B should be removed.

When a task loses sponsorship, the attributes contributed by its remaining sponsors (if any) may fall below the threshold of eligibility for execution. Such a task becomes *stayed* [79, 80]. Stayed tasks continue to exist but are not executed, though they may run again in the future if they receive new sponsorship. If a stayed task's state becomes inaccessible (and hence a candidate for garbage collection) the task will be deemed truly irrelevant and its state will be deallocated.

A task may thus lose sponsorship at an arbitrary moment, be stopped dead in its tracks, and be garbage-collected without ever again resuming execution. In a side-effect-free program, this is fine, but in a program with side effects, there is always the danger of interrupting a task's execution in the middle of a co-ordinated sequence of side effects, leaving a data structure incomplete or inconsistent—for example, leaving locks locked. Other Lisp systems have a construct called unwind-protect [85, 90] that allows a programmer to deal with this problem by specifying "clean-up actions" that should be executed before a computation is aborted.

A better solution comes from the observation that if it will be a mistake to abort a task at a given point, then it is mistake to declare it irrelevant at that point: actions not yet performed by that task are in fact required by other tasks, though possibly in an indirect way. The solution is to effectively associate a sponsor with each data structure updated by a sequence of side effects that must not be aborted. Before beginning a sequence of side effects on a data structure, a task first adds the data structure's sponsor to its own set of sponsors. When finished with the data structure, the task can revert to its old set of sponsors. Any task accessing the data structure should also supply sponsorship to the data structure's sponsor. The data structure's sponsor thus serves as a conduit for attributes from data structure accessors to data structure mutators, ensuring that a task in the process of updating the data structure will be permanently halted only if no task ever accesses the data structure again. This idea is at the root of the *class* concept developed by Osborne [79].

The above discussion implicitly assumes that, when a task is blocked from progressing, it is easy to identify the task or subcomputation that should be sponsored in order to remove the obstacle. This is true when writing side-effect-free programs in which all tasks are created using future, but in programs with side effects or explicit use of determine!, it can be hard to tell which task will perform the awaited side effect or resolve the touched future. The class concept mentioned above can be used by the programmer to declare tasks that may potentially perform an awaited operation, so they can be sponsored by tasks that await the operation. Unfortunately, use of the raw class concept can be error-prone, since the consequence of forgetting to register a task may be that a necessary task does not receive sponsorship and the computation gets stuck. Higher-level constructs that capture common patterns of sponsorship are needed here.

When a sponsor sponsors many tasks, it must apply some policy in supplying attributes to those tasks. In simple cases, all tasks may be viewed as equally important to achieving the sponsor's goal, and the same attributes are accordingly supplied to all sponsored tasks. In more complex cases, there may be an element of speculation in how to achieve the sponsor's goal, leading to an uneven distribution of attributes by a sponsor. For example, it may be desirable for a sponsor associated with a parallel-OR expression (por X Y) to sponsor X more heavily than Y, perhaps because X often returns a true answer quickly. A vast number of sponsor policies are possible, and current work [79, 80] only scratches the surface concerning how to express them.

Even more complex issues arise from nested speculative computations such as (por (pand A B) (pand C D)), where the optimal policy for the por sponsor depends on internal details of the sponsored pand subcomputations, and may involve a complex shuffling of attributes back and forth between the two disjuncts as information emerges from the execution of the individual computations A through D. For modularity, it is desirable if the sponsoring policy for a subcomputation such as (pand A B) can be specified by considering only some summary characterization of A and B, without investigating the context in which the pand expression is used. Even understanding what the optimal sponsoring policy for such cases is, or what characterizations it should be based on, requires further research into the optimal scheduling of nested speculative computations such as nested por-pand expressions.

This section gives only an abbreviated overview of the general problem of speculative computing, along with comments on some promising solutions. For a much more complete discussion of the issues, along with a discussion of related literature, the reader is referred to Osborne [79, 80].

5.2.4 Summary

Tasks can be classified as *mandatory* or *speculative*. Among mandatory tasks, there is only a very weak guarantee of fairness of scheduling: a runnable task will not be kept idle when there is nothing else to execute. Among speculative tasks, execution can be controlled by a network of *sponsors* that distribute *attributes* to tasks; in a current prototype of a speculative computing system [79, 80], these attributes are simply numerical priorities that control a priority-based scheduler. With suitably defined attributes and sponsors, we can look to the speculative part of a Multilisp scheduler to provide most of the richness of behavior that we want out of schedulers in general-purpose computing systems.

5.3 Continuations

Among the few features of sequential Scheme that do not adapt naturally to a parallel environment with futures, *continuations* cause the most trouble. This section first introduces some basic concepts associated with continuations and then explores the good and bad points of several different ways of adding continuations to Multilisp. While none of these approaches can be "proven correct," an approach suggested by Katz and Weise [51, 52] looks like the best according to the criteria of Section 5.1. Other approaches [44, 48] do not meet these criteria as well but contain interesting ideas relating both to continuations and speculative computing.

In sequential Scheme, evaluation of the procedure application

(call-with-current-continuation f)

causes the continuation of that procedure application to be *captured*, packaged up as a procedure, and passed as the sole argument to the procedure f [82]. A common idiom for using continuations is thus (call/cc (lambda (k) ...k...)), where the continuation captured by call/cc is bound to the variable k and may be accessed within the body ...k... of the lambda expression. (call/cc is a common abbreviation for call-with-current-continuation.)

A continuation itself looks like a Scheme procedure and may be applied to an argument. (In some formulations, it may also accept no arguments or multiple arguments.) If a continuation is applied to an argument v (this operation is often referred to as *throwing* v to the continuation), then execution will resume at the point where the continuation was captured by call/cc and the value v will be returned from that application of call/cc. For example, (call/cc (lambda (k) (+ 1 (k (+ 2 3))))) returns the value 5. Continuations thus provide a powerful "nonlocal goto" facility.

If the call to f simply returns a value v, then v is returned as the value of the call to call/cc, so the value of (call/cc (lambda (k) (+ 1 (+ 2 3)))) is 6.

Standard denotational approaches to defining the semantics of sequential programming languages with side effects (such as Scheme) use the concept of a continuation as a "container" denoting the portion of a computation that remains to be done after a particular subcomputation completes [82, 87]. From a semantic standpoint, call/cc simply provides access to these continuations as manipulable objects, and therefore introduces no difficulty in semantic definition (though some argue that it leads to a less desirable semantics [72]).

From an operational standpoint, a continuation may be viewed as the stack and register contents that together represent the current computation state and encode the computation's future path (*e.g.*, procedure return points). *Every* expression evaluation has a continuation, which is the context to which the expression's value will be returned; the special function of call/cc is to capture this continuation as a manipulable object. Effectively, call/cc captures the stack and register contents that together represent the continuation of the call to call/cc (*i.e.*, the continuation to which call/cc would return its value) and copies them for safekeeping into a continuation object. Whenever the continuation object is applied to a value v, the saved stack and register contents are re-installed as the current stack and register contents, v is installed in the appropriate result register, and computation continues from that state. The result is that a return from the original invocation of call/cc occurs, with v being the value returned.

A continuation may be invoked more than once, as the rather artificial example in Figure 3 shows. In this example, a continuation is captured by call/cc and bound to the variable k. This continuation is then returned as the value of the call to call/cc and bound to the variable v. This "normal" return from call/cc invokes (implicitly) the continuation bound to k. Then the continuation is invoked again, by evaluating (v #f), so the call to call/cc returns again! This time, the false value #f is passed to the continuation and hence returned from call/cc and bound to v. Execution then returns to the if expression, but since the value of v is false this time, v's false value is simply returned as the value of the whole let expression.

While the particular program structure of Figure 3 is of little use, fancier versions can be used for failure-driven loops or iterator control structures in which control is repeatedly thrown back to a continuation until an acceptable return value is produced.

```
(let ((v (call/cc (lambda (k) k))))
  (if v (v #f) v))
```

Figure 3: An example of multiple use of a continuation

(An example of this kind is given in [51].) Continuations are also useful in implementing coroutine-like control structures.

It is useful to distinguish between *single-use* and *multiple-use* continuations. As we have seen, a continuation, once captured, may be invoked any number of times, each invocation leading to a new return from the invocation of call/cc that captured the continuation. The general, multiple-use style of using continuations can lead to several returns from a single procedure call. Thus, in general, it is important to prevent the information captured in a continuation from being destroyed when the continuation is used. In practice, this means that when a continuation is invoked, "control stack" information must be copied from the continuation to a working stack, so that the usual (destructive) push and pop operations on the working stack will not destroy the information captured in the continuation.

In many important cases, however, a continuation is only used once before being discarded. When it is known that a given continuation will only be used once, there are opportunities to reduce costs in many sequential Scheme implementations by eliminating some copying steps. We will see that single-use continuations can be less troublesome in parallel Lisps as well. (Note that a "normal" return from the procedure called by call/cc when a continuation was captured, which leads to a return from the call/cc application itself, also counts as a use of the continuation, since it, like any other use, causes a return from the call/cc application.)

5.3.1 Compositional Continuations

A semantically different but related concept, also referred to as "continuations," has been developed by Felleisen and others [22, 23]. To avoid confusion, we refer to these "continuations" as $\mathcal{F}$-*continuations*. $\mathcal{F}$-continuations are captured by an $\mathcal{F}$ operator analogous to call/cc. A major difference between $\mathcal{F}$-continuations and continuations is that $\mathcal{F}$-continuations are *compositional*: an invocation of a continuation discards the caller's control state and never returns, but an invocation of an $\mathcal{F}$-continuation retains the caller's control state and returns to the caller the value that the captured computation would originally have returned to the top-level continuation of the computation.

In (call/cc f), the procedure f receives a captured continuation. Additionally, the call to f, like any other procedure call, has an implicit continuation, which is the continuation that will receive the result (if any) returned by the call to f. When call/cc is used, these two continuations are in fact the same. When $\mathcal{F}$ is used in the expression ($\mathcal{F}$ f), however, they are different: f receives an $\mathcal{F}$-continuation that captures the continuation of the expression ($\mathcal{F}$ f), but the implicit continuation for the call to f is *the top-level continuation of the computation*. For example, (call/cc (lambda (k) 0)) captures the current continuation, discards it, and returns 0 to the caller of call/cc; ($\mathcal{F}$ (lambda (k) 0)) likewise discards the captured $\mathcal{F}$-continuation, but then returns 0 as the top-level value of the computation! $\mathcal{F}$ thus differs from call/cc in two ways: it constructs an $\mathcal{F}$-continuation, which behaves differently from a continuation when invoked, and it uses a different implicit continuation for the call to its argument function f.

Prompts [23], denoted by #, are a subsequent elaboration that allow the programmer to restrict the effect of $\mathcal{F}$. Syntactically, a prompt looks like an operator that can enclose an expression E in the form (# E). A prompt effectively defines a "firewall" around which the control state ("stack") is split by $\mathcal{F}$, the newer portion being captured in the $\mathcal{F}$-continuation and the older portion being retained in the continuation for the call to $\mathcal{F}$'s argument f. When ($\mathcal{F}$ f) is evaluated in the presence of prompts, the implicit continuation for the call to f is the continuation for the expression just inside the closest dynamically enclosing prompt, and the $\mathcal{F}$-continuation passed to f captures the control state from the point of the application of $\mathcal{F}$ out to that prompt. When prompts are used, $\mathcal{F}$-continuations are still compositional, but now the value returned from invoking an $\mathcal{F}$-continuation is the value that the captured computation would have returned to its closest dynamically enclosing prompt. The introduction of prompts eliminates the special status of the "top-level continuation" in the original formulation of $\mathcal{F}$; to obtain the old semantics we can simply enclose the entire computation within a prompt.

A typical application for $\mathcal{F}$-continuations is in the construction of "iterator" or "backtracking" control structures. For example, a tree-walk procedure can be defined to return a node of the argument tree plus an $\mathcal{F}$-continuation. Invoking this $\mathcal{F}$-continuation will return, to its invoker, another node and another $\mathcal{F}$-continuation that can be further invoked to continue the search [23, 44].

It is possible to build $\mathcal{F}$ and prompts using call/cc and side effects. It is likewise possible to define call/cc in terms of $\mathcal{F}$ [83]; hence, neither mechanism has greater logical power than the other. We discuss $\mathcal{F}$-continuations here not because they add fundamental logical power, but for two other reasons: they provide a convenient abstraction that is clumsy (though possible) to build out of standard continuations, and they serve as the basis for a proposal for continuations in a concurrent Scheme [44] to be discussed below.

5.3.2 Criteria for Continuations in Multilisp

Unfortunately, in defining the semantics of a parallel programming language such as Multilisp, the notion of packaging up "the entire future of the computation" (which may include many concurrently executing threads of computation) into one object is not particularly useful or natural. This leaves us with no natural, definitive standard for "continuations" in a parallel language. Yet continuations are undeniably useful in sequential Scheme for implementing sophisticated control structures, and it is undesirable to have to trade them away to get the power of parallel computing.

What criteria should a continuation mechanism for Multilisp meet? The criteria given in Section 5.1 furnish a starting point. Since these criteria neither completely

```
(future
  (call/cc
    (lambda (k)
      (+ (future 1)
         (future (k (+ 2 3)))))))))
```

Figure 4: An example of continuations used in the "downward" and single-use style

```
(let ((v (future (call/cc (lambda (k) k)))))
  (if v (v #f) v))
```

Figure 5: An example of continuations used in the "upward" and multiple-use style

nor precisely define what we want, and there is no generally accepted formal notion of "continuation" in the semantics of parallel programs, it is not surprising that the motivation for proposed continuation mechanisms for Multilisp-like languages is stated intuitively, not formally. However, we can identify a sequence of increasingly challenging tests to apply to proposed mechanisms:

1. Programs that use call/cc but no concurrency constructs should yield the same results as in a sequential Scheme.

2. Programs that use continuations exclusively in the single-use style should yield the same results as in a sequential Scheme, even if future is wrapped around arbitrary subexpressions. As an example, consider the trivial but illustrative expression shown in Figure 4, derived from our earlier call/cc example (call/cc (lambda (k) (+ 1 (k (+ 2 3)))))) by wrapping future around several subexpressions. This example illustrates a "downward" use of continuations, where the continuation is passed "deeper" into the computation to be used, as distinguished from an "upward" use in which the continuation is passed "out" of the context in which it was captured, and is invoked from elsewhere. (Technically, the "downward" use of a continuation k is characterized by the fact that k is part of the continuation that is in effect when k is invoked.) It is possible to have "upward" use of continuations in single-use mode, as in coroutining, but examples tend to be more complex.

3. Programs should yield the same results as in a sequential Scheme, even if future is wrapped around arbitrary subexpressions, with no restrictions on how continuations are used. A trivial example, exhibiting both the "upward" and multiple-use styles of continuation use, is shown in Figure 5 (a slightly modified version of Figure 3). If we remove the future construct, this program will return the false value #f when run by a sequential Scheme implementation, after returning twice from the invocation of call/cc. We would like to see the same behavior when the program with future runs in Multilisp.

These tests say nothing about modularity, except to the extent that being able to wrap future around arbitrary subexpressions of a program without changing its meaning is something one would hope for in a system that supports modularity. Nor do the tests address the meaning of continuations in programs that include side effects or explicit determine! operations. It is hard to say anything general or precise about such situations, but we can hope that a definition of continuations that makes sense in side-effect-free Multilisp programs continues to be useful and usable when the full range of Multilisp's capabilities are used.

5.3.3 Continuations and future

A major hurdle in defining a continuation mechanism for a language including future is the clash between the multiple-use potential of continuations and the "resolve-once" character of futures: in an expression such as (future X), use of continuations could cause the expression X to return several times, possibly with different values, but only one of these values can be saved as the value of the future. One approach to this problem is simply to ignore it and implement call/cc exactly as in sequential Scheme, by saving the execution stack of the current task when a continuation is captured and reinstating it (in the current task) when the continuation is invoked. The perils of using this approach in an otherwise unmodified Multilisp system are well documented by Katz and Weise [51]; however, as preparation for the discussion to follow, we consider first this simple way of adding call/cc to Multilisp.

Curiously, in programs that use both future and call/cc, MultiScheme may return different answers from other Multilisp implementations (such as Concert Multilisp) even if no continuation is used more than once. In the example of Figure 4, Concert Multilisp will resolve the outer future to 5, effectively yielding the same result as sequential Scheme does when the future forms are removed, but MultiScheme will never resolve the outer future at all, so the expression in Figure 4 will look like a nonterminating computation to any enclosing expression. The difference can be traced to the differences in the two systems' implementations of future, shown in Figures 1 and 2. In Figure 4, the task that returns from the call/cc invocation is not the same as the task that created the outer future. In Concert Multilisp, the future to resolve when call/cc returns is part of the continuation, so this change of tasks does not change the future that will be resolved, but in MultiScheme, the future to resolve is associated with the current task, and therefore the future created for (future (k (+ 2 3))) will be resolved, even though the value to which it will resolve is being returned from call/cc. Neither system can return a value for the multiple-use expression of Figure 5, although each system finds its own amusing way to fail.

It is clear that both Concert Multilisp and MultiScheme pass test (1) in Section 5.3.2, since both act just like a sequential Scheme when concurrency constructs are not used. It is equally clear that MultiScheme fails tests (2) and (3): Figures 4 and 5 furnish examples. Concert Multilisp fails test (3) but passes test (2). To see why Concert Multilisp passes test (2), note that no errors will occur in resolving futures since there are no multiple returns from expressions. Moreover, we can informally view the future to be resolved by a task as the link from the "base" of its continuation to the "top" of its parent's continuation. In Concert Multilisp, the association between a

```
1.      (define (call/cc-using-future f)
2.        (let ((the-future (make-future)))
3.          (fork (let ((k (lambda (v)
4.                            (determine! the-future (cons v '())))
5.                          (quit))))
6.                  (k (f k))))
7.            (car the-future)))
```

Figure 6: Defining use-once continuations in terms of future

continuation and the future that will receive its value is immutable, thus providing an immutable link to the same parent continuation as in sequential Scheme.

Interestingly, if we consider only single-use continuations, there is a rather simple way to implement the behavior of call/cc using the same primitive operations used to build future. Figure 6 shows the definition of a call/cc-like procedure call/cc-using-future, based on futures. This implementation is actually quite close to the standard technique for implementing call/cc: in call/cc-using-future, the stack is saved in the parent process, which becomes suspended at the car operation on line 7, only to be resumed when the "continuation" is invoked and resolves the future created on line 2. Note that car acts to prevent invocations of call/cc-using-future from returning before the "continuation" k is invoked; the indirection of resolving the future to (cons v '()) instead of just v here allows an unresolved future to be returned from an invocation of call/cc-using-future. Thus, if single-use continuations suffice, the state-capturing capability already needed when touching must suspend a task can be turned to use for call/cc as well, so continuations need no special support. Unfortunately, this capability is not powerful enough for multiple-use continuations. (It is interesting—but not surprising in light of the similarity between Figures 1 and 6— that use of this implementation for call/cc produces Concert Multilisp's continuation semantics, whether it is executed in MultiScheme or in some other Multilisp system.)

The literature offers three contrasting approaches to defining the meaning of multiple-use continuations in parallel programs: the solution proposed by Katz and Weise [51]; the approach taken by Ito and Matsui in PaiLisp [48]; and the *process continuations* of Hieb and Dybvig [44], based on the $\mathcal{F}$ operator and prompts.

5.3.4 The Approach of Katz and Weise

Katz and Weise change the Multilisp definition of future so it captures its continuation and saves it. Then if the expression X in (future X) returns more than once, the additional return values are communicated directly to the continuation of future. Figure 7 shows an implementation of this idea. f, k, and *first* in the figure are variable names chosen not to conflict with any free variables of X. k is bound to the future form's continuation, captured using call/cc. (Henceforth we use call/cc to refer to the standard version that can capture multiple-use continuations, not the

```
(call/cc
  (lambda (k)
    (let ((f (make-future))
          (first #t))
      (fork (k f))          ; fork parent
      (let ((value X))      ; evaluate child
        (if (atomic-swap! first #f)
            (begin (determine! f value)
                   (quit))
            (k value))))))
```

Figure 7: Implementation of (future X) from Katz and Weise [51]

call/cc-using-future version discussed above.) f is bound to the future used for communication between X and its parent task. *first* is a flag that is used to distinguish the "first" return from X (whose value is used to resolve the future) from all subsequent returns (whose values are passed directly to the continuation k). (atomic-swap! *first* #f) first fetches the value of the variable *first* and then stores #f into *first*, all in one atomic operation. The value originally fetched from *first* is returned as the value of the atomic-swap! form. Since #t is a constant meaning "true" and #f is a constant meaning "false," the first return from X that executes the atomic-swap! operation will execute the determine! operation on the future f and the remaining returns from X will find *first* to be false and will send the value returned by X directly to the continuation k.

An interesting and unsettling possibility opened up by this solution is the possibility of multiple returns from an expression such as

$$\texttt{(call/cc (lambda (k) (cons (future (k 5)) '()))),}$$

where the corresponding future-free expression

$$\texttt{(call/cc (lambda (k) (cons (k 5) '())))}$$

would return only once (with the value 5). The multiple returns in the former case come about because the constructor cons is not strict, and hence the fact that (future (k 5)) yields a future that will never resolve does not prevent cons from returning a value. Consequently, in addition to the expected return of 5, we get a (possibly unexpected) return of a cons cell. This problem can be solved by associating an additional attribute called *legitimacy* with each task, and propagating legitimacy following a tree walk that mimics the evaluation order of sequential Scheme programs; the details are described in [51]. Using this solution, the failure of the legitimate call (k 5) to return to its caller prevents legitimacy from being conferred on the cons operation, in turn marking the return of the cons cell from the whole expression as illegitimate, while the return of 5 is marked as legitimate. Illegitimate tasks can be filtered out by building "fences" that can only be crossed by legitimate tasks. With the addition of legitimacy tracking, the

Katz and Weise approach passes all three of our tests given in Section 5.3.2, assuming that a "fence" is put around every computation at the top level.

Many parallel programming languages have some kind of "wait" or "barrier" construct that waits until all activity spawned by a particular expression or statement has completed; the qwait construct of Qlisp [30] is an example. Multilisp has no such construct, partly because it violates modularity to be able to look inside a procedure's invocation and ask whether any internal activity is still in progress: a procedure ought to be able to announce its completion to the outside world while internal "housekeeping" tasks that it may have spawned (e.g., to rebalance a tree used as an internal data structure) are still active. Barrier constructs are very useful, however, in cases where explicit termination detection is awkward to program efficiently, such as detecting completion of a marking step on a graph. Legitimacy fences serve a function similar to that of a barrier construct, however, and may serve to give an attractive and solid definition of such a construct's semantics. An interesting question suggested by this point of view is whether it makes sense to provide a construct that allows the spawning of a "housekeeping" task outside of its parent's "legitimacy stream"—that is, in a way that the parent's legitimate completion is independent from that of the housekeeping task.

It is interesting to consider the speculative-computing aspects of the future implementation given in Figure 7. When continuations are used, any number of returns (including zero) is possible from a given expression. Nevertheless, this implementation gambles that there will be one return (by creating a future for it and immediately enqueuing it for execution), but gambles against additional returns (by waiting until they happen before propagating them). Similarly, when a value is first returned by the future body, it is optimistically used to resolve the future without checking its legitimacy, which may not be known yet (though enough record-keeping is done to make sure that the legitimacy of the value can ultimately be ascertained).

A more conservative implementation would insist on proof that a future body will return, and that a value is legitimate, before proceeding, but might expose far less concurrency. A more reckless (and somewhat implausible) implementation could gamble, say, that a future body X will return at least twice by creating two futures and immediately forking two invocations of the parent continuation k. Suitable logic to handle returns by X, plus suitable legitimacy filtering, would yield an equally correct implementation of future, but with different performance characteristics. Thus, the Katz-Weise implementation strategy makes it clear that there is a whole spectrum of scheduling policies for future, from rigidly conservative to wildly speculative.

The Katz-Weise approach certainly has drawbacks. Capturing the continuation of every future expression has a significant cost in time, and retaining the continuation until there is no possibility of additional returns from the expression may have a significant cost in space. Legitimacy propagation adds further costs. Moreover, some programs will create large numbers of illegitimate tasks, whose useless, speculative execution will use up a large fraction of the available processing resources. (It would be interesting to see how successfully this problem could be controlled by specifying suitable sponsors for speculative returns from future.) In programs with side effects, illegitimate tasks might perform spurious side effects that the corresponding sequential

Scheme program might not have performed. Such side effects could be prevented by installing a legitimacy-checking "fence" before every side-effect operation, but at a heavy cost in lost concurrency. Finally, the redefinition of future shown in Figure 7 helps programs that use the "bundled" future construct, but not those that explicitly use "unbundled" constructs such as determine!. Nevertheless, the Katz-Weise approach meets every one of our stated criteria for a continuation mechanism for Multilisp, and thus deserves to be considered as the semantic standard against which other proposals for continuations in Multilisp are measured.

5.3.5 Continuations in PaiLisp

PaiLisp [48] defines continuations rather differently. In PaiLisp, a continuation can be captured using call/cc in the standard way. (call/cc in PaiLisp creates a multiple-use continuation; an optimized procedure call/ep is available for creating a single-use continuation.) The difference lies in the meaning of invoking a continuation. A PaiLisp continuation records the identity of the task that captured it. If a continuation is invoked by the same task that captured it, the resulting behavior is exactly as in sequential Scheme (or Multilisp): the saved control state (stack) stored in the continuation is substituted for the current control state and execution resumes by returning from the call/cc invocation that captured the continuation. If, on the other hand, a continuation is invoked by a different task, the saved control state stored in the continuation is substituted for the current control state *of the task that captured the continuation*, forcing it to abandon its current computation and pick up at the spot where call/cc captured the continuation (*i.e.*, forcing a goto in the task that captured the continuation). In the task that invoked the continuation, the call to the continuation just returns and execution continues undisturbed.

PaiLisp passes test (1) from Section 5.3.2, since it behaves identically to sequential Scheme when all computation is done by the same task. Regarding test (2), the "downward" case illustrated in Figure 4 is clearly handled correctly: evaluation of (k (+ 2 3)) will redirect the execution of the parent task away from the outer + operation and back to the return from call/cc, causing the entire expression to correctly yield the value 5. In some cases, however, the fact that the call to the continuation returns, with a value of "undefined" [48], could cause errors to occur that would not have occurred in the corresponding future-free program. It is easy to "program around" this difference, but it does represent a change in the semantics of call/cc and continuations. In the "upward," single-use case (*e.g.*, coroutines), small program changes (calls to the PaiLisp primitive procedure suspend inserted after calls to continuations) will likewise usually be needed to generate the behavior of the original sequential Scheme program.

Test (3) brings up the possibility of multiple, concurrent invocations of the same continuation. This in itself creates no problem for any of the parallel Lisp models discussed above, since every invocation would be executing in a different task, but in PaiLisp, a second invocation of a continuation k whose first invocation is still running will presumably abort the current path of execution in k's task and restart it at k, thus effectively aborting the first invocation of k. It is difficult to see how to solve this problem without fundamentally changing the nature of continuations in PaiLisp. For this reason (as well as the fact that PaiLisp does not permit multiple attempts to resolve a future, which however could easily be fixed using the Katz-Weise ideas in Figure 7), we must consider that PaiLisp does not pass test (3). Thus PaiLisp continuations occupy an intermediate position on our scale, generating correct results (according to our criteria) more often than MultiScheme but less often than Concert Multilisp.

In PaiLisp, a principal function of continuations is to be part of a small kernel language PaiLisp-Kernel, which can be used via macro expansion or procedure definition to define full PaiLisp as well as Multilisp and Qlisp. PaiLisp's definition of continuations is remarkably useful for this purpose and can be used to define constructs ranging from monitors [46] to parallel OR [48]. Since invoking a PaiLisp continuation can change the flow of control in another process, PaiLisp continuations can be used to kill or send a signal to another process, assuming that the target process has co-operated by creating the necessary continuations. None of the continuation mechanisms discussed above can do this, so PaiLisp continuations offer some basic support for multiple-approach (but not order-based) speculative computing that the previously discussed continuation mechanisms lack. On the other hand, PaiLisp-Kernel as it stands offers no way to communicate attributes such as priorities to the scheduler, and hence would have to be extended before being an adequate base for building a full implementation of speculative computing with sponsors.

We may conclude that PaiLisp continuations are an interesting construct with demonstrated usefulness in defining parallel Lisp languages based on a small kernel language, but that they are not as successful as the Katz-Weise approach in meeting our criteria for a continuation mechanism to be presented to parallel Lisp application programmers. Perhaps some version of PaiLisp continuations should exist side by side with standard continuations, using a name other than call/cc for the procedure that captures a PaiLisp continuation.

5.3.6 The Approach of Hieb and Dybvig

The Hieb-Dybvig approach adapts the $\mathcal{F}$ operator and prompts [22, 23] to "tree-structured" parallel computing. They assume that there is a tree structure that includes all tasks and is generated by the parent-child relationships between tasks. They further assume that a parent task returns a value only after all of its child tasks have returned values. Relative to $\mathcal{F}$, they add new flexibility in selecting the subtree whose state is to be captured (effectively, the prompt up to which the state is to be captured) and change a few details. Their approach abandons the idea of a single, universal continuation-capture procedure such as call/cc. Instead, they introduce a spawn operator that creates a new node in the task tree and constructs a *process controller* object corresponding to the new node. A process controller is analogous to a customized version of the $\mathcal{F}$ operator that captures the control state back to the spawn operator that created it. The object created when a process controller is invoked is analogous to an $\mathcal{F}$-continuation and is called a *process continuation*. Like $\mathcal{F}$-continuations, process continuations are compositional and hence differ from standard continuations; we always use the term "process continuation" below when referring to the former.

(spawn f) applies the procedure f to the newly created process controller object. A simple use of spawn is shown in the following expression:

```
(spawn (lambda (c) (+ 1 (c (lambda (k) 3)))))
```

When this expression is evaluated, the variable c is bound to the process controller object created by spawn. When c is invoked, k is bound to the resulting process continuation, which will accept a value and add 1 to it. However, in this case the process continuation is discarded and 3 is returned directly as the value of the whole expression (*i.e.*, as the result of the spawn). In a more complex example such as

```
(let ((pk (spawn (lambda (c) (+ 1 (c (lambda (k) k)))))))
  (pk (pk 0)))
```

the process continuation bound to k is returned from the spawn expression and bound to the variable pk. pk is thus bound to a function that adds 1 to its argument, so the value of the above let expression is 2. We can see from this example that process continuations are multi-use: a process subtree can be restarted several times from the point in its execution at which a continuation was captured.

Unlike any of the previously discussed call/cc mechanisms, a process controller can capture the state of a whole subtree of tasks. Specifically, application of a process controller c to a procedure f suspends all tasks in the subtree rooted at c's associated process tree node and packages their state into a process continuation k. f is then applied to k; the continuation for this call to f is the continuation of the spawn invocation that created c. (It is illegal to invoke a process controller c if c's associated process tree node is not part of the continuation of the call to c.)

Since process continuations are compositional, if a process continuation k is invoked, all tasks in k's associated subtree resume execution where they were suspended, but when a value is finally returned from k's root node, the value appears as the value of the invocation of k. Thus the value returned by the following expression is 2:

```
(let ((pk (spawn (lambda (c) (pcall + 1 (c (lambda (k) k)))))))
  (pk (pk 0)))
```

((pcall F A B) evaluates F, A, and B in parallel and then applies the resulting function to the resulting values.) It is pleasing that the introduction of pcall, which is the only difference between this expression and the previous example, does not change the result.

Process controllers and process continuations can be useful even in sequential programming, where they can be used as a generalization of $\mathcal{F}$ and $\mathcal{F}$-continuations for purposes such as building iterators and backtracking control structures. Additionally, they can be used in parallel programs to generate "iterators" that search in parallel for the next value to yield, but then suspend all branches of the search until a further value has been demanded, at which point all branches of the search can be resumed [44].

The tree of process controllers that builds up as a program executes is similar in some ways to a sponsor network, although it is more restricted in form since it is onstrained to be a tree rather than an arbitrary graph. Invoking a process controller o suspend its controlled tasks likewise has some features in common with the staying of a group of tasks that have lost their sponsorship; thus, like PaiLisp continuations, process controllers could be used to implement parallel OR. In fact, it is rather simpler o use process controllers than PaiLisp continuations to kill off the remaining parts of a process tree that has become irrelevant. This is especially true when there are nested speculative constructs: invoking a process controller will automatically suspend execution of all descendant tasks of that controller, no matter how deep the task tree has become.

Unfortunately, like PaiLisp continuations, process controllers by themselves offer no mechanism for communicating attributes such as priorities to the scheduler, so they are not useful for order-based speculative computing. Moreover, a process has no way o protect itself from being suspended or terminated at an arbitrary point by another process invoking a process controller that is a common ancestor. Thus a process has no way, for example, to protect itself from being terminated while holding a lock. The similarities between process controllers and speculative computing mechanisms suggest hat a set of common implementation techniques might be useful for both process continuations and speculative computing; on the other hand, process controllers and process continuations seem too restricted in their current form for a full speculative computing system to be built on top of them.

The restriction to tree-structured parallel computing is another limitation of process continuations. In a language with futures, such as Multilisp, the tree induced by parent-child task relationships can still be defined, but it is not as useful because a parent task may return while its child is still executing, and a task may become blocked waiting for a task that is not its child. A definition of process continuations for Multilisp would have to grapple with questions such as what should be done if a task T invokes a process controller that is associated with an ancestor task A of T, but A has already returned a value. Since process continuations differ from call/cc continuations even in sequential programs, it makes no sense to apply our compatibility criteria directly. However, we can view process continuations as a new sequential Scheme construct, and it would be interesting to know whether a parallel version of process continuations could be defined that would work in Multilisp and meet our criteria for compatibility with the sequential version.

5.3.7 Summary

Of the several continuation mechanisms surveyed above, that of Katz and Weise [51] looks like it defines the best semantics for making continuations and futures work together, meeting all of the criteria set forth in Section 5.3.2 for compatibility with continuations in sequential Scheme. Other mechanisms surveyed, notably PaiLisp continuations [48] and process continuations [44] do not meet the compatibility criteria as well but do offer interesting capabilities to control and terminate the execution of tasks, something that the Katz-Weise approach does not provide. These other mechanisms thus provide some support for speculative computing, but since the control they offer basically only allows starting and stopping task execution, they are considerably less expressive (though possibly also less expensive) than the sponsor model for speculative computing, especially for order-based speculative computing.

If we take the Katz-Weise approach as our standard, various interesting questions arise concerning its interaction with speculative computing. As mentioned above, it would be interesting to see how speculative-computing ideas could help in focusing processing resources on the computations that are (or are the most likely to become) legitimate, and avoid expending processing on tasks that will never become legitimate.

A quite different problem concerns whether (and how) the sponsorship of a task should change if it invokes a continuation. Sponsorship of a task is typically (though not always) predicated on the current estimate of the importance of a value that the task is expected to compute. A task that invokes a continuation has effectively switched to another computation that may compute a different value. One might argue that sponsorship should be associated with continuations rather than tasks: a continuation's sponsor would sponsor any task that invoked that continuation. Unfortunately, it is hard to say anything general about what a task will do when continuations are used—a task that invokes a continuation may have switched to an entirely different computation, or it may simply have taken a temporary, coroutine-like detour on the way toward computing the result associated with its original continuation. This difficulty is the motivation for MultiScheme's implementation of future (shown in Figure 2): while MultiScheme's implementation may not meet the criteria of Section 5.3.2 as well as others, it at least makes it easy to know which future will receive a value when a task finishes executing and therefore which task to sponsor while awaiting that future's value [73].

Unfortunately, the Katz-Weise continuation semantics really look more desirable, so we need to find another way to handle the sponsorship issue. Continuations are inherently an unstructured enough control mechanism that general and useful theorems about the flow of control in programs that use continuations are hard to find. This situation is very similar to the situation that arises with side effects. It thus seems likely that the best way to handle sponsorship when continuations are used is similar to the approach applied in the case of side effects: a simple and easily understood default policy, augmented with mechanisms for the programmer to control sponsorship when the default policy does not produce the desired behavior.

The definition of a sound continuation mechanism is of interest in its own right, but continuations are also useful for error and exception handling, discussed next.

5.4 Errors and Exceptions

An interesting problem created by future and delay involves how to handle errors and exceptions during program execution. A common approach to handling such events in sequential programming languages is to reflect them to a dynamically enclosing context (e.g., from a procedure to its caller) [31, 47, 66, 90], but applying this approach to Multilisp leads to some unusual problems. Consider an expression (future (/ 3 0))—or, perhaps worse—(delay (/ 3 0)). In both cases, evaluation of the expression (/ 3 0), which will cause an error, may be delayed long enough that the dynamically enclosing context has completed its work and no longer exists. Therefore, a policy of notifying the dynamically enclosing context cannot always be carried out. (This is another case where it is helpful to restrict concurrency to be tree-structured, as Hieb and Dybvig [44] do—see Section 5.3.6.)

Exception handling is, of course, a capability that is far from standardized even in sequential programming languages. (Scheme, for example, defines no specific error-handling mechanism [82].) The importance of compatibility with a sequential version is therefore somewhat less here than in the case of continuations; however, we would like to handle errors and exceptions in a fashion that makes sense when applied to a sequential program, and is compatible with that fashion (as dictated by the criteria of Section 5.1) when extended to parallel programs.

What exception-handling capabilities are important? Basically, the programmer needs the ability to specify handlers for exception conditions that may arise. As a special case—typically the default—the handler can be a standard system debugger, thus unifying the handling of exceptions with that of errors (which we may define as unanticipated exceptions). Whether a handler is programmer-supplied or is a standard system procedure, several options should be available to it:

1. Resuming the computation that signalled the exception, perhaps specifying a result to be returned by the exception-raising operation.

2. Throwing a specified value to a specified continuation (typically the continuation is that of an enclosing computation that is to be aborted because of the exception).

3. Abandoning the entire computation, returning to the top-level command loop or its equivalent.

Especially when the handler is a debugger, some additional capabilities are useful to support the user's interactive exploration of what may have gone wrong:

4. Accessing the state of the interrupted computation.

5. Starting and stopping other parts of the computation (*e.g.*, siblings or "cousins" of the exception-raising task).

Continuations and speculative computing mechanisms can both be valuable in providing these capabilities. Capabilities (1)–(3) listed above can all be provided through suitable use of continuations. (1) can be supported by creating a continuation when an exception is raised and passing it to the exception handler for possible use. (2) can be supported by prearrangement (explicit call/cc operations to capture and save the necessary continuations) or perhaps in conjunction with (4) by a mechanism for creating "ex post facto continuations" (capturing continuations that still exist in a control stack somewhere but were not explicitly captured by call/cc operations in the program). (3) can be handled easily by prearrangement if the top-level command loop captures a suitable continuation before executing user code.

This use of continuations presents the problem of illegitimate returns, discussed in Section 5.3.4. An expression such as

```
(call/cc (lambda (k) (cons (future (/ 3 0)) '())))
```

may already have returned a value when the divide-by-zero exception is raised. If the exception handler then throws a replacement value to the continuation bound to k, there will be two returns from the expression. The second return (caused by the exception handler) is the only legitimate one. Indeed, this scenario differs little from the example

```
(call/cc (lambda (k) (cons (future (k 5)) '()))),
```

given in Section 5.3.4, except that the mechanism for throwing to k is more direct in the latter case. Fortunately, the Katz-Weise definition of future (Figure 7) provides a basic mechanism to deal with this; however, processing resources would be freed sooner if sponsorship could be removed quickly from the aborted (illegitimate) computation, staying its tasks. (It is interesting to note the similarity between our needs here and the functionality provided by process controllers, discussed in Section 5.3.6.)

Returning to the above list of exception-handling capabilities, the details of supporting (4) are clearly implementation-dependent; however, it is obviously desirable to have available the basic facilities needed by interactive debuggers to display stack backtraces and examine and modify variable-binding environments. Also useful would be provisions for seeing what tasks exist and what tasks are waiting for particular values or events. Facilities for navigating the sponsor network would also be valuable, since the sponsor network should offer a more hierarchical and modular view of the subcomputations currently in progress than can be obtained by looking at individual tasks. Finally, provisions for modifying as well as examining the sponsor network would support capability (5) above, by allowing the programmer to selectively add or remove sponsorship for portions of the overall computation.

A final issue related to debugging involves the ability to interrupt and examine runaway programs. Although a programming error often manifests itself as a runtime error, sometimes it just shows up as non-termination. Systems for sequential programming typically have an interrupt character (such as control-C) that can be typed to suspend program execution and invoke the debugger, which can then be used to examine the state of the program under test and terminate, resume, or modify its execution path, much as if a run-time error had occurred at that point. One approach to building such an interrupt facility for a parallel Lisp is for it to suspend *all* tasks: this is done in the MultiScheme system [73]. The major drawback of this approach is that it is incompatible with "system programming," where several interacting programs may coexist in the same environment and some of them are vital, say, to displaying output on the user's terminal. In such a system, halting *all* tasks when an interrupt is requested will be overly strong medicine. A better idea would be for every computation started from the user's top-level command loop to have its own sponsor. Then it would be appropriate simply to stay that sponsor when the interrupt character is typed, and start a debugger sponsored by a new sponsor. Debugger commands could then be used, following the interrupt, to make any additional desired adjustments in sponsorship of computations, but system maintenance tasks not sponsored by the user's command loop would continue running unless explicitly stayed by the user.

5.4.1 Debugger User Interface

Typical sequential Lisp systems handle an exception by suspending the original computation and invoking a *breakloop* that provides the user all the capabilities of a top-level read-eval-print loop. From a breakloop, the user can examine the state of the computation, perform other computations, and resume the original computation. If another exception occurs during interaction with the breakloop, a nested breakloop is invoked.

In this approach, every exception invokes a breakloop. The straightforward parallel extension of this idea is for any task receiving an exception to invoke a breakloop. When errors occur in many tasks, many breakloops will be invoked. In Concert Multilisp, a *censor* is used to control which of multiple breakloops has access to the terminal; the user can command the censor to shift its focus from one breakloop to another. In Butterfly Lisp [3], a separate window is created to run each breakloop. In both cases the user may have to contend with an abundance of breakloops, and if related tasks continue to run, the cause of the error may be obscured. MultiScheme [73] prevents the generation of multiple breakloops by stopping all tasks when an exception occurs, but the user can inspect only one task from the subsequent breakloop, and the policy of stopping all tasks can have the other problems discussed above. Mul-T addresses the problem with its *group* concept, described in Section 5.4.3.

5.4.2 Concert Multilisp's Exception Handling

The idea of handling exceptions using sponsors and continuations is motivated by new ideas in speculative computing and continuation management, and has never been implemented in its entirety. As a partial solution to the same problems, Concert Multilisp adopted the philosophy of communicating errors and exceptions to *users* of a value—operations that touch the value—rather than always to the dynamically enclosing context [35, 38]. This philosophy parallels that of the "error values" in some functional languages [92]. Concert Multilisp's error values, known as *exception values*, have the property that, when touched by a task T, they raise an exception in T. This can lead T's associated future to resolve to an exception value, propagating the exception to all tasks that touch T's value. However, Concert Multilisp also contains mechanisms a programmer can use to control or limit the propagation of exceptions when desired. This propagation of exceptions takes the place of throwing to a continuation to exit an exception handler.

Each Concert Multilisp task has an associated *exception handling procedure*. By default, a task created using future or delay inherits the same exception-handling procedure as its parent task, but this default can be overridden by giving an exception-handling procedure for the child task as an explicit second operand to future (or delay). When an exception is raised, a description of the exception is constructed and passed to the current task's exception-handling procedure along with a *suspension* of the task (a single-use continuation that can be used to resume the task). The exception handler of the top-level task created by the Concert Multilisp listener loop is a system-supplied debugger, which will be invoked to handle all exceptional conditions unless explicitly overridden in the program.

Propagation of errors and exceptions through exception values has a curious consequence: it is possible for a long-lived data structure to contain exception values if the computation of some parts of the data structure could not complete normally. On the positive side, the existence of exception values at least makes it possible to represent a data structure not all of whose elements can be computed. On the negative side, however, exception values can be viewed as "time bombs" or "land mines" that can be planted in data structures to sabotage later computations [35, 38].

5.4.3 The Mul-T Debugging Environment

Mul-T's debugging environment is based on *groups*, which are collections of tasks resulting from the evaluation of a single expression typed by the user. Groups can be started, stopped, resumed, and killed independently of other groups. Basic support functions that are not naturally associated with any specific group, such as exception handling and access to the terminal, are performed by distinguished tasks [61].

Groups in Mul-T support a pleasing parallel extension of the breakloop idea. All tasks created during evaluation of an expression typed by the user belong to the same group G. If an exception occurs, the group G is stopped, suspending all of its constituent tasks. At this point the user regains control and may examine and alter the state of any of the stopped tasks. Even though several tasks may be stopped, the computation is represented by a single stopped group. Mul-T's group concept thus represents a restricted case of the sponsor-based mechanism advocated above.

There may be several stopped groups at a given time, analogous to the nested breakloops of sequential Lisps. The most recently stopped group is called the *current group*, and the task in which the exception occurred is called the *current task*. The usual Lisp debugging commands apply by default to the current task of the current group, so Mul-T's debugger "feels" like a sequential Scheme debugger. But the commands also allow referring to other tasks or other stopped groups. An extra benefit of decoupling stopped computations is that the user may resume them in any order, in contrast to sequential Lisp systems where only the most recently suspended computation may be resumed.

In Mul-T, control of the interactive terminal stream lies in a distinguished task separate from all tasks performing user computations. Further, there is a distinguished exception-handler task for each processor in the system. These special-purpose "server" tasks run only during exception handling or group termination and coordinate with the Mul-T scheduler to insure that

- After an exception is signalled by one task in a group, no other tasks in the group will run.
- Only one processor at a time runs the terminal control task.

5.4.4 Summary

Error and exception handling takes on a new look in the presence of parallel computing and futures, since the control stack on which many debugging approaches are based no longer has such a simple form. However, the previously discussed ideas for implementing continuations and speculative computing seem able to solve most of the problems introduced. There are still a number of loose ends. One is the question of how to handle exceptions signalled by speculative or illegitimate tasks. Should handling of such exceptions be deferred until the task is known to be relevant (or legitimate)? Another question concerns the architecture of the debugging system that an exception handler might invoke; some comments on debugging tools appear in Section 7. Nevertheless, the basic outlines of a reasonable approach to error and exception handling in Multilisp now seem clear.

5.5 Data Parallelism

It is instructive to consider the distinction between "data parallelism" and "control parallelism." Data parallelism is achieved by performing the same operations concurrently on many elements of an aggregate data structure [45], while in control parallelism at most one instance of any given part of the program is executing at any one time. A parallel algorithm for elementwise addition of two vectors is a typical application of data parallelism; a pipeline of processes performing successive transformations on a stream of data values is a typical use of control parallelism. It is often asserted (correctly) that data parallelism is the only kind that increases as larger versions of the same problem are solved, while control parallelism only increases when programs get larger. Therefore, if massively parallel computers of the future apply algorithms of moderate complexity to very large data sets, data parallelism will have to be the primary source of concurrency.

Data parallelism has further been identified with SIMD architectures, while it is sometimes asserted that MIMD architectures can exploit only control parallelism, thus rendering them inferior to the SIMD approach. MIMD architectures can indeed exploit control parallelism, which is difficult for SIMD machines, but there is nothing preventing MIMD machines from also exploiting data parallelism. Indeed, Multilisp, which is very much a MIMD computing model, exploits data parallelism every time future is used in a parallel, recursive exploration of all the nodes in a tree. Inability to exploit data parallelism is thus not the Achilles' heel of MIMD architectures that it is sometimes made out to be.

Nevertheless, programming languages motivated by the challenges of exploiting data parallelism in the SIMD world contain ideas that can profitably be adapted to the MIMD world as well. In particular, aggregate data types such as the *xappings* of Connection Machine Lisp [86] and aggregate operations on those types are very valuable in providing ways to rapidly spawn large amounts of concurrent activity. future, on the other hand, only spawns one new task each time it is executed. While large numbers of tasks can be spawned quickly by using future recursively in a tree-like structure, use of future on the linear-list data structures often used by Lisp programmers to represent data aggregates does not spawn tasks quickly enough [38]. Built-in aggregate data types such as xappings would give programmers quick, easy access to massive data parallelism without requiring them to design explicit tree or array structures to represent the data aggregates [41]. Language extensions in this direction should be explored.

5.6 Summary

The basic semantics of **future** and scheduling in Multilisp are sufficient for many parallel programs that involve only mandatory computation. On the other hand, the weak specification of scheduling in Multilisp, though it provides useful flexibility for implementations, makes it difficult to implement algorithms involving speculative computing. *Sponsors* can be used to supply the additional control needed. Mul-T's *groups* are seen to be a limited kind of sponsor useful in managing multiple stopped computations.

Continuations are a frequently useful feature of sequential Scheme that do not mix well with the traditional definition of **future** in Multilisp. The redefinition of **future** due to Katz and Weise and shown in Figure 7 solves the semantic problem, though at some increase in the cost of **future**. In combination with sponsors, this Katz-Weise approach allows a new, improved view of how to handle errors and exceptions in Multilisp.

Finally, extant **future**-based parallel Lisps do not include primitive aggregate data types that promote rapid spawning of large amounts of concurrent computation. Languages such as Connection Machine Lisp, developed for use on SIMD architectures, may offer some help in addressing this weakness.

6. Implementation

Efficient implementation of sequential Scheme and other languages with run-time type tagging and garbage collection has received considerable attention and met with considerable success [12, 15, 16, 59], but futures and concurrency introduce new implementation challenges. The major implementation challenges (beyond those of a sequential Scheme) for Multilisp are

- Suppressing excessive task and future creation.
- Task scheduling and task queue management.
- Storage allocation and parallel garbage collection.
- Touching.
- Dynamic binding.

We consider each of these in turn.

6.1 Reducing the Cost of future

A useful "benchmark" for the cost of task and future creation is the expression (touch (future 0)), whose execution involves exactly one creation of a task and a future and exactly one synchronization operation on the future. Mul-T makes a serious attempt at "industrial-strength" performance; the result is that Mul-T takes approximately 196 instructions to evaluate this expression [61]. Although this is considerably less than it takes to do the same thing on several other parallel Lisp systems [61], it is much more than the 8 instructions taken by a call to (and return from) the trivial procedure (lambda () 0). The experimentally measured execution time for the expression (touch (future 0)) is about 100 μsec when executed on one NS32532 processor of the Encore Multimax. This suggests that the processor is delivering only about 2 MIPS on this instruction mix, which emphasizes data-structure manipulation and memory-to-memory instructions to a greater extent than a typical computational instruction mix does. (This measurement actually gives a pessimistic estimate of the overhead associated with future. In many cases no tasks will block on a future, reducing the overhead to approximately 119 instructions [61].)

6.1.1 Inlining

In many parallel Lisp programs, creating a task for every use of future leads to creation of tasks far in excess of the number of processors available to execute them. In this case, Multilisp's extremely relaxed requirements for fairness in scheduling (see Section 5.2.1) create an opportunity to optimize the implementation of future. In the expression (future X), execution of the parent task concurrently with the evaluation of X is *permissible* but is not *required*. It is thus generally permissible for an implementation to evaluate X fully before proceeding with execution of the parent task: in other words, to treat future as an identity operator. We refer to this treatment as *inlining* because the expression X is effectively evaluated "in line" as a subroutine, rather than concurrently as a separate task. We may view inlining as a run-time mechanism for increasing the granularity of tasks and hence reducing the proportion of processor time that is devoted to task management overhead. This run-time "chunking" or granularity-increasing mechanism can supplement (or, in optimistic scenarios, even replace) the programmer's efforts to place future constructs so as to avoid excessively fine granularity while still exposing enough parallelism.

It is worth noting that the benefits of inlining are greatest for the "bundled" future construct. If a program contains the "unbundled" primitives of Figure 1, then inlining can still be applied but its benefits will be reduced, unless a compiler can recognize a particular constellation of these primitives as being equivalent to future. For example, if inlining were applied to the fork primitive in Figure 1, the task creation and management cost would be eliminated, but the costs of make-future, determine!, and later touches of the future would remain.

Inlining can improve performance if (1) we can accurately identify future expressions whose tasks are "excess" in the sense that they are not needed to utilize the full parallel processing power of the machine and (2) processing an inlined future is cheaper than processing a future that creates a task. The latter condition definitely holds: inlining (future X) avoids the costs of setting up a new task (*e.g.*, allocating and initializing space for its stack), the queue management associated with scheduling the new task for execution, and even the cost of allocating and initializing a future object to act as a placeholder for X's value. Further savings are realized when the value of the inlined expression (future X) is touched: since no future was ever actually created for X, touching the value of the inlined (future X) is no more expensive than touching the value of X itself.

A simple strategy, *load-based inlining*, is for a processor to inline all futures it encounters when the number of tasks on its queues is greater than or equal to some threshold T. The rationale for this strategy is that these queued tasks represent a backlog of work that is available if any processor becomes idle. In practice, a threshold of 1 (allowing a backlog of just one task per processor to suppress further task creation) works fairly well—about as well as any other threshold—for many programs [61, 76]. Load-based inlining can be implemented cheaply and the cost of an inlined future construct is quite low [61, 62].

Load-based inlining is vulnerable to *task starvation* caused either by *bursty task creation* or *parent-child welding*. Bursty task creation refers to the fact that opportunities to create tasks may be distributed unevenly across a program. At the moment when a task is inlined, it may appear that there are plenty of other tasks available to execute, but by the time these tasks finish executing, there may be too few opportunities to create more tasks. Consequently, processors may go idle that could have been kept busy if less inlining had been done earlier in the program's execution. Parent-child welding refers to the fact that inlining permanently "welds" together a parent and child task: if an inlined child becomes blocked waiting for a future to resolve (or for some other event), the parent is blocked as well and is not available for execution. On the other hand, if a non-inlined child blocks, its parent is still runnable.

In extreme cases, parent-child welding can even result in deadlock. A child task can become blocked waiting for an event that will only occur when its parent resumes execution; if the child must finish before the parent can resume, the computation will never finish [61, 76]. Such deadlock can never occur in the simple case of Mul-T programs generated by starting from a side-effect-free sequential program and just wrapping future around selected subexpressions; nevertheless, the fact that inlining can cause deadlock in a program that otherwise would always produce an answer is a serious concern.

6.1.2 Lazy Task Creation

Load-based inlining is implemented in Mul-T; in the cases where it works well, the benefits are large [61], so an inlining mechanism without the problems discussed above would be attractive. *Lazy task creation* [76] is such a mechanism. It is essentially a revocable inlining mechanism: when a future is encountered, its task is provisionally inlined, but enough information is retained to enable the inlining decision to be retroactively reversed at a later time. To allow this, tasks must have a stack structure such that the "seam" between the portions of stack pertaining to the parent and child task executions can be found, and that the stack can be split apart at that point to yield two independent stacks—one for the parent and one for the child—even after the child has gone some distance into its execution. This provides a way to "unweld" a blocked child from its parent so that the parent can resume execution, thus solving the task starvation problems discussed above, including the deadlock problem. Even a running child can be "unwelded" from its parent, furnishing an additional task if it is needed because some other processor has just finished a task.

Lazy task creation provisionally inlines *every* future and splits a task only when a processor needs a new task to execute. With suitable implementation techniques, the extra cost of making inlining decisions revocable is small [76]. Lazy task creation thus offers the best of both worlds: the performance advantages of inlining are obtained in every situation except where task splitting yields additional useful parallelism.

A special attraction of inlining and lazy task creation is that it promises to reduce the performance cost of semantic enhancements that make future and task creation more expensive. For example, the Katz-Weise future implementation of Figure 7 is significantly more expensive than the simple Multilisp future implementation of Figure 1 because of the call/cc operation and maintenance of the variable *first*. Legitimacy propagation adds yet further costs. If, through lazy task creation, the vast majority of future constructs are inlined, these costs can be avoided most of the time. All the expressive power of the Katz-Weise approach remains available, but its computational burden is considerably reduced. Similar comments apply to speculative computing support: if a simple future construct means, "Create a child task with the same sponsor as the parent," then lazy task creation is quite appropriate and the costs of sponsor management and speculative task scheduling are lowered.

Neither load-based inlining nor lazy task creation is particularly effective in increasing task granularity in the case of fine-grained linear recursive programs (loops), as when applying a procedure to every element of a linear list [76]. A possible way to solve this problem is to eliminate such loops as completely as possible and replace them with operations on suitable aggregate data types whose representations would be tree- or vector-like, allowing granularity enhancement to be more effective. Adding built-in aggregate data types such as Connection Machine Lisp's xappings [86] would promote this goal.

3.2 Scheduling

We now turn from the topic of when to create tasks to the question of how to manage the tasks that have been created and in what order to schedule them for execution. The scheduling semantics specified in Section 5.2.1 allow considerable latitude in task scheduling decisions, which is exploited by inlining and lazy task creation to reduce the number of tasks created. This latitude can also be exploited to schedule tasks in a way that preserves locality of reference and avoids filling up memory by having too many parallel tasks in existence simultaneously.

A classical parallel-processing problem occurs when there is too *much* parallelism in a program. A highly parallel program may reach a deadlocked state where every task, to make progress, requires additional storage (*e.g.*, to make yet more tasks), and no more storage is available. This can happen even though a sequential version of the same program requires very little storage. The sequential version effectively executes the tasks one after another, reusing the same storage pool. The parallel machine runs out of storage by trying to execute all tasks at the same time.

Ideally, parallel tasks should be created until the processing power of the parallel machine is fully utilized (*saturated*) and then execution within each task should become sequential. This execution order has been called BUSD ("*B*readth-first *U*ntil *S*aturation, then *D*epth-first") [76]. First-in, first-out (FIFO) is a natural queuing discipline to produce breadth-first (fair) execution, which is good for spawning a lot of parallel tasks but can have large memory requirements. Conversely, last-in, first-out

(LIFO) queuing naturally produces depth-first (unfair) execution. By mimicking the "LIFO queuing" performed by a stack in sequential programming, LIFO queuing tends to conserve space by beginning a new subcomputation only after a previous subcomputation (and all computations nested within it) have finished, and for the same reason tends to produce shorter task queue lengths. LIFO is also the execution order produced by inlining, which is performed under lazy task creation chiefly when the machine is saturated; thus, lazy task creation tends to produce BUSD execution [76].

Thanks to the weakness of Multilisp's scheduling semantics, both queuing disciplines are legal. Moreover, the time to complete a mandatory parallel computation is generally not very sensitive to task execution order, as long as runnable (but not running) tasks are not allowed to coexist with idle processors. (Speculative computations are, of course, more sensitive to scheduling order.) Multilisp schedulers can thus try to approximate BUSD execution by using a mixed strategy with both FIFO and LIFO aspects, without fear of either violating Multilisp's semantics or picking a seriously suboptimal execution order for the application program at hand.

6.2.1 Scheduling in Concert Multilisp

In the Concert Multilisp scheduler, each task has two possible states: *active* and *pending*. Generally, each processor has at most one active task, which is executed until it finishes or becomes blocked. When a processor P evaluates an expression such as (future X), the *child* task remains active on P and the *parent* task is suspended and pushed onto P's LIFO pending queue. If the system is saturated, the parent task will remain suspended until the child task has finished, as would occur in sequential (or inlined) execution, thus limiting task queue growth to the same magnitude as stack growth in a sequential implementation. In practice, the task queue growth (and general storage requirements) of programs are often dramatically lower when using this policy than when using FIFO task queues.

When a processor's active task finishes or blocks, the processor looks at its queue of pending tasks to find one to activate. If this queue is empty, it looks in the pending task queues of other processors to find a task to "steal" and activate [34]. Thus a task will eventually be executed by the same processor that created it, unless some other processor has run out of tasks. This strategy should help preserve locality of memory references.

An additional benefit of this scheduling policy is that, in saturation, tasks that would be waiting for a future tend to be suspended while tasks calculating the values of futures tend to be active. Thus, references to futures that have not yet resolved are only a small fraction of all references to futures, so referencing tasks seldom need to be suspended [78]. But if there are idle processors in the system, one of them can pick up the parent task while the child task is still active, and thus parallelism is not reduced.

If an active task blocks, waiting for a future or a semaphore, its processor will search for another task to activate. This is a departure from the strict LIFO discipline, but there is no evidence that it constitutes a serious loophole in the strategy of resource usage control via unfairness.

When a processor needs to steal a task from another processor, the order in which other processors' pending queues are searched can influence locality. The Concert multiprocessor had a natural "clustering" or locality hierarchy among the processors [36, 39] and it made sense to search pending queues in the searching processor's own cluster first. Even in the absence of any significant "clustering" in the hardware architecture, imposing an arbitrary clustering hierarchy on the scheduler's search pattern seems to improve locality [78]. The reasons for this are poorly understood, but perhaps a hierarchical scheduler search pattern increases the chances that, when a task migrates, it will migrate back to a processor where it or a related computation previously executed, rather than "wandering off" in a random walk across all the nodes of the multiprocessor.

When the multiprocessor is not saturated and there are many idle processors, the scheduler must avoid causing excessive nonlocal memory traffic and lock contention. In one approach to reducing these costs, when a processor fails to find a pending task to steal, it registers itself as "idle" and then awaits a wakeup when a pending task appears; of course, this waiting and wakeup must be implemented carefully to avoid race conditions. A simpler expedient, employed in Concert Multilisp, is to associate an "outside searcher bit" with each cluster. A processor finding nothing to steal within its own cluster performs a test-and-set operation on its cluster's outside searcher bit, and proceeds to search other clusters only if the bit was found to be 0 (meaning that there are currently no other outside searchers from that cluster). This limits the number of processors concurrently attempting to access task queues in clusters other than their own and hence reduces contention. Moreover, before searching a given cluster's task queues, a searching processor can check that cluster's outside searcher bit. If the bit is set, indicating that a processor within that cluster has recently searched unsuccessfully for pending tasks in that cluster, the cluster can be skipped (it will eventually be revisited if no other pending tasks are found), reducing the amount of work required to find a cluster with work available to be stolen, if such a cluster exists.

It is interesting to wonder whether a processor stealing a task from another processor's pending queue should take the most recently or least recently enqueued task on that queue. In Concert Multilisp, the most recently enqueued task is taken, preserving the LIFO queuing discipline. But it could be argued that the least recently enqueued task is likely to be the root of a larger computation for the stealing processor to work on, more closely approximating BUSD execution and leading to greater locality and less stealing later on. This hypothesis deserves a careful experiment.

When a processor P resolves a future, any tasks awaiting that future's value must be re-enqueued for execution. Concert Multilisp pushes all of these tasks onto the pending task queue of P. Locality might be better enhanced if they were re-enqueued on the processor where they last ran, but this strategy has never been tried in Concert Multilisp.

3.2.2 Scheduling in Mul-T

In Mul-T, each processor has two LIFO queues, one for newly created tasks (the *new task queue*) and one for tasks ready to run again after blocking (the *suspended task queue*) [61]. When a task is created, it is put on the new task queue of the processor creating the task. When a blocked task becomes runnable again, it is placed on the suspended task queue of the processor that was running it when it blocked (in contrast to Concert Multilisp's policy). When a processor finishes a task, it looks in several places for another task to run, observing the following priority order:

1. Its own suspended task queue.

2. Its own new task queue.

3. The new task queues of all other processors.

4. The suspended task queues of all other processors.

This policy aims to increase locality by resisting the migration between processors of partially completed work (which may have built up some useful state on its local processor) while making newly created work (which may be less expensive to move) available for migration if needed for load balancing. (The effectiveness of this strategy in actually increasing locality has not been studied.) An interesting difference between Mul-T's queuing policy and Concert Multilisp's is that in (future X), Mul-T enqueues the *child* task (on the new task queue) and continues with the parent task. This policy is attractive in Mul-T because the expense of suspending the parent task is relatively higher than in Concert Multilisp, but this policy departs from the ideal of BUSD execution order. Even so, task queue growth and storage use are not generally observed to be excessive, so the unfairness introduced by Mul-T's LIFO queues must be an effective damper on task creation even though a strictly depth-first execution order is not used.

6.2.3 Scheduling under Lazy Task Creation

Under lazy task creation, scheduling has a rather different look. Since tasks are only created upon demand, there is never a reason to enqueue a newly created task—its demander can immediately take it and execute it. At first sight, it might appear that task queues are never needed, but there are still situations where tasks may be enqueued: for example, when a future with several waiting tasks resolves. Nevertheless, the frequency of task enqueuing and dequeuing operations is sharply reduced: this is a principal benefit of lazy task creation.

When a processor finishes its current task, lazy task creation makes it much more likely that no suspended task will be immediately available to execute; the processor must obtain work by finding a processor executing a task with a "seam" in it and breaking the task at the seam. The problem of searching for a nonempty task queue is thus replaced by the similar problem of finding a seam that can be broken. While experience with lazy task creation is still preliminary, we can expect the same contention and locality issues to arise in both cases.

Lazy task creation suggests new strategies to use when waiting for and resolving futures. When a task with a seam in it must block to wait for a future to resolve (or for any other event) the processor executing the task can simply break the task at the seam closest to the top of the stack, enqueue the top part to wait on the future, and continue execution just below the broken seam. This avoids the need to access any queues to search for work. It also means that waiting tasks never have seams, so they need not be searched by idle processors looking for seams. When a processor resolves a future just before completing execution of a task, if any tasks were waiting on the future, one of them can be resumed immediately by the processor instead of being enqueued, again reducing task-queue manipulation costs.

6.2.4 Scheduling of Speculative Computations

Speculative computing introduces significant new scheduler implementation challenges. Schedulers for mandatory computations basically try to expend a minimum of effort in finding an available computation, using only very inexpensive and crude heuristics for choosing among available tasks to enhance locality or reduce memory requirements. A scheduler for speculative computations is expected to exert reasonable efforts to implement the scheduling policy dictated by the distribution of attributes from sponsors to tasks. For example, if tasks have a priority attribute, then a scheduler should avoid executing a low-priority task on one processor while a higher-priority task sits idle elsewhere. To guarantee that such a priority inversion *never* occurs would be very costly, requiring something like a check of all processors' activities every time a task's priority changes or a task becomes available for execution. On the other hand, allowing such priority inversions to persist for a long time is also costly, because processing resources are not being devoted to the optimal set of tasks. The speculative scheduler's job is to balance these two costs by detecting priority inversions fairly quickly and fairly cheaply.

The design of a scheduler for speculative computations is reported by Osborne [79], but we have little other experience with implementations of speculative schedulers. Thus, little is known about either the best techniques or their costs. Developing good techniques and a good understanding of their performance is an important research topic. If effective and efficient speculative schedulers can be implemented, they will be useful for more than sponsor-based speculative computing: their ability to handle tasks with different priorities could help in performing parallel real-time computing as well.

6.2.5 Compiler and Operating-System Interaction with Scheduling

Even with the granularity enhancement possible through inlining, task creation and scheduling operations in a future-based parallel Lisp tend to be very frequent and must be efficient. Moreover, there will generally be a large number of tasks in existence at any given moment. Thus, the same implementation challenges faced by "threads libraries" for parallel programming are present for Multilisp as well.

In existing Multilisp implementations, scheduling operations are kept cheap by creating only one operating-system process for each physical processor. Each such process runs a user-mode scheduler that manipulates tasks without informing the operating system of their existence. This strategy works fairly well as long as the tasks' activities are computational, but is awkward if a task performs a system call that blocks, since every task blocked in the operating system takes one of the physical processors out of circulation.

Another problem with user-mode task scheduling surfaces when a multiprocessor is shared among several users. An operating-system process running a simple user-mode scheduler looks busy even when there are no tasks to schedule and it is merely searching for work. This prevents other users' programs, which might have some real computing to do, from being scheduled. In general, more thought needs to go into the interface between operating-system schedulers and user-mode schedulers. The operating-system scheduler, which is responsible for the overall allocation of resources among the users of a shared system, needs a way to get information about users' individual requirements from the user-mode schedulers. It also needs a way to "push back" on the user-mode schedulers, telling each one how many processors (and perhaps how much memory) it is allowed to use. Since system loads change from moment to moment, this feedback mechanism needs to operate continuously, not just when starting to run a new program. These problems of allocation of system resources among users become especially interesting when speculative computing is involved—at some level, a scheduler needs to allocate resources between user A's speculative computation at priority p and user B's at priority q. It seems as though something like a controller sponsor is needed at the operating-system level.

Another system-oriented problem comes from the large number of tasks that may exist at one time. Conventionally, each task would have a contiguous region of memory to use as a stack. The conventional technique for stack overflow detection is to put an unmapped "guard page" at the end of the region allocated for the stack and detect the page fault that occurs when an access beyond the end of the allocated stack segment is attempted. Page sizes tend to be fairly large, so the expense of dedicating an entire page to a task's stack becomes unattractive as the number of tasks grows. Moreover, some operating systems have problems creating an address space with a large number of "holes" in it, as would be required for the guard-page approach when there are many tasks.

An alternative (used in Mul-T [61]) is to have the compiler insert explicit bounds-checking instructions when the stack is extended (as by a procedure call), but this slows down execution. Another alternative is to abandon the linear stack format and instead use a linked list of stack frames. This can be done with fairly good performance [76] but still has costs that are avoided when a simple contiguous stack is used. It is possible that alternative hardware architectures could help here [76], but for existing architectures, none of the available alternatives is perfect.

6.2.6 Summary

Scheduling for a parallel Lisp has several goals: it should be cheap, it should minimize storage requirements and promote locality, and it may have to handle speculative tasks of differing priorities. Simple user-mode schedulers using LIFO queues seem to handle the first two requirements well when tasks are primarily computational, but speculative computing and operating-system interaction introduce new requirements whose solutions have not been explored much.

6.3 Storage Allocation and Garbage Collection

A major difference between Lisp-like languages and conventional C- or FORTRAN-like languages is the availability of garbage collection in Lisp. With a garbage collector to find and reclaim inaccessible storage, a programmer need not write code to determine when objects are no longer in use and can be deleted. This service is even more valuable in parallel computing than in sequential computing, because parallel computing brings new complexities whose solutions are more important (and harder to automate) than storage management and because if an object is used by several concurrent tasks, it is awkward to determine when all of the object's users have finished with it so it may be deleted safely.

The principal garbage-collector design options for parallel systems are the same as for sequential systems. Here, we focus exclusively on copying garbage collectors (as opposed to the mark-and-sweep variety), which are more widely used and seem a better choice for the large address spaces we would like to consider. Three important varieties of copying garbage collectors are the *stop-and-copy*, *on-the-fly*, and *incremental* varieties. In each variety, *mutator* tasks perform operations of the program being executed, including storage-allocation operations; *scavenger* tasks perform garbage-collection operations. In a stop-and-copy collector, mutators execute until storage is exhausted. All mutators are then suspended and all processors scavenge until a garbage collection is complete, after which the mutators can resume execution [17, 73, 75]. In on-the-fly collection, some processors always mutate and other processors always scavenge. Synchronization protocols impose the necessary discipline on interactions between mutators and concurrently running scavengers [20]. When incremental collection [10] is used, each processor can alternate between periods of time spent as a mutator and a scavenger. Synchronization protocols similar to those needed for on-the-fly collection are also needed here [34], but the division of labor between mutation and scavenging is more flexible.

Stop and copy is the simplest and most commonly used of these garbage collection schemes, since it is the only one in which mutating processors are not exposed to intermediate states of the scavenger. Incremental garbage collection is the most complex of the three, since the other two can be viewed as special cases of incremental collection arising from particular decisions about how to schedule processors between mutation and scavenging. On the other hand, the full generality of incremental garbage collection, with each processor able to switch between the two kinds of activity, is little more complex than on-the-fly garbage collection, since the complexity of ensuring correct interaction between mutating and scavenging processors exists in both cases. Concert Multilisp uses an incremental garbage collector [34], but other parallel Lisps have used stop-and-copy garbage collectors [61, 73, 75].

Although incremental garbage collection is the most complex, it is also the most flexible in the allocation of processor time, since each processor is free to switch between mutation and scavenging as needed. This flexibility takes some pressure off the garbage collector's load-balancing mechanisms. Efficient operation of a stop-and-copy garbage collector requires an even distribution of work among the processors during scavenging to avoid idle time caused by processors that finish scavenging early. Achieving this in a parallel stop-and-copy garbage collector is difficult [17]. In on-the-fly garbage collection, unless the level of necessary garbage-collection activity is estimated very accurately in advance, either scavenger processors will sometimes need to wait for mutator processors to generate more garbage, or *vice versa*. Using an incremental garbage collector, both of these load-balancing problems can be solved adaptively, simply by switching processors between scavenging and mutation as needed. Thus although incremental garbage collection is somewhat more complex, it has the potential to respond to changing conditions in a much more forgiving way. Incremental garbage collection used to be thought impractical without special hardware support [77] but recently some techniques for using standard virtual-memory hardware to support incremental garbage collection have been developed [5].

An interesting garbage-collection problem, especially in the presence of speculative computing, is picking the right *root set* (the set of objects from which an object must be accessible if its storage is not to be reclaimed). All Lisps, including parallel Lisps, use the bindings in the top-level environment as part of the root set. Additionally, Concert Multilisp uses all runnable or running tasks as the root set, so nothing accessible to a runnable task will be deleted. A consequence of this policy is that a runnable task is its own reason for existence: no runnable task will ever be deleted.

MultiScheme, by contrast, uses only active read-eval-print loops, plus certain tasks in critical sections (in addition to the top-level environment) [75]. This allows a runnable task to be deleted if its *goal future* (the future it will resolve) is not ultimately accessible from an active read-eval-print listener loop that is waiting for a result [73, 75]. If a task's goal future is inaccessible in this way, then MultiScheme declares the task to be irrelevant; this choice of root set means that irrelevant tasks are automatically deleted every time a garbage collection occurs.

In a sponsor-based system for speculative computing, a task is irrevocably declared to be irrelevant if it has no sponsor (or all of its sponsors are inaccessible) and the future with which it was created is inaccessible. Thus, a task should be retained if it has a sponsor that is accessible either from the top-level environment or from the "top-level sponsor" that sponsors the user's top-level command loop. Consequently, it makes sense for the root set to consist of the top-level environment plus the top-level sponsor.

In a sponsor-based system, a sponsor will need to have pointers to all the tasks it sponsors. It is also useful for a task to have pointers to all of its sponsors (*e.g.*, so the task can inform its sponsors of its successful completion). Such pointers can interfere with the deletion of objects that the garbage collector really should delete. For example, an otherwise inaccessible sponsor S might be retained simply because it sponsors a task T that is accessible through another sponsor S'. S would be retained because of its accessibility via the back-pointer from T. The retention of S would cause any other tasks sponsored by S, which might otherwise be inaccessible, to also be retained. Another example of such inappropriate retention occurs if an otherwise inaccessible task is blocked waiting for a future to resolve (or for some other event): a task should not be retained simply because it is waiting for an accessible future [73, 75].

These problems can be solved by using *weak pointers* [73, 75]. If all paths from a root to an object include one or more weak pointers, then the object is deemed to be inaccessible and is deleted. (Weak pointers to a deleted object can be replaced by a distinguished value so that the object's deletion can be detected if the weak pointer is subsequently used.) Weak pointers should be used for the back-pointers from a task to its sponsors so that the mere fact of sponsoring an accessible task will not protect a sponsor from being declared inaccessible. Similarly, weak pointers should be used in queues of waiting tasks, so the mere fact of waiting will not protect a task from deletion. Weak-pointer support can be added to a garbage collector with only a modest increase in complexity and little cost in performance [73, 75].

6.4 Touching

As described in Section 4, futures are typically implemented by adding a "placeholder" data type to the set of primitive data types. Every time a strict operation is performed, the necessary touch is implemented as a check on the operand's type to see if it is a placeholder. If it is, this check is followed by a dereferencing operation to fetch the true value from the placeholder (or suspend the task if the value is not yet available).

Touch operations are very frequent in most Multilisp programs. Many operands that are touched are in fact futures, but even more are usually not futures. Moreover, when a future is touched, it is much more common for the future to have already resolved than to be unresolved. This means that an efficient implementation of touching is of paramount importance when the touched value is not a future, of considerable importance when the touched value is a resolved future, and of some importance when the touched value is an unresolved future.

There are many kinds of situations where a value must be touched:

- Operands of operators such as +, car, and >, which require operands only of a certain type.
- The operator position in a procedure call. (The value of F in $(F\ X)$ must be touched before it is used as a procedure.)
- Arguments to the procedure eq?, which tests whether two pointers refer to the same object.
- The predicate position in conditional constructs such as if or cond (*e.g.*, the value of P in (if $P\ A\ B$)). This follows from the previous case if we consider that conditional constructs use eq? to compare their predicates to the false value #f.
- Arguments to type-checking functions such as number? or pair?, which test their operands for membership in a certain type.

The first two categories are situations in which a safe implementation needs to perform a type check in any event; the touch in this case can be treated fairly efficiently by making it the first part of the error handler that is invoked when an operand is not of the expected type, introducing no extra overhead in the case when the touched value is not a future. The final three categories are situations in which no type error is possible and thus no type check is usually done. Here it is hard to avoid introducing some extra touching cost unless processors have special support for manipulating tagged data, but it can be held to about two instructions (in the case where the touched value is not a future) if the representation of futures is chosen carefully.

In the Mul-T system, a future is represented by a pointer to the placeholder data structure, but the low-order bit in the pointer is turned on to mark the pointer as a future. The NS32000 code used by Mul-T for touching a value residing in register rn is as follows:

```
        tbit   $0,rn  ; test the low-order bit
        beq    OK     ; if 0, then not a future
        jsr    chase-future-in-rn
OK:     Continue with the computation.
```

To make the simple cases run faster, Mul-T duplicates some of the touching code into separate subroutines chase-future-in-r1, chase-future-in-r2, etc. To further reduce the touching cost, Mul-T's compiler eliminates the touch-checking code in certain situations where it can prove that a value can never be a future: for example, when the value has already been touched in a previous statement, or was produced by an operator that never generates a future. Even so, the performance lost due to touch checks in Mul-T varies from about 20% to about 70%, even in programs that generate no futures [61]. Aggressive compiler data-flow analysis to eliminate more touches might reduce this cost somewhat, but it is also possible that hardware support for tagged-data manipulation will be necessary to reduce the cost of touches significantly.

6.5 Dynamic Binding

Early Lisps used a policy of *dynamic binding*, where the bindings of free variables not bound in the current procedure would be sought in the environment of the procedure's caller, and so on up the call chain [70]. This binding policy was especially attractive because of the *shallow binding* implementation technique, which associates a *value cell* at a fixed address with each variable name. Entry to a variable-binding construct such as a procedure or let expression is accomplished by saving (on the stack) the current value-cell contents for each variable to be rebound, and then installing the newly bound values. Exit from the construct is accomplished by reversing the process and restoring the previous value-cell contents (by popping them off the stack).

Modern Lisps have tended instead toward a policy of *lexical binding*, where the bindings of a procedure's free variables are sought in the procedure's definition environment [82, 85]. The semantics of lexical binding are generally acknowledged to be preferable for most kinds of variables, since (among other advantages) they prevent mysterious changes in a procedure's operation due to conflicts between variable names used in the procedure and in its caller.

This tendency is fortunate, since the shallow-binding implementation of dynamic binding does not adapt well to parallel computing. The problem is that concurrently active computations may need to have different bindings for the same variable, creating conflicts over the use of the variable's value cell. *Deep binding* is an alternative implementation technique for dynamic binding, based on an *association list* (or *alist*). The alist is a list of bindings that is passed to a procedure from its caller. Entry to a variable-binding construct is accomplished simply by consing new bindings onto the front of the alist, and exit is implemented simply by restoring the previous alist. Deep binding adapts well to parallel computing, but variable accesses can be much more expensive since they require searching down the alist until a binding of the variable of interest is found.

Since standard lexical-binding implementations are efficient and adapt well to parallel computing, it is appealing to support only lexical binding in a parallel Lisp. Unfortunately, dynamic binding is really the ideal semantics for some variables which are associated with attributes that we wish to pass implicitly from caller to callee, for example, the current set of sponsors or the current exception-handling procedure. Such attributes can be recorded in *ad hoc* ways. For example, Concert Multilisp reserves a special slot in the data structure representing a task to point to the task's current exception handler, but this approach requires modification of basic levels of the implementation (adding a new slot to the task structure) every time a new dynamically bound variable is introduced. Alternatively, an alist mechanism can be introduced, as in Mul-T or MultiScheme (MultiScheme also contains a rather ingenious "trap-on-reference" mechanism for recognizing references to dynamic, or *fluid*, variables and directing them to the alist [73]), but access can become expensive if the alists become long. Understanding of the proper level of support for dynamic binding in parallel Lisps awaits further experience.

6.6 Summary

Task management is an essential function of a parallel Lisp implementation and can be divided into two parts: granularity enhancement and scheduling. Granularity enhancement refers to "chunking" together of logically separate tasks to amortize task management overhead over larger units of computation; scheduling refers to the management of the tasks that remain after granularity enhancement. Implementations of both parts can benefit by exploiting the permissiveness of Multilisp's scheduling specification. This permissiveness is exploited by inlining and lazy task creation for the purpose of increasing granularity, and by unfair scheduling using LIFO queues for the purpose of reducing storage requirements and increasing locality. Lazy task creation can be used, not just with the basic Multilisp future construct, but also with the Katz-Weise future construct (Figure 7) and with speculative tasks having the same sponsorship as their parents, resulting in appealing reductions in the extra costs of these mechanisms. Both lazy task creation and unfair scheduling induce an execution order that tends toward the ideal of BUSD (*B*readth-first *U*ntil *S*aturation, then *D*epth-first) execution. The result of applying these techniques in Mul-T is a high-performance parallel Lisp system that shows significant speedups over efficient sequential programs [61, 62, 76].

Other parallel Lisp implementation issues include garbage collection, touching, and dynamic binding. Incremental garbage collection promises the most flexible allocation of work between mutation and scavenging, which is important in keeping processors usefully occupied, but most parallel Lisp implementations have avoided it because of its extra complexity and co-ordination costs. New ideas for using virtual-memory hardware to help in incremental garbage collection [5] could change this in the future. Touching imposes significant overhead (20%–70%) on compiled parallel Lisps, even after some compile-time optimization; either more aggressive optimization techniques or architectural (hardware) support would pay a big dividend here. Finally, dynamic binding is needed in parallel Lisps but its efficient implementation is difficult. More experience with the dynamic-binding needs of real application programs is needed in finding the right tradeoff between efficiency, complexity, and generality here.

7. Tools for Parallel Programming

It is useful to think of program development as consisting of three phases: programming, debugging, and tuning. The development of a program is unlikely to be a simple sequential pass through these three phases; usually each phase will be visited multiple times. Nevertheless, each phase is an activity that a program development environment should support. The above discussion has focused on language design and implementation questions: in other words, on support for the programming phase of program development (though debugging has also been mentioned). In this section, we focus on tools that are useful as part of a program development environment. While these tools can aid the programming process, they help mainly in the other phases of the process: locating problems that cause incorrect output (debugging) or inferior performance (tuning). The tools discussed here help in two ways: finding good places to use **future** in a program and understanding the execution that results from a particular set of **future**-placement decisions.

Novice Multilisp programmers often find it tricky to use **future** well. A program, *Savant*, has been developed to automatically insert **future** into a side-effect-free program in the most profitable places [32]. Although Savant follows rather simple rules, it puts futures in most of the same places where an experienced programmer would. By studying these rules, a novice can more quickly attain proficiency in using **future**: their codification is thus a valuable by-product of the development of Savant.

Tools for observing and visualizing the execution of parallel programs are another necessity for the parallel programmer. One tool developed for Concert Multilisp produces graphical *parallelism profiles* for programs. Figure 8 shows parallelism profiles for executing a parallel Quicksort algorithm [34]. The horizontal axis on the profile marks the passage of time in seconds, and the vertical axis indicates the number of processors busy at a given moment. Black ink indicates "real computing" also performed in an execution of the corresponding sequential algorithm (created by removing all uses of **future**) and the shades of gray correspond to two different kinds of overhead that result from using futures.

Such profiles are far more useful than simple wall-clock times or speedup figures in understanding how a parallel program is performing and why. For example, if performance is mediocre, the profiles allow us to tell whether the cause is excessive **future** overhead, uniformly low available parallelism, or a long sequential section in an otherwise highly parallel program. This information is valuable in understanding how performance might be improved.

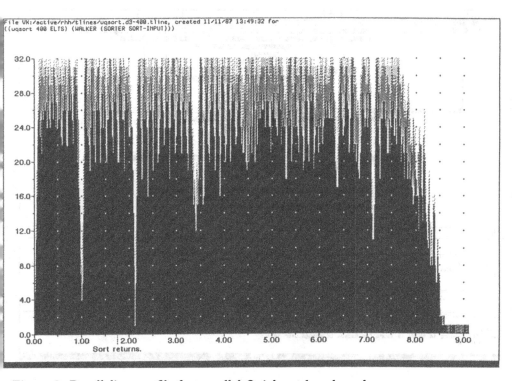

Figure 8: Parallelism profile for parallel Quicksort benchmark

Unfortunately, it is not always easy to determine the reason for a phenomenon observed in a parallelism profile. For example, in Figure 8, the reason for the occasional pronounced dips in the number of busy processors is not at all obvious. While the performance improvement that could result even if all these dips were completely eliminated is small in this case, we might still learn something useful from understanding their cause. Moreover, many other programs exhibit longer versions of such bottlenecks that completely dominate performance.

The need for more detailed insight into the interactions between tasks in a parallel program led to the development of the ParVis parallel program visualization tool [9]. To use ParVis, a parallel program is first run in an instrumented mode that generates a trace of significant events during program execution, such as the creation, termination, blocking, and resumption of tasks. Collecting this trace increases program run time by a small fraction, like 10% or less. It is important that this fraction is small, since we do not want to perturb program timing too much in the process of observing it.

ParVis itself is a visualization tool that can be run after the program under investigation has finished executing. It reads the trace file and produces a graphical display of the relationships between tasks in the traced program. Figure 9 shows a portion of a ParVis display of the execution of a parallel, doubly recursive program for computing Fibonacci numbers; the self-similar structure of task relationships in this program can

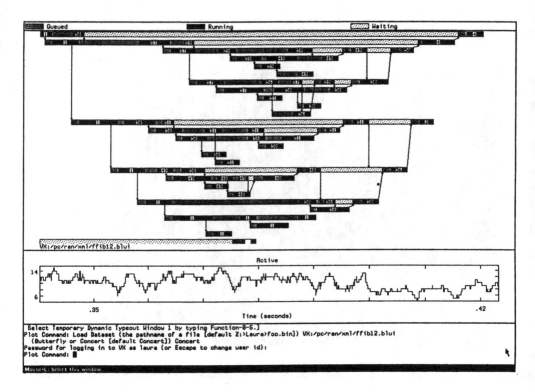

Figure 9: Example ParVis screen display for a parallel Fibonacci program

be seen easily. ParVis can be instructed interactively to zoom in on different parts of the display and can select and highlight tasks that satisfy predicates defined by the user. It can thus perform actions such as, "Highlight all tasks that were executing at time T and all tasks that were waiting, directly or indirectly, for their results." Use of these capabilities can yield detailed insight into the intertask relationships that caused a particular feature on a parallelism profile.

Time in a ParVis display flows from left to right; each task is displayed as a horizontal band whose left edge indicates the time at which the task was created and whose right edge indicates the time at which the task terminated. The stipple pattern displayed within the band changes to reflect the history of task status changes: a dark gray pattern is displayed during periods when the task was actually running, a lighter gray pattern indicates periods when the task was runnable but not actually running, and a light, speckled pattern is used for periods when the task was blocked (*e.g.*, waiting for a future to resolve). The numbers displayed within the "running" periods identify the processor that was running the task; this can be useful for detailed explorations of scheduling behavior. Arrows show relationships between tasks. Arrows point

- From the creator of each task to the beginning of that task.
- From a running-to-blocked transition to the task whose result is awaited.

- From the end of a task to each blocked-to-runnable transition caused by the completion of that task.

The ParVis system that produced Figure 9 has several limitations. It becomes too slow for comfortable interactive use if the trace in use has more than about 1000 tasks, while a realistic program executing under Mul-T could easily generate thousands of tasks per processor per second. Another limitation is that the amount of detailed information in large traces can overwhelm the user. Aids for browsing through this database and identifying patterns of interest are badly needed. As a start in this direction, a *filter language* has been included in ParVis [9]. The filter language allows a user to define predicates that are satisfied by the tasks of interest; those tasks can then be highlighted in the display. Another browsing facility that might be valuable would be a way of rearranging tasks in the display so that a group of tasks of interest could be displayed physically close together. A re-implementation of ParVis with careful attention paid to efficient and incremental processing of the trace database should solve the performance problem; more experience with various user interfaces is necessary to find the best browsing tools.

Finally, the ParVis style of display has all kinds of unexplored potential as a way to access additional information about program execution. In the implemented ParVis system, positioning the mouse over a particular task will cause the **future** expression that spawned that task to be displayed. An interesting and probably very useful extension of this idea would be to be able to position the mouse at any point in any task and ask for the value at that time of any variable visible to that task. Any such capability would have to be supported by an "Instant Replay" system [65] that could regenerate precisely the values used by the traced execution so they could be displayed. Implementing the replay capability is a significant, though not insuperable, technical challenge in itself; but the ParVis interface would be wonderful for displaying the results.

8. Concluding Remarks

The feasibility of building an efficient parallel implementation of Lisp with **future** has been demonstrated [61, 62, 76]; using the ideas discussed in this paper it should be possible to build a second generation of parallel Lisps that are as efficient but semantically more elegant and powerful. The language-design criteria given in Section 5.1 offer a guide in this process. To evaluate the real user needs that these parallel Lisps must satisfy, however, we need more parallel Lisp users—more significant applications must be programmed in parallel Lisps. To make this possible, good tools to facilitate parallel Lisp program development must be developed, and they, along with high-performance parallel Lisp systems, must be made widely available. An important threshold will have been crossed when parallel Lisps are used for serious programming by users other than the parallel Lisp developers themselves.

The ideas discussed in this paper have been oriented more toward perfecting environments for parallel computing based on **future** than changing them, but more radical changes can be considered. Several approaches could be tried to relieve the burden on programmers to identify all parallelism explicitly using **future**. For example, Multilisp programs execute sequentially by default—parallelism is exploited only where the **future** construct is used. How about the alternative of making **future**-style parallelism the default (*e.g.*, by implicitly wrapping **future** around almost every expression) and requiring explicit action by the programmer to request sequential execution? This has never been explored, in part because of the cost of all the implicit **future** constructs, but with new ideas such as lazy task creation it looks more feasible, if an elegant language-level formulation can be designed.

Sophisticated compile-time analysis is often able to restructure Lisp programs into a parallel form [42, 63]. Accordingly, another avenue to pursue would be to see how such analysis can be used to supplement the programmer's own use of the **future** construct. Ideally, the programmer would be called upon to identify only that parallelism that compile-time analysis will not discover, and much of the low-level parallelism would be exploited automatically.

While this paper has focused on parallel Lisps based on the **future** construct, the ideas discussed are applicable in many other contexts. Most of them are applicable, almost without change, to implementation of functional languages on parallel systems [7, 71, 91]. Even when we go farther afield, say, to FORTRAN programs automatically restructured for parallel execution, the problems of scheduling, and the need for tools that help visualize a parallel program's execution, are still great.

9. Acknowledgments

Special thanks go to Morry Katz for his inspiration and clear thinking about continuations and futures, and for pointing out the problems of checking for multiple attempts to resolve the same future. I am grateful to Takayasu Ito, whose encouragement and patience finally led to the writing of this paper and whose thoughtful comments significantly improved it. I also thank Randy Osborne for his careful reading and valuable comments. The Cambridge Research Lab of Digital Equipment Corporation provided a warm and supportive place to write the paper. Concert and Multilisp, which furnished the environment in which the ideas in this paper germinated, were developed by many members of the Parallel Processing Group at M.I.T. Several of these contributors are cited below; others must remain unnamed due to space limitations, but are nevertheless very gratefully acknowledged.

10. References

1. Abelson, H., and G. Sussman, *Structure and Interpretation of Computer Programs*, M.I.T. Press, Cambridge, Mass., 1984.

2. Agarwal, A., R. Simoni, J. Hennessy, and M. Horowitz, "An Evaluation of Directory Schemes for Cache Coherence," *15th Annual Int'l. Symp. on Computer Architecture*, Honolulu, June 1988, pp. 280–289.

3. Allen, D., S. Steinberg, and L. Stabile, "Recent developments in Butterfly Lisp," *AAAI 87*, July 1987, Seattle, pp. 2–6.

4. Anderson, T., *The Design of a Multiprocessor Development System*, M.I.T. Laboratory for Computer Science Technical Report TR-279, Cambridge, Mass., Sept. 1982.

5. Appel, A., J. Ellis, and K. Li, "Real-time Concurrent Collection on Stock Multiprocessors," *ACM SIGPLAN '88 Conf. on Programming Language Design and Implementation*, Atlanta, June 1988, pp. 11–20.

6. Arvind, K. Gostelow, and W. Plouffe, *An Asynchronous Programming Language and Computing Machine*, U.C. Irvine Report TR114a, 1978.

7. Arvind, R. Nikhil, and K. Pingali, *Id Nouveau: Language and Operational Semantics*, CSG Memo, Computation Structures Group, M.I.T. Laboratory for Computer Science, Sept. 1987.

8. Baek, H.J., *Parallel Retrieval Algorithms for Semantic Nets*, S.B. thesis, M.I.T. E.E.C.S. Dept., Cambridge, Mass., June 1986.

9. Bagnall, L., *ParVis: A Program Visualization Tool for Multilisp*, S.M. thesis, MIT E.E.C.S. Dept., Cambridge, Mass., Feb. 1989.

10. Baker, H., *Actor Systems for Real-Time Computation*, M.I.T. Laboratory for Computer Science Technical Report TR-197, Cambridge, Mass., March 1978.

11. Baker, H., and C. Hewitt, "The Incremental Garbage Collection of Processes," M.I.T. Artificial Intelligence Laboratory Memo 454, Cambridge, Mass., Dec. 1977.

12. Bartlett, J., *SCHEME→C: A Portable Scheme-to-C Compiler*, WRL Research Report 89/1, DEC Western Research Laboratory, Palo Alto, Ca., Jan. 1989.

13. Bradley, E., *Logic Simulation on a Multiprocessor*, Technical Report TR-380, M.I.T. Laboratory for Computer Science, Cambridge, Mass., November 1986.

14. Bradley, E., and R. Halstead, "Simulating Logic Circuits: A Multiprocessor Application," *Int'l. J. of Parallel Programming 16:4*, August 1987, pp. 305–338.

15. Chambers, D., and D. Ungar, "Customization: Optimizing Compiler Technology for SELF, a Dynamically-Typed Object-Oriented Programming Language," *ACM SIGPLAN '89 Conf. on Programming Language Design and Implementation*, Portland, Oregon, June 1989, pp. 146–160.

16. Clinger, W., A. Hartheimer, and E. Ost, "Implementation Strategies for Continuations," *1988 ACM Symp. on Lisp and Functional Programming*, Snowbird, Utah, July 1988, pp. 124–131.

17. Courtemanche, A., *MultiTrash, a Parallel Garbage Collector for MultiScheme*, S.B. thesis, M.I.T. E.E.C.S. Dept., Cambridge, Mass., Jan. 1986.

18. Crowther, W., *et al.*, "Performance Measurements on a 128-Node Butterfly Parallel Processor," *1985 Int'l. Conf. on Parallel Processing*, St. Charles, Ill., Aug. 1985, pp. 531–540.

19. Dennis, J.B., "Data Flow Supercomputers," *IEEE Computer 13:11*, Nov. 1980, pp. 48–56.

20. Dijkstra, E., et al., "On-the-fly Garbage Collection: An Exercise in Co-operation," *Language Hierarchies and Interfaces (Lecture Notes in Computer Science 46)*, Springer-Verlag, 1976.

21. Encore Computer Corp., *Multimax Technical Summary*, Encore Computer Corp., Marlborough, Mass., Rev. E, Jan. 1989.

22. Felleisen, M., D. Friedman, B. Duba, and J. Merrill, *Beyond Continuations*, Indiana University Computer Science Dept. Tech. Report 216, Bloomington, In., 1987.

23. Felleisen, M., "The Theory and Practice of First-Class Prompts," *15th Annual ACM Symp. on Principles of Programming Languages*, San Diego, Ca., Jan. 1988, pp. 180–190.

24. Forgy, C.L., "Rete: A Fast Algorithm for the Many Pattern / Many Object Match Problem," *Artificial Intelligence J. 19*, Sept. 1982, pp. 17–37.

25. Friedman, D., and D. Wise, "Aspects of Applicative Programming for Parallel Processing," *IEEE Trans. Comp. C-27:4*, April 1978, pp. 289–296.

26. Gabriel, R., *Performance and Evaluation of Lisp Systems*, M.I.T. Press, Cambridge, Mass., 1985.

27. Gabriel, R., and J. McCarthy, "Qlisp," in J. Kowalik, ed., *Parallel Computation and Computers for Artificial Intelligence*, Kluwer Academic Publishers, 1988, pp. 63–89.

28. Goldman, R., and R. Gabriel, "Qlisp: Experience and New Directions," *ACM/ SIGPLAN PPEALS 1988—Parallel Programming: Experience with Applications, Languages, and Systems*, New Haven, Conn., July 1988, pp. 111–123.

29. Goldman, R., and R. Gabriel, "Preliminary Results with the Initial Implementation of Qlisp," *1988 ACM Symp. on Lisp and Functional Programming*, Snowbird, Utah, July 1988, pp. 143–152.

30. Goldman, R., R. Gabriel, and C. Sexton, "Qlisp: Parallel Processing in Lisp," *Proc. U.S./Japan Workshop on Parallel Lisp (Lecture Notes in Computer Science)*, Springer-Verlag, 1990.

31. Goodenough, J., "Exception Handling: Issues and a Proposed Notation," *Comm. ACM 18:12*, Dec. 1975, pp. 683–696.

32. Gray, S., *Using Futures to Exploit Parallelism in Lisp*, S.M. thesis, M.I.T. E.E.C.S. Dept., Cambridge, Mass., Jan. 1986.

33. Gurd, J., C. Kirkham, and I. Watson, "The Manchester Prototype Dataflow Computer," *Comm. ACM 28:1*, January 1985, pp. 34–52.

34. Halstead, R., "Multilisp: A Language for Concurrent Symbolic Computation," *ACM Trans. on Prog. Languages and Systems*, October 1985, pp. 501–538.

35. Halstead, R., and J. Loaiza, "Exception Handling in Multilisp," *1985 Int'l. Conf. on Parallel Processing*, St. Charles, Ill., Aug. 1985, pp. 822–830.

36. Halstead, R., T. Anderson, R. Osborne, and T. Sterling, "Concert: Design of a Multiprocessor Development System," *13th Annual Int'l. Symp. on Computer Architecture*, Tokyo, June 1986, pp. 40–48.

37. Halstead, R., "Parallel Symbolic Computing," *IEEE Computer 19:8*, August 1986, pp. 35–43.

38. Halstead, R., "An Assessment of Multilisp: Lessons from Experience," *Int'l. J. of Parallel Programming 15:6*, Dec. 1986, pp. 459–501.

39. Halstead, R., "Overview of Concert Multilisp: A Multiprocessor Symbolic Computing System," *ACM Computer Architecture News 15:1*, March 1987, pp. 5–14.

40. Halstead, R., "Parallel Symbolic Computing Using Multilisp," in J. Kowalik, ed., *Parallel Computation and Computers for Artificial Intelligence*, Kluwer Academic Publishers, 1988, pp. 21–49.

41. Halstead, R., "Design Requirements for Concurrent Lisp Machines," in K. Hwang and D. DeGroot, eds., *Parallel Processing for Supercomputers and Artificial Intelligence*, McGraw Hill, New York, 1989, pp. 69–105.

42. Harrison, W.L., "The Interprocedural Analysis and Automatic Parallelization of Scheme Programs," *Lisp and Symbolic Computation 2:3/4*, 1989, pp. 179–396.

43. Henderson, P., and J.H. Morris, "A Lazy Evaluator," *Proc. 3rd ACM Symp. on Principles of Prog. Languages*, 1976, pp. 95–103.

44. Hieb, R., and R.K. Dybvig, "Continuations and Concurrency," *1990 ACM Conf. on the Principles and Practice of Parallel Programming (PPoPP)*, Seattle, March 1990.

45. Hillis, W.D., and G.L. Steele, "Data Parallel Algorithms," *Comm. ACM 29:12*, Dec. 1986, pp. 1170–1183.

46. Hoare, C.A.R., "Monitors: An Operating System Structuring Concept," *Comm. ACM 17:10*, October 1974, pp. 549–557.

47. Ichbiah, J.D., *et al.*, "Preliminary ADA Reference Manual," *SIGPLAN Notices 14:6*, Part A, June 1979.

48. Ito, T., and M. Matsui, "A Parallel Lisp Language PaiLisp and its Kernel Specification," *Proc. U.S./Japan Workshop on Parallel Lisp (Lecture Notes in Computer Science)*, Springer-Verlag, 1990.

49. Katz, M., *ParaTran: A Transparent, Transaction Based Runtime Mechanism for Parallel Execution of Scheme*, S.M. thesis, M.I.T. E.E.C.S. Dept., Cambridge, Mass., May 1986.

50. Katz, M., *ParaTran: A Transparent, Transaction Based Runtime Mechanism for Parallel Execution of Scheme*, Technical Report TR-454, M.I.T. Laboratory for Computer Science, Cambridge, Mass., July 1989.

51. Katz, M., and D. Weise, "Continuing Into the Future: On the Interaction of Futures and First-Class Continuations," *1990 ACM Conf. on Lisp and Functional Programming*, Nice, France, June 1990.

52. Katz, M., and D. Weise, "Continuing Into the Future: On the Interaction of Futures and First-Class Continuations (A Capsule Summary)," *Proc. U.S./Japan Workshop on Parallel Lisp (Lecture Notes in Computer Science)*, Springer-Verlag, 1990.

53. Keller, R., and F. Lin, "Simulated Performance of a Reduction-Based Multiprocessor," *IEEE Computer 17:7*, July 1984, pp. 70–82.

54. Kessler, R., and M. Swanson, "Concurrent Scheme," *Proc. U.S./Japan Workshop on Parallel Lisp (Lecture Notes in Computer Science)*, Springer-Verlag, 1990.

55. Knight, T., "An Architecture for Mostly Functional Languages," *ACM Symposium on Lisp and Functional Programming*, Boston, Mass., Aug. 1986, pp. 105–112.

56. Knueven, P., P. Hibbard, and B. Leverett, "A Language System for a Multiprocessor Environment," *Fourth International Conf. on the Design and Implementation of Algorithmic Languages*, Courant Institute of Mathematical Studies, New York, June 1976, pp. 264–274.

57. Kornfeld, W., and C. Hewitt, "The Scientific Community Metaphor," *IEEE Trans. on Systems, Man, and Cybernetics*, January 1981.

58. Krall, E., and P. McGehearty, "A Case Study of Parallel Execution of a Rule-Based Expert System," *Int'l. J. of Parallel Programming 15:1*, Feb. 1986, pp. 5–32.

59. Kranz, D., R. Kelsey, J. Rees, P. Hudak, J. Philbin, and N. Adams, "Orbit: An Optimizing Compiler for Scheme," *Proc. SIGPLAN '86 Symp. on Compiler Construction*, June 1986, pp. 219–233.

60. Kranz, D., *ORBIT: An Optimizing Compiler for Scheme*, Yale University Technical Report YALEU/DCS/RR-632, February 1988.

61. Kranz, D., R. Halstead, and E. Mohr, "Mul-T: A High-Performance Parallel Lisp," *ACM SIGPLAN '89 Conf. on Programming Language Design and Implementation*, Portland, Oregon, June 1989, pp. 81–90.

62. Kranz, D., R. Halstead, and E. Mohr, "Mul-T: A High-Performance Parallel Lisp (Extended Abstract)," *Proc. U.S./Japan Workshop on Parallel Lisp (Lecture Notes in Computer Science)*, Springer-Verlag, 1990.

63. Larus, J., and P. Hilfinger, "Restructuring Lisp Programs for Concurrent Execution," *ACM/SIGPLAN PPEALS 1988—Parallel Programming: Experience with Applications, Languages, and Systems*, New Haven, Conn., July 1988, pp. 100–110.

64. Lau, W., *Lexical Analysis of Noisy Phonetic Transcriptions*, S.M. thesis, M.I.T. E.E.C.S. Dept., Cambridge, Mass., Feb. 1986.

65. LeBlanc, T., and J. Mellor-Crummey, "Debugging Parallel Programs with Instant Replay," *IEEE Trans. Comp. C-36:4*, April 1987, pp. 471–482.

66. Liskov, B.H., and A. Snyder, "Exception Handling in CLU," *IEEE Trans. Softw. Eng. SE-5:6*, Nov. 1979, pp. 546–558.

67. Lucassen, J., and D. Gifford, "Polymorphic Effect Systems," *15th Annual ACM Conf. on Principles of Programming Languages*, Jan. 1988, pp. 47–57.

68. Ma, M., *Efficient Message-Based System for Concurrent Simulation*, Ph.D. thesis, M.I.T. E.E.C.S. Dept., Cambridge, Mass., January 1989.

69. Marti, J., and J. Fitch, "The Bath Concurrent Lisp Machine," *Proc. EURO-CAL '83 (Lecture Notes in Computer Science 162)*, Springer-Verlag, March 1983, pp. 78–90.

70. McCarthy, J, et al., *LISP 1.5 Programmer's Manual*, M.I.T. Press, Cambridge, Mass., 1962.

71. McGraw, J., *et al.*, *SISAL — Streams and Iteration in a Single-assignment Language*, Language Reference Manual (version 1.0), Lawrence Livermore National Laboratory, Livermore, Calif., July 1983.

72. Meyer, A., and J. Riecke, "Continuations May Be Unreasonable: Preliminary Report," *1988 ACM Symp. on Lisp and Functional Programming*, Snowbird, Utah, July 1988, pp. 63–71.

73. Miller, J., *MultiScheme: A Parallel Processing System Based on MIT Scheme*, Technical Report TR-402, M.I.T. Laboratory for Computer Science, Cambridge, Mass., Sept. 1987.

74. Miller, J., "Implementing a Scheme-Based Parallel Processing System," *Int'l. J. of Parallel Programming 17:5*, Oct. 1988, pp. 367–402.

75. Miller, J., and B. Epstein, "Garbage Collection in MultiScheme," *Proc. U.S./Japan Workshop on Parallel Lisp (Lecture Notes in Computer Science)*, Springer-Verlag, 1990.

76. Mohr, E., D. Kranz, and R. Halstead, "Lazy Task Creation: A Technique for Increasing the Granularity of Parallel Programs," *1990 ACM Conf. on Lisp and Functional Programming*, Nice, France, June 1990.

77. Moon, D., "Garbage Collection in a Large Lisp System," *1984 ACM Symp. on Lisp and Functional Programming*, Austin, Tex., Aug. 1984, pp. 235–246.

78. Nuth, P., *Communication Patterns in a Symbolic Multiprocessor*, Technical Report TR-395, M.I.T. Laboratory for Computer Science, Cambridge, Mass., June 1987.

79. Osborne, R., *Speculative Computation in Multilisp*, Technical Report TR-464, MIT Laboratory for Computer Science, Cambridge, Mass., Dec. 1989.

80. Osborne, R., "Speculative Computation in Multilisp," *Proc. U.S./Japan Workshop on Parallel Lisp (Lecture Notes in Computer Science)*, Springer-Verlag, 1990.

81. Rees, J., N. Adams, and J. Meehan, *The T Manual*, fourth edition, Yale University Computer Science Department, January 1984.

82. Rees, J., and W. Clinger, eds., "Revised[3] Report on the Algorithmic Language Scheme," *ACM SIGPLAN Notices 21:12*, Dec. 1986, pp. 37–79.

83. Sitaram, D., and M. Felleisen, "Control Delimiters and their Hierarchies," *Lisp and Symbolic Computation 3*, 1990, pp. 67–99.

84. Solomon, S., *A Query Language on a Parallel Machine Operating System*, S.B. thesis, M.I.T. E.E.C.S. Dept., Cambridge, Mass., May 1985.

85. Steele, G.L., *Common Lisp: The Language*, Digital Press, Burlington, Mass., 1984.

86. Steele, G.L., and W.D. Hillis, "Connection Machine Lisp: Fine-Grained Parallel Symbolic Processing," *1986 ACM Conf. on Lisp and Functional Programming*, Cambridge, Mass., Aug. 1986, pp. 279–297.

87. Stoy, J., *Denotational Semantics: The Scott-Strachey Approach to Programming Language Theory*, M.I.T. Press, Cambridge, Mass., 1977.

88. Sugimoto, S., et al., "A Multi-Microprocessor System for Concurrent Lisp," *Proc. 1983 International Conf. on Parallel Processing*, June 1983.

89. Swanson, M., R. Kessler, and G. Lindstrom, "An Implementation of Portable Standard Lisp on the BBN Butterfly," *1988 ACM Symp. on Lisp and Functional Programming*, Snowbird, Utah, July 1988, pp. 132–142.

90. Symbolics Corp., *Symbolics Common Lisp: Language Concepts*, Symbolics Corp., Cambridge, Mass., August 1986.

91. Turner, D., "A New Implementation Technique for Applicative Languages," *Software — Practice and Experience 9:1*, Jan. 1979, pp. 31–49.

92. Wetherell, C., "Error Data Values in the Data-Flow Language VAL," *ACM Trans. on Prog. Languages and Systems 4:2*, April 1982, pp. 226–238.

1. Trademarks

Butterfly is a trademark of Bolt, Beranek, and Newman, Inc.

Connection Machine and *Lisp are trademarks of Thinking Machines Corporation.

FX/8 is a trademark of Alliant Computer Systems Corporation.

Multimax is a trademark of Encore Computer Corporation.

Series 32000 is a registered trademark of National Semiconductor Corporation.

A Parallel Lisp Language PaiLisp and its Kernel Specification

Takayasu ITO and Manabu MATSUI
Department of Information Engineering
School of Engineering
Tohoku University
Sendai, JAPAN 980

Abstract

Parallel Lisp languages have been proposed and developed for parallel programming of Lisp programs in Artificial Intelligence and Symbolic Computing. PaiLisp is a parallel Lisp language based on a shared-memory parallel architecture. PaiLisp has been designed so as to include

1. parallel constructs such as future and pcall of Multilisp, and exlambda for mutual exclusion and spawn and par for process creation

2. parallelized Lisp constructs such as parallel conditional expressions, parallel mapcar, parallel and/or, etc.

The first version of PaiLisp, designed in 1986, was based on Franzlisp and the next version was based on Common Lisp. The current version of PaiLisp is based on Scheme. That is, the current version of PaiLisp may be viewed as an extension of Scheme with parallel Lisp constructs mentioned above.

In this paper we present

1. **The language specification of PaiLisp**
   PaiLisp is specified as Scheme with parallel Lisp constructs.

2. **PaiLisp-Kernel, which is a compact kernel of PaiLisp**
   PaiLisp-Kernel is designed as Scheme with only 4 parallel constructs {spawn, suspend, exlambda, call/cc}, where call/cc is extended in a parallel situation.

3. **Description of PaiLisp using PaiLisp-Kernel**
   A concrete description of PaiLisp using PaiLisp-Kernel is given. This means that an implementation-oriented operational semantics of PaiLisp is given in terms of PaiLisp-Kernel.

1   Introduction

Lisp has been used as the most popular programming language in practice of Artificial Intelligence and Symbolic Computing. Since the early 1980's parallel execution of Lisp programs and parallel Lisp language have been studied extensively in response to AI applications and progress of parallel architecture. Early parallel Lisp attempts are seen in parallelized Lisp interpreters and data flow models for parallel execution of Lisp programs. Currently active research in parallel Lisp has been inspired by two parallel Lisp languages, Multilisp conducted by Halstead[3] and Qlisp conducted by McCarthy and Gabriel[1].

PaiLisp is a parallel Lisp language based on a shared memory architecture. Its design is inspired by parallel constructs of Multilisp and Qlisp, and its parallelized Lisp constructs come from parallel execution of Lisp programs based on a data flow model of computation studied by the authors in 1983[4,5]. That is, PaiLisp is designed so as to include

(1) parallel constructs such as **future**, **pcall** and **delay** of Multilisp and **spawn**, **par**, **suspend**, **exlambda**, **signal/wait** and an extended **call/cc**;

(2) parallelized Lisp constructs such as parallel conditional expressions, parallel mapcar, parallel and/or, etc.; these parallel constructs come from a data flow model of parallel execution of Lisp programs

PaiLisp was originally designed so as to introduce the concurrency of (1) and (2) into Franzlisp and Common Lisp. But the current version of PaiLisp is based on Scheme for several technical reasons: Scheme was favored over Common Lisp for introducing "concurrency" since it is a compact and static language with clear semantics. In this paper we present

1. **The language specification of PaiLisp**
   PaiLisp is designed as Scheme with parallel constructs.

2. **PaiLisp-Kernel, which is a compact kernel of PaiLisp**
   PaiLisp-Kernel is a compact kernel language of PaiLisp, by which the meanings of all the PaiLisp constructs can be expressed. PaiLisp-Kernel is designed as Scheme with only 4 parallel constructs: **spawn**, **suspend**, **exlambda** and an extended **call/cc**, where call/cc is extended in a parallel situation.

3. **description of PaiLisp using PaiLisp-Kernel**
   A concrete description of PaiLisp using PaiLisp-Kernel is given; that is, the kernel specification of PaiLisp is given.

4. **PaiLisp-Kernel in PaiLisp-Kernel**
   A meta-circular interpreter of PaiLisp-Kernel is given in **Appendix I**.

The major contributions of this paper are

- the extraction of PaiLisp-Kernel from PaiLisp

- the precise description of parallel Lisp constructs using PaiLisp-Kernel

- a proposal of call/cc in a parallel situation.

2 PaiLisp: A Parallel Lisp Language

A data flow model of parallel execution of Lisp programs was studied from a theoretical standpoint, as is reported in [4,5]. Being motivated by this theoretical study the first author decided to design and construct a MC68000-based multi-microprocessor system with shared memory (PAI-68K) for implementation of parallel Lisp interpreter. The outline of this effort is reported in [6].

The first version of PaiLisp was designed in 1986 by T.Ito and A.Kon as a continuing effort of developing a parallel Lisp interpreter on PAI-68K, an MC68000-based multi-microprocessor system with shared memory. This first version of PaiLisp was based on Franzlisp, and its description was given in terms of an extended C with concurrency and Lisp basic functions. The next version of PaiLisp was based on Common Lisp, but it was soon abandoned, since the first author realized that it was very difficult to add concurrency into Common Lisp in a simple and clear way.

The current version of PaiLisp is based on Scheme. This decision to use Scheme as the base language comes from our efforts of finding a kernel language, by which we can describe the meanings of all other constructs in PaiLisp. This problem of finding a kernel language of parallel Lisp occurred to the first author when he had a conversation whith Professor John McCarthy after his talk at the Qlisp project in January, 1987. All parallel Lisp constructs of PaiLisp were essentially introduced in 1986. The big progress since 1986 is in extracting PaiLisp-Kernel, a compact kernel of PaiLisp.

In this paper we give the details of PaiLisp as follows:

1. This section (Section 2) gives an outline of PaiLisp, and the parallel constructs of PaiLisp are verbally explained.

2. Section 3 gives PaiLisp-Kernel, which is defined as Scheme plus only 4 parallel constructs, and PaiLisp-Kernel in PaiLisp-Kernel is also given.

3. Section 4 gives the description of PaiLisp using PaiLisp-Kernel. This is shown by giving a PaiLisp-Kernel program for each parallel construct of PaiLisp.

The design of PaiLisp has been influenced by Multilisp and Qlisp in addition to a data flow model of parallel execution of Lisp programs.
That is, PaiLisp is designed so as to include

1. parallel constructs such as **future** and **delay** of Multilisp and **spawn, par, suspend, exlambda, signal/wait** and an extended **call/cc** introduced in PaiLisp;

2. parallelized Lisp Constructs such as parallel evaluation of arguments, parallel conditional expressions, parallel mapcar, parallel logical and/or, etc. along with a data flow model of parallel execution of Lisp programs in [4,5].

Table1 gives an overview of PaiLisp, comparing it with Multilisp and Qlisp. PaiLisp-Kernel is a compact kernel of PaiLisp to be defined as an extension of Scheme with the following four constructs to support concurrency:

$(spawn\ \langle e \rangle)$	for process creation,
$(suspend)$	for suspendion of process execution,
$(exlambda\ (x)\ \langle e \rangle)$	for creation of exclusive closure,
$(call/cc\ \langle f \rangle)$	for control of continuation,

	PaiLisp	Multilisp	Qlisp
[invocation and control of parallel processes]			
mutual exclusion	exlambda	replace replace-if	QLAMBDA
synchronization	wait signal (call/cc) (suspend)	suspend activate	suspend resume
process creation	spawn	...	...
parallel execution	par	pcall future	QLET QLAMBDA
future value	future	future	(QLET)
delayed evaluation	delay	delay	
[parallelized Lisp constructs]			
parallel evaluation of arguments	pcall eager	pcall	QLET
parallel evaluation of list structure	pmapcar	...	...
parallel conditional expresions	pcond pcond#	... ...	... ...
parallel AND/OR	par-and par-or	... ...	... ...
[other constructs]			
control among processes	call/cc	(call/cc)	catch ,throw
process suspension	suspend	...	(suspend)
infinite looping	loop	...	(loop)
Base Language	Scheme	Scheme	Common Lisp

Table 1: Comparisons of PaiLisp, Multilisp and Qlisp

Remark: The constructs of Multilisp and Qlisp are based on [3] and [1], respectively.

where call/cc is an extension of Scheme's call/cc in a concurrent situation.The details of PaiLisp constructs will be defined and explained below. As is seen from this table Multilisp and PaiLisp use Scheme as their base languages, while Qlisp uses Common Lisp as its base language. PaiLisp has many parallelized Lisp constructs since the beginning of its design, although the latest versions of Multilisp and Qlisp support these parallelism in some way.

2.1 Parallel Lisp Processes in PaiLisp

In designing a parallel Lisp language it is necessary to clarify the concept of parallel processes in Lisp. Lisp is a language to deal with linked data structures through pointers. A typical machine model for parallel Lisp is a shared memory parallel architecture, whose simplest configuration is given in Figure 1. A model of parallelizing Lisp is a parallel computation model in which sequential Lisp programs share their environments and data as in Figure 2. A Lisp process (simply, a process) is a computation process expressed by a Lisp program under this model.

As a parallel language the following basic operations for processes are required for parallel Lisp.

1. **creation and initiation of processes**
   Creation of Lisp processes and initiation of their executions must be described in a language.

2. **suspension and resumption of process executions**
   It is required to describe that execution of a process is temporarily suspended and its execution will be resumed later (by effect of other processes).

3. **Killing of processes**
   Killing of process means that its execution will be forced to terminate by some other process(es) under certain conditions. It is required to describe how to kill processes in order to avoid unnecessary computations.

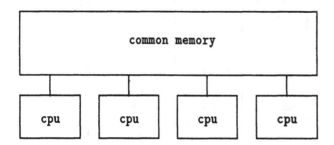

Figure 1: Model of shared memory parallel architecture

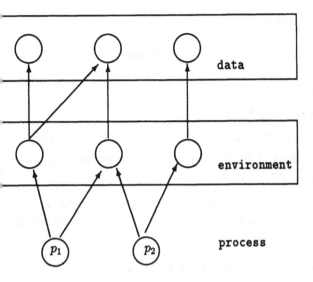

Figure 2: Model of Lisp processes , environment and shared data

How to describe these basic operations in PaiLisp is explained in the next paragraph. As is discussed in the next section this insight into the basic operations for Lisp processes has become the basis of our kernel language design. Parallel Lisp processes in Pailisp are formed from

1. **the basic operations on Lisp processes**
   These were designed and cleaned up to establish PaiLisp-Kernel, a compact kernel for PaiLisp.

2. **primitives for mutual exclusion**
   Exclusive function closure and semaphore primitives are used.

3. **future**
   This is an interesting construct introduced by Halstead[3].

4. **parallel constructs based on a data flow model of Lisp**
   A data flow model for parallel execution of Lisp programs was first introduced in [4]. PaiLisp possesses a set of parallel Lisp constructs that comes from the data flow model. They are classified as follows:

   [F] parallel evaluation of functional arguments

   [C] parallel evaluation of conditional and logical expressions

   [L] parallel evaluation on list structure

5. **delayed evaluation and infinitary looping**
   These constructs are often convenient to describe concurrent processes.

   The above basic operations of creation, suspension and killing of processes will be actually shown to be *basic* in the sense that these basic operations and Scheme are universal to describe behaviors of PaiLisp constructs. This will be done in Section 4, giving the description of PaiLisp constructs in terms of PaiLisp-Kernel.

The idea of giving these descriptions can be explained as follows:

1. In case of parallel execution of arguments of $(F\ E_1\ E_2)$;

   (a) spawn the processes for executing E_1 and E_2

   (b) suspend execution of the process which has called execution of $(F\ E_1\ E_2)$;

   (c) after termination of executions of E_1 and E_2, resume the process which has been suspended at (b) and then apply F.

   This will be described as $(pcall\ F\ E_1\ E_2)$. Notice that this **pcall** is different from Multilisp's **pcall**. The approximate analog to Multilisp's **pcall** is **eager** in PaiLisp, which is expressed using **future** as follows:

   $$(eager\ F\ E_1\ E_2) = ((future\ F)(future\ E_1)(future\ E_2))$$

   {See 4.2 for a detailed discussion.}

2. In case of execution of $(future\ E)$,
   future has two phases: generate its future-value and to wait for its true value.

   (a) for generation of the future-value, it is necessary to spawn a process for E and to initiate its execution;

   (b) the suspended process will be resumed when the value of E is actually computed.

   To realize **future** some careful treatment is required for generation of the future-value and for syschronization to acquire its value. This will be discussed in Section 4 when the kernel description of PaiLisp is given.
   Using **future** it is possible to write parallel execution of $(F\ E_1\ E_2)$ as follows:

   $$((future\ F)\ (future\ E_1)\ (future\ E_2))$$

   which can be also expressed as $(eager\ F\ E_1\ E_2)$ in PaiLisp. It should be noticed that this parallel execution of functional form possesses more parallelism than $(pcall\ F\ E_1\ E_2)$.{See **4.2** for a more careful discussion.}

2.2   An Overview of PaiLisp

An overview of PaiLisp is given in Table 1. In this paragraph we give some comments and overall explanations on PaiLisp. PaiLisp is designed as a Scheme-based parallel Lisp with 17 parallel constructs as in Table 1. These 17 constructs may be categorized as follows:

1. constructs for process creation, suspension, killing and control;

2. constructs for parallelism based on **future,par**, **pcall** and a data flow model of parallel execution of Lisp programs.

These parallel constructs possess some overlap in their descriptive power. For example, $pcall\ F\ E_1\ E_2$) may be approximated using **future** as $F\ (future\ E_1)(future\ E_2))$, but their operational meanings and actual efficiency would be different. The parallel execution of conditional expressions cannot be described by future alone, since we must be able to describe how to cancel the unnecessary executions in the conditional expression. {This will be explaind in detail in Section 4.}

Scheme as the base language of PaiLisp

As has been mentioned repeatedly, the current vertion of PaiLisp is based on Scheme. Scheme has the following features:

1. lexical scoping

2. procedures as first class objects

3. call-with-current-continuation to express continuation

4. removal of tail recursion

In PaiLisp all of these Scheme features are inherited with some extensions. **call-with-current-continuation** is a powerful control structure which allows to describe **catch** and **throw**. In PaiLisp this continuation construct is extended for parallel processes. {In the previous version of PaiLisp (in 1987) Common Lisp was the base language. Dynamic variables of Common Lisp cause some difficulty for good and efficient implementation, and the hugeness of Common Lisp may prevent us from giving the formal semantics and consistent implementation of (Common Lisp based) PaiLisp. For these reasons Scheme has been adopted as the base language of the current version of PaiLisp.}

Process concept of PaiLisp

The concept of parallel Lisp processes in PaiLisp was intuitively explained in 2.1. A parallel process of PaiLisp may be considered as a collection of individual processes, each of which can be identified by its process name. Each individual process will be specified by

> its process name (Pn),
> its execution status {run,killed,suspended,waiting} (S),
> its value obtained by computation up to the current point (cv),
> its continuation after the current point $(Cont)$,
> and
> its access information to the exclusive resource (Ex).

Thus an individual process P of PaiLisp will be specified by the quintuple:

$$P = \langle Pn, S, cv, Cont, Ex \rangle$$

A precise meaning of PaiLisp constructs will be specified in terms of this process concept of PaiLisp, although our desciptions of PaiLisp constructs are rather informal and intuitive in this paper.

2.3   Parallel constructs in PaiLisp

In this section we explain the syntax and semantics of parallel constructs of PaiLisp.

2.3.1   Constructs for process invocation and control

In this paragraph we explain the meanings of (*spawn e*), (*suspend*) and (*call/cc f*) of PaiLisp.

1) (*spawn e*)

This is a basic construct for process creation in PaiLisp. (*spawn e*) creates a process to compute the expression *e*, and its computaion will be carried out concurrently with the parent process that executes this **spawn** statement. The environment at (*spawn e*) will be inherited lexically by this newly created process. The parent process which executes (*spawn e*) will continue its execution without waiting for termination of the execution of the newly created process. The value returned by the spawn statement is unspecified at the level of its language specification and the value of e will be discarded.

In a sense this **spawn** is a simplified construct like **future**; that is, **spawn** is a version of **future** which does not return its future value. From an operational standpoint (*spawn e*) may be understood to have the follwing meaning:
Assume that

> a process P is in the **run** state
> and
> (*spawn e*) will be actually executed.

The value that P gets as the result of evaluating (*spawn e*) is **unspecified** at the level of its language specification. The value returned by the spawn statement is a value to be computed under its current environment.

A process name P_n for (*spawn e*) will be created. {P_n should not have the naming conflict within the current parallel process.} The initiation of the process P_n will take place with the following rule:

> the expression e will be evaluated,
> and after its completion P_n will fall into the **killed** state.

The parent process which contains (*spawn e*) will continue its execution with the value of (*spawn e*) explained above.

2) (*suspend*)

This is a basic construct to be used for suspension and resumption of process execution.

3) (*call/cc f*)

This is an extension of Scheme's call-with-current-continuation to a parallel situation, to be used to describe control-transfer among parallel processes.
f must be a procedure with one argument. (*call/cc f*) creates a procedure with one argument to denote its current continuation, and *f* will be applied to this procedure.

Compared with Scheme's continuation the continuation in PaiLisp is extended as follows:

1. In a continuation the name of the process which generates the continuation will be recorded;

2. When a continuation is called, the process which executes the continuation (the rest of the continued computation) is the process that generated the continuation. When the called process is blocked by an exclusive closure or a condition variable, this process will be removed from the corresponding queue. When a process that did not generate the continuation called it, the process calling the continuation will continue its execution concurrently. The value returned by the process that has called the continuation will be unspecified in this case.

By this extension the continuation can be used as a method of controlling execution of processes from other processes. In execution of (*spawn e*) a new process that executes *e* will be created. The continuation of execution of *e* in this case can be used for killing of process. This is an example of use of continuation for controlling process executions.

Remark Let A be a task that invokes a continuation closure, and let B be a task that captured the continuation, where A and B are different.
If B is currently executed when A invokes the continuation, the execution of B will be continued until the end of an indivisible atomic process being executed; then, the switching control of the continuation will take place.
If B has already completed its execution, then the invocation for the continuation will be ignored; hence A will continue its execution.
This was the original meaning, but it will be better to define the invocation of the continuation closure generated by completed process so as to resume its process execution.

Example ⟨Use of call/cc and suspend ⟩

```
(begin
    (call/cc (lambda (wakeup)
                (spawn (begin
                           (print 1)
                           (wakeup 'dummy)
                           (print 2)))
                (suspend))))
    (print 3))
```

In this program it is guaranteed that the execution of (print 1) always precedes to (print 2) and (print 3).

```
(let ((kill 'dummy))
    (call/cc (lambda (wakeup)
                (spawn (call/cc (lambda (k)
```

```
                                      (set! kill k)
                                      (wakeup 'dummy)
                                      ........)))
                    (suspend)))
      AA...)
```

In this case, after assigning the continuation into kill the parent process will be resumed by wakeup; for this purpose, when *AA...* is executed the continuation to kill the child process will be placed in the variable kill.

```
(m-suspend f) = (call/cc (lambda (k)
                           (spawn (f k))
                           (suspend)))
```

This is an approximate description of Multilisp's suspend[3].

2.3.2 Constructs for Mutual Exclusion

4) $(exlambda\ (x_1, ..., x_n)\ e_1, ..., e_m)$

exlambda creates a new queue q and an exclusive closure
$[(exlambda\ (x_1, ..., x_n)\ e_1, ..., e_m), env, q]$, where env is the current environment. When an exclusive closure is used by a process, the process that calls this closure will be suspended in its execution until this closure is released. {This exlambda is a kind of refinement of qlambda of Qlisp[1].}

5) $(signal\ cvar\ e)$ and $(wait\ cvar)$

These constructs can be used only within an exclusive closure. wait means

temporary suspension of execution of the process and release of its access to the exclusive closure.

The information required for resuming the execution of a suspended process will be added to the queue of the condition variable cvar.
signal will be used to resume the execution of the process suspended by wait, and it will return the value of e as the result of its application to an exclusive closure. {The idea here is similar to Hoare's monitors.}

Example ⟨Problem of Five Dining Philosophers⟩
The following program for Problem of Five Dining Philosophers explains PaiLisp programming with exlambda and signal/wait.

```
(define (phil right left)
   (loop (THINK)
         (get-fork right)
         (get-fork left)
         (EAT)
         (release-fork right)
         (release-fork left)))
(define (make-fork)
```

```
    (let ((free #t) (c (make-cond-var)))
      (exlambda (cmd)
          (cond ((eq cmd 'get)
                  (if (not free) (wait c))
                  (set! free #f))
                ((eq cmd 'release)
                  (set! free #t)
                  (signal c 'dummy))))))
 (define (get-fork fork) (fork 'get))
 (define (release-fork fork) (fork 'release))
 (define (five-phil)
    (let ((fork1 (make-fork))
          (fork2 (make-fork))
          (fork3 (make-fork))
          (fork4 (make-fork))
          (fork5 (make-fork)))
      (par
        (phil fork1 fork2)
        (phil fork2 fork3)
        (phil fork3 fork4)
        (phil fork4 fork5)
        (phil fork5 fork1))))
```

This example is for explaining PaiLisp programming and in particular for explaining how to use and create condition variables. Notice that this program for Problem of Five Dining Philosophers is not deadlock-free.

2.3.3   future

The future is an interesting and important construct introduced by Halstead[3] into a parallel Lisp language Multilisp. future is important as a construct to express *true concurrency.*

6) (*future e*)

(*future e*) returns a special virtual value for e, called the future value for e. The parent process that called this future statement will continue its execution, and simultaneously with this execution a new process which computes e will be created and executed. The process that called this statement can continue its execution, using the future value for e.

But when an operation on the future value of e requires its true value, its process will be suspended until the value of e is obtained. For example, in case of (*car* (*future e*)) "*car*" requires the actual value of e for its execution, so that its execution will be suspended until the true value of e is obtained.

2.3.4   Constructs based on data flow model for Lisp

The parallel constructs based on a data flow model for Lisp come from the first author's idea proposed in [4] and [5], in which parallel evaluation of functional arguments, parallel conditional expressions and parallel operations on list data structures were introduced. The parallelism based on the data flow model was the basis of our implementation of a parallel Lisp interpreter on a shared memory parallel machine PAI-68K developed at our laboratory[6].

7) $(par\ e_1, ..., e_n)$

This means the parallel execution of $e_1, ..., e_n$ until completion of their executions. The result of **par** is unspecified, and the results of computing $e_1, ..., e_n$ will be discarded.

8) $(pcall\ f, e_1, ..., e_n)$ and $(eager\ f, e_1, ..., e_n)$

$(pcall\ f, e_1, ..., e_n)$ means that after completion of parallel execution of $e_1, ..., e_n$ the expression f will be evaluated and then the function f will be applied to the values of $e_1, ..., e_n$.

$(eager\ f, e1, ..., en)$ means $((future\ f)(future\ e_1), ..., (future\ e_n))$. Notice that pcall of PaiLisp is different from Multilisp's pcall but **eager** of PaiLisp is the approximate analog to Multilisp's pcall.{See 4.2 for a more careful discussion.}

9) $(pcond\ (p_1\ e_1)(p_2\ e_2)...(p_n\ e_n))$

In case of **pcond** the predicates $p_1, p_2, ..., p_n$ will be evaluated in parallel. If $p_1, ..., p_{i-1}$ are false and p_i is true, then e_i will be computed and the value of e_i will be returned as the value of pcond, terminating all other executions of predicates.

10) $(pcond\#\ (p_1\ e_1)(p_2\ e_2)...(p_n\ e_n))$

In case of **pcond#** the predicates $p_1, p_2, ..., p_n$ and their bodies $e_1, e_2, ..., e_n$ will be evaluated in parallel. If $p_1, ..., p_{i-1}$ are false and p_i is true, then the value of e_i will be returned as the value of **pcond#**, terminating all other executions for predicates and bodies. Also, whenever the value of p_k is determined to be false the evaluation of e_k will be terminated.

11) $(par\text{-}and\ e_1, e_2, ..., e_n)$

In this case $e_1, e_2, ..., e_n$ will be executed in parallel. If one of them yields false, then the value of par-and will become false, terminating all other executions. If no expression yields false after execution of every expression of $(e_1, e_2, ..., e_n)$, then the value of e_n will be returned as the result of **par-and**.

12) $(par\text{-}or\ e_1, e_2, ..., e_n)$

In this case $e_1, e_2, ..., e_n$ will be executed in parallel. If one of them yields non-false (or non-NIL), then its non-false value will be returned as the result of par-or, terminating all other executions. If no expression yields non-false (or non-NIL), then the result of **par-or** will become false (that is, #f).

13) $(pmapcar\ f\ L)$

pmapcar applies the function f to each element of the list $L = (L_1, L_2, ..., L_n)$ in parallel, and the resulting list is the value of **pmapcar**. The application of f to each list element will be done by future, that is, $(future\ (f\ Li))$.

2.3.5 Other Constructs

It may be possible to introduce other constructs into PaiLisp, but we included only two other constructs in PaiLisp:

14) $(delay\ e)$

delay does not produce a process to compute e immediately, but it returns a special virtual value called the delay value for e, which contains all the information necessary to compute e.

At the first time when the true value of e is requested the actual execution to compute e will take place.

Delayed evaluation is a purely sequential construct, but it is included here since it enables us to describe infinitary data structures.

15) $(loop\ e_1, e_2, ..., e_n)$

loop executes $e_1, e_2, ..., e_n$ repeatedly in this order. This repetition will continue until an escape from loop by calling a continuation created using call/cc takes place.

In order to emphasize the importance of describing the infinitary repetition in a concurrent process this loop construct was introduced.

Several other constructs were considered: for example,

a) Non-deterministic Choice

$(alt\ (p_1\ e_1)(p_2\ e_2)...(p_n\ e_n))$ In this case $p_1, p_2, ..., p_n$ will be executed in parallel and one of the predicates which return non-NIL will select its body non-deterministically.

b) Multiple Conditional future

$(m\text{-}future\ f\ (p_1\ e_1)(p_2\ e_2)...(p_n\ e_n))$
$= ((future\ f)\ (future\ (pcond\#\ (p_1\ e_1)))...(future\ (pcond\#\ (p_n\ e_n))))$
This is a generalization of future, while spawn was a restriction to future.

c) call/ep

This is a restricted call/cc that does not allow the following case:

call/cc returns its value and call/cc invokes the continuation

This call/ep (call-with-escape-procedure) will be disussed in 3.1.2 .

d) Constructs from Channel-Lisp

Channel-Lisp[8] is another model of parallel Lisp that modular Lisp programs communicate through Occam-like channels. It would be useful to introduce some constructs and mechanisms from Channel-Lisp for modular/structured programming of Lisp concurrent programs. In particular the ideas of channel communication between Lisp processes and stream programming in Lisp would be valuable to write an elegant modular concurrent Lisp program.

3 PaiLisp-Kernel

PaiLisp may be viewed as Scheme with 17 parallel constructs, as was explained above. PaiLisp may be too powerful and redundant, compared with Multilisp and Qlisp. But we were able to extract a very compact kernel of PaiLisp, by which we can describe the meanings of all the constructs of PaiLisp.

In this section we explain the details of PaiLisp-Kernel, clarifying some basic concepts in parallel Lisp processes.

3.1 Basic Constructs in PaiLisp-Kernel

PaiLisp-Kernel is Scheme with four parallel process constructs as follows:

1. $(spawn \langle e \rangle)$:
   process generation for $\langle e \rangle$

2. $(suspend)$:
   temporary suspension of process execution

3. $(exlambda (\langle x_1 \rangle \cdots \langle x_n \rangle) \langle e_1 \rangle \cdots \langle e_m \rangle)$:
   generation of exclusive closure for $\langle e_1 \rangle, \cdots, \langle e_m \rangle$

4. $(call/cc \langle f \rangle)$:
   control by means of continuation, an extension of call/cc in Scheme

The previous section has given some detailed explanations of these four constructs, but their detailed meanings will become clear in what follows.

3.1.1 Parallel Lisp processes

A parallel Lisp process consists of Lisp operations to be executed concurrently and their states. It has one of three states {run, blocked, killed}. A blocked state will be classified into one of three cases {waiting by exclusive closure, waiting by synchronization condition, suspended}; in case of waiting by exclusive closure and synchronization condition, it is necessary to record them into the corresponding process state. There are two kinds of operations in parallel Lisp processes: operations for processes and operations for shared resources.

[**A**] Operations on Shared Resources

    a. Access to Shared Resources by Exclusive Closure
        PaiLisp is a parallel Lisp based on a shared memory architecture.
        For exclusive access to shared resources the following exclusive closure realized
        by exlambda is in the language:

$$(exlambda (\langle x_1 \rangle \cdots \langle x_n \rangle) \langle e_1 \rangle \cdots \langle e_m \rangle)$$

        which generates an exclusive function closure. This is essentially same as the
        closure generated by $(lambda (\langle x_1 \rangle \ldots \langle x_n \rangle) \langle e_1 \rangle \cdots \langle e_m \rangle)$ except that it can be
        applied from only one process at a time. While a process is applying it, another

process trying to apply it will wait until the former completes its application. When several processes are waiting, they will be recorded in a FIFO queue in the order of their application.

b. Synchronization by signal/wait

PaiLisp-Kernel is Scheme plus {spawn, suspend, exlambda, call/cc}. When we consider the synchronization problem it is often convenient to use the signal/wait operations, Here we explain the synchronization problem in terms of signal/wait. However, as will be shown in Section 4, these operations can be described in terms of PaiLisp-Kernel; thus, there should be no change in the definition of PaiLisp-Kernel. Within exclusive closure it is possible to use synchronization realized by $(wait\ \langle cvar \rangle)$ and $(signal\ \langle cvar \rangle\ \langle e \rangle)$. The value of the condition variable $\langle cvar \rangle$ is a special Lisp datum to be generated by the function $(make\text{-}cond\text{-}var)$.

A process which executes $(wait\ \langle cvar \rangle)$ will fall into the blocked state. The exclusive access to the lexically innermost exclusive closure which contains the $(wait\ \langle cvar \rangle)$ will be released, and that closure will become applicable by other processes.

When $(signal\ \langle cvar \rangle\ \langle e \rangle)$ is executed, a process waiting on the condition variable $\langle cvar \rangle$ will be unblocked and go into the run state. The unblocked process gets the access right to the exclusive closure. If there is no process with the condition variable $\langle cvar \rangle$, the access right to the condition variable will be released.

signal should be invoked by a process that originally entered the exclusive closure, and signal should cause the invocations of the closure to return, producing the value of e. e should be evaluated before the signal operation actually takes place.

The processes which wait on condition variables will be recorded in the FIFO queue of condition variables in the order of executing wait, and they will be treated in the order of arrival. {For an example of use of signal/wait, see Example in 2.3.1}

N.B.: The first version of PaiLisp-Kernel was Scheme plus {spawn, suspend, exlambda, call/cc, signal, wait}, M.Matsui actually gave a description of signal/wait by PaiLisp-Kernel, as is given in Section 4.

[B] How to realize "initiation","suspension","resuming" and "killing"of processes

a. Initiation

$(spawn\ \langle e \rangle)$ generates a process to execute $\langle e \rangle$ and initiates its execution. The environment for spawn will be inherited lexically. After generation of a process spawn returns a value without termination of execution of $\langle e \rangle$. The value to be returned is unspecified at the level of specification. The parent process called spawn and the newly created process will be executed in parallel.

b. Suspension and resuming

$(suspend)$ will be used for temporary suspension (blocking) of a process. The parent process which executes $(suspend)$ falls into the blocked state. It will become unblocked when the continuation generated by (*suspend*) is called by other processes and its execution will be resumed.

c. Killing

Killing of process created by (*spawn* ⟨e⟩) can be done by invoking the continuation of ⟨e⟩. When the continuation of ⟨e⟩ is called, its process states falls into "killed" according to the definition of (*spawn* ⟨e⟩), so that the process will be killed. {For an Example of killing and resuming, see Example in 2.3.1}

3.1.2   Extension of continuation in Parallel Lisp

The continuation is a powerful control mechanism originally introduced in Denotational Semantics of Sequential Programs, and it has been introduced into Scheme as an important language construct. call/cc is the form used in Scheme to express call-with-current-continuation. In PaiLisp we extend this call/cc as follows:

1. (*call/cc* ⟨f⟩) generates a procedure with one argument to denote the current continuation and applies ⟨f⟩ to it.

2. When a continuation is called, the process that "continues" is the process that created the continuation. When a process that did not create the continuation calls the continuation, the process that called the continuation will continue its execution concurrently. In this case the value returned by the process that has called the continuation will be unspecified.

3. When the process called by continuation is locked by exclusive closure or signal/wait, it will be removed from the corresponding queue.

> **Remark:** The continuation extended as above is a very powerful and general control mechanism, but its implementation and execution cost may be high. Therefore we examined an efficient and restricted version of call/cc which has been named as call/ep to mean call-with-escape-procedure.
> call/ep is a restricted call/cc in which the escape procedure can be invoked only under the control of call/ep which produced its procedure. That is, if an escape procedure were not called, the current continuation should contain the action to return the value from call/ep which produced the escape procedure.
> It may be considered that in call/ep the continuation can be used only once or returned normally from call/cc.
> catch/throw and block,return-from can be realized by this call/ep. According to our experiences to describe PaiLisp using PaiLisp-Kernel and Scheme programming most cases of using call/cc could be replaced by call/ep.
> However it is possible to write a Scheme program in which call/cc cannot be replaced by call/ep. For example, the following is such an example:

```
(let ((loop #f) (n 2))
   (call/cc (lambda (k) (set! loop k)))
```

```
(print n)
(if (zero? n)
    #t
    (begin (set! n (- n 1)) (loop #f))))
```

3.1.3   On choosing Basic Primitives of PaiLisp-Kernel

Using PaiLisp-Kernel we can describe all the constructs of PaiLisp, as is shown in the next section. We give some comments on the primitives of PaiLisp-Kernel.

1. **spawn** is more elementary than **future**, since it is **future** which does not return its future value.

2. The well-structured statements like **par** are favorable from the standpoint of programming, but we do not know a universal set of well structured constructs to describe all parallel Lisp processes.

3. **call/cc** is more powerful than **catch/throw**, and moreover, in case of **catch/throw** their dynamic nature inherent in use of **tag** often causes the degradation of program understandability.

4. At the first thought **signal** and **wait** were included in PaiLisp-Kernel,but it was found (by M.Matsui) that these constructs could be described as in this paper. {See the next section.}

3.2   Description of PaiLisp-Kernel in PaiLisp-Kernel

It is possible to express an interpreter for PaiLisp-Kernel in PaiLisp-Kernel. This meta-circular interpreter **eval** interpretes and executes an S-expresson to denote a program in PaiLisp-Kernel. The meta-circular interpreter whose complete description is given in **Appendix I** consists of

1. descriptions for top-level, evaluator, enviroments for variables, apply, primitive functions and closure,

   and

2. descriptions for parallel constructs {spawn, suspend, call/cc, exlambda}

The following are the comments and remarks for the description of the meta-circular interpreter given in **Appendix I**.

1. The interpreter **eval** takes 2 arguments *exp* and *lenv*, where *exp* is an expression in PaiLisp-kernel to be interpreted and *lenv* is local the environment for **eval** to evaluate exp. **eval** analyses the syntax of *exp* and calls the corresponding procedure to deal with it.

2. The environment is expressed as an alist of bindings of variables.
   {See variable and several auxiliary functions listed there.}

3. **primitive** is expressed as a pair of (*primitive* .⟨label⟩). This ⟨label⟩ will be used for selecting what shall be done in **apply-primitive**.

4. **apply-proc** does the function applications according to the types of functions, that is, primitive functions, closure, exclusive closure, and continuation.

5. **closure** is defined as a list with args, body to be executed, and lenv to denote its local environment.

6. (*spawn e*) spawns a new **eval** to interpret **e**.

7. The interpreter will execute its **suspend** for **suspend**. This is expressed in (*apply-primitive fn args*).

8. **call/cc** will be dealt with by generating the continuation ⟨cont⟩ at the interpreter level; it will be dealt with as a pair (*continuation* .⟨cont⟩). The call of the continuation will be done by calling the continuation at the interpreter level.

9. The exclusive closure is defined as a list with arguments, body to be executed, lenv to denote its local environment and lock for the exclusive execution.
   lock is an exclusive closure at the interpreter level for exclusive execution of application of the exclusive closure. The application of an exclusive closure will be done by **apply-exclosure**.

N.B. The meta-circular interpreter in Appendix I is an updated and revised version by Matsuo Nonaka (a graduate student of the first author). He improved the description to be self-consistent on the basis of Scheme.

Remark The meta-circular interpreter of PaiLisp-Kernel may be considered to be an implementation-oriented operational semantics of PaiLisp-Kernel. On the basis of this description and the clarification of parallel Lisp processes an attempt to give formal semantics of PaiLisp-Kernel has been taken by A.Umemura and the first author, using a formal deductive formalism of operational semantics proposed by G.Plotkin and G.Kahn. That is, a state transition of a PaiLisp process is expressed as a Gentzen-style deduction.

4 Description of PaiLisp using PaiLisp-Kernel

Pailisp can be described by PaiLisp-Kernel. This will be established, showing how to descibe every construct of PaiLisp using PaiLisp-Kernel. Let "K" be the transformation from PaiLisp into PaiLisp-Kernel. Then

$$K[exp]$$

means the result of the transformation of exp by K. We define this transformation K for each PaiLisp construct. We assume that naming conflicts among arguments of lambda expressions and variables in let expressions are prevented by appropriate renaming of variables.

4.1 Description of $(par \ \langle E_1 \rangle \langle E_2 \rangle \cdots \langle E_3 \rangle)$

In execution of **par** the child processes to compute $\langle e_i \rangle$ will be generated and the termination of **par** requires the termination of all the child processes; thus, the child processes with shorter execution time will be waited for termination of other processes. The initiation of a child process can be done by **spawn**, and **waiting** will be done by **call/cc** and **suspend**.

```
1   K[(par <E1> ... <En>)]
2   = (call/cc (lambda (return)
3           (let* ((n <n>)
4                 (unlock
5                 (exlambda ()
6                   (if (= n 1)
7                       (return '<unspecified>))
8                   (set! n (- n 1)))))
9               (spawn (begin K[<e1>] (unlock)))
10              ...
11              (spawn (begin K[<en>] (unlock)))
12              (suspend))))
```

The parent process will generate **return** which denotes the continuation for suspension or waiting. {(2)}
The child processes to compute $\langle E_i \rangle$ will be generated.{(9-11)}
After this action the parent process will be suspended until the termination of the child processes{(12)}.
unlock is an exclusive closure to manage the variable n to denote the number of cchild processes which are not terminated yet.{See (5-8)} Everytime **unlock** is called the value of n will be decreased {(8)}. When the last child process calls **unlock**, the parent process suspended will be resumed by the continuation **return**.

4.2 Descriptions of $(pcall \ \langle F \rangle \ \langle E_1 \rangle \cdots \langle E_n \rangle)$ and $(eager \ \langle F \rangle \ \langle E_1 \rangle \cdots \langle E_n \rangle)$

(1) Description of *pcall*
As in case of **par**, the processes to compute $\langle E_1 \rangle, \cdots, \langle E_n \rangle$ will be generated , and their values will be stored in $t_1, \cdots, t_n$.{(5-15)}
The parent process (resumed for execution) will apply $\langle F \rangle$ to them.

```
1   K[(pcall <F> <E1> ... <En>)]
2   = (let ((t1 '<unspecified>)
3           ...
4          (tn '<unspecified>))
5      (call/cc (lambda (return)
6                  (let* ((n <n>)
7                         (unlock
8                          (lambda ()
9                             (if (= n 1)
10                               (return '<dummy>))
11                            (set! n (- n 1)))))
12                  (spawn (begin (set! t1 K[<E1>]) (unlock)))
13                  ...
14                  (spawn (begin (set! tn K[<En>]) (unlock)))
15                  (suspend))))
16      (K[<F>] t1 ... tn))
```

Let us denote Multilisp's pcall as m-pcall. Then the description of $(m\text{-}pcall\langle F\rangle\langle E_1\rangle \cdots \langle E_n\rangle)$ can be given as follows:

```
1   K[(m-pcall <F> <E1> ... <En>)]
2   = (let ((f '<unspecified>)
3          (t1 '<unspecified>)
4           ...
5          (tn '<unspecified>))
6      (call/cc (lambda (return)
7                  (let* ((n <n+1>)
8                         (unlock
9                          (exlambda ()
10                            (if (= n 1)
11                               (return '<dummy>))
12                            (set! n (- n 1)))))
13                  (spawn (begin (set! f K[<F>]) (unlock)))
14                  (spawn (begin (set! t1 K[<E1>]) (unlock)))
15                  ...
16                  (spawn (begin (set! tn K[<En>]) (unlock)))
17                  (suspend))))
18      (f t1 ... tn))
```

From these description of pcall and m-pcall we can see the difference of PaiLisp's pcall and Multilisp's pcall precisely, and moreover we can see why Multilisp's pcall extracts more parallelism than PaiLisp's pcall. A nice aspect of the kernel language is to clarify the meanings of language constructs in this way.

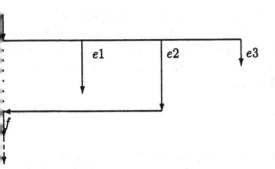

Figure 3: Example of $(pcall\ \langle f \rangle\ \langle e_1 \rangle\ \cdots\ \langle e_n \rangle)$
$\langle f \rangle$ will be applied to $\langle e_1 \rangle, \cdots, \langle e_n \rangle$ after their termination.

(2) Description of *eager*
eager can be defined using future as follows:

```
K[(eager <F>   <E1> ... <En>]
 = ((future <F>) (future <E1>) ... (future <En>))
```

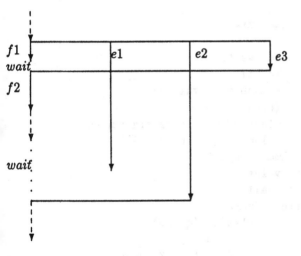

Figure 4: Example of $(eager\ \langle f \rangle\ \langle e_1 \rangle\ \cdots\ \langle e_n \rangle)$
Even a part of application of $\langle f \rangle$ and the execution of using the future value of $\langle f \rangle$ may be executed in parallel with $\langle e_1 \rangle \cdots \langle e_n \rangle$.

4.3   Descriptions of $(future\langle E \rangle)$ and $(delay\langle E \rangle)$

(1) Description of $(future\langle E \rangle)$
$(future\ \langle E \rangle)$ returns a special virtual value for $\langle E \rangle$, named the future value for $\langle E \rangle$. The parent process that called this future statement will continue its execution, and simultaneously with this execution a new process which computes e will be created and executed. The process that called this statement can continue its execution, using the

future value for $\langle E \rangle$. When the actual value is required, the force operation for the future value will be performed. If the actual value is computed, this actual value will be returende, but if not, the **waiting** realized by **suspend** and **call/cc** will take place. The future value will be denoted as a datum with a special type *pdata*. The following three operations will be defined for a datum with pdata.

make-pdata: Given a procedure with no argument, this will make a datum the type *pdata*, containing that procedure.

pdata-procedure:This will fetch a procedure stored by *make-pdata*. When the actual value of the *future* is requested, this procedure with no argument will be called.

pdata?: This is the test predidate for *pdata*.

The lock operation for an exclusive closure will be used for waiting; {See (5-12)}. When the actual true value is required,(*lock 'wait ⟨continuation⟩*) will be called; {See (26)}. When the actual true value is given,it will be called in the form of (*lock 'result ⟨value⟩*).

```
1 K[(future <E>)]
2 = (let ((value '<unspecified>)
3         (avail #f)
4         (queue '()))
5    (let ((lock (exlambda (cmd arg)
6                   (cond
7                     ((eq? cmd 'wait)
8                      (cond (avail
9                              (lambda () value))
10                           (else
11                            (set! queue (cons arg queue))
12                            (lambda () (suspend)))))
13                    ((eq? cmd 'result)
14                     (set! value arg)
15                     (set! avail #t)
16                     (letrec ((wake
17                                (lambda (queue)
18                                  (cond
19                                    (not (null? queue))
20                                      ((car queue) arg)
21                                      (wake (cdr queue)))))))
22                       (wake queue)))))))
23      (spawn (lock 'result K[<E>]))
24      (make-pdata (lambda ()
25                    (call/cc (lambda (k)
26                               ((lock 'wait k)))))))))

27 K[(delay <E>)]
28 = (let ((value '<unspecified>)
29         (avail #f))
30    (let ((lock (exlambda ()
```

```
31                      (cond ((not avail)
32                             (set! value K[<E>])
33                             (set! avail #t)))
34                      value)))
35          (make-pdata lock)))

36   (define (force x)
37     (if (pdata? x)
38         (force ((pdata-procedure x)))
39         x))

40   (define car
41     (let ((kernel-car car))
42       (lambda (x) (kernel-car (force x)))))

43   (define cdr
44     (let ((kernel-cdr cdr))
45       (lambda (x) (kernel-cdr (force x)))))
```

(2) Description of (delay ⟨E⟩)

delay can be described by means of pdata, as in future. In case of delay the procedure stored in pdata must be modified in the following way. The process called at the
first time will compute its true value; after then, its true value will be returned. avail is
the flag to tell if the true value is computed; if not computed yet, it will be computed
{(32-33)}. force should be defined as (36-39).
Using this force, car and cdr must be defined as in (40-45). Many other functions and
predecates must be defined in this way; some of them are listed in Appendix II.

4.4   Description of (pmapcar ⟨F⟩ ⟨L⟩)

The description of pmapcar can be given as a procedural definition, using future as
follows:

```
(define (pmapcar f 1)
   (cond
     ((null? 1) '())
     (else (cons (future (f (car 1)))
                 (pmapcar f (cdr 1))))
```

Instead of this definition it is possible to define pmapcar as follows:

```
(define (pmapcar f 1)
   (cond
     ((null? 1) '())
     (else (cons (future (f (car 1)))
                 (future (pmapcar f (cdr 1)))))  ))
```

This looks better than the former definition, since this extracts more parallelism. However, the overhead for process generation of the latter is almost twice of the former, so that we prefer the former definition here.

4.5 Description of $(pcond\ (\langle P_1\rangle\langle E_1\rangle)\cdots(\langle P_n\rangle\langle E_n\rangle))$

In order to give the description of pcond, the following must be described:

> how to create processes to compute $\langle P_1\rangle,\cdots,\langle P_n\rangle$;
> how to wait for their results;
> and
> how to kill processes whose executions become unnecessary.

In order to kill some processes it is required to preserve the continuation at the time of process creation.start-process (3-15) is introduced for this purpose. start-process gets a closure. A process to execute this closure will be created by spawn (8-13), and the continuation to kill this process will be stored in the process-list(8-10).
kill-all kills all the created processes using the continuation stored in the process-list.
pcond can be realized by start-process and kill-all as follows:

```
1   K[(pcond (<P1> <E1>) ... (<Pn> <En>))]
2   = (let* ((process-list '())
3              (start-process
4               (lambda (p)
5                 (let ((p-res '<dummy>)
6                       (p-lock (exlambda (e) (e))))
7                   (call/cc (lambda (wake-up)
8                     (spawn (call/cc (lambda (k)
9                       (set! process-list
10                          (cons k process-list))

11                      (p-lock (lambda ()
12                                (wake-up '<dummy>)
13                                (set! p-res (p)))))))))
14                   (suspend)))
15                 (lambda () (p-lock (lambda () p-res))))))
16             (p1 (start-process (lambda () K[<P1>])))
17             ...
18             (pn (start-process (lambda () K[<Pn>]))))
19      (letrec ((kill-all
20                (lambda (l)

21                  (if l (begin ((car l) '<dummy>)
22                               (kill-all (cdr l)))))))
23         (cond
24          ((p1) (kill-all process-list) K[<E1>])
25          ...
26          ((pn) (kill-all process-list) K[<En>]))))
```

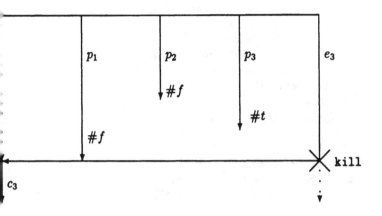

Figure 5: Behavior of *pcond*

4.6 Description of $(pcond\# \ (\langle P_1 \rangle \ \langle E_1 \rangle) \cdots (\langle P_n \rangle \ \langle E_n \rangle)))$

This description is similar to the case of **pcond**, but there are the following differences:

1. When $\langle P_i \rangle$ is false it is necessary to stop the evaluation of $\langle E_i \rangle$. **start-process** in this *pcond#* creates a pair of processes for $\langle P_i \rangle$ and $\langle E_i \rangle$.(18-19)

2. When $\langle P_i \rangle$ is true **kill-all** kills all the processes except the process to compute $\langle E_i \rangle$.

3. When $\langle P_i \rangle$ is true the synchronization for $\langle E_i \rangle$ and $\langle P_i \rangle$ must be done.

```
1  K[(pcond# (<P1> <E1>) ... (<Pn> <En>))]
2  = (let* ((process-list '())
3          (start-process
4            (lambda (p e)
5              (let ((p-res #t)
6                    (p-lock (exlambda (e) (e)))
7                    (e-res '<dummy>)
8                    (e-lock (exlambda (e) (e)))
9                    (e-kill '<dummy>))
10                (call/cc (lambda (wake-up)
11                  (spawn (call/cc (lambda (k)
12                    (set! process-list (cons k process-list))
13                    (p-lock (lambda ()
14                            (wake-up '<dummy>)
15                            (set! p-res (p))
16                            (if (not p-res)
17                                (e-kill '<dummy>)))))))
18                  (suspend)))
19                (if p-res
20                    (call/cc (lambda (wake-up)
```

```
21                            (spawn (call/cc (lambda (k)
22                              (set! process-list
23                                    (cons k process-list))
24                              (set! e-kill k)
25                              (e-lock (lambda ()
26                                        (wake-up '<dummy>)
27                                        (set! e-res (e)))))))
28                            (suspend))))
29                   '(,(lambda ()
30                        (p-lock (lambda () p-res)))
31                      ,e-kill
32                      ,(lambda ()
33                         (e-lock (lambda () e-res)))))))
34        (pe1 (start-process (lambda () K[<P1>])
35                            (lambda () K[<E1>])))
36        ...
37        (pen (start-process (lambda () K[<Pn>])
38                            (lambda () K[<En>]))))
39     (letrec ((kill-all
40               (lambda (e l)
41                 (cond
42                  ((not (null? l)) (if (not (eq? e (car l)))
43                                       ((car l) '<dummy>))
44                                   (kill-all e (cdr l))))))
45      (cond
46       (((car pe1)) (kill-all (cadr pe1) process-list)
47                    (caddr pe1))
48       ...
49       (((car pen)) (kill-all (cadr pen) process-list)
50                    (caddr pen)))))
```

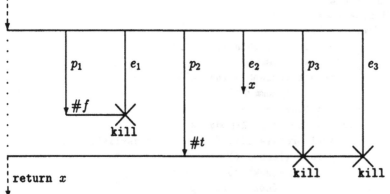

Figure 6: Behavior of (*pcond#* (p_1 e_1) (p_2 e_2) (p_3 e_3))

4.7 Descriptions of $(par\text{-}and\langle E_1 \rangle \cdots \langle E_n \rangle)$ and $(par\text{-}or\langle E_1 \rangle \cdots \langle E_n \rangle)$

(1) Description of $(par\text{-}and\langle E_1 \rangle \cdots \langle E_n \rangle)$
par-and can be realized as follows:

a. Whenever one of $\langle E_1 \rangle, \cdots, \langle E_n \rangle$ becomes *false*, **par-and** returns the value *false*, killing all other computations. This killing will be done by means of **continuation** as in the case of **pcond**.

b. When none of $\langle E_1 \rangle, \cdots, \langle E_n \rangle$ becomes *false*, **par-and** returns the value of $\langle E_n \rangle$.

```
1   K[(par-and <E1> ... <En>)]
2   = (call/cc (lambda (return)
3       (let* ((process-list '())
4              (kill-lock (exlambda (e) (e)))
5              (tmp '<dummy>)
6              (1 <n>)
7              (1-unlock
8               (exlambda ()
9                     (if (= 1 1)
10                    (return tmp)
11                    (set! 1 (- 1 1)))))))
12      (letrec ((kill-all
13               (lambda (k pl)
14                 (cond ((null? pl) '<dummy>)
15                       ((eq? k (car pl))
16                        (kill-all k (cdr 1)))
17                       (else
18                        ((car 1) '<dummy>)
19                        (kill-all (cdr 1)))))))
20       (let ((start-process
21             (lambda (e)
22               (kill-lock (lambda ()
23                 (call/cc (lambda (r)
24                 (spawn (call/cc (lambda (k)
25                   (set! process-list
26                         (cons k (process-list)))
27                 (r '<dummy>)
28                 (let ((res (e)))
29                   (cond
30                   ((not res)
31                    (kill-lock
32                    (lambda ()
33                      (return #f)
34                      (kill-all  k process-list))))
35                   (else
36                    (1-unlock)))))))))
```

```
37                           (suspend))))))))
38          (start-process (lambda () K[<E1>]))
39          ...
40          (start-process (lambda () K[<En-1>]))
41          (start-process (lambda () (set! tmp K[<En>]) tmp))
42          (suspend))))))
```

(2) Description of $(par\text{-}or\langle E_1\rangle \cdots \langle E_n\rangle)$
par-or can be described similarly.

a. Whenenver one of $\langle E_1\rangle, \cdots, \langle E_n\rangle$ becomes non-NIL, **par-or** returns this non-NIL value as its result, killing all other executions.

b. If none of $\langle E_1\rangle, \cdots, \langle E_n\rangle$ becomes non-NIL, then **par-or** returns *false* as its value.

```
1   K[(par-or <E1> ... <En>)]
2   = (call/cc (lambda (return)
3       (let* ((process-list '())
4              (kill-lock (exlambda (e) (e)))
5              (l <n>)
6              (l-unlock
7               (exlambda ()
8                  (if (= l 1)
9                      (return #f)
10                     (set! l (- l 1)))))))
11        (letrec ((kill-all
12                  (lambda (k pl)
13                    (cond ((null? pl) '<dummy>)
14                          ((eq? k (car pl))
15                           (kill-all k (cdr l)))
16                          (else
17                           ((car l) '<dummy>)
18                           (kill-all k (cdr l))))))))
19          (let ((start-process
20                 (lambda (e)
21                   (kill-lock (lambda ()
22                     (call/cc (lambda (r)
23                       (spawn (call/cc (lambda (k)
24                         (set! process-list
25                               (cons k (process-list)))
26                         (r '<dummy>)
27                         (let ((res (e)))
28                           (cond
29                            (res
30                             (kill-lock
31                              (lambda ()
```

```
32                              (return res)
33                              (kill-all k process-list))))
34                          (else
35                              (1-unlock)))))))
36                      (suspend))))))))
37          (start-process (lambda () K[<E1>]))
38          ...
39          (start-process (lambda () K[<En>]))
40          (suspend))))))
```

4.8   Description of *exlambda*, *signal* and *wait*

In PaiLisp exlambda,signal and wait are introduced for mutual exclusion in concurrent programming by PaiLisp.

It can be seen that the **signal/wait** operations can be realized using **call/cc** in PaiLisp-Kernel. However, since exlambda does not have a list datum to express its access right it is necessary to give a description of exlambda to express its access right in an explicit manner. The transformation function $K[E]$ and its auxiliary function $K_1[e, \text{lock}, k]$ will be defined and used to describe **exlambda,signal/wait**.

$$K[E] = K_1[E, NIL, NIL]$$

In $K_1[e, \text{lock}, k]$ the arguments **lock** and **k** have the following meanings:

lock: an exclusive closure to be used to get/release the access right of **exlambda**

k: the continuation to be used for escape at **signal**.

(1) exlambda

$(exlambda\ (\langle x_1 \rangle \cdots \langle x_n \rangle)\ \langle e_1 \rangle \cdots \langle e_n \rangle)$ is a closure that

a. gets the access right for an exclusive closure$\{(41)\}$

b. computes $\langle e_1 \rangle, \cdots, \langle e_n \rangle$ in order$\{(42\text{-}45)\}$

c. releases the access right for the exclusive closure$\{(46)\}$

d. returns the value of e_n $\{(47)\}$

The operation a is as follows $\{(7\text{-}12)\}$:

> it checks "flag";
> if it is in use, the continuation for resumption will be recorded in
> queue and the process will be suspended;
> otherwise, the flag will be set as "in-use".

The operation c is as follows$\{(14\text{-}18)\}$:

> if the queue is free, then the flag will be set free;
> otherwise, the first process in queue will be resumed.

Also, the continuation k which is used for escape at **signal** will be generated.$\{(39)\}$

```
1    K[(exlambda (<x1> ... <xn>) <e1> ... <em>)]
2    = (let* ((flag #f)
3            (queue '(make-queue))
4            (lock (exlambda (cmd . args)
5                      (cond
6                        ((eq? cmd 'get)
7                         (let ((r (car args)))
8                           (cond
9                             (flag (add-to-queue r queue)
10                                   (lambda () (suspend)))
11                             (else (set! flag #t)
12                                   (lambda () '<unspecified>)))))
13                        ((eq? cmd 'release)
14                         (cond
15                           ((not (queue-empty? queue))
16                            ((take-1 queue) '<unspecified>))
17                           (else
18                            (set! flag #f))))
19                        ((eq? cmd 'wait)
20                         (let ((cvar (car args))
21                               (r (cadr args)))
22                           (add-to-queue r (cvar-queue cvar))
23                           (cond
24                             ((not (queue-empty? queue))
25                              ((take-1 queue) '<unspecified>))
26                             (else
27                              (set! flag #f)))))
28                        ((eq? cmd 'signal)
29                         (let ((cvar (car args)))
30                           (cond
31                             ((not (queue-empty? (cvar-queue cvar)))
32                              ((take-1 (cvar-queue cvar))
33                               '<unspecified>)))
34                             ((not (queue-empty? queue))
35                              ((take-1 queue) '<unspecifiied>))
36                             (else
37                              (set! flag #f)))))))))
38        (lambda (<x1> ... <xn>)
39          (call/cc (lambda (k)
40                     (let ((tmp '<unspecified>))
41                       (call/cc (lambda (r) ((lock 'get r))))
42                       K1[<e1>, lock, k]
43                       ....
44                       K1[<em-1>, lock, k]
45                       (set! tmp K1[<em>, lock k])
46                       (lock 'release)
47                       tmp)))))
```

(2) wait

(*wait* ⟨c⟩) calls lock, and it will be registered in the queue ⟨c⟩; then the process itself will be suspended. The queue of the exclusive closure will be checked, and if there is any process being waited, it will be taken and executed else the flag to indicate "in-use" will become #f.{(20-27)}

```
48  K1[(wait <c>), <lock>, <k>]
49  = (call/cc (lambda (r)
50               (<lock> 'wait K[<c>] r)
51               (suspend)))
```

(3) signal

In case of (*signal* ⟨c⟩ ⟨e⟩), ⟨e⟩ will be computed; then lock will be called and the queue for ⟨c⟩ will be checked. If there is a process which is waiting on ⟨c⟩, then its process will be resumed for execution. If there is no such process, the queue of the exclusive closure will be checked, and if there is any process waiting for execution it will be resumed, else the flag to indicate "in-use" will become #f. The application of continuation ⟨k⟩ to value(⟨e⟩) causes the escape from the exclusive closure.{(30-37)}

```
52  K1[(signal <c> <e>), <lock>, <k>]
53  = (let ((tmp K[<e>]))
54      (<lock> 'signal K[<c>])
55      (<k> tmp))
```

(4) Some Auxiliary Functions for *queue* and *cvar*

```
56  (define (make-queue)
57    (let ((tmp (cons '<unspecified> '())))
58      (set-car! tmp tmp)
59      tmp))

60  (define (queue-empty? queue)
61    (null? (cdr queue)))

62  (define (add-to-queue r queue)
63    (let ((tmp (cons r '())))
64      (set-cdr! (car queue) tmp)
65      (set-car! queue tmp)))

66  (define (take-1 queue)
67    (let ((tmp (cdr queue)))
68      (cond
69        ((eq? (car queue) tmp)
70         (set-car! queue queue)
71         (set-cdr! queue '()))
```

```
72      (else
73       (set-cdr! queue (cddr queue))))
74      (car tmp)))

75  (define (make-cvar)
76    '(*cvar* . ,(make-queue)))

77  (define (cvar-queue cvar)
78    (cdr cvar))
```

The pictorial explanations of behaviors of **make-queue**, **add-to-queue** and **take-1** are given in **Appendix III**.

4.9 Remarks

There may arise many comments and questions , reading the descriptions of this section. Here we list only some of them.

1. After writing these descriptions we found that some non-local jump might occur by a call of continuation closure (created by call/cc) according to the current definitions. Some critical issues may arise and exist in relation with **call/cc** and **exlambda**.

2. According to the current description of **exlambda** it is possible to escape from the inside of **exlambda**. The **release** will not be taken so that a process that waits the exclusive closure will be blocked forever.
   When a process P which created a continuation closure resides in an exclusive closure, a call of the continuation closure by another process should become effective only when P finishes its task within the exclusive closure.

3. The problem raised by M. Katz[13] was also our concern when we defined our **call/cc** of PaiLisp. This problem will occur when we parallelize a program with call/cc, using **future**.
   In order to guarantee the equivalence of results of a sequential Scheme program and its PaiLisp version using **future** we will need some modification of the semantics of **call/cc**. This is suggested when we explained the meaning of **call/cc** in 2.3.1.

4. There are some unsettled technical issues as is seen from the above remarks. Also, there are several issues that need to be refined in PaiLisp and PaiLisp-Kernel; for example, **make-cond-var** had to be included in PaiLisp constructs, and **pmap** is better than **pmapcar**. Resolving these issues is left for future study.

Acknowledgements

After the workshop Robert H. Halstead, Jr. made various stimulating comments and discussions on our descriptions of this paper. In addition, he helped us to improve our English explanations. Matsuo Nonaka (a graduate student of the first author) re-examined the meta-circular interpreter of PaiLisp-Kernel and the description of PaiLisp using PaiLisp-Kernel. He kindly collaborated us to prepare the appendices. R. Osborne read our draft carefully. We are grateful to their interests on PaiLisp and their collaborations to improve PaiLilsp and to prepare this manuscript. We thank Y.Iizuka and S.Tsuchiya for typing the manuscript.

$$\left[\begin{array}{l} \textit{This work on PaiLisp was supported by Grant} - in - Aid \\ \textit{for Scientific Reseach (A) } 01420029, \textit{under The Ministry of} \\ \textit{Education ,Science and Culture, Japan} \end{array} \right]$$

References

[1] R. P. Gabriel and J. McCarthy *Queue-based multiprocessing Lisp*, ACM Symp. on Lisp and Functional Prog. (1984)

[2] R. Goldman and R. P. Gabriel *Preliminary results with the initial implementation of Qlisp*, ACM Symp. on Lisp and Functional Prog. (1988)

[3] R. Halstead,Jr. *Multilisp: A language for concurrent symbolic computation*, ACM Symp. on Lisp and Functional Prog. (1984)

[4] T. Ito and S.Wada *Models of parallel execution of Lisp functions and their evaluations*,Information Processing Society of Japan. Report of SIG on Symbolic Processing, SYM26-5 (1983) (in Japanese)

[5] T. Ito, T. Tamura and S. Wada *Theoretical comparisons of interpreted/compiled executions of Lisp on sequential and parallel machine models*,IFIP Congress '86 (1986)

[6] T. Ito, et al. *An MC68000-based multiprocessor system with shared memory and its application to parallel Lisp interpreter*, Symp. on Computer Systems, Information Processing Society of Japan (1987)

[7] T.Ito *R&D Activities of Lisp Systems in Japan*, NSF/Monbusho Seminar on US/Japan Scientific Co-operation in Computer Software (1987)
{The outline of the first version of PaiLisp was reported at this seminar.}

[8] T.Ito and H. Oyaizu *Channel-Lisp: A parallel Lisp language based on channel communication*, Proc. Princeton Conf. on Information Sciences and Systems (1990)
{Channel-Lisp was originally published as T.Ito and H.Oyaizu, *Design of a parallel Lisp language based on channel communication* , Proc. Conference of Software Science and Technology (1988) (In Japanese)}

[9] T. Ito and T. Yuasa *Some non-standard issues on Lisp standardization*, International Workshop on Lisp Evolution and Standardization (1988)

[10] J. Rees and W. Clinger (ed.) *Revised³ Report on the altorithmic language Scheme*, SIGPLAN Notices 31 (1986)

[11] S. Sugimoto, et al. *A multi-microprocessor system for Concurrent Lisp*, Int'l Conf. on Parallel Processing (1983)

[12] J. Weening *A parallel Lisp simulator*, Stanford CSD Report STAN-CS-88-1206 (1988)

[13] M. Katz *Continuing into future*, This Proceedings

APPENDIX I
PaiLisp-Kernel in PaiLisp-Kernel

This meta-circula interpreter of PaiLisp-Kernel is an updated version by Matsuo Nonaka (a graduate student of the first author).

```
;;;
;;; Top Level
;;;
    (define (top-level-loop)
      (display "Kernel-> ")
      (let ((exp (read)))
        (cond ((eq? exp 'exit)
               (display "Good-bye!"))
              (else
               (display (call/cc
                          (lambda (continuation)
                            (set! err continuation)
                            (top-level-eval exp))))
               (newline)
               (top-level-loop)))))

    (define (top-level-eval exp)
      (cond ((and (pair? exp)
                  (eq? (car exp) 'define))
             (var-define (cdr exp)))
            (else (eval exp '()))))

    (define (var-define x)
      (cond ((symbol? (car x))
             (set! genv (cons (cons (car x)
                                    (eval (cadr x) '()))
                              genv)))
            ((symbol? (caar x))
             (var-define '(,(caar x) (lambda ,(cdar x) ,@(cdr x)))))
            (else
             (err '*define-error*)))
      '*unspecified-define*)
```

Remarks

1. To save space, some details of the program are abbreviated; for example, in the definition of **eval**, the definitions of cond?, do-cond, case?, do-case, etc. are abbreviated.

2. The variable **genv** which represents a global environment is a association list that consists of a list of pairs of variable and its value. Addition to **genv** will never happen simultaneously, because only the top level process can execute **ver-define**.

3. The global variable **err** must be bound to some value in advance.

```
;;
;;   Evaluator
;;
     (define (eval exp lenv)
       (cond ((const? exp) (const-val exp))
             ((var? exp) (var-value exp lenv))
             ((quote? exp) (quote-val exp))
             ((lambda? exp) (make-closure exp lenv))
             ((if? exp) (do-if exp lenv))
             ((cond? exp) (do-cond exp lenv))
             ((case? exp) (do-case exp lenv))
             ((and? exp) (do-and exp lenv))
             ((or? exp) (do-or exp lenv))
             ((set!? exp) (var-assign exp lenv))
             ((let? exp) (do-let exp lenv))
             ((let*? exp) (do-let* exp lenv))
             ((letrec? exp) (do-letrec exp lenv))
             ((begin? exp) (do-begin exp lenv))
             ((quasiquote? exp) (quasiquote-val exp lenv))
             ((exlambda? exp) (make-exclosure exp lenv))
             ((spawn? exp) (do-spawn exp lenv))
             (else
              (apply-proc (evlis exp lenv)))))


;;
;;   Variable references
;;
     (define (var? exp) (symbol? exp))

     (define (var-value var lenv)
       (let ((tmp1 (assoc var lenv)))
         (if (null? tmp1)
             (let ((tmp2 (assoc var genv)))
               (if (null? tmp2)
                   (err '*unbound-variable*)
                   (cdr tmp2)))
             (cdr tmp1))))


;;;
;;;  Literal expression
;;;
     (define (quote? exp)
       (eq? (car exp) 'quote))

     (define (quote-val exp) (cadr exp))

     (define (const? exp)
       (or (boolean? exp)
           (number? exp)
           (char? exp)
           (string? exp)
           (null? exp)))

     (define (const-val exp) exp)
```

```
;;;
;;; Lambda expression
;;;
    (define (lambda? exp)
      (eq? (car exp) 'lambda))

    (define (make-closure exp lenv)
      (let ((vars (cadr exp))
            (body (cddr exp)))
        '(*closure* ,vars ,body ,lenv)))

;;;
;;; Conditionals
;;;
    (define (if? exp)
      (eq? (car exp) 'if))

    (define (do-if exp lenv)
      (if (eval (cadr exp) lenv)
          (eval (caddr exp) lenv)
          (if (null? (cdddr exp))
              '*unspecified-if*
              (eval (cadddr exp) lenv))))

;;;
;;; Assignments
;;;
    (define (set!? exp)
      (eq? (car exp) 'set!))

    (define (var-assign exp lenv)
      (let ((var (cadr exp))
            (val (eval (caddr exp) lenv)))
        (let ((tmp1 (assoc var lenv)))
          (if (null? tmp1)
              (let ((tmp2 (assoc var genv)))
                (if (null? tmp2)
                    (err '*undefined-variable*)
                    (begin (set-cdr! tmp2 val)
                           '*unspecified-assign*)))
              (begin (set-cdr! tmp1 val)
                     '*unspecified-assign*)))))

;;;
;;; Sequencing
;;;
    (define (begin? exp)
      (eq? (car exp) 'begin))

    (define (do-begin exp lenv)
      (eval-seq (cdr exp) lenv))
```

```
(define (eval-seq body lenv)
  (let ((tmp (eval (car body) lenv)))
    (if (null? (cdr body))
        tmp
        (eval-seq (cdr body) lenv))))
```

```
;;;
;;; Exlambda Expression
;;;
```

```
(define (exlambda? exp)
  (eq? (car exp) 'exlambda))
```

```
(define (make-exclosure exp lenv)
  (let ((vars (cadr exp))
        (body (cddr exp))
        (lock (exlambda (e) (e))))
    '(*exclosure* ,vars ,body ,lenv ,lock)))
```

```
;;;
;;; Spawn
;;;
```

```
(define (spawn? exp)
  (eq? (car exp) 'spawn))
```

```
(define (do-spawn exp lenv)
  (spawn (eval (cadr exp) lenv))
  '*unspecified-spawn*)
```

```
;;;
;;; Apply Procedure
;;;
```

```
(define (procedure? obj)
  (or (primitive? obj)
      (closure? obj)
      (exclosure? obj)
      (esc-proc? obj)))
```

```
(define (apply-proc exps)
  (let ((proc (car exps))
        (args (cdr exps)))
    (cond ((primitive? proc)
           (apply-primitive (primitive-name proc) args))
          ((closure? proc)
           (apply-closure proc args))
          ((exclosure? proc)
           (apply-exclosure proc args))
          ((esc-proc? proc)
           (apply-esc-proc proc (car args)))
          (else (err '*apply-error*)))))
```

```
(define (evlis exps lenv)
  (cond ((null? exps) '())
        (else (cons (eval (car exps) lenv)
                    (evlis (cdr exps) lenv)))))
```

```
;;;
;;; Apply Primitive Function
;;;
    (define (make-primitive name)
      (cons '*primitive* name))

    (define (primitive? x)
      (and (pair? x)
           (eq? (car x) '*primitive*)))

    (define (primitive-name primitive) (cdr primitive))


    (define (apply-primitive name args)
      (cond ((eq? name 'not) (not (car args)))
            ((eq? name 'boolean?) (boolean? (car args)))
            ((eq? name 'pair?) (pair? (car args)))
            ((eq? name 'symbol?) (symbol? (car args)))
            ((eq? name 'number?) (number? (car args)))
            ((eq? name 'char?) (char? (car args)))
            ((eq? name 'string?) (string? (car args)))
            ((eq? name 'vector?) (vector? (car args)))
            ((eq? name 'procedure?) (procedure? (car args)))
            ((eq? name 'null?) (null? (car args)))
            ((eq? name 'list?) (list? (car args)))
            ((eq? name 'eq?) (eq? (car args) (cadr args)))
            ((eq? name 'cons) (cons (car args) (cadr args)))
            ((eq? name 'car) (car (car args)))
            ((eq? name 'cdr) (cdr (car args)))
            ((eq? name 'set-car!) (set-car! (car args) (cadr args)))
            ((eq? name 'set-cdr!) (set-cdr! (car args) (cadr args)))
            ((eq? name '=) (= (car args) (cadr args)))
            ((eq? name '<) (< (car args) (cadr args)))
            ((eq? name '>) (> (car args) (cadr args)))
            ((eq? name '+) (apply + args))
            ((eq? name '*) (apply * args))
            ((eq? name '-) (- (car args) (cadr args)))
            ((eq? name '/) (/ (car args) (cadr args)))
            ((eq? name 'apply) (apply-proc args))
            ...
            ((eq? name 'call/cc)
             (call/cc (lambda (k)
                       (apply-proc '(,(car args) ,(make-esc-proc k))))))
            ((eq? name 'suspend) (suspend))
            (else (err '*undefined-primitive*))))

;;;
;;; Apply Closure
;;;
    (define (closure? x)
      (and (pair? x)
           (eq? (car x) '*closure*)))
```

```
(define (closure-vars closure) (cadr closure))
(define (closure-body closure) (caddr closure))
(define (closure-lenv closure) (cadddr closure))

(define (apply-closure closure args)
  (eval-seq (closure-body closure)
            (var-bind (closure-vars closure)
                      args
                      (closure-lenv closure))))

(define (var-bind vars args lenv)
  (cond
    ((null? vars) lenv)
    ((symbol? vars) (cons (cons vars args) lenv))
    (else (cons (cons (car vars) (car args))
                (var-bind (cdr vars) (cdr args) lenv)))))
```

```
;;;
;;; Apply Exclosure
;;;
(define (exclosure? x)
  (and (pair? x)
       (eq? (car x) '*exclosure*)))

(define (exclosure-vars excl) (cadr excl))
(define (exclosure-body excl) (caddr excl))
(define (exclosure-lenv excl) (cadddr excl))
(define (exclosure-lock excl) (caddddr excl))

(define (apply-exclosure excl args)
  ((exclosure-lock excl)
   (lambda ()
     (eval-seq (exclosure-body excl)
               (var-bind (exclosure-vars excl)
                         args
                         (exclosure-lenv excl))))))
```

```
;;;
;;; Apply Escape-Procedure
;;;
(define (make-esc-proc system-esc)
  (cons '*esc-proc* system-esc))

(define (esc-proc? x)
  (and (pair? x)
       (eq? (car x) '*esc-proc*)))

(define (esc-proc-system-esc esc-proc) (cdr esc-proc))

(define (apply-esc-proc esc-proc arg)
  ((esc-proc-system-esc esc-proc) arg))
```

APPENDIX II
Forced Definitions of Primitive Operations

1. Operations that require "force"

car   cdr . etc.

```
(define car
  (let ((kernel-car car))
    (lambda (x) (kernel-car (force x)))))

(define cdr
  (let ((kernel-cdr cdr))
    (lambda (x) (kernel-cdr (force x)))))
```

pair?   symbol?   number?   etc.

```
(define pair?
  (let ((kernel-pair? pair?))
    (lambda (x) (kernel-pair? (force x)))))

(define symbol?
  (let ((kernel-symbol? symbol?))
    (lambda (x) (kernel-symbol? (force x)))))
```

eq?   eqv?   equal?   etc.

```
(define eq?
  (let ((kernel-eq? eq?))
    (lambda (x y) (kernel-eq? (force x) (force y)))))
```

+   −   *   /   etc.

```
(define +
  (let ((kernel-+ +))
    (lambda args (apply kernel-+ (map force args)))))

(define -
  (let ((kernel-- -))
    (lambda args (apply kernel-- (map force args)))))
```

set−car!   set−cdr!   vector−set!   etc.

```
(define set-car!
  (let ((kernel-set-car! set-car!))
    (lambda (x y) (kernel-set-car! (force x) y))))

(define set-cdr!
  (let ((kernel-set-cdr! ser-cdr!))
    (lambda (x y) (kernel-set-cdr! (force x) y))))
```

2. Operations that do not require "force"

cons   list   vector?   etc.

APPENDIX III
Pictorial Explanations of Behaviors of Functions on "Queue"

[The Structure of the queue]

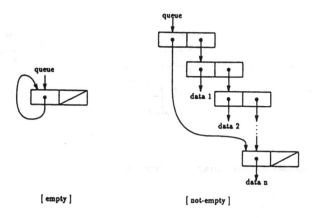

[empty]   [not-empty]

The car of the queue is a pointer to the last element of the queue. If the queue is empty, it points to the queue itself.

The cdr of the queue is a pointer to the first element of the queue. If the queue is empty, it holds NIL value.

[The add-to-queue operation]

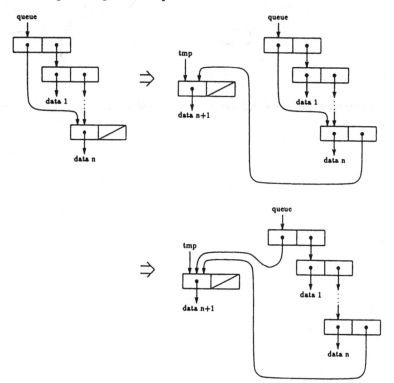

Using the pointer to the last element, the add-to-queue function can connect the new element to the last element without using intermediate pointers.

[The take-1 operation]

When the queue consists of only one element

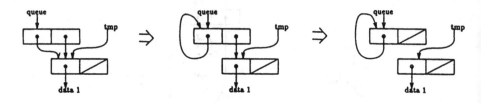

When the queue consists of more than one element

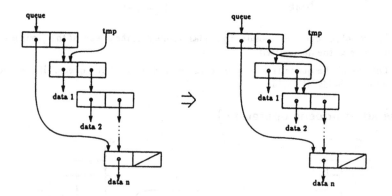

The first element of the queue is discarded and returned as the value of the function take-1.

Continuing Into the Future:
On the Interaction of Futures and First-Class
Continuations
(A Capsule Summary)

Morry Katz*
(katz@cs.stanford.edu)

Daniel Weise†
(daniel@mojave.stanford.edu)

Abstract

One of the nicest features of the *future* construct originally presented in Multilisp [2] is its near orthogonality with respect to a functional subset of Scheme [1]. Introducing futures into most functional programs does not affect the value returned, even though the parallel execution order might differ from the sequential. When futures and continuations are used in the same program, however, parallel and sequential executions can yield different results. No existing implementation of futures has yet addressed this issue. We make futures and continuations interact properly through a simple, yet important, change to the implementation of the future construct. This change causes a second problem to manifest itself: the creation of extraneous computation threads. The second problem is addressed by making an additional change to the future construct.

1 Summary

It is the philosophy of the authors that a functional program containing continuations should not have its sequential semantics altered through the introduction of futures. In a talk delivered at the Workshop on Parallel Lisp by one of us (Katz), we presented a preliminary version of this paper in which we demonstrated modifications to the implementation of the future construct which guarantee identical parallel and sequential semantics. Since the workshop, we have developed a simpler and more elegant implementation of the future construct which achieves the same goal. A final version of our paper will appear in the proceedings of the 1990 ACM Conference on Lisp and Functional Programming [4]. In Halstead's paper in this publication, he discusses the implications of our work and how it relates to other research being done in the field of parallel lisp [3].

*Supported by Stanford University Computer Science Department.
†Supported by Defense Advanced Research Projects Agency contract # N00014-87-K-0828.

2 References

[1] H. Abelson, et. al. Revised[3] Report on the Algorithmic Language Scheme. MIT AI Memo 848a.

[2] Robert H. Halstead, Jr. Multilisp: A Language for Concurrent Symbolic Computation. *ACM Transactions on Programming Languages and Systems* 7,4 (Oct. 1985), 501-538.

[3] Robert H. Halstead, Jr. New Ideas in Parallel Lisp: Language Design, Implementation, and Tools. Paper presented at the U.S./Japan Workshop on Parallel Lisp, Sendai, Japan, June 1989, to be published in *Lecture Notes in Computer Science*, Springer-Verlag, Berlin.

[4] Morry Katz and Daniel Weise. Continuing Into the Future: On the Interaction of Futures and First-Class Continuations. To be published in *Proceedings of the 1990 ACM Conference on Lisp and Functional Programming*.

Speculative Computation in Multilisp*

Randy B. Osborne
Digital Equipment Corporation
Cambridge Research Lab†
ran@crl.dec.com

Abstract

We demonstrate by experiments that performing computations in parallel before their results are known to be required can yield performance improvements over conventional approaches to parallel computing. We call such eager computation of expressions *speculative* computation, as opposed to conventional *mandatory* computation that is used in almost all contemporary parallel programming languages and systems. The two major requirements for speculative computation are: 1) a means to control computation to favor the most promising computations and 2) a means to abort computation and reclaim computation resources.

We discuss these requirements in the parallel symbolic language Multilisp and present a *sponsor model* for speculative computation in Multilisp which handles control and reclamation of computation in a single, elegant framework. We describe an implementation of this sponsor model and present performance results for several applications of speculative computation. The results demonstrate that our support for speculative computation adds expressive and computational power to Multilisp, with observed performance improvement as great as 26 times over conventional approaches to parallel computation.

1 Introduction

The future construct in Multilisp (described in Section 1.1) has proven very versatile and successful for achieving parallelism in symbolic computation [Hal86a]. However, experience with parallel symbolic computation has led to the recognition that "speculative" styles of computation may be more effective for certain applications, notably searches, than the "mandatory" style of computation obtained using future [Hal85, Hal86b, Hal86a]. Speculative computation is eager evaluation where the result(s) of the evaluation may be unnecessary. Speculative computation involves a gamble whereby one trades additional, possibly unnecessary, computation for potentially faster execution.

---

*This research was performed as part of the author's doctoral work at the M.I.T. Laboratory for Computer Science.

†One Kendall Square, Bldg. 700, Cambridge, MA. 02139

Speculative computation has two requirements. First, because computation resources are generally limited, we would like to reclaim the resources devoted to unnecessary computation. Thus speculative computation requires the ability to "abort"[1] computation and reclaim computation resources.

The second requirement follows naturally from the first, assuming that computation resources are limited: given that some of the computation may be unnecessary, we would like to arrange the use of resources to favor the most promising computations. Thus speculative computation requires the ability to control computation resources.

We discuss these requirements in this paper and the issues with supporting speculative computation in Multilisp. We present a model for speculative computation in Multilisp which should furnish an archetype for speculative computation in other parallel languages. We describe an implementation of this model and present performance results for several applications of speculative computation.

1.1 Multilisp

Multilisp [Hal85] is a version of the Scheme programming language extended with explicit parallelism constructs. Multilisp is based on a shared memory paradigm and includes side-effects (hence the explicit parallelism constructs). (future E) creates a task to evaluate E and immediately returns a placeholder for the result. This placeholder (known as a *future*) may be manipulated just as if it was the result of evaluating E. If a task attempts a strict operation on such a placeholder (i.e. an operation, such as +, requiring the value represented by the placeholder), the task suspends until the placeholder is *determined* with the result of evaluating E. This task is said to *touch* the placeholder. We generalize this notion to say that the strict operation task touches the task evaluating E.

(delay E) is exactly like future except the task created to evaluate E does not begin execution until the placeholder is touched. The Appendix describes two additional features of Multilisp which we use later.

1.2 Previous Work

We briefly review the most significant previous work in speculative computation.

Burton [Bur85] appears to be the first to have addressed both requirements — controlling computation and reclaiming unnecessary computation — for speculative computation. Burton proposed adding a parallel construct essentially like future, but with an additional priority argument, to a simple functional language. The "speculative" tasks created by this construct were to be scheduled for execution according to their priorities, thus providing a means to control computation. Burton suggested an approach like [GP81] for aborting useless tasks. Burton never implemented this proposed support for speculative computation.

---

[1]We put abort in quotes because, as we discuss later, we do not necessarily have to kill useless computation.

There are two problems with Burton's proposed support. First, his priorities are fixed. Thus the computation resources allocated to speculative activities cannot be reassigned with the availability of better information. His priorities lack transitivity (see Section 4.1), for example. Second, his control via priorities lacks modularity. The priorities occupy a global space: there is no hierarchical structure. Thus a programmer must manage a global space of priorities, making it difficult to develop and understand pieces of a program independent of the whole (see Section 4.1).

Two other groups have investigated speculative computation in functional languages based on distributed graph reduction models. In his work on Distributed Applicative Processing Systems (DAPS), Hudak developed a model with distributed mark and sweep garbage collection to reclaim useless tasks [HK82] but with no priorities or means to control computation. More recently, Partridge and Dekker presented a scheme with integer priorities and distributed reference counting to reclaim useless tasks [PD89]. The priority of a task in their scheme is the maximum of the priority contributed to it by each of its (possibly multiple) parents. Let p denote the current priority of a parent task. Then, initially a parent task contributes priority $p-1$ to each of its child tasks. Upon demanding a child task, the parent contributes priority p to the child task. Priorities cannot decrease. Due to this constraint and the constrained relationship between parent and child priorities, these priorities lack flexibility in controlling computation. These priorities also lack modularity, as in Burton's work. One important difference between our work and these functional language efforts is that Multilisp includes side-effects.

There has also been work on supporting speculative computation in the parallel Lisps MultiScheme [Mil87] and Qlisp [GG89]. MultiScheme has disjoin for spawning "first-of" styles of speculative computation (see Section 3.1) and garbage collection of tasks for reclaiming unnecessary computation. Recently, Epstein [Eps89] extended MultiScheme beyond this rudimentary support for speculative computation. Like Burton, Epstein added priorities for controlling computation, except Epstein's priorities are transitive (as in [PD89]): a computation has at least the priority of the computations blocked on it. Epstein also used this priority system to reclaim unnecessary computation by explicitly "downgrading" the priority of unwanted computation. Our ideas are similar, but go further. Epstein's ideas fall short in two ways. First, downgrading fails to reclaim all the descendants of an unnecessary computation. Epstein relied on garbage collection to reclaim such descendants, but this strategy suffers problems, as we discuss in Section 4.2.1, especially in the presence of side-effects. Second, Epstein's control via priorities lacks modularity. Finally, Epstein apparently did not investigate (due to time constraints) the performance of any applications utilizing speculative computation.

Qlisp's support for speculative computation centers around "heavyweight" futures which can implement "first-of" types of speculative computation. Qlisp also has garbage collection of tasks and explicit killing for reclaiming unnecessary computation. However, Qlisp lacks any means to control computation (other than aborting it). The Qlisp work is on-going.

Soley [Sol89] explored speculative computation in a functional dataflow language. His main emphasis was reclaiming unnecessary computation. He did add priorities to control computation but the associated overhead was large and priorities were not transitive.

Researchers in parallel logic languages have long been interested in a form of speculative computation they call Or-parallelism. However, to date all the work we know of has concentrated on aborting useless computation and lacked any means, such as priorities, to control computation. (See e.g. [Lus88, CG87, Ued87, Sha87].) To our knowledge, the one exception is the work of Chikayama et al [CSM88]. They are investigating shōens for speculative computation in logic languages. A shōen is a manager for controlling computation (through priorities) and the resources devoted to computation.

Our work addresses both requirements for supporting speculative computation — controlling speculative computation and reclaiming unnecessary computation — in an imperative environment. We argue that the implementation must support these requirements for suitable efficiency and expressiveness.

1.3 Overview

In Section 2 we give a precise definition of speculative computation and related terms. In Section 3 we present some examples of speculative computation to which we refer throughout the paper. In Section 4 we discuss the issues with speculative computation motivated by the examples. In Section 5 we present our sponsor model for speculative computation. In Section 6 we describe our implementation of a subset of this model which we call the touching model. Finally, in Section 7 we report the results of experiments with the examples in Section 3.

2 Definitions

2.1 Speculative Computation

We classify computation into three groups:

1. computation known to be required,

2. computation known not to be required, and

3. computation not known to be required or not required.

This classification is with respect to a given state of knowledge at a given time and a given specification of the program in which the computation is embedded. The state incorporates perfect knowledge about the past and whatever information may be known about the future, such as input data and analysis of the program. The program specification is a set of conditions on the results and side-effects produced by the program (and perhaps also conditions on the inputs and the execution environment) such that the program is considered correct if every execution of the program (subject to the input and environment conditions) is guaranteed to meet these conditions. We use the program specification to define what it means for a computation to be required or not required. A computation is required if, with the given state of knowledge, the computation is definitely always necessary to meet the program specification. Likewise, a computation is not required if, with the given state of knowledge, the computation is definitely not ever necessary to meet the program specification. As a program executes, the state of knowledge increases. Thus during program execution the above classification constitutes a succession of improving approximations with time, starting with some *a priori* designations.

Computation in group 1, i.e. computation that is known to be required, is **relevant** computation. Computation in group 2, i.e. computation that is known not to be required, is **irrelevant** computation. Computation in group 3 is **speculative** computation. We also refer to relevant computation as **mandatory** computation. Thus a speculative computation may become mandatory during its course of computation, as more information becomes available to indicate that it is necessary. For instance, a mandatory computation may select a particular speculative computation from among several; that computation becomes necessary and the rest become unnecessary. Or, further input data or control information obtained with time may indicate that a speculative computation is actually necessary.

Eager computation is computation that is started early, before it is required, but with certainty that it will be required.[2] Speculative computation is computation that is started before it is required, like eager computation, but without any assurance that it will be required later, unlike eager computation.

If all computation is functional, the classification of computation is simpler. In this case, a demand-driven interpreter evaluating a program defines the specification of that program. Thus, whether or not a computation is required reduces to whether or not a demand-driven interpreter ever (irrevocably) demands the computation. For a nondeterministic operator like parallel **or** (described in Section 3.1), we define a **choice** computation to be any computation which such an operator may choose. When a demand-driven interpreter demands the result of such a nondeterministic operator, we define the interpreter to provisionally demand all the operator's choice computations. (To avoid problems with non-termination, we assume a *fair* demand-driven interpreter that provisionally demands all choice computations equally.) At the "choice time" when the nondeterministic operator chooses a choice computation, the demand-driven interpreter irrevocably demands the chosen computation and "undemands" all of the operator's non-chosen computations. The chosen computation is, of course, required and the non-chosen computations, provisionally demanded and then undemanded, are not required.

Thus for a functional program P we have the following simpler definitions. A computation C in P is relevant if a fair demand-driven interpreter evaluating P either will or does demand C irrevocably (i.e. never undemands C). Computation C is irrelevant if a fair demand-driven interpreter will never demand C irrevocably. Finally, computation C is speculative if we cannot determine, based on the given state of knowledge, whether or not a demand-driven interpreter will ever demand C irrevocably.

With side-effects, a demand-driven interpreter is not sufficient to define relevance. Computation not explicitly demanded by such an interpreter may be required, and hence

---

[2]This is not the universal meaning of eager computation — some people use it to mean speculative computation.

relevant, for the side-effects that it may perform, such as writing a shared variable, or releasing a lock or semaphore. Thus with side-effects we must use the general classification given earlier. However, side-effects raise some thorny issues with this classification (such as how do we determine if a given computation with side-effects is necessary to meet the program specification). We do not pursue these issues here.

Note that with our definitions, speculative computation may exist in conventional programs and even in sequential programs.

2.1.1 Classifications of Speculative Computation

We distinguish three flavors of speculative computation based on the way in which resources are used for speculation:

1. **multiple-approach** speculative computation

   In this flavor, the speculation is in pursuing multiple approaches simultaneously, as in "first-of" speculative computation, where not all the approaches are necessary (but at least one is). A dominant characteristic of this flavor is aborting irrelevant computation, i.e. aborting unnecessary approaches.

2. **order-based** speculative computation

   In this flavor, the speculation is in the **order** in which the computations are performed. Not all the computations are necessary so this order is important. There may be an optimal order but this may not be known *a priori*. Thus the goal is to use an order which has good average behavior (as in minimum average completion time). Order-based speculative computation is invariably resource constrained: the order matters because there are insufficient resources to perform all computations simultaneously.

3. **precomputing** speculative computation

   In this flavor, the speculation is in precomputing some quantity for possible future use. Unlike in multiple-approach speculative computation, where at least one approach is necessary, precomputation is not necessarily required. Also, unlike multiple-approach speculative computation, precomputing speculative computation computation often does not involve any aborting of computation (because the precomputation terminates before it is known if the result is required).

In practice most speculative computation involves a mix of these three flavors, especially multiple-approach and order-based speculative computation. Indeed, ordering becomes important as soon as there are insufficient resources.

2.2 Optimistic Computation

What most people mean by optimistic computation is subset of speculative computation in which there is a particular concern to undo **all** side-effects ever performed by an aborted computation, so it appears that the computation never occurred. That is, side-effects obey an atomic transaction or encapsulation [BZ89] model in which all or no side-effects persist. Our notion of speculative computation includes styles of speculation which do not fit into this all-or-nothing model.

3 Examples

We present five quite different examples of speculative computation which we use to motivate discussion in the rest of the paper.

3.1 Parallel search

Search is a particularly rich domain for speculative computation. In searching for a target in subspaces S_1, S_2, ..., S_n, we could search the subspaces concurrently (subject to availability of machine resources) and terminate all remaining searches when we find the target to avoid wasting machine resources. These subspace searches are examples of "first-of" speculative computation.

Without language support for speculative computation, as in conventional Multilisp, we must either abandon the goal of terminating useless subsearches or we must have each subsearch explicitly check for termination. The former is inefficient and the latter can be awkward and suffer from lack of expressiveness (as we discuss in Section 4.2.2). Thus the benefits of support for speculative computation are efficiency and ease of performing parallel search. These benefits are important because of the importance of parallel search in symbolic computation such as in Artificial Intelligence.

Probably the simplest examples of parallel search are parallel or and and, which we call por and pand respectively. (por E_1 E_2 ... E_n) returns the value of the first E_i to evaluate to a non-nil value and nil if all the E_i evaluate to nil. In contrast, (pand E_1 E_2 ... E_n) returns nil when any E_i to evaluates to nil and true if all the E_i evaluate to non-nil. In both cases, any remaining E_i evaluations may be aborted after a result is returned. These two nondeterministic operators represent perhaps the most important potential application of speculative computation because of the ubiquity of or and and.

Parallel search is an example of multiple-approach speculative computation.

3.2 Branch prediction: parallel if

In the expression (if *pred consequent alternate*) we might like to evaluate *pred*, *consequent*, and *alternate* concurrently to reduce the total execution time. If *pred* evaluates to true, we accept the result of evaluating *consequent* and abort the evaluation of *alternate* (if it is still in progress). If *pred* evaluates to false, we accept *alternate* and abort *consequent*.[3] Computing *consequent* and *alternate* in parallel is an example of (deterministic) multiple-approach speculative computation.

---

[3] And if *consequent* and *alternate* evaluate to the same value, we could abort *pred*.

This branch prediction example demonstrates another benefit of speculative styles of computation: the relaxation of synchronization constraints to reduce the critical path length. By relaxing the synchronization constraints, we mean relaxing the constraints on when computation is actually performed, while still obeying the overall data and control constraints. As with parallel search, the objective is the reduction of the critical path in an *efficient* manner.

3.3   Producer-consumer parallelism: The Boyer Benchmark

Written as a parallel Multilisp program, the Boyer Benchmark [Gab85] is an example of producer-consumer parallelism with an interesting twist. Given an input expression, the Boyer Benchmark determines whether the expression is a tautology based on a database of rewrite rules. The producer successively rewrites the input expression according to the rewrite rules to obtain an if-then-else tree. The consumer, which operates concurrently with the producer, traverses this if-then-else tree, checking for consistency between each predicate and its consequent and alternate. The interesting twist is that not all the rewrites are necessarily required by the tautology checker. For example, the rewrite rule for and is (and a b) → (if a (if b #t #f) #f). If a happens to be #f, there is no need to rewrite expression b. However, the producer does not know this until the consumer terminates without demanding this rewrite. (a may not be so simple, or a may be shared by some other expression.) Thus the rewrites represent speculative computation.

In an attempt to reduce the execution time we could perform all rewrites eagerly, gambling (in a form of branch prediction) that they will be required. However, this application of speculative computation fails if there are too few processor resources (see Section 7.2) because the machine becomes saturated with speculative rewrites which swamp out the tautology checker computation. That is, unnecessary rewrites use resources that otherwise would be devoted to necessary rewrites and tautology checking and thus lengthen the execution time. To counteract this problem, we could perform all rewrites lazily but then the execution time may be long due to insufficient parallelism.

To solve this problem, we need a way to order the allocation of resources to speculative activities according to their relative promise. For Boyer two ordering levels are sufficient: one for the tautology checker (i.e. consumer) and one for the rewrites (i.e producer) whereby the consumer can preempt the producer for processor resources. However, we also need some way to promote a rewrite to the consumer level when we find it necessary. That is, we need what we call *dynamic* ordering. With such static and dynamic ordering, the Boyer Benchmark is an example of order-based speculative computation.

(There is also the issue of aborting all the useless rewrites when the tautology checker terminates, but aborting has already received adequate mention.)

3.4   Ordering: the traveling salesman problem

Consider a branch and bound algorithm to solve the traveling salesman problem. We would like to expand nodes representing partial tours in parallel according to some heuristic so we can focus our machine resources on the most promising partial tours first. One way to achieve the desired ordering of node expansions is via an explicit priority queue (programmed in the language). However, this is an awkward solution. A better solution is to extend the static ordering — which we already argued was necessary for cases like the previous example — to an arbitrary infinitum of orderings. In both the Boyer Benchmark and the traveling salesman problem the fundamental problem is the same: ordering the allocation of resources to activities according to their relative promise.

The speculation in the traveling salesman problem is in the *order* in which resources are allocated to node expansion, i.e. it is order-based speculative computation. This notion of ordering is the key idea missing in most other approaches to speculative computation. Aborting exists in the traveling salesman problem, but it is implicit aborting: a node checks the cost of the node with respect to the current best cost of a complete tour and simply terminates if the cost exceeds the best cost.

3.5 Precomputing streams

A stream is a possibly infinite list of objects [AS84]. The illusion of infinity is maintained by generating the list lazily: elements are added to the tail of the list incrementally as demanded (thus advancing the tail). The idea in precomputing a stream is to extend the tail of the stream, by computing several elements ahead, before these elements are actually demanded. This idea is a form of branch prediction — the hope is to reduce the critical path by doing a certain amount of precomputing. Such element precomputing is an example of precomputing-based speculative computation. We do not pursue precomputing styles of speculative computation further in this paper.

4 Issues

In this section we describe the main issues with speculative computation. The idea behind speculative styles of computation is to use excess machine resources to reduce the average execution time. Because these excess resources are limited, it is important to use them efficiently. Therefore, in general, we must control speculative computation and we must reclaim irrelevant computation.

4.1 Controlling computation

Because not all speculative computation is necessary, the order in which we allocate resources to computation is important, as the Boyer example demonstrates. We want to allocate resources to computation to favor the most promising computations. This requires some sort of ordering of computation. For concreteness, let us assume priorities for specifying this ordering.

Issue 1: Determining the relative promise, i.e. priority, of computations

In general, the programmer must decide the relative promise of computations, as controlling computation relies on meta-knowledge about a program's function, inputs, and purpose as well as its operating environment. The optimal assignment of priorities is a scheduling problem which we mention briefly in connection with Issue 4.

Issue 2: Interaction of computation

The promise of computations, i.e. priorities, must be transitive. Without this transitivity, interaction of computation may subvert the desired ordering. For instance, suppose that computation C_1 demands the result of (uncompleted) computation C_2. If C_1's priority is greater than C_2's, then C_1's progress is effectively that of the lower-priority C_2, subverting the desired ordering of C_1 with respect to other computations.

Transitivity (of priorities) provides the dynamic ordering of resources to computation that is so essential in the Boyer Benchmark.

Issue 3: Modularity

We need a way to preserve the functionality of a group of related speculative computations, such as in the Boyer Benchmark and the traveling salesman problem, wherever the group appears. We call this the *modularity principle*: we should be able to embed any speculative computation or group of speculative computations as subcomputation(s) within some larger speculative computation. For example, we should be able to have the traveling salesman problem as a disjunct in por while retaining both the desired ordering of the disjuncts with respect to each other and the desired local ordering of the traveling salesman computations with respect to each other.

To support this modularity, we want each "module" to have a new, local priority space relative to the parent priority. This allows modules to be nested in hierarchical fashion.

This modularity is important. It allows arbitrary nesting of speculative computation with the assurance that local ordering relationships will be retained. This increases the ease of programming and expressiveness. If all priorities occupy the same flat priority space the lack of modularity can be quite troublesome. For example, if the traveling salesman problem is a disjunct in a por, all the priorities in the traveling salesman problem must be carefully adjusted so as not to interfere with the other disjuncts.

Issue 4: More complex control

Sometimes we need complex, dynamic control of computation. Consider por. We may start with some *a priori* idea of the relative priority for the disjuncts but this assignment may change as information is garnered from the disjuncts and some disjuncts complete. Furthermore, the result of the por may be demanded by some other computation. Should this demand be propagated to all disjuncts or just the most promising ones or propagated according to some other policy? The answer is affected by the computational requirements of the disjuncts, other computations in the system competing for the resources, and the urgency of the demand. This is the sort of scheduling problem that we must analyze to ultimately determine the control we want. We investigated optimal scheduling in some simple cases in [Osb89] and in current work we are analyzing optimal scheduling of nested pors and pands.

Until we know more about the optimal control of speculative computation (at least in certain situations), control specification will have to be *ad hoc* and experimental. In the rest of this paper we focus on basic control mechanisms.

Finally, we wish to point out that there are other types of control, like controlling the duration of execution, and multiplexing computations, that we also want for speculative computation in addition to the ordering provided by priorities.

4.2 Reclaiming computation

To use machine resources efficiently we must reclaim irrelevant computation. The essential issue is the reclamation of processor resources devoted to irrelevant computation so that these resources may be recycled for other computation. (We assume that processors are expensive and few in number and that memory is cheap and plentiful. Hence our emphasis on processor resources.) Reclamation of computation state, i.e. the storage used by a computation, is an independent issue.

The two important issues for computation reclamation are:

1. Reclamation speed

   We must reclaim irrelevant computation quickly.

2. Run-away phenomenon

   This phenomenon occurs when an irrelevant computation spawns descendants faster than they can be reclaimed. It must be avoided.

There are two approaches to computation reclamation: implicit reclamation and explicit reclamation. Each approach has problems.

4.2.1 Implicit Reclamation

In implicit reclamation the system discovers that a computation is irrelevant and reclaims it. However, there is no operational test that the system can perform to determine if a computation is irrelevant. Instead, implicit reclamation systems approximate the relevance of a computation by its accessibility. (We ignore reference count systems since they cannot reclaim cyclic structures.) A computation is represented by a task object and a computation is considered relevant if and only if its task object is accessible from some root set. Therefore implicit computation reclamation amounts to the garbage collection of computation, an idea first suggested by [BH78].

There are two problems with implicit computation reclamation, both following from the assumption that a computation is relevant if and only if it is accessible:

1. A computation may be irrelevant but still accessible.

2. Inaccessibility implies irrelevance only if all the computation is functional.

   In the presence of side-effects, as in Multilisp, an inaccessible computation can still be relevant through the side-effects it may perform.

We also believe that implicit reclamation is too inefficient. With implicit reclamation, irrelevant computation is only reclaimed when a garbage collection occurs, which we argue is too infrequent and costly. The problem is that the frequency of implicit reclamation is tied to the frequency of garbage collection cycles, which depends on factors such as memory size and rate of storage allocation that do not necessarily have anything to do with the creation, rate of creation, or even presence of irrelevant computation. An application that does little consing, for instance, will have very infrequent computation reclamation.

There are two ways to address the problem of the infrequency of implicit reclamation:

1. Invoke garbage collection more frequently (than is required by storage concerns).

   This method is unattractive because it incurs the large cost of garbage collection (tracing all the objects), more frequently, whether or not there is any irrelevant computation present.

2. Invoke the garbage collector explicitly whenever we believe there is enough irrelevant computation to justify the cost.

   This alternative still suffers from the cost of tracing **all** objects, including non-task objects. Furthermore, it is unattractive if we are continually generating irrelevant computation.

3. Use generation garbage collection [LH83].

   Generation garbage collection can significantly reduce the cost of garbage collection by reducing the average number of accessible objects that must be traced. This reduces the tracing cost. However, this reduced cost does not entirely solve the problems with implicit reclamation. Three major problems still remain:

   (a) The reclamation time is still coupled to the consing rate.

   (b) We still must trace all accessible objects in a generation, whether or not the objects are task objects.

   (c) An irrelevant computation might still take a long time to be reclaimed if it or an inaccessible object which points to it (directly or indirectly) gets promoted to older generations.

Implicit reclamation does not have any run-away phenomena: all computation is stopped during a garbage collection and not restarted until proven accessible.

4.2.2 Explicit reclamation

In explicit reclamation the user identifies irrelevant computation and either the user or the system reclaims such computation.

The simplest form of explicit reclamation is explicit termination checking whereby the user both identifies and terminates irrelevant computation. In explicit termination checking, the programmer "wires" reclamation into the application. The programmer arranges for each computation he or she may want aborted to periodically check some termination condition and simply terminate, returning a value if this condition is true. This value is either a special terminal value (perhaps a "no-value" as in [Sol89]) or a nonsense value. In any event, computation is essentially short-circuited by a true termination condition. There are two important points with this type of reclamation. First, the reclamation is performed totally at the language level (in the source code), by merely changing the course of computation, and not by appeal to some extra-language facility, such as garbage collection. Second, computation deemed irrelevant terminates, returning a value, and is not aborted in mid-stream before returning a value.

Explicit checking has several problems. The main problem is inserting the termination checks in the source code. Every descendant computation and (potentially) every function must have termination checks. This checking is awkward to arrange in many cases, and it is impossible to arrange in some cases because not all the source code may be available. Some function calls may be "unknown" in the sense that the functions may be defined in modules outside a user's scope. For instance, a function may be defined previously in the environment, or defined subsequently in the environment by dynamic loading, or a function may be part of a system utility or library. How do we perform termination checking in these "unknown" functions? How do we do termination checking in the descendant computations that such functions may spawn? A static placement of termination checks in the source code cannot always track the dynamic execution of a program.

Three problems remain even if it is possible to insert all the necessary termination checks in the source code. The first problem is ensuring that reentrant source code remains reentrant. If the statically inserted termination checks in the source code check statically assigned locations, then all invocations of a function check the same location. This links the termination of all simultaneous invocations of a function even if the invocations are part of independent speculative activities. Such linking effectively prevents reentrant code — different speculative activities cannot call the same system utility simultaneously for instance. We can solve this problem by using dynamically bound variables for termination checks — then the statically inserted checks check dynamically bound locations. However, dynamic binding is expensive in parallel processing (because of the need for deep binding). The second problem is nested termination. Each nesting of speculative activities, e.g. each nesting of **por**, has to have an independent termination check. However, we cannot always statically determine the dynamic nesting behavior of computations and thus we cannot always insert the necessary termination checks. The third problem is sharing of computation. All parties that could potentially share the result of a computation must understand if that computation could terminate prematurely and must know what action to take if the computation does terminate prematurely. For example, a disjunct D in a por may spawn a descendant computation whose result is shared with some function F external to the por. What happens if some other disjunct returns a true value first and disjunct D is terminated? What value is returned to function F? In the presence of side-effects it is all too easy for this type of sharing to occur. Once again, we cannot always statically determine the dynamic nature — sharing in this case — of computation.

While explicit termination checking may be useful in simple cases where static analysis suffices, it lacks sufficient expressive power to be a general solution.

For general explicit reclamation we need to separate the identification of irrelevant computation from its reclamation. The user can "declare" computation irrelevant, but as just discussed, the user cannot always reclaim computation at the language level. For a general solution we need system support to reclaim computation.

First, we need source code-independent computation reclamation: we need to reclaim computation by (potential) checks below the language level in the dynamic execution of a computation, not by static termination checks embedded in source code. This addresses the problem with unknown functions. The checks could take the form of either interrupts or polling, as in explicit checking (but below the language level, unlike in explicit checking). With polling, the interpreter must perform such checks or the compiler must generate code to perform such checks in all code (user and system). Polling can take one of two forms. Either a speculative activity keeps one flag that all of its computations and their descendants poll, as in explicit termination checking, or each computation has its own flag which it polls and a speculative activity maintains a list of all the flag locations in its computations and their descendants. The former alternative means that a computation has, in general, a list of flag locations to poll (because of nested speculative activities and sharing of computation). Efficiency thus dictates the latter alternative which has a smaller runtime cost while performing a computation but a larger startup cost (to register the flag location) when initiating a computation. We therefore assume the latter alternative in the following discussion. One can view interrupts as merely an optimization of this latter alternative: an interrupt supplies a positive checking result without polling.

Second, we need dynamic naming of computations to solve the problems with reentrant code and nested computations. If using interrupts, we need dynamic naming of computations to uniquely identify computations for interrupts, and if using polling we need dynamic naming of checking locations so we can generate checking code statically but still perform checks dynamically. For polling, we can achieve the dynamic naming of checking locations by associating the checking location (i.e. flag location) with the (dynamic) name of the computation.

Third, we need automatic naming of descendant computations. We need to be able to name all the descendants of a computation to declare them irrelevant and cause their reclamation (by either interrupts or polling). The system must automatically record such names to solve the problem with unknown functions which spawn descendants.

Fourth, we need some form of reference counts for shared computation to avoid reclaiming such computations while at least one sharer is relevant.

Fifth, we need reversible reclamation. With declarations, a programmer may declare a relevant computation irrelevant. Although a programmer (or programming system) can potentially have an understanding of an entire program, the programmer may choose not to, may not be able to, or may simply make an error. Thus a relevant computation may demand a computation declared irrelevant, either directly, by demanding the result of the "irrelevant" computation, or indirectly, by requiring the side-effect(s) that the "irrelevant" computation will perform (e.g. release a lock or semaphore).

If a computation is killed — irreversibly reclaimed — when it is declared irrelevant, then *lockout* deadlock will result if some other computation should later demand its result. One solution to this problem is to signal an error when a killed computation is demanded, in effect declaring it an error to mistakenly declare a computation irrelevant.

This solution has two problems. First, a killed computation may be demanded at a point in time and space far from the point at which it was mistakenly declared irrelevant. Thus the error signalled may be far removed from the actual error, making it difficult to understand and repair. A single mistake could result in multiple errors, as different computations demand the same killed computation. Second, the user's idea of a computation's relevance may change with time. Initially, the best information available may suggest that a computation is irrelevant. However, information could later be produced (e.g. from new input data) which may suggest that the computation is in fact relevant. There is no way within this first solution to express this "imperfect" relevance knowledge.

A better solution is to merely suspend a computation when it is declared irrelevant, thereby reclaiming its computation resources (which we argued earlier is the important issue), while still maintaining its computation state. Thus the computation may be restarted later if a relevant computation demands its result (or if it must perform a relevant side-effect). The ability to resume computation declared irrelevant is important because it is often difficult to foresee the relevance of computations, especially in large systems, due to all the ways computation can interact.

Thus, we need reversible reclamation — we must be able to restart computation that is inadvertently reclaimed though user error or failure to (correctly) analyze side-effect dependencies.

Finally, to prevent run-away phenomena, the key requirement is to prevent the spawning of new descendant computations until reclamation reaches all computation.

In summary, the special system support required to reclaim computation is:

1. Source-code independent reclamation by either interrupts or polling below the language level. Interpreter or compiler support is required to automatically insert the polling checks.

2. Dynamic naming of computation (for interrupts and polling locations)

3. Automatic naming of descendant computations

4. Reference counts for shared computation

5. Reversible reclamation

6. Interlock of spawning and reclamation to prevent run-away phenomena

4.3   Side-effects

As with conventional parallel computation, the main issue with side-effects is proper synchronization. The emphasis on relaxing synchronization constraints and aborting computation give rise to three additional issues. The first is persistence of side-effects: when a computation is aborted, what happens to the effects it has performed? One possibility is to completely undo all side-effects performed by an aborted computation, yielding "all-or-nothing" semantics for side-effects. The second issue, which is very much related to the first, is interference. With speculative styles of computation we might temporarily violate precedence constraints — to speed execution — and repair the execution order later. This could lead to interference, i.e. name conflicts, that would otherwise not occur. For example, in branch prediction both branches could side-effect the variable x. We must ensure that x has the proper value afterwards. This entails both a synchronization issue (ensuring the proper final value for x) and a persistence issue (what if the consequent side-effected y and the alternate did not — which effect persists?). Both of these problems can be addressed (at considerable expense) by encapsulation methods in which each speculative thread has a copy of the store and the copies are merged afterwards.

We do not address these issues of persistence and interference in our work because we believe they are not important in our intended application domain (mostly functional applications — we believe side-effects should be used sparingly) and because we believe available solutions are too expensive for anything other than coarse-grained parallelism.

The third issue is the relevance of side-effects. Specifically, some side-effects may be relevant in the sense that deadlock may occur if they are not performed, e.g. if a computation holding a lock is aborted. This aspect of side-effects makes it tricky to determine if a computation is relevant, since it may only be relevant for its effect and not its result. In fact, this is precisely the subtlety that causes the problems with implicit reclamation.

4.4   Errors and exceptions

Speculative computation raises the following two new issues in error and exception handling:

1. Control-related errors

   A computation controlling the resource use of other computations may encounter an error or exception condition. How does this affect the controllee(s)?

2. Irrelevant errors

   Errors may be or become irrelevant by virtue of occurring in an irrelevant computation or in a computation which later becomes irrelevant. Recognizing this, how are errors and exception conditions treated?

We have some ideas on how to address these issues based on the groups in Mul-T [KHM89], but we have not pursued them in our work.

5   The Sponsor Model

Our model for speculative computation in Multilisp is based on the notion of sponsors introduced by [KH81]. The allocation of resources to tasks is controlled by the *attributes* a task possesses. Sponsors supply these attributes, which may be priorities for example. Each task may have zero or more sponsors which contribute attributes to that task. Thus, the sponsors of a task collectively determine the computation resources allocated to that task. A task without a sponsor does not run. The attributes contributed by a task's sponsors are combined according to a *combining-rule* to yield the *effective attributes* of the task.

There are four types of sponsors in our model:

1. External sponsors — These sponsors supply absolute attributes. We discuss later why we call them external.

2. Toucher sponsors — When one task touches another (see Section 1.1), the toucher task sponsors the touchee task with the effective attributes of the toucher task. This sponsorship is removed when the touchee task determines its *future* object (and hence no longer needs sponsorship).

3. Task sponsors — A task may sponsor any other task. The sponsor attributes in this case are the effective attributes of the sponsoring task. Toucher sponsors are merely a special case of task sponsors, except that the addition and removal of toucher sponsors occurs automatically with touch and determine respectively, whereas the addition and removal of task sponsors is always explicit. Task sponsors offer a way, for example, for a task to sponsor its children.

4. Controller sponsors — The three previous types of sponsors are all passive — they merely act as fixed attribute sources or pass on attributes from other sources. Controller sponsors receive sponsorship and actively distribute it among the tasks in their control domain according to some built-in control strategy. Controller sponsors implement the complex and dynamic control that we sometimes want.

The collection of sponsors in an application form a sponsor network. External sponsors are the source of all attributes. These attributes are distributed in a dynamic fashion by passive toucher sponsors according to the dynamic interconnection of sponsors by touching, by passive task sponsors according to their explicit connection with other sponsors, and by active controller sponsors according to their control strategy. The external sponsors can be thought of as external sources of attributes for this sponsor network; hence, we call them external.

Controller sponsors are the cornerstone of modularity in our sponsor model. We call a controller sponsor and its collection of sponsored tasks a **group**. The controller sponsor essentially introduces a new ordering space for tasks in that group. Thus the ordering of tasks in a group may be local to that group. Groups may be nested with all local ordering relative to the immediate parent group or to other groups, depending on the controller sponsor. Thus groups allow us to solve the modularity problems with the traveling salesman problem and the Boyer Benchmark: we can simply create a group for each of these applications with local ordering. These groups can then be embedded in any fashion desired in other speculative computation.

We have omitted some important details of this model, such as inter-group touching, for space reasons. See [Osb89] for further details of this model.

6 Implementation

6.1 The Touching Model

We implemented an initial subset of the sponsor model that we call the touching model. The only attributes in this model are priorities. Each task has an external sponsor which provides what we call the *source* priority of the task. The external sponsor, toucher sponsors, and controller sponsors of a task T combine to determine the task's effective priority according to the following *max combining-rule*:

$$effpri(T) = \max(sourcepri(T), \max_{j \in touch(T)} (effpri(j)), \max_{k \in control(T)} (cntlpri(k, T)))$$

where $effpri(i)$ is the effective priority of task i, $sourcepri(i)$ is the source priority of task i, $cntlpri(i, j)$ is the priority that controller i contributes to task j, $touch(i)$ is the set of tasks touching task i, and $control(i)$ is the set of controller sponsors for task i. There are no task sponsors in this model and only a primitive form of controller sponsors which we describe in Section 6.2.

Any change in the effective priority of a task may lead to changes in the effective priority of the tasks sponsored by that task, and so on. The recursive process of updating the effective priorities according to the max combining-rule is called *priority propagation*. There can be cycles during priority propagation (see [Osb89]), but with our primitive controller sponsors all such cycles correspond to a "touch" chain cycle of tasks:[4] all the tasks in the touch chain cycle are deadlocked on each other. Because touch chain cycles are an error condition in Multilisp, we do not worry about the cycles they may cause during priority propagation.

All priorities are in the interval $[0, MAX]$. Only the tasks with the highest effective priority run at any point in time (i.e. scheduling is preemptive), except for tasks with effective priority 0. Such tasks are not runnable; they are *stayed*, meaning that their processor resources have been reclaimed. (Thus the preemptive scheduling mechanism provides source code-independent reclamation.) In order for a task to be stayed, the source priority of the task must be 0 and the effective priority of all the task's touchers and controllers must be 0, i.e. the task must be un-sponsored. (Setting the sponsor priority to 0 accomplishes the same thing as removing the sponsor.) The computational state of a stayed task is retained (until it becomes inaccessible and is garbage collected). Thus a stayed task may be restarted by re-sponsoring the task so that the task's effective priority becomes > 0 — this provides reversible reclamation.

---

[4]Recall that there are no task sponsors in our touching model.

Computation reclamation is explicit, as suggested in Section 4.2.2. "Declaring a task irrelevant" means setting the source priority of the task to 0 and propagating any resultant change in the task's effective priority (to any task it may be sponsoring and so on). We call this process *staying*. Note that *staying* a task ("declaring the task irrelevant") does **not** imply that the task will be *stayed* ("considered irrelevant") since the task could still have sponsors, indicating that the task is relevant from the viewpoint of other tasks demanding its value. Thus the effective priority provides a reference count.

The max combining-rule provides demand transitivity and solves the problem of mistakenly staying computation, such as might occur with shared computation and side-effects. If we mistakenly stay a task we automatically resume it when we later touch it. Extending this idea, we can even solve the problem with aborting relevant side-effects. We simply have to ensure that our demand for a side-effect ensures sponsorship of the computation that will perform the side-effect. We describe how to do this and give examples in [Osb89].

Thus the max-combining rule allows us to handle controlling and reclaiming computation in one simple and uniform framework.

6.2 Language Features

We had two important goals in this implementation. The first goal was to retain the **future** construct. The second goal was to minimize the impact of our support for speculative computation on the performance of conventional styles of computation. To accomplish this second goal we distinguished *mandatory tasks* and *speculative tasks*. Mandatory tasks always have effective priority *MAX* and cannot be stayed. Speculative tasks can have any effective priority $\in [0, MAX]$ and may be stayed. Thus mandatory tasks correspond to the tasks in conventional styles of computation and speculative tasks correspond to the tasks in speculative styles of computation. However, these are merely operational terms and do preempt our definitions given earlier: a mandatory task may perform speculative computation and a speculative task may perform mandatory computation. Because mandatory tasks cannot be stayed and cannot be preempted, they can be implemented more efficiently than speculative tasks.

The top level, read-eval-print-loop, task is a mandatory task. All the children of a mandatory task are also mandatory tasks, provided that the children are created with **future**.

(**spec-future** *exp pri*) creates a speculative task with source priority *pri* to evaluate *exp* and immediately returns a placeholder for the result, just as **future** does. All the children of a speculative task are also speculative. If a speculative task executes **future**, the child task is a speculative task with its source priority inherited from its parent.

Orthogonal to this notion of inheritance is the notion of contagion. If a mandatory task touches a speculative task, the speculative task becomes mandatory.

(**make-group** *exp pri*) is the same as **spec-future** except it returns a group object. A group in this implementation is merely the name for a **make-group** task and all its descendant tasks, i.e. the tree of tasks rooted by a **make-group** task. Thus **make-group** provides automatic naming of descendant tasks. Presently, there is no controller sponsor associated with these groups. (We plan to add full controller sponsors in the future.)

(**stay-group** *group*) performs the staying operation on all members of the group *group*, i.e. it stays all group members. It returns an unspecified value. Thus a group provides a (dynamic) name for reclamation and **stay-group** provides automatic staying of descendants.

(**my-group-obj**) returns the group object representing the executing task's group. A task's group is always the newest ancestral group.

The primitives (**get-priority** *obj*) and (**change-priority** *obj new-pri*) provide a way to examine and change a task's source priority. See [Osb89] for details.

Sometimes we need to prevent a speculative task from being stayed. For example, we want to avoid deadlock if a task is stayed in a critical region. One way to achieve this goal is with the following constructs.

(**promote-task**) temporarily promotes the executing task to be a mandatory task.

(**demote-task**) demotes a task, if necessary, from temporary promotion to mandatory status.

(**rplacx-eq-mand** *pair new old*), x= **a** or **d**, has the same semantics as the **rplacx-eq** construct in Multilisp (see Appendix), except it temporarily promotes the task to mandatory status if the **eq** test succeeds. This construct is useful for spin-locks.

(**make-class** *class-type*) creates and returns a class object. A class is collection of tasks and a sponsor in the fashion of the groups mentioned in Section 5. Unlike with the group created with the **make-group** construct, the members of a class are arbitrary and not necessarily all descendants of a common parent. We have implemented three types of classes, each of which corresponds to a different type of primitive controller sponsor:

1. class-all, in which the class sponsor sponsors all the members of the class,

2. class-any, in which the class sponsor sponsors an arbitrary member of the class, and

3. class-pqueue, in which the class sponsor sponsors only the top priority task in the class.

(**add-to-class** *obj class*): if *obj* is an undetermined *future* object *f* or a class object *c*, then **add-to-class** adds either the task associated with *f* or the class object *c* to the class *class*. Otherwise, **add-to-class** does nothing. It returns an unspecified value.

(**remove-from-class** *obj class*) functions like **add-to-class** but instead removes *obj* from the class *class*.

A class may be sponsored by either the maximum priority task blocked on a placeholder or the maximum priority task waiting on a semaphore.

(**make-future** &optional *class*) creates and returns a placeholder (as described in the Appendix) and sponsors the class *class* (if specified) with the maximum priority task blocked on the placeholder. This sponsorship is removed when the placeholder is determined.

(**make-sema** &optional *class*) creates and returns a binary semaphore object and sponsors the class *class* (if specified) with the maximum priority task waiting on the placeholder.

Classes provide another way to prevent deadlock due to staying a task in a critical region. The idea is to ensure that any task in the critical region is the member of a class and ensure that any task requiring access to the critical region sponsors that class (e.g. by waiting on a semaphore for access to the critical region). This class in turn sponsors any tasks in the critical region. See [Osb89] for details.

6.3   Implementation Details

The implementation is an extension of the original byte-code interpreter implementation of Multilisp [Hal85]. The major features we added are preemptive scheduling based on priorities, touch propagation, and staying. The preemptive scheduling is implemented with priority queues and polling. In order to stay all the descendants of a group we maintain a "tasknode" tree of all tasks and their children. We mitigate run-away phenomena by preventing the creation of new tasks in a group while we are staying that group. See [Osb89] for further implementation details.

6.4   An Example: por

We present an implementation of **por** as an example of our language features. As a side benefit this example also illustrates some of the issues in speculative computation.

An implementation of **por** has four general requirements:

1. Initialization – create a task to evaluate each disjunct[5]

2. Race officiating – return the first true value

3. Termination detection – return nil if all the disjuncts evaluate to nil

4. Computation reclamation – abort any remaining (useless) tasks after the first true value is returned

Figure 1 shows an implementation of **por** meeting these requirements. The argument to this version of **por** is a list of (thunk . priority) pairs. The priority in each pair is the initial priority of the associated thunk. These priorities let the user convey the relative promise of the thunks.

First we give an overview of the implementation ignoring the class and group constructs. The implementation creates a placeholder for the result (line 3) and calls the procedure **spawn-tasks** (line 17) to spawn a task to evaluate each thunk in the argument list (line 6). Each task performs race officiating and termination detection. If the thunk

---

[5]This may not always be the optimum policy: creating a task for each disjunct may increase the execution time if there are insufficient processors available.

```
(define (por thunk-pri-list)
  (let* ((lock (cons '*no-result* (make-future)))          ; 1
         (class (make-class *class-all*))                  ; 2
         (result (make-future class)))                     ; 3

    (define (spawn-tasks thunk-pri n)
      (if (null thunk-pri)
          (determine-future (cdr lock) n)                  ; 4
          (let ((thunk (get-thunk (car thunk-pri)))
                (priority (get-priority (car thunk-pri))))
            (add-to-class                                  ; 5
              (spec-future (eval-thunk thunk) priority)    ; 6
              class)
            (spawn-tasks (cdr thunk-pri) (+ n 1)))))

    (define (eval-thunk thunk)
      (let ((val (thunk)))
        (if val
            (if (rplaca-eq lock '*result* '*no-result*)    ; 7
                (begin
                  (determine-future result val)            ; 8
                  (stay-group (group-block (my-group-obj))))) ; 9
            (if (eq (car lock) '*no-result*)               ;10
                (term-detect (cdr lock))))))               ;11

    (define (term-detect n)
      (if (rplacd-eq lock (- n 1) n)                       ;12
          (if (= n 1)                                      ;13
              (determine-future result nil))               ;14
          (term-detect (cdr lock))))

    (add-to-class                                          ;15
      (group-future                                        ;16
        (make-group (spawn-tasks thunk-pri-list 0) *max-pri*)) ;17
      class)
    result))
```

Figure 1: An implementation of por

evaluates to a true value and it is the first thunk to do so (line 7), the task determines the result placeholder to that value (line 8) and stays all the other tasks (line 9). If the thunk evaluates to nil, the task performs termination detection (line 11): if all the other thunks have already evaluated to nil, the task determines the result placeholder to nil (line 14).

Now we explain the implementation in further detail. Line 1 initializes a lock cell. Its **car** is used for race officiating synchronization. Initially the **car** is **'*no-result*** to signify that no thunk has yet evaluated to true. The **cdr** of the lock cell is used for termination detection. Initially it is a placeholder for the number of thunks. The **make-group** construct in line 17 serves two purposes. First, it creates a group in which to spawn all the **eval-thunk** tasks and thus provides a name (referenced in line 9 via **(group-block (my-group-obj)))** by which all the tasks comprising the **por** can be stayed. Second, it creates a new task to spawn the **eval-thunk** tasks so that **por** returns the result placeholder as soon as possible. The make-group task has maximum priority ***max-pri*** (equal to MAX) so that all the **eval-thunk** tasks are spawned as rapidly as possible.

Termination detection works in a distributed fashion as follows. The procedure **spawn-tasks** maintains a count of the number of thunks spawned and in line 4 determines the placeholder in the **cdr** of the lock cell with this number. Thereafter the **cdr** of this cell holds the number of thunks still running. When a thunk evaluates to nil, the thunk task first performs the optimization in line 10 and if necessary calls the **term-detect** procedure. This procedure spins until it can atomically decrement the count in line 12. If only one task remains when it eventually succeeds (line 13), the result placeholder is determined to nil as described before.

The class created in line 2 is used for two purposes. The first purpose is to cause any demand for the **por** result manifested by touching the result placeholder to be propagated to all the disjunct tasks by the class-all sponsor policy. This is the reason for the **add-to-class** in line 5. The second purpose is to ensure some amount of modularity. We want to be able to embed this **por** within other speculative computation, where it could be stayed and restarted, without danger of deadlock. If the **por** is stayed we must ensure that all the tasks comprising it are restarted when the result placeholder is touched. We presently lack full-fledged controller sponsors to perform this function so we achieve it instead by making sure all the tasks comprising the **por** are members of the class created in line 2. This is the reason for the **add-to-class** in line 15 (as well as line 5). The **group-future** in line 16 extracts the future object for the make-group task from the group object.

6.5 Problems

The main problem with the present implementation is the lack of full controller sponsors. Although classes are useful for solving deadlock problems with side-effects (see [Osb89]), they are an inadequate substitute for controller sponsors. For example, the class sponsor in the above **por** implementation fails to fully address the modularity problem. The desired relative priorities of disjuncts are not necessarily maintained if the **por** is stayed and restarted (because staying sets the source priority to 0 and restarting does not reset it) and descendants of the winning disjunct cannot continue once the **por** returns (because all

Version	Inferencing time	
	Average	Std. Dev.
Sequential and	2.98	0.05
Mandatory pand	2.39	0.07
Speculative pand	2.28	0.13

Table 1: Emycin inferencing times (in seconds; statistics for 20 runs)

descendants of the por are stayed when it returns). This later problem can be addressed by creating a group for each disjunct and staying only the non-winning disjunct groups. However, this solution is too awkward.

7 Results

7.1 pand: Emycin

This application is a follow-up on the Emycin work of Krall and McGehearty [KM86]. We started with the parallel kernel they developed for this rule-based expert system and investigated the use of pand for combining inference rules. We used the same gems database as Krall and McGehearty described in [KM86]. This database uses and heavily to combine inference rules.

We experimented with three versions of the Emycin kernel differing only in the version of and. The three versions were:

1. Sequential and

2. Speculative pand – the and analog of the speculative por function presented in Section 6.4.

3. Mandatory pand – the speculative pand version, implemented instead with mandatory tasks and without groups and staying, i.e. without the ability to abort unnecessary computation.

Table 1 shows the results on the Concert Multiprocessor [HAOS86] with 32 processors. The version with speculative pand is only slightly faster than the version with mandatory pand. The parallelism profiles in Figures 2, 3, and 4 are very informative. (The kernel is a parallel program; thus even the base sequential and version in Figure 2 has parallelism.)

The parallelism profile for sequential and in Figure 2 features three peaks of parallelism, each of which almost saturates the machine, separated by deep valleys of very little parallelism. The first peak in the mandatory pand version in Figure 3 is much longer due to all the rules that can fire in parallel. This additional parallelism mostly fills in the first valley. The increased computation delays the start of the second peak from 1.3 seconds to 1.6 seconds and changes the relative timing of computation so that the width of

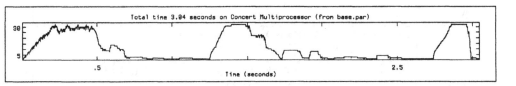

Figure 2: Parallelism profile with sequential **and**

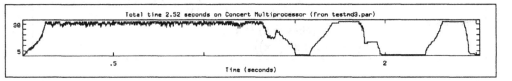

Figure 3: Parallelism profile with mandatory **pand**

the second valley decreases. Thus the mandatory version fills in some of the valleys in the sequential version and thereby decreases the total execution time. In Figure 4 the speculative **pand** version completely fills in the first valley (though there is a little dip at 0.4 seconds about where the first valley previously started). This complete fill-in is due to aborting useless computation. The parallelism in the mandatory version only partly overlaps this valley because the useless computation lengthens the critical path. The result is that the first peak in the speculative version ends at about 1.3 seconds whereas the second peak in the sequential version ends at about 1.7 seconds. However, there is still a long sequential section in the valley, starting at about 1.6 seconds, with only one or two active rules. If this section with only one or two active processors were removed in all versions, the speculative version would be fastest by a significant margin. Although aborting useless computation does reduce the time until the end of the second peak, it does not significantly reduce the overall inferencing time for the gems database.

There are two reasons for this poor performance improvement. First, most conjunct tasks in the Emycin kernel are very short and thus the relative overhead of speculative **pand** is quite large. To separate the intrinsic merit of speculative computation from overhead artifacts, we artificially reduced the relative overhead of **pand** by adding delay loops to the four main procedures of the Emycin kernel. The speedup of the speculative **pand** version relative to the mandatory **pand** version increased with the delay amount, confirming the overhead factor, and reached an asymptote of about 15%.

The second, and more significant reason, is that many conjuncts are shared between **ands** with the gems database. Thus there is a great deal of dependency between **pand**

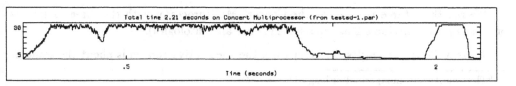

Figure 4: Parallelism profile with speculative **pand**

Name	Input Expression
tc2	(implies (and (implies a b) (implies b c)) (implies a c))
test-case	(implies (and (and (implies (f x) (g x)) (implies (g x) (h x))) (implies (h x) (i x))) (implies (f x) (i x)))
test-case2	(implies (and (and (and (implies (f x) (g x)) (implies (g x) (h x))) (implies (h x) (i x))) (implies (i x) (j x))) (implies (f x) (j x)))

Table 2: Boyer test cases

invocations. For an artificial database with no shared conjuncts we observed about 50% speedup with speculative **pand** over mandatory **pand**.

Even with the poor performance improvement, the Emycin kernel with the gems database is a very interesting application of **pand** because many of the **pands** are nested and many conjuncts are shared among multiple **pands**. This nesting and sharing makes explicit termination checking too difficult (see Section 4.2.2) and makes outright killing of conjuncts unworkable. Finally, the short execution time of most conjuncts makes implicit reclamation ineffective: most useless tasks would simply run to completion before garbage collection occurred. (No garbage collection occurred during any of our runs.)

7.2 Boyer Benchmark

We wrote three versions of the Boyer Benchmark described in Section 3.3. All three versions were identical except for the parallelism construct in the rewriter, i.e. producer. The tautology checker, i.e. consumer, in these three versions uses mandatory tasks created with **future**. Thus the tautology checker tasks run at top priority (MAX). The eager version uses **futures** in the rewriter (which run at MAX priority) and thus performs rewrites eagerly. The lazy version uses **delays** and thus performs rewrites lazily. The speculative version uses **spec-futures** with priority p[6] and thus performs rewrites eagerly subject to available processors. Thus the speculative version has two ordering levels: one for the tautology checker tasks and one for the rewriter tasks. If a tautology checker task touches a rewriter task, the rewriter task is promoted to priority MAX, thus providing the *dynamic* ordering that we mentioned in Section 3.3.

We ran these three versions on the Concert Multiprocessor with the three variations of *modus ponens* in Table 2 as inputs (which are all tautologies).

Table 3 shows the results. In every case, the speculative version is about the same or

---

[6]The priority p is unimportant as long as $0 < p < MAX$.

Input	Version	Number of Processors			
		8	16	24	32
tc2	eager	5.6	3.4	3.0	3.0
	lazy	8.0	7.9	8.0	8.2
	speculative	5.1	3.3	3.0	3.0
test-case	eager	39.8	22.1	16.3	15.1
	lazy	18.5	18.2	18.7	19.4
	speculative	14.8	10.6	10.3	10.3
test-case2	eager	335	185	170	211
	lazy	34.8	34.6	35.2	36.8
	speculative	30.2	28.1	27.8	30.6

Table 3: Execution time (in seconds) of Boyer Benchmark

Input	Version	Number of Processors			
		8	16	24	32
tc2	eager	1.1	1.0	1.0	1.0
	lazy	1.6	2.4	2.7	2.7
test-case	eager	2.7	2.1	1.6	1.5
	lazy	1.3	1.7	1.8	1.9
test-case2	eager	11	6.6	6.1	6.9
	lazy	1.2	1.2	1.2	1.2

Table 4: Speed of speculative version relative to speed of eager and lazy versions

faster (and sometimes much faster) than both the eager and lazy versions.[7]

Table 4 makes the relative performance of the three versions clear. The speed of the speculative version relative to the speed of the eager and lazy versions displays two trends (though in opposite directions for each version). For the eager version, this speed ratio decreases as the number of processors increases and increases as the input size increases. As the number of processors increases with the eager version there are more "surplus" processors at every point in time to perform unnecessary rewrites, thus reducing the relative effect of unnecessary rewrites. As the input size increases the number of unnecessary rewrites increases, thus increasing the relative execution time. As the number of processors gets very large, the execution time for the eager version should approach that for the speculative version. For the lazy version, the speed ratio increases as the number of processors increases and decreases as the input size increases. As the number of processors increases with the lazy version there is insufficient parallelism — due to the lazy evaluation of all rewrites — to utilize all processors, thus increasing the relative

---

[7]The anomalies in the execution time of the eager and speculative versions for test-case2 and 32 processors are due to bus contention. The execution time for the eager version with test-case2 and 32 processors is also highly variable due to frequent garbage collection activity.

execution time. As the input size increases, there is more necessary work available to utilize the processors. For large inputs, the execution time of the lazy version should approach that for the speculative version.

Another way of looking at the results is as follows:

- The eager version is better than the lazy version if the processors are not saturated with mandatory computation, as with many processors or a small input. Then the eager version exploits the extra processors to perform the rewrites speculatively and reduce the execution time.

- The lazy version is better than the eager version if the processors are saturated with mandatory computation, as with few processors or a large input. Then the lazy version prevents mandatory computation from being crowded out by speculative computation.

- The speculative version is the same or better than the eager and lazy versions for all conditions. It prevents mandatory computation from being crowded out by speculative computation while still utilizing the extra concurrency of the speculative computation. That is, it dynamically adjusts the tradeoff between concurrency and crowd-out of mandatory computation.

These results indicate the importance of ordering speculative computation. (To re-iterate, this application has only 2 spec-futures, and performs no aborting.) The key feature of spec-future here is that it creates a second-class type of task that only runs if there are free processors. That is, spec-future is not fully lazy nor fully eager; it adapts dynamically to the load. This frees the user from scheduling concerns as the machine and input size vary.

7.3 Traveling salesman problem

We used two different programs to solve the traveling salesman problem using the same branch and bound algorithm. The qtrav program uses an explicit global priority queue (written in Multilisp) to achieve the desired ordering of node expansions. qtrav creates n worker tasks which continually pull nodes off this queue, expand them into child nodes, and re-insert them in the priority queue. The strav program instead uses the ordering mechanism for speculative tasks. It creates a speculative task for each node expansion with the priority set to effect the desired ordering of node expansions.

Figure 5 shows the execution time of qtrav and strav on the Concert Multiprocessor for three sets of cities, a16, a18, and a20, of 16, 18, and 20 cities respectively. The graph shows only the qtrav results for the optimum number of worker tasks.

The graph indicates that strav is always faster than qtrav. The difference in execution times increases as the number of cities and number of processors increases. qtrav encounters a distinct knee around 24 processors and actually slows down (for a18 and a20) as the number of processors increases from 24 to 32. This behavior is caused by priority queue contention.

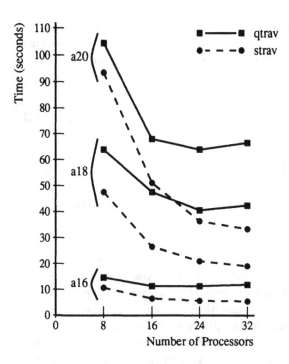

Figure 5: Traveling salesman results on Concert

It is not surprising that strav is faster than qtrav given that strav essentially pushes the priority queue overhead down one layer of interpretation, from the language level to the implementation. strav provides more than speed. It also moves a good deal of resource management (the management of task ordering in this case) from the user level to the implementation. Automating this resource management makes it easier to exploit resources in three ways:

1. We do not have to write (or even think about) the priority queue code. Instead, we can use the more efficient implementation code to perform task ordering.

2. We are insulated from concerns over the machine size. The implementation automatically distributes the priority queues to avoid excessive contention with a large number of processors.

3. We do not have to worry about appropriate parameter values, such as the number of workers.

Consequently, strav is easier to program and understand than qtrav.

7.4   Eight-puzzle

The Eight-puzzle game is a popular children's game with eight tiles numbered 1 to 8 respectively arranged in some fashion on a three-by-three square game board, as in Figure

6. A move consists of sliding a numbered tile into the (adjacent) empty square. The object of the game is to arrange the numbered tiles in clockwise order around the perimeter of the board with the empty square in the center, as in Figure 7.

<table>
<tr><td>2</td><td>1</td><td>6</td></tr>
<tr><td>4</td><td></td><td>8</td></tr>
<tr><td>7</td><td>5</td><td>3</td></tr>
</table>

Figure 6: Starting position

<table>
<tr><td>1</td><td>2</td><td>3</td></tr>
<tr><td>8</td><td></td><td>4</td></tr>
<tr><td>7</td><td>6</td><td>5</td></tr>
</table>

Figure 7: Solution

We wrote four versions of a Multilisp program — one sequential and three parallel versions — to solve the Eight-puzzle. All the parallel versions create a task to examine each board position in the search tree. The first parallel version, which we call the mand version, uses mandatory tasks and thus cannot abort unnecessary computation. The second parallel version, which we call the spec version, uses speculative tasks all at the same priority — thus it lacks the ability to order computation. After the spec version finds the first solution, it aborts (i.e. stays) all the remaining search tasks. Thus the spec version is essentially like por. The final parallel version is a refinement of the spec version with ordering, i.e. different task priorities. The task priorities in this version, which we call the spec2 version, implement the heuristic ordering of board examination suggested in [Nil80]. Each board b has a heuristic cost $C(b)$ given by $D(b) + W(b)$ where $D(b)$ is the depth of board b in the search tree and $W(b)$ is the number of (numbered) tiles misplaced with respect to the solution board. For example, $W(b) = 7$ for the board in Figure 6. Boards are examined in order of increasing heuristic cost. Thus the spec2 version uses the built-in (distributed) priority queues to achieve a desired ordering, like the strav version in Section 7.3. The spec2 version is an example of simultaneous multiple-approach and ordering-based speculative computation.

Table 5 shows the time to find the first solution starting with the board position in Figure 6 for four different versions of game tree search. The shortest solution for this starting board is 18 moves [Nil80]. The indicated times are for eight processors on an Encore Multimax (Model 320).[8]

The execution time of the spec2 version is far superior to that of the other versions, provided that the search depth is sufficient to include a solution (i.e. ≥ 18). For a search depth of 20, the sequential version took longer than we cared to measure and the spec version exhausted the heap and crashed. The spec2 version did not exhaust the heap and was 26 times faster than the mandatory version![9] Thus careful control of the ordering reduced both the execution time and the memory requirements.

---

[8]Multimax is a trademark of Encore Computer Corporation.

[9]This superlinear speedup is a typical characteristic of multiple-approach speculative computation: the speedup depends on the position of the solution in the "subtrees" and the order in which these subtrees are searched.

Search	Search version			
depth	sequential	mand (no staying)	spec (no ordering)	spec2 (heuristic order)
10	77 sec.	11.1 sec.	11.7 sec.	14.5 sec.
15	23 min.	192 sec.	crash	crash
20	?	23 min.	crash	54 sec.

Table 5: Eight-puzzle execution time

The mandatory version did not exhaust the heap because the scheduling of mandatory tasks encourages depth-first examination of the search space (see [Osb89]). The spec version, without ordering, encourages a breadth-first examination of the search space which requires much more storage than a depth-first examination. The priorities in the spec2 version encourage a "directed" breadth-first search, focusing the breadth on the most promising search paths.

If the search depth is insufficient to include a solution, the spec2 version is slower than the mandatory version. For a search depth of 10, the spec2 version is only 1.3 times slower. For a search depth of 15, the spec2 version exhausted the heap and crashed.

This Eight-puzzle application demonstrates once again the importance of ordering (for execution time) and the expressive power gained by our support for speculative computation. As in Section 7.3, built-in support for ordering (in the form of priority queues) makes programming easier and improves efficiency by eliminating the layer of interpretation that would be associated with explicit ordering (i.e. priority queues) at the language level.

This application also demonstrates the importance of ordering for controlling memory usage. The ordering for minimum resource use is not the necessarily the same as the ordering for minimum execution time, as demonstrated by the contrast between the performance of the mandatory and spec2 versions for a search depth of 15. In this fundamental tradeoff between execution time and memory use, we have focused on execution time and ignored memory use. This is a weakness of our work that must be addressed in the future.

8 Conclusions

Speculative styles of computation exploit excess resources in an attempt to reduce the critical path length and hence execution time of applications. The success of this approach depends on exploiting excess resources *efficiently*. The key requirements for efficient speculative computation are:

- a means to reclaim unnecessary computation, and

- a means to control computation, i.e. control the allocation of resources to computation.

We discussed these requirements in the context of Multilisp and we presented a sponsor model for speculative computation which addresses these requirements. This model handles control and reclamation of computation in a single, elegant framework.

We implemented a subset of the sponsor model called the touching model. The touching model was intended as a simple prototype and consequently suffers from a number of deficiencies. The most serious deficiency is lack of modularity. Nevertheless, we were able to successfully exploit speculative computation with this implementation for several applications.

The applications we considered demonstrate the following:

1. the importance of aborting useless computation

   Emycin demonstrates the importance of aborting useless computation.

2. the importance of ordering computation

   Boyer, travsales, and Eight-puzzle all demonstrate the importance of ordering computation. In the case of Boyer, ordering sped execution by about a factor of about 2 (with 16 processors) and in the case of Eight-puzzle, ordering sped execution by a factor of 26 (with 8 processors) over a naive approach.

3. the expressive and computational power added by our support for speculative computation

   The expressive power comes from 1) the ability to control computation — with priorities for ordering, explicit computation reclamation (staying), and controller sponsors — and 2) the interaction of computation — with the max combining-rule. With our support for speculative computation we can realize a small gain with Emycin where other approaches either realize no gain, as with implicit reclamation, or fail, as with a naive approach like explicit termination checking. Furthermore, our support makes it easier to manage machine resources, and thus makes programming easier. The computational power comes from the significant improvement in performance — a factor of about 2 with Boyer and a factor of 26 with Eight-puzzle.

Much work remains. In the short term we plan to add full controller sponsors and modularity to the implementation. In the longer term there are three main areas of work.

1. Computation control

   We need to further address the question: what control is desired? We need to study the optimal scheduling of speculative computation to determine the control mechanisms required and the ultimate benefit of speculative computation.

2. Applications

   We need to investigate many more applications to further assess the requirements and benefits of speculative styles of computation and the suitability of our model and language constructs.

3. Implementation

We need to understand the fundamental costs of supporting speculative styles of computation. To address this, and facilitate experimentation with larger applications, we are (at the time of this writing) converting to a compiled implementation. We are integrating our sponsor model and support for speculative computation into the Mul-T [KHM89] parallel computing environment.

9 Appendix

In this appendix we describe two features of Multilisp used in this paper that we did not describe in Section 1.1.

Sometimes it is convenient to have a *future* without an associated task for write-once synchronization, like the I-structures in the dataflow language Id [Nik88].

(**make-future**) creates and returns an empty placeholder (*future*).

(**determine-future** *fut exp*) explicitly determines the undetermined placeholder (*future*) *fut* to the value of *exp*. It returns an unspecified value. Each task created by a **future** or **delay** ends with an implicit **determine-future**. It is permissible, though not encouraged, to explicitly determine a *future* created with **future** or **delay** with **determine-future**. It is an error to determine (explicitly or implicitly) a *future* more than once.

The following two atomic operations are extensions of the **set-car!** and **set-cdr!** mutators in Scheme.

(**rplaca-eq** *pair new old*) performs the following **eq** check and possible swap atomically: If the **car** of *pair* is **eq** to *old*, the **car** of *pair* is replaced by *new* and *pair* is returned. If the **car** of *pair* is not **eq** to *old*, nil is returned.

(**rplacd-eq** *pair new old*) performs the same **eq** check and possible swap as above atomically, but based on the **cdr** of *pair* rather than the **car**.

10 Acknowledgments

Bert Halstead provided numerous suggestions that contributed greatly to this work. We thank Ed Krall, Pat McGehearty, and the Microelectronics and Computer Technology Corporation (MCC) for permission to use the parallel kernel mentioned in Section 7.1. We also thank Laura Bagnall Linden for ParVis [Bag89], a wonderful program visualization tool which we used extensively during the experimental part of this work. Figures 2, 3, and 4 were extracted from ParVis displays.

11 References

[AS84]   H. Abelson and G. Sussman. *Structure and Interpretation of Computer Programs*. M.I.T. Press, Cambridge, MA., 1984.

[Bag89]   L. Bagnall. ParVis: A program visualization tool for Multilisp. Master's Thesis, Electrical Engineering and Computer Science, M.I.T., January 1989.

[BH78]   H. Baker and C. Hewitt. The incremental garbage collection of processes. A.I. Lab Memo 454, M.I.T., March 1978.

[Bur85]   F. W. Burton. Speculative computation, parallelism, and functional programming. *IEEE Trans. on Computers*, pages 1190–1193, December 1985.

[BZ89]   R. Bubenik and W. Zwaenepoel. An operational semantics for optimistic computations. Technical Report TR89-85, Department of Computer Science, Rice University, February 1989.

[CG87]   K. Clark and S. Gregory. Parlog: Parallel programming in logic. In E. Shapiro, editor, *Concurrent Prolog: Collected Papers*, Volume 1, Chapter 3. M.I.T. Press, 1987.

[CSM88]   T. Chikayama, H. Sato, and T. Miyazaki. Overview of the parallel inference machine operating system (PIMOS). In *Int'l. Conf. on Fifth Generation Computer Systems*, pages 230–251, 1988.

[Eps89]   B. Epstein. Support for speculative computation in MultiScheme. Bachelor's Thesis, Brandeis University, May 1989.

[Gab85]   R. Gabriel. *Performance Evaluation of Lisp Systems*. M.I.T. Press, 1985.

[GG89]   R. Goldman and R. Gabriel. Qlisp: Parallel processing in Lisp. *IEEE Software*, pages 51–59, July 1989.

[GP81]   D. Grit and R. Page. Deleting irrelevant tasks in an expression-oriented multiprocessor system. *ACM Trans. on Prog. Languages and Systems*, pages 49–59, October 1981.

[Hal85]   R. Halstead. Multilisp: A language for concurrent symbolic computation. *ACM Trans. on Prog. Languages and Systems*, pages 501–538, October 1985.

[Hal86a]   R. Halstead. An assessment of Multilisp: Lessons from experience. *International Journal of Parallel Programming*, December 1986.

[Hal86b]   R. Halstead. Parallel symbolic computing. *IEEE Computer*, pages 35–43, August 1986.

[HAOS86]   R. Halstead, T. Anderson, R. Osborne, and T. Sterling. Concert: Design of a multiprocessor development system. In *13th Annual Symp. on Computer Architecture*, pages 40–48, June 1986.

[HK82]   P. Hudak and R. Keller. Garbage collection and task deletion in Distributed Applicative Processing Systems. In *Proceedings 1982 ACM Conf. on Lisp and Functional Prog.*, pages 168–178, 1982.

[KH81]   W. Kornfeld and C. Hewitt. The scientific community metaphor. *IEEE Trans. on Systems, Man, and Cybernetics*, pages 24–33, January 1981.

[KHM89]   D. Kranz, R. Halstead, and E. Mohr. Mul-T: A high-performance parallel Lisp. In *SigPlan Conf. on Prog. Language Design and Implementation*, pages 81–90, 1989.

[KM86]   E. Krall and P. McGehearty. A case study of parallel execution of a rule-based expert system. *Int'l. Journal of Parallel Programming*, pages 5–32, January 1986.

[LH83]   H. Lieberman and C. Hewitt. A real-time garbage collector based on the lifetimes of objects. *Communications of the ACM*, pages 419–429, June 1983.

[Lus88]   E. Lusk et al. The Aurora Or-parallel Prolog system. In *Proc. of Int'l. Conf. on Fifth Generation Computer Systems*, pages 819–830, 1988.

[Mil87]   J. Miller. MultiScheme: A parallel processing system based on MIT Scheme. Technical Report TR-402, Laboratory for Computer Science, M.I.T., September 1987.

[Nik88]   R. Nikhil. Id (version 88.0) reference manual. Computation Structures Group Memo 284, Laboratory for Computer Science, M.I.T., March 1988.

[Nil80]   N. Nilsson. *Principles of Artificial Intelligence.* Morgan Kaufmann, 1980.

[Osb89]   R. Osborne. Speculative computation in Multilisp. Technical Report TR-464, Laboratory for Computer Science, M.I.T., November 1989.

[PD89]   A. Partridge and A. Dekker. Speculative parallelism in a distributed graph reduction machine. In Bruce Shriver, editor, *Proceedings of 22nd Annual Hawaii Int'l Conf. on System Sciences*, Volume 2, pages 771–779, 1989.

[Sha87]   E. Shapiro. Concurrent Prolog: A progress report. In E. Shapiro, editor, *Concurrent Prolog: Collected Papers*, Volume 1, Chapter 5. M.I.T. Press, 1987.

[Sol89]   R. Soley. On the efficient exploitation of speculation under dataflow paradigms of control. Technical Report TR-443, Laboratory for Computer Science, M.I.T., 1989.

[Ued87]   K. Ueda. Guarded Horn clauses. In E. Shapiro, editor, *Concurrent Prolog: Collected Papers*, Volume 1, Chapter 4. M.I.T. Press, 1987.

Garbage Collection in MultiScheme
(Preliminary Version)

James S. Miller
Brandeis University
Waltham, MA 02254-9110
USA

Barbara S. Epstein
Encore Computer Corp.
Marlboro, MA 01752-3089
USA

Abstract

On stock hardware, our garbage collector commonly takes under 4% of a system's time and less than 0.2 seconds at each occurrence. It provides an unsurpassed mechanism for reclaiming memory and processing resources in a parallel system. Furthermore, the elementary algorithm is easily extended to a parallel implementation that achieves significant performance improvement without slowing down the operation of user programs.

The garbage collector is also an important component of the system when investigating speculative computation. The requirement that the garbage collector recycle tasks that are no longer performing useful work impacts not only the design of internal data structures, but also affects the semantics of continuations in a parallel system.

This research was supported in part by the Defense Advanced Research Projects Agency and was monitored by the Office of Naval Research under contract numbers N00014–83–K–0125, N00014–84–K–0099, N00014–86–K–0180, and MDA903–84–C–0033. Additional funds and resources were provided by BBN Advanced Computers Inc., and the Hewlett-Packard Corporation.

1 Introduction

On stock hardware, MIT Scheme's[12] garbage collection commonly takes under 4% of a system's time and less than 0.2 seconds at each occurrence. It provides an unsurpassed mechanism for reclaiming memory and processing resources in a parallel system. Furthermore, the elementary algorithm is easily extended to a parallel implementation in MultiScheme that achieves significant performance improvement without slowing down the operation of user programs.

Our recent work is a direct extension of the work on parallel garbage collection described by Courtemanche[7] and Miller[13]. We report results achieved by a number of researchers at BBN Advanced Computers, Inc., the Massachusetts Institute of Technology, and Brandeis University. Collectively, this work has been directed at both the practical problems related to achieving a high performance parallel garbage collector on stock hardware (primarily the work of Rozas, Courtemanche, Miller, and Johnson) and at exploring ways in which the garbage collector can support novel uses of parallelism at the user level (Miller and Epstein).

On some Lisp systems, garbage collection has been so slow that it has forced users to turn to other implementation languages; this is unfortunate, since an efficient algorithm has been well known for over twenty years. This compacting two-space algorithm, published in 1969[9], is described in Section 2 along with some variations that improve performance in a serial implementation. Creating a parallel variant of this algorithm is straightforward, but tuning it to perform well is somewhat more difficult. Section 3 describes both the algorithm and some of the performance issues that arise in actual practice.

An efficient garbage collector is an important goal in and of itself, but by adding one new data type (the **weak pair**) that provides a link between the user and the garbage collector, we acquire an entirely new kind of power. The implementation of the weak pair is simple (see Section 4.1) and forms the basis for a number of interesting features:

- The system automatically discards tasks that are no longer performing useful work.

- Hash functions on arbitrary Scheme objects can be implemented without forcing retention of the hashed objects.

- We can create **populations**[17] to store sets of objects without forcing retention of the objects.

- The system can detect and correct an important set of common errors (failure to release locks, close files, etc.).

The first of these features, the garbage collection of useless tasks, was suggested as long ago as 1977[4], but in a more restricted setting. In a system supporting Halstead's **future** construct[10], the system's data structures be carefully constructed from weak pairs in order to garbage collect tasks. As part of this structuring, MultiScheme separates the notion of a **task** (an active computational entity, similar to an **actor**[11]) from a **continuation** (the actor's script). This separation is *not* arbitrary, and Section 4.2 provides the rationale, based on a requirement that tasks be automatically garbage collected. The section also discusses the slightly thorny issue of choosing a root for garbage collection that simultaneously retains tasks of interest to the user and discards tasks that are actively but uselessly computing.

We close (Section 5) with a discussion of a form of parallel processing, called **speculative computation**, that becomes viable with the effective garbage collection of tasks. Speculative computation uses "spare" computational power to effectively explore a range of options, some of which may not be essential to the problem at hand. We have extended MultiScheme to provide a notion of task priority as a means for controlling the scheduling of computational resources. In addition to merely using the priority when choosing the next task, MultiScheme dynamically modifies priorities as a program runs. In conjunction with the garbage collection of tasks this prevents a useless task from hogging resources, while preventing deadlocks from the premature removal of a useful task.

2 A Serial Two-Space Collector

The basic garbage collection algorithm used in MultiScheme is the well-known[9] two space compacting algorithm of Minsky, Fenichel, and Yochelson (for a simple but complete description and implementation see [2]). The algorithm works by copying all of active memory, compacted and relocated, into a new region of memory. We position a scan pointer at the start of the new area of memory, copy the root of the garbage collection from old space to new space, and position a free pointer to the word after the root (i.e. to the first free location in the new area of memory). Then we repeatedly relocate the object to which scan points, advancing scan to the next object after each relocation. (Recall that scan always points into the new part of memory, and hence at a copy of some object from the old space.) Relocating an object is easy:

- If the object isn't a pointer, it is left unchanged. Fixnums[15], for example, just cause the scan pointer to be incremented. For long objects consisting of non-pointer (binary) data (eg. strings, long integers, or machine language code), there is a header word indicating how far the scan pointer is to be advanced to skip over the data.

- If the object is a pointer, it will point into the old address space. Under most circumstances, the object to which it points is copied into the new space and free is advanced past the copy. The original version (in old space) is modified so that its first word contains a forwarding pointer to the newly created copy. (A forwarding pointer is sometimes called a broken heart.)

- If the object we want to relocate is a pointer, but the first word of the object it points to is a forwarding pointer, the object has already been copied into new space. The forwarding pointer specifies where the copy is; rather than make another copy the pointer we are relocating is made to point to the existing copy.

This process of relocating objects repeats until scan meets free, at which time all the contents of the old memory that can be referenced have been relocated into the new area of memory. By copying into a spare heap the same size as the active one we are assured that all of the active memory can be copied, and the algorithm will terminate. A proof of correctness is based on noting the invariant that memory between the start of new space and the current value of scan contains pointers only to copies of objects (in the new space), memory between scan and free contains copies of active objects, and memory beyond free is not referenced.

Readers familiar with Baker's incremental garbage collector[4] or the more recent generation-based[19] garbage collectors will also find this algorithm familiar, since it forms the basis of all of these techniques. The two space collector has a running time proportional to the amount of memory in active use, unlike the more familiar mark-sweep garbage collector that takes time proportional to the maximum size of the heap.

2.1 Static Spaces Improve Performance

This garbage collector is quite efficient, since the code fits in most instruction caches and memory reference to the new space is highly localized. Unfortunately, a simple implementation will scan and copy large quantities of memory that are permanently needed by the system. This is a well-understood problem that has prompted the implementation of "generational" garbage collectors[19].

MIT's CScheme system (on which ours is based) takes an intermediate approach. It provides two static areas of memory, known as the pure and constant areas. The **pure** area contains only non-pointer objects and immutable pointers into the static areas — thus its contents are never modified by garbage collection and it need not be scanned. The **constant** area contains arbitrary (including mutable) objects; while this area must be scanned in order to relocate objects to which it points, the contents of the area are never copied.

The user has the ability to move arbitrary objects into either of these two areas, and moving an object recursively moves all objects to which the initial one points. It is important to guarantee that objects in the pure area never point into the heap. This is done by moving those subcomponents that can be mutated by operations internal to the Scheme system into the constant area instead of the pure area. The user-visible mutation operations (eg. set-car!, set-cdr!, and vector-set!) specifically test for mutation of objects in the pure area and produce an error rather than store a pointer to the heap into the pure area . Users can intercept this error in order to move the object from the pure area into the constant area and then perform the mutation.

These two areas provide a degree of flexibility that users can exploit to cut down the amount of time taken to perform a garbage collection. By moving immutable objects (such as large data structures constructed at load time or by initialization procedures) into the pure area, these objects are neither scanned nor copied at garbage collection time. They are also removed from the heap itself, so the frequency of garbage collection is reduced. Mutable objects can be moved to constant space, where they will be scanned but not copied. Again, objects in constant space do not occupy space on the heap and decrease the frequency of garbage collections.

As an example of the usefulness of the pure and constant areas, consider the runtime system which is written in Scheme. The majority of the code and its data structures are moved into one or the other of the static areas when Scheme is initially bootstrapped. The result is dramatic — we often observe a factor of 7 improvement in the speed of garbage collection over the same system without the code moved into the static area. This number falls as the running program generates active data on the heap since the speed of a garbage collection is determined by the amount of active storage.

The implementation of these areas is a very simple variant on the previous algorithm. We add a new "circumstance" under which an object isn't copied: if it is located in either the pure or constant area. In addition, before copying the root of the garbage collection to new space, we place the scan pointer at the beginning of the constant area and the free pointer at the start of the new heap space. We then scan all of constant space. This will copy into the new space any objects referenced from the constant area (recall that the pure space has no such references). The root is then copied into new space wherever **free** points, and the algorithm proceeds as above.

There are two additional factors that arise as a consequence of compilation:

1. Interpretation of a program causes large quantities of data structure to be consed for passing arguments (i.e. to create environments or closures). A great deal of the compiler's analysis is specifically aimed at reducing the need for these data structures. A good compiler can eliminate the vast majority of this consing by making use of registers and a stack. One brief test based on MIT's compiler indicated that compiling a program reduced the consing to 44% of the amount performed by an interpreted version of the program. By compiling both the program and the runtime system procedures it called, the reduction was to 12% of the original amount. The pretty printer, a cons intensive program, was used for this test, so these results are extremely encouraging.

2. In MIT's system an interpreted program consists of list structure, while a compiled program is largely binary data. While the compiled code is sometimes as much as 30% larger than the interpreted version, only about 28% of the compiled code is scanned by the garbage collector. For simplicity (see [16]) compiled code isn't placed in the pure area. Overall, the entire MIT runtime system requires about twice the amount of storage to be scanned when it is compiled as when it is interpreted. There is reason to believe, however, that this particular program has an anomolously large amount of scanned code. Several other large programs exhibit much smaller expansion.

These two factors tend to act in opposite directions. The first dramatically reduces the frequency of garbage collection without noticeably changing the time required for an individual garbage collection pass. The second increases the time required for each individual pass, but doesn't alter the frequency of the passes. In practice we find that our system with a compiled runtime and no user code takes 0.85 seconds for a garbage collection pass on our HP9000/320 system based on a 16MHz Motorola 68020. The same system when interpreted requires only 0.58 seconds – a factor of 1.4 degradation imposed by compiling the system. On the other hand, the compiled system may garbage collect only one-half as often as the interpreted system. Just to get a sense of the balance between these two factors, we tried a very simple test program. The system spent 2% of its time garbage collecting with an interpreted runtime system and 4% when the runtime system was compiled. Clearly, other test programs would change this balance.

3   A Parallel Garbage Collection Algorithm

Despite the efficiency of the two-space collector on simple programs, many programs generate large active data structures on the heap and consequently undergo large numbers of relatively slow garbage collections. The CScheme compiler itself can spend as much as 70% of its time garbage collecting when processing a large program with a small heap size. One solution, of course, is to increase the heap size thereby reducing the frequency of garbage collections. This does nothing to speed up an individual garbage collection pass, and may degrade performance on a virtual memory system.

Fortunately, the garbage collection algorithm itself is easily modified to operate in parallel. MultiScheme contains an implementation of such a parallel garbage collector, and it provides an interesting case study in practical parallel algorithm design. An initial parallel implementation was proposed by Miller[13] and subsequently implemented, described, and measured by Courtemanche[7]. The basic idea is to divide the work of scanning the new space equitably between the processors.

A garbage collection is initiated by a processor that has noticed the need for more space. It alerts the other processors and starts a barrier synchronization that is complete when all other processors agree to stop running user code and begin the garbage collection phase (see [14] for MultiScheme's support of garbage collection initiation). Each processor is responsible for scanning part of the constant space and copying part of the garbage collection root, then begins scanning part of the data copied into the new heap space. The partitioning of constant space occurs every time an object is moved into either pure or constant space so it need not be recomputed when the garbage collection starts. The root of the garbage collection includes the processor-private stack areas used by the Scheme interpreters; each such stack is scanned by its associated processor[1]. The remainder of the root is shared by all of the processors, and is scanned by the processor that initiated the garbage collection.

This initial scanning causes some objects to be copied into the new heap space, and the algorithm must continue by scanning these objects. This raises two problems: how did the scanning (which occurs in parallel on all of the processors) manage to copy objects into a single shared heap area without interspersing their contents and destroying their integrity? Furthermore, how can we divide the work of scanning these copied objects? In Courtemanche's collector this was accomplished by dividing the heap space into fixed-sized **consing partitions** when the system first starts. At garbage collection time, each processor grabs one of these partitions as an **output partition**, used as the destination for objects copied while it is scanning. Whenever copying an object would over-fill the partition, it is **released** to a queue of filled partitions that will eventually be scanned and a new output partition is taken from the new heap space. When the initial scan phase concludes, all processors enter a loop that attempts to dequeue and scan a filled partition. If no partition is available from the queue, the current output partition is scanned instead. The algorithm completes when there are no partitions on the queue and all processors have finished scanning their own output partitions.

3.1 Static Memory Allocation

Courtemanche's system was based on pre-allocating heap space to specific processors. That is, when the system was booted the memory was divided into fixed sized regions

---

[1]For architectural reasons, the MultiScheme implementation on the BBN Butterfly makes a copy of all compiled code in each interpreter's local memory. In addition to its stack, each processor scans its own copy of this code area.

and each processor was allocated one region to be used solely by that processor as a heap. This gave the system convenient control over the binding of processors to the memory that they used for space allocation. It allowed for co-locality of a processor and its heap[2], but at the expense of increasing garbage collection frequency when the processors allocated space at different rates. That is, if only one processor actively allocated heap space it would require a garbage collection as soon as it filled up its own heap.

There is an obvious solution to this problem of uneven space allocation, but at the cost of losing some control over locality. The current implementation of Butterfly Scheme[5] dynamically allocates memory to processors. It continues to statically divide the memory between the processors, but maintains a globally visible data structure that indicates the amount of each partition that is in actual use. At system initialization (and after each garbage collection) each processor grabs a fixed quantum of memory from its own partition. As it needs to allocate memory it does so by using part of this initial quantum. When it runs out of space it goes back to the global data structure to see if its partition has sufficient space to fulfill the request; if so, it bites off another chunk of its own partition and continues running. Otherwise it checks all of the other processors' partitions. Only if no space is available on *any* processor does it initiate a garbage collection.

Even with this change, however, a hidden penalty arises when the processors have vastly different amounts of memory on their heaps. The cost of searching through the global data structure to find a processor whose consing partition has sufficient space is significantly higher than the cost of merely allocating space from the processor's own consing partition. Both Courtemanche's system and the current BBN Scheme system try to alleviate this problem by having the garbage collector divide the active memory equally among the processors' heaps. They do this by subdividing each of the consing partitions into multiple **heaplets**. At the start of a garbage collection, each processor takes the first heaplet from its own consing partition to use as its output partition. The remaining heaplets are considered to be organized in a spiral consisting of the lowest remaining heaplets in all of the consing partitions, then the next higher heaplets, and so on. When a processor fills its output partition it takes the next available heaplet in the spiral for its new output partition. At the end of a garbage collection, therefore, all of the processors' consing partitions are filled to roughly the same extent – they differ by no more than one in the number of filled heaplets in the partition.

This does, however, lead to a phenomenon that Courtemanche called **partition wastage** (sic). At the end of a garbage collection each processor will use as its **free** pointer the **free** pointer of the highest heaplet used during the garbage collection from its partition. The portion of memory that is free in any other heaplets within the partition is thus wasted – Courtemanche's partition wastage. His measurements show that, as might be expected, partition wastage rises linearly with the number of processors in the system.

---

[2]On the Butterfly, MultiScheme deliberately didn't aim for co-locality. Instead, it tried to randomly distribute memory references across the Butterfly switch.

3.2 Dynamic Memory Allocation

In addition to the partition wastage problem there is another problem with the memory allocation systems described above. As the number of processors grows, the consing partition must shrink unless the virtual address space grows proportionately. And here we encounter a problem with current architectures: they support 32 bit pointers to byte addresses but have no data type bits. Even on today's commercial parallel processors this is barely sufficient: a 512 processor machine with a mere 4 megabytes per node requires 31 bits to address all of the available memory. This is a particularly severe problem in a Lisp system that uses a two space collector since it will use half the address space for each of the two semi-spaces.

But the practical limits are considerably smaller. The current implementation of MultiScheme (using 8 bits for type codes) has a maximum heap size of 4 megapointers. On a 128 processor machine this means that the individual consing partition is only 32K pointers, and from this we must take space for the static and program areas. One well-known problem of a two-space collector is that it divides this small amount of space in half by dividing the heap into two parts. Minsky's original implementation did not suffer from this problem: his second space was allocated on the magnetic drum. BBN Butterfly Scheme uses a similar technique – the second space is allocated in virtual memory that isn't accessible through ordinary Scheme pointers because it lies outside of the 4 megapointer reference range. At the end of the garbage collection this inaccessible memory is copied back down into the Scheme heap. Since the Butterfly typically has far more physical memory than is available in a single shared virtual address space, this mechanism tends to keep both the old and new space in physical memory. As a result the copy operation is relatively fast. It can be even faster under an operating system like Mach, where it can be replaced by a set of page map operation that use the virtual memory hardware instead of performing memory operations.

Despite this, any reasonable initial quantum taken by all processors from their 32K pointer consing partition virtually guarantees that the system is constantly garbage collecting. Worse yet, no vectors can be allocated that exceed the length of a processor's consing partition since no processor will ever have this much free space. The problem is quite dramatic.

Consider the following (uninteresting) program:

```
(define (test)
  (define (loop n name)
    (if (= n 0)
        'done
        (begin (vector-cons 100000 'junk) ; Make a large (garbage) vector
               (write name)               ; Show who's working
               (loop (- n 1) name)))))     ; Loop around again
  (for-each touch                          ; Start and wait for 6 tasks
          (list (future (loop 10 'a)) ... (future (loop 10 'f)))))
```

This program has six tasks (named a through f) regardless of the number of processors used to run the program. Running on a machine with a maximal heap size of 2.6 mega-pointers we would expect this to require three garbage collections since it allocates (and discards) 6 megapointers of memory. Using ten processors this is precisely the observed result. Increasing this to twenty processors, however, caused in excess of 60 garbage collections! The reason, upon investigation, turned out to be that the size of a consing partition with twenty processors was just under 100K pointers. Thus each attempt to vector-cons caused a garbage collection[3]!

The solution is again simple, and was implemented by Kirk Johnson and Jim Miller. In this solution there is a single global free pointer used by all processors to allocate large chunks of heap space. When a processor runs out of room in its current heap, it allocates a new chunk using the global pointer. It then allocates smaller amounts as required during execution. When a processor needs to allocate a chunk that exceeds the upper limit of the actual shared heap it uses a privately allocated "emergency area" instead and immediately requests a garbage collection.

This mechanism both reduces the frequency of garbage collections when the load on the system is unbalanced, and entirely eliminates the partition wastage. The implementation has proven efficient, provided that the "chunks" are large enough to reduce contention for the global free pointer.

3.3 Performance Bottlenecks

Courtemanche showed that his algorithm achieved linear speed-up to five processors, but then performance remained constant. He identified two specific problems with his garbage collection mechanism that accounted for this phenomenon: inadequate partitioning of the constant space, and processor starvation. The first was the result of an apparently harmless simplification of the partitioning algorithm for constant space, and was easily repaired.

Processor starvation is more serious. Courtemanche attributes it to a lack of active storage available for scanning. As the number of processors increases there is no work for the additional processors to perform. Ultimately, as the number of processors becomes very large they generate contention just trying to locate scanning to be performed and the system, in fact, slows down. This problem was the subject of recent work at BBN by Guillermo Rozas. Rozas examined the sources of contention and processor idle time during garbage collection. He identified eight different problem areas:

1. Idle time waiting for the initial synchronization barrier. This barrier is required to guarantee that all processors have stopped allocating space on the heap and "flipped" into the new space.

2. Contention for the data structure used to allocate partitions to be scanned.

---

[3]The observant reader may point out that the algorithm described here would, in fact, prevent the system from ever allocating a vector of 100K elements. In fact, the BBN implementation has a special case for handling allocation of large objects that allows this case to succeed once at the end of each garbage collection.

3. Contention for the data structure used to allocate output partitions.

4. Contention for moving a single object. This occurs when two (or more) processors are actively scanning memory and both need to move the same object into new space.

5. Idle time because no partition is available to be scanned. This occurs when other processors are still scanning memory, since they might cause a new partition to be available at a later time.

6. Idle time waiting for the synchronization barrier indicating termination of the scanning operation.

7. Idle time waiting for the synchronization barrier indicating that all post-scanning operations have been completed.

8. Idle time waiting for the processor that initiated the garbage collection to complete Scheme level code needed by the system to complete the garbage collection cycle.

Of these, by far the least common is the conflict between multiple processors for moving the same object. In fact, to lessen the impact of this problem to a completely negligible level we carefully arrange to store the forwarding pointer in old space *before* the copy operation begins. Thus, another processor will see a completed relocation as early as possible. The location in old space that holds the forwarding pointer is used as a lock to guarantee the atomicity of the copy operation.

The remaining seven items occur often and can be a source of significant performance degradation as the number of processors grows. To help eliminate the contention generated by using a simple spin to detect synchronization or lock release, Rozas added a set of tunable delays. By making some of the delays proportional to the number of interpreters, the contention is reduced at the cost of a lengthened minimum delay.

4   Garbage Collection of Tasks

MultiScheme's model of parallelism, based on the future, is directly inherited from Halstead's Multilisp[10]. A future is composed of two parts: a task representing work to be performed and a placeholder representing a value being computed by one or more tasks. Tasks are created for the explicit purpose of calculating a value, and each of these values allows for the synchronization of the task computing the value (producer) and any tasks that need the value to continue their own computation (consumers). We refer to this as value-oriented parallelism as opposed to the more common task-oriented parallelism generally found in parallel versions of languages like C, PASCAL, and FORTRAN.

Because placeholders act just as the values they represent, the synchronization supported by MultiScheme is highly dynamic and resembles the mechanisms used in dataflow computation models. Storing a placeholder in a widely visible data structure is a reasonable (and common) activity, even in a side-effect free program like the one in Figure 1.

```
(define (make-tree f low high)
  (let ((delta (- high low)))
    (if (zero? delta)
        (f low)
        (let* ((interval (if (even? delta) delta (- delta 1)))
               (mid-point (+ low (/ interval 2))))
          (cons (future (make-tree low mid-point))
                (future (make-tree (+ mid-point 1) high)))))))

(define (search tree value) ...)

(search (make-tree square 1 10) x)      ; For some value x
```

Figure 1: Parallel Tree Search

In this example, tree is probably *not* fully constructed when the call to search starts. Thus, the code within search must be responsible for synchronizing with the tasks that are creating the tree. This synchronization is dynamic, since the tasks have not even been created before the search commences.

The parallel tree search of Figure 1 raises another problem in addition to that of dynamic synchronization. If the function f is hard to compute, we should abort the building of sub-trees as soon as the correct value has been located by the search procedure. This problem is well-known in serial computing, and has led to lazy evaluation and the stream-based model of computation. But a parallel system, unfortunately, gains its speed advantage from eager evaluation. One way out of this dilemma is to remove tasks from the system as soon as they are known to be unneeded, an approach suggested by Hewitt and Baker in [4]. Another commonly proposed alternative (often in conjunction with a construct like Common Lisp's catch) is to kill tasks when they become useless. These two approaches strongly resemble the same two options for memory allocation – garbage collection vs. explicit release.

Just as prematurely releasing memory in an explicit memory management system causes problems arising from dangling pointers, deliberate "task homicide" can result in unexpected and undesirable premature reclamation of tasks. The dangling pointer problem of memory allocation has its direct analog in a form of deadlock in the parallel processor system. Imagine that we modify the program of Figure 1 by adding the following code:

```
(let ((tree (make-tree 2 20)))
  (if (search tree 3)
      '(FOUND 3)
      (search tree 27)))
```

Recall that **make-tree** creates the tree using parallel tasks, and thus the call to (**search tree 3**) may begin before the tree is fully constructed. If **search** kills off "useless" tasks — those constructing parts of the tree that the search didn't have to examine — then the subsequent (**search tree 27**) may well try to search a part of the tree that has not been constructed and whose tasks have been killed by the earlier search. The program deadlocks.

While MultiScheme provides procedures to kill tasks[14], their use is generally discouraged. Instead, the standard mechanisms for creating tasks (the **future** construct and the ones described below for speculative computation) interact with the garbage collector to provide automatic reclamation of unneeded tasks. In order to perform this reclamation, MultiScheme requires mechanisms to reference tasks without preventing their reclamation and to identify tasks that must continue to run. The former is supported by **weak pairs**, discussed in Section 4.1. The latter is handled by our choice of task-related data structures and the root of garbage collection, as discussed in Section 4.2.

4.1 Low-Level Support

The MultiScheme system incorporates two modifications originally intended to support the garbage collection of tasks. Both have since been merged into the sequential implementation of Scheme, since they provide useful services beyond their original design goal.

The first modification is the addition of a new data type, the **weak pair**. This resembles a standard cons cell[4], but with the property that the car of the cell reverts to '() if there are no references to the object in the car other than through the cars of weak pairs. Support for these objects[5] is easily implemented in a two-space garbage collector, since it provides space for four pointers at garbage collection time for each pair that is retained (the original two in old space, plus two more in new space). These are used as follows:

1. One old space pointer is used as usual to contain a forwarding pointer indicating the new location of the cell.

2. The second old space pointer would ordinarily be unused. It is used to store the original car of the cell.

3. One new space pointer is used as usual to contain a copy of the cdr of the cell.

4. The second new space pointer allows each processor to maintain a list, headed by the processor-private variable **weak-list**, of all the weak pairs copied by this processor into new space during the garbage collection. The type code on this cell indicates that it does *not* contain a pointer to be traced by the garbage collector when it is subsequently scanned.

---

[4] For purely aesthetic reasons, the standard operations for use with cons cells do not operate on weak pairs. A separate set of operations (**weak-car**, etc.) are provided instead.

[5] Objects similar to the weak pair may exist in other Lisp systems. But the authors are unaware of any implementation descriptions elsewhere in the literature.

At the end of the garbage collection, the cdrs of the weak pairs in new space are correct. The cars, however, must be located and corrected. This is done in parallel, by having each processor follow the chain of weak pairs headed by its **weak-list** variable. For each cell, the original car (still available in old space, cell 2) is examined. If the type code indicates a non-pointer, or the address indicates an object in pure or constant space, the new car is just the same as the old car. Otherwise, the object originally stored in the car is examined to see if a forwarding pointer is present: if so, the new car becomes a pointer to the relocated object; if not, the new car is set to '().

There are three things worth noticing about this algorithm. First, it is performed in parallel by having each processor responsible for updating the weak pairs that it copied during the regular scan phase. Second, it does *not* itself allocate memory, and hence can be safely performed during the garbage collection operation. Finally, it must have access to both old and new space, and hence is best considered a part of the garbage collection operation itself rather than as a Scheme procedure that must run immediately after the garbage collection is complete.

The weak pair mechanism has proven quite useful. It is a convenient base on which to implement the **weak set** (formerly **population**) abstraction of T[17] and the object hash tables of MIT Scheme[12]. These, in turn, provide the mechanism upon which to build a variety of user conveniences including the automatic closing of files reclaimed through garbage collection.

A second mechanism, **precious objects**, has been proposed to augment the weak pair, and is only now beginning to be explored. The goal of the weak pair mechanism is to allow the garbage collector to reclaim certain objects despite references to them. By contrast, precious objects allow the garbage collector to report its *desire* to reclaim certain objects without actually reclaiming them. Precious objects are implemented by allowing the user to designate an additional root for garbage collection, called the **precious object list**. The garbage collector first performs its normal operations without considering this list. After the collection is complete (either before or after handling weak pairs, depending on the desired interaction between the two features), the precious object list is scanned and split in two: one list contains those objects that are "alive" (i.e. those containing a forwarding pointer indicating that they were relocated, plus those in constant space and non-pointer objects) and the other list contains those that would otherwise be reclaimed. This second list is then used as the root to commence another garbage collection pass — thus preserving the precious objects. This list is made available to users after the garbage collection.

Precious objects can form the base of a number of user services, including the automatic release of resources when they are no longer in use. This is very important for catching and reporting certain user errors (eg. forgetting to release a lock). It is also useful for interfacing with external services. The MIT Scheme interface to the X Windows package, for example, will use this mechanism to release resources in the X server when a Scheme program ceases to need them.

The precious objects mechanism is desirable but it has not yet been exploited since it can be mimicked using the (pre-existing) weak pair mechanism. MIT Scheme, for example, automatically calls the Unix **close** operation when all references to a file (through the port data objects) are lost. This is done by building a weak list of all the ports in the system. After each garbage collection, this list is scanned for entries whose **car** has become '() indicating that the port is no longer in use. A parallel list is also maintained containing the information needed to locate the actual operating system resource that must be released, and the appropriate call to **close** is issued. The entry is then spliced out of both lists. This trick, providing parallel structures for user-accessible and system internal data structures, allows any system with weak pairs to mimic a system with precious objects (albeit in a slightly inelegant manner).

4.2 System Issues

Garbage collection of tasks seems easy once we have made the small changes to the garbage collector that provide the weak pair mechanism. We need only arrange the system's data structures to use a carefully chosen combination of ordinary and weak pairs. We examine every pointer to a task and ask whether it provides a reason to retain the task (in which case it must be an ordinary cons cell) or if it is for purely internal uses (and is implemented with a weak pair).

MultiScheme's value-oriented parallelism leads directly to one kind of reference: when a value becomes available, all of the tasks that are waiting for its value must be reactivated. The connection from the placeholder receiving the value to the tasks that are activated when it arrives is maintained using weak pairs. This allows the garbage collector to reclaim tasks whose computation has been halted awaiting the arrival of a value. Two issues, however, remain: how do we reclaim tasks that are *not* waiting for values (for example, tasks that are useless but are in an infinite loop), and what prevents all tasks from being garbage collected?

These questions force us to consider carefully the nature of the graph traversed by the garbage collector. We must examine both the edges of the graph and the root used to locate the "useful" portion of the graph. Let us begin by assuming that we can choose an appropriate set of root tasks and memory objects, thus concentrating on the construction of the graph itself. Since we have adopted a value-oriented approach we make the flow of a data value through the graph the dominant consideration. That is, we retain a task only if it is computing a value that is still needed by the on-going computation. In terms of MultiScheme, this means that we require a task precisely when the placeholder for the value it is computing is required — the graph must have an edge connecting each placeholder with the task[6] computing its value. At first glance, this seems simple enough: when we encounter a **future** we create a placeholder and a task and simply make the placeholder reference the corresponding task. In fact, MultiScheme has a slot, called the **motivated task**[14], in the placeholder for just this purpose.

But MultiScheme inherits from Scheme the ability to reify a continuation into a procedure by using **call-with-current-continuation**[18]. What is the nature of the continuation for a task newly created by **future**? Clearly, when the task completes its

---

[6]When we discuss speculative computation in Section 5 we will see that there may be multiple tasks computing the value of a single placeholder. Thus, there may be multiple edges emanating from a single placeholder.

computation it must store the computed value in the appropriate placeholder and stop execution. But what, exactly, is the "appropriate placeholder"? There are two equally legitimate possibilities, hinging critically on the desired relationship between a continuation and a task:

1. The continuation for a newly created task has a specific placeholder built into it. In this model, the *continuation* contains the information connecting a task with a placeholder. The user can be completely unaware of the existence of tasks. The only role tasks play is as structures internal to the scheduling of the system itself.

2. The continuation for a newly created task stores the computed value into whatever placeholder is associated with the task that is executing. Thus the *task* (not the continuation) contains the information linking a task to a placeholder.

To make the difference clearer, we can write the Scheme procedure used to implement the future macro for each interpretation. Assume the transformation:

```
(future exp) ⤳ (spawn-task (lambda () exp))
```

In our first interpretation the code would be roughly:

```
(define (spawn-task thunk)
  (let ((placeholder (make-placeholder)))
    (make-task                 ; Task holds continuation only
      (lambda (value)          ; Continuation
        (determine! placeholder value)))
    placeholder))              ; Value of future
```

In our second, we would use:

```
(define (spawn-task thunk)
  (let ((placeholder (make-placeholder)))
    (make-task placeholder ;  Task holds placeholder (its  goal), too
      (lambda (value)          ; Continuation
        (determine! (task.goal (current-task))
                    value)))
    placeholder))              ; Value of future
```

The difference in code, clearly, is minor. But the impact on the semantics of both continuations and tasks is major, as is the impact on the garbage collection of tasks. We can see the difference in semantics clearly by considering the interaction with MultiScheme shown in Figure 2. Consider our first semantics. In this case, when (define value-2 ...) is evaluated, value-2 receives a placeholder as its value. The continuation for the newly created task explicitly references this particular placeholder. After exporting this

```
(define cont '())
(define value-1 '())
(define value-2
  (future (call-with-current-continuation
           (lambda (continuation)
             (set! cont continuation)
             (let loop-forever () (loop-forever)))))))))
; Wait for  cont to have a non-null value
(set! value-1 (future (cont 'STOP)))

; What are the values of  value-1 and  value-2?
```

Figure 2: The Semantics of a Task

continuation to the variable cont the task goes into an infinite loop (hopefully to be reclaimed by the garbage collector).

When (set! value-1 ...) is evaluated, a second task and placeholder are created. But this new task calls the continuation created for the original task (stored in cont). Since this continuation explicitly references the particular placeholder stored in value-2, the termination of the task causes value-2 to have the value STOP. Value-1 contains a placeholder, but it will never receive a value.

The situation is similar in the second semantics, but the result is very different. Neither continuation references a specific placeholder. Instead they both look to the task that is executing at the time the continuation is invoked in order to locate the placeholder. It is the *second* task that ultimately calls the task termination continuation, and that task was created with the intention of supplying a value to the placeholder stored in value-1. Thus it is value-1 that receives the value STOP and value-2 will never receive a value.

From a language design point of view, either semantics can be defended. There is perhaps a slight preference for the first semantics, since extending this choice allows us to build a MultiScheme variant that supports the equivalent of or-parallelism in PROLOG. Extension in this direction requires that the act of supplying a value to a placeholder *not* allow the placeholder to be replaced by the value. Instead it must remain to record the tasks that have used the value so that a new value arriving later will cause the same tasks to be resumed again — the familiar forking of processes when multiple values are available at a choice point.

From the system design point of view, however, there is a marked advantage to the second semantics related directly to our desire to garbage collect tasks. By making the task an explicit object and the repository for the placeholder that will receive a value, we make the user responsible for maintaining the information needed to correctly reclaim tasks. When a task is created with a placeholder as its goal, we add the task to the list of motivated tasks that is part of the placeholder data structure. This information is essentially static — initialized when a task is created and not subsequently modified.

By contrast, the first semantics requires this information to be updated whenever a task invokes a continuation. By itself, this change is minor; but the ramifications are severe. Since we cannot predict the behavior of an arbitrary task, we must assume that it might invoke *any* continuation that is visible to it. Since this invocation would lead to supplying a value for the placeholder associated with the continuation, we must assume that *any* task might be responsible for computing the value of *any* (visible) placeholder. But this means that we can never reclaim a task! For this reason, we have chosen to promote the task to a user-visible object. The resulting system has three independent components related to parallelism:

Placeholder
> The representative of a value not yet computed. These are essentially invisible to the computation, but provide the value synchronization of the underlying model of parallelism.

Continuation
> The representation of work to be performed. At any time a computation can create a procedure representing the work it has remaining (by calling `call-with-current-continuation`).

Task
> The representation of an active computational agent, similar in spirit (but not detail) to an actor. A task has a placeholder whose value it is computing, and a continuation (the actor's script) representing the work it is performing to compute that value.

We now understand how to construct the edges of the graph traced by the garbage collector. Every placeholder has an edge (called the **motivated task**) connecting it to the task that is computing its value. The connections indicating the tasks that must be awakened when a value has been computed, however, are *not* edges of the graph traversed by the garbage collector.

There are two obvious choices for the root of garbage collection. We could either use all tasks active at the time of garbage collection or use those reachable from the global naming environment. Both of these have defects: the former fails to reclaim useless tasks that are in infinite loops (and hence always running when a GC begins), and the latter fails to retain tasks spawned by user input. Our solution is relatively simple and seems to work well in practice. The garbage collector uses as its root ...

1. ... the global naming environment. This is essential in any case, and serves to retain any processes calculating globally visible data structures.

2. ... the stack of any task running with a reduced interrupt mask at the time of the garbage collection. Tasks that are in a critical section change interrupt levels to lock out user interrupts. This root serves to prevent them from being reclaimed until the critical section is complete.

3. ... the set of tasks representing active read–eval–print (rep) loops. Each invocation of a rep loop creates a new task and this set of tasks is maintained in a global variable. Thus, this is really handled through the use of the global naming environment.

5 Speculative Computation

The ability to garbage collect tasks allows us the freedom to explore uses of parallelism in which we do not know a *priori* that the tasks we are creating are necessary — an area known as **speculative computation**. Based on the mechanism used to gain performance, we distinguish two kinds of speculative computation: **eager evaluation** and **multiple approaches,**

In eager evaluation, we gain speed by overlapping the execution of an essential task with that of one or more other tasks, and use the value of the essential task (when it is finally computed) to determine which of the other tasks is valid. This approach arises from a natural desire to evaluate the predicate of an if statement concurrently with both the consequent and the alternative. The performance improvement is determined by the difficulty of computing the predicate. It is easy to define a **speculative-if** macro that provides precisely this power:

```
(speculative-if predicate consequent alternative) ↝
(let ((conseq (future consequent))
      (alt (future alternative)))
  (if predicate (touch conseq) (touch alt)))
```

For some problems, the appropriate predicate to use with eager evaluation is essentially "use whichever one computes an answer fastest." For example, problems involving complicated searches (such as those arising naturally in artificial intelligence and theorem proving) tend to have this characteristic. For these kinds of problems it may be productive to devote processing power to following several alternative problem solving strategies, in the hopes that at least one of them will ultimately provide a viable solution. We refer to this as **multiple approach speculation**, and it is accessible to MultiScheme users through the procedures disjoin and await-first[14].

In both cases, of course, we must worry about possible side-effects that might lead to non-determinism or errors in one of the speculative branches of the computation. Because the garbage collector will remove any tasks that aren't working toward a useful goal, however, we needn't worry about explicitly killing "competitive" branches once one of them is resolved. On the other hand, there is no reason to squander processing resources if this can be easily avoided. We have implemented an intermediate solution[8] to this dilemma by adding priorities to MultiScheme tasks and using a timer to cause task preemption.

The model of process scheduling described in [14] is based on an undifferentiated pool of tasks from which some architecture-dependent mechanism (encapsulated in the procedure get-work) selects tasks to run. We have modified this model to allow the user to specify a priority for a task and we require get-work to choose a higher priority task before any lower priority tasks that may be available. By combining this with a timer interrupt mechanism that forces tasks to relinquish the processor after a finite interval, we provide a service that over time causes higher priority tasks to take precedence over lower priority tasks.

Using this basic mechanism we have added two higher-level features, called **promotion** and **downgrading**. Promotion occurs when a task must suspend execution while waiting for the value of a placeholder to be computed. Since this task can do no further work until the value of the placeholder is known, we promote the priority of the tasks that are computing the value of the placeholder to that of the waiting task. If these tasks are waiting for some other placeholder's value, then the tasks computing that value must be promoted as well, and so on. The act of touching a placeholder (i.e. waiting for its value to be computed) thus causes the tree of tasks rooted at the placeholder and generated by the **motivated task** and **waiting for slots** to be promoted to the maximum of their current priority and the priority of the task that performed the touch.

Downgrading operates similarly, but "in reverse." When the placeholder created by a call to disjoin receives a value (because one of the multiple problem solving approaches has yielded a value), the priorities of any sibling tasks (i.e. tasks whose values were alternatives to the one that has succeeded in computing a value) are lowered to a very small value. This change in priority is also propagated down the tree of tasks in the same way. With this in mind, we can rewrite our earlier **speculative-if** macro:

```
(speculative-if predicate consequent alternative) ⤳
(let ((conseq (future consequent (speculative-priority)))
      (alt (future alternative (speculative-priority))))
  (if predicate
      (begin
        (reduce-priority alt (ultra-low-priority))
        (touch conseq))
      (begin
        (reduce-priority conseq (ultra-low-priority))
        (touch alt)))))
```

The details of the propagation mechanism are of some interest, and are described in detail in [8]. In essence, we try to maintain an invariant that a task's priority must be at least as high as the priority of any task waiting for the value it is computing. A change in priority is propagated down this tree until either a task is found that is actively computing (i.e. we reach a leaf of the tree), or we encounter a task whose priority already violates this invariant, or modifying the task's priority would violate the invariant.

5.1 Toy Example: A Rule-Based System

To demonstrate the speculative computation mechanisms we will examine a simplified interpreter for a rule-based system. The example is based on a program originally developed for teaching an introductory undergraduate course in signal processing[1]. It is a rule-based expression simplifier supplying enough power to handle a set of rules for simple symbolic algebra. Like most rule interpreters it consists of a pattern matcher, a rule firing mechanism, and a control structure component. Both the pattern matcher and the control structure can utilize speculative parallelism, but for simplicity this example deals only with the control structure. For a more complete description of the other components of the system, see [1] and [13].

The rule interpreter has an inner loop that takes an expression and tries to match it against all of the rules. If a rule matches the expression, the rule firing mechanism is invoked to produce a modified (presumably simpler) expression. If no rule matches, then the expression is already in its simplest form. The problem we are attempting to solve, then, is converting the sequential control structure of "multiple solution techniques augmented with a default result" into a corresponding speculative (parallel) control structure. In doing so, we will assume that rules may be fired *in any order* that terminates and will still arrive at a correct final result — the only restriction is that we will not "give up" on simplifying an expression until all rules have failed to simplify it. This assumption is *not* valid in general for rule sets and poses an important practical limitation to the solution described here.

The primitive mechanisms available for speculative computation directly from Multi-Scheme (`disjoin` and `await-first`) provide the ability to wait for any one of a set of placeholders to receive a value. The problem we have here, however, is more complex. We must detect the case in which none of the standard solution approaches provides a result (i.e. none of the rules match) and provide a default behavior. We must code the rule matcher in a way that allows this to be detected, and we have chosen a rather simple but perhaps inelegant technique: the rule matcher returns a specific result indicating failure and we loop until either a match succeeds or all matches fail. This is packaged together in the following procedure:

```
(define (fail) fail)
(define (first-value placeholders default-value)
  (define (failed? object)
    (and (not (placeholder? object))      ; Has a value, and...
         (eq? object fail)))               ; the value is a failure
  (if (null? placeholders)
      default-value                        ; No alternative
      (let ((result (await-first placeholders)))
        (if (failed? result)
            (first-value                   ; Failed: try again
             (filter-out failed? placeholders) default-value)
            result))))                     ; Success
```

With this procedure, we can rewrite the sequential control structure component:

```
(define (scan rules expression)
  (if (null? rules)
      expression
      (match-rule (car rules)
                  expression
                  (lambda () (scan (cdr rules))))))
```

into the speculative parallel version:

```
(define (scan rules expression)
  (first-value
    (map (lambda (rule) (future (match-rule rule expression fail))
         rules))
    expression))
```

If we are able to estimate the likelihood of success for any given rule (either statically or dynamically), we can consider supplying a priority with each rule. The only change that is needed to scan is to add this priority to the future expression:

```
(future (match-rule rule expression fail)
        (calculate-priority rule))
```

MultiScheme then attempts to schedule the matching tasks for the rules on a priority basis.

6   Conclusions and Future Work

We are happy with the performance of our garbage collector on stock serial hardware; with improvements in hardware performance we anticipate achieving garbage collection in "the blink of an eye[7]" Since garbage collection need not interfere with either data collection or control signalling, a serial Lisp system using this collector can be seriously considered for use in hard real-time systems.

Unfortunately, the parallel implementation does not perform as well. This is due in part to the technological lag between serial processors used in inexpensive desktop workstations and those in current parallel processors. Presumably this will change with time. Also, the contention generated during parallel garbage collection remains significant. We plan to complete a set of measurements (currently underway) aimed at quantifying this contention with the goal of tuning the garbage collector as a function of the number of processors available.

---

[7]Psychologists put this figure of merit — the maximum amount of time that can elapse without altering the perception of effective control — at 0.05 seconds.

Our initial work in taking these measurements has shown us the difficulties involved in both gathering statistics and visualizing them. We are using a standard set of tools available on the BBN Butterfly, and by practical experience are gaining insight into their uses and limitations. We plan to capitalize on this experience by generating a similar set of tools within the MultiScheme environment. We expect to provide a dynamic (rather than our current post-mortem[3]) visualization tool, triggered by a measurement task that runs periodically in the spirit of Clamen's original work[6].

Our work on measuring the garbage collector raises another issue that has long been a concern. Having a substantial program of genuine practical interest provides tremendous motivation and the insight needed to develop tools appropriate to the problem at hand. Our interest in the garbage collector has helped spur the development of tools for visualization of parallel programs written in C (since that is the implementation language for the garbage collector itself). By developing a high performance Lisp environment on a parallel processor, we hope to attract implementors of one or more major Lisp applications. In conjunction with these implementors, we will have both the necessary resources and (more importantly) the necessary motivation and experience to capitalize on the technological base provided by parallel processors.

References

[1] Hal Abelson and G. J. Sussman. Procedural abstractions in lisp programming. Tentative title, submitted to *Byte* Magazine, August 1987.

[2] Harold Abelson, Gerald Jay Sussman, and Julie Sussman. *Structure and Interpretation of Computer Programs*. MIT Press, 1985.

[3] Laura Bagnall et al. The butterfly lisp user interface. Submitted to *Workshop on Parallel and Distributed Debugging*, 1987.

[4] H. Baker and C. Hewitt. The incremental garbage collection of processes. Technical Report AI Memo 454, Mass. Inst. of Technology, Artificial Intelligence Laboratory, December 1977.

[5] BBN Advanced Computers Inc., Cambridge, MA. *Butterfly Common Lisp and Butterfly Scheme Release Notes*, February 1989. Release 1.0.

[6] Stewart Michael Clamen. Debugging in a parallel lisp environment. Bachelor's thesis, Mass. Inst. of Technology, 1986.

[7] Anthony James Courtemanche. Multitrash, a parallel garbage collector for multiScheme. Bachelor's thesis, Mass. Inst. of Technology, 1986.

[8] Barbara S. Epstein. Support for speculative computation in multiScheme. Bachelor's thesis, Brandeis, 1989.

[9] R. Fenichel and J. Yochelson. A Lisp garbage collector for virtual memory computer systems. *Comm. of the ACM*, 12(11):611–612, 1969.

[10] R. Halstead. Multilisp: A language for concurrent symbolic computation. In *ACM Trans. on Prog. Languages and Systems*, pages 501–538, October 1985.

[11] C. Hewitt. Viewing control structures as patterns of passing messages. *Journal of Artificial Intelligence*, 8(3):323–364, 1977.

[12] Mass. Inst. of Technology, Cambridge, MA. *MIT Scheme Reference, Scheme Release 7*, 1988.

[13] James Miller. *MultiScheme: A Parallel Processing System Based on MIT Scheme.* PhD thesis, Mass. Inst. of Technology, August 1987. Available as MIT LCS/TR/402.

[14] James Miller. Implementing a Scheme-based parallel processing system. *International Journal of Parallel Processing*, 17(5), October 1988.

[15] James Miller and Christopher Hanson. *IEEE Draft Standard for the Programming Language Scheme.* IEEE. forthcoming.

[16] James Miller and Guillermo Rozas. Free variables and first-class environments. *Journal of Lisp and Symbolic Computation*, to appear.

[17] Jonathan Rees, Norman Adams, and James Meehan. The t manual. Technical report, Yale University, January 1984. Fourth edition.

[18] Jonathan Rees and William Clinger (*editors*). Revised[3] report on the algorithmic language Scheme. *ACM Sigplan Notices*, 21(12), December 1986. Also available as MIT AI Memo 818a.

[19] David Ungar. Generation scavenging: A non-distruptive high performance storage reclamation algorithm. *ACM SIGPLAN Notices*, 19(5):157–167, May 1984.

Qlisp: An Interim Report

Ron Goldman, Richard P. Gabriel, Carol Sexton
Lucid, Inc.

Abstract

One of the major problems in writing programs to take advantage of parallel processing has been the lack of good multiprocessing languages—ones which are both powerful and understandable to programmers. In this paper we describe multiprocessing extensions to Common Lisp designed to be suitable for studying styles of parallel programming at the medium-grain level in a shared-memory architecture. The resulting language is called Qlisp.

A problem with parallel programming is the degree to which the programmer must explicitly address synchronization problems. Two new approaches to this problem look promising: the first is the concept of heavyweight futures, and the second is a new type of function called a partially, multiply invoked function.

1. Introduction

The quest for higher-speed computers continues, and as the physical limitations on uniprocessor speed inhibit continued improvements, the need for parallel computers becomes more pressing. However, a computer that cannot be programmed is worthless, and so it makes sense to turn our attention to programming languages that can express parallel computations.

We have decided to focus our attention on medium-grained parallelism within the confines of artificial intelligence and symbolic computing. Our interest in researching language design is to study how to write parallel programs. To that end we are not initially concerned about introducing the minimal number of new constructs or in the fine details of syntax. Rather, we are trying to create a rich blend of language constructs that will allow programmers to describe parallel algorithms in a variety of

This research was supported by DARPA under contract N00039-84-C-0211.

styles—simplification will follow. In doing so we are hoping to help artificial intelligence programming in the future.

Therefore, we are investigating parallel extensions to the programming language Common Lisp [7]. The resulting language is called Qlisp. Other research into extending Lisp to support parallel programming is described in [4], [6] and [8].

This paper describes the Qlisp language, giving examples of its use. We also discuss additional extensions based on our experience programming in Qlisp. Performance results of the initial implementation of Qlisp are reported in [3].

1.1 History

Qlisp was initially designed by John McCarthy and Richard Gabriel [2] while they were affiliated with the Lawrence Livermore National Laboratory's S1 Project. The S1 was to have been a 16-processor multiprocessor, with each uniprocessor being a Cray-class supercomputer. Until 1987 the only implementations of Qlisp were interpreter-based simulators. Since late 1987 we have been engaged in implementing Qlisp on an Alliant FX/8 parallel computer; this implementation is based on Lucid Common Lisp, a commercial Common Lisp system.

The Qlisp project supports an exploratory programming component which is researching the effectiveness of Qlisp for symbolic mathematics. The inclusion of an application component of the Qlisp research has been important for gaining critical experience before design and implementation decisions are frozen. Experience gained during the implementation process has resulted in a number of changes to the original design of Qlisp.

1.2 Design Goals

The design of Qlisp was aimed at satisfying the following goals:

- The language will support medium-grained parallelism. Medium-grained parallelism matches well the intuitions programmers have about how to parallelize programs. Fine-grained parallelism often requires special hardware support, which is unlikely to be found in stock hardware except for vector processors. Most vector processors are designed for numeric computation. A commercial multiprocessor will typically be designed to support multiple users, and medium-grained parallelism is the best one can do on such hardware. Coarse-grained parallelism can often be achieved with simple message-passing techniques.

- The language will support the explicit expression of parallelism. There will be little or no support for implicit parallelism such as that provided by vectorizing or parallelizing compilers. Medium-grained parallelism often involves dealing with side-effects, and reasoning about when it is safe to parallelize in the presence of side-effects usually requires domain-specific knowledge.

- The target computer will support a shared address space. It is not important whether the shared address space is implemented using shared memory, except for performance requirements. Symbolic computation typically involves manipulating large shared data structures, which are best handled in a shared address spaces. We do not wish the programmer to worry about access to data structures in non-uniform memory.

- The language will support a variable number of processors. The number of processors a parallel computation requires may depend on the data. In this case it would be important to be able to adapt the number of processes used to solve a problem to the number of processors available.

- The language will provide mechanisms for limiting the number of processes. The cost of creating and maintaining a process can be high. If a process cannot be immediately run, that cost may overshadow the potential gains from spawning it. Also, the number of instructions to spawn the process may be larger than the number of instructions needed for the computation it performs. Therefore, limiting the parallelism can often improve performance.

2. The Qlisp Language

The approach used for Qlisp is queue-based multiprocessing. The programmer must explicitly indicate in the program when parallelism is possible by using the special parallel constructs described below. When a running program executes a statement specifying parallelism, it then adds a collection of new tasks to a queue for subsequent evaluation. When a processor completes a task it goes to this queue for its next task. Basing parallelism on runtime queues means that a program is not written or compiled for a specific number of processors. The number available could even change during the course of a computation. Tasks need not be of similar length, since a processor finishing a short task merely takes another from the queue.

2.1 Futures

Whenever a new process is created to perform some computation, the process will have associated with it a special datatype called a future [1]. This future is a promise to eventually deliver the value that is being computed by the process. Initially the future has no value and is unrealized. The future is realized when the process associated with it finishes its computation. If some other process needs to know the value of an unrealized future in order to perform some operation (such as addition), then it must block and wait until the future has been realized. However many operations, such as **cons**, assignment, or parameter passing, only require a pointer to the future and do not need to wait for it to be realized.

To explicitly wait for a future to be realized, the construct

$$\text{(get-future-value }form\text{)}$$

can be used. When called, **get-future-value** will evaluate *form*, and then, if its value is a future, wait for it to be realized; it then returns the future's value.

2.2 SPAWN

The simplest way to introduce parallelism into a Qlisp program is to use the construct

$$\text{(spawn }(prop)\ \ form\text{)}$$

to create a new process to evaluate *form*. The form *prop* is a propositional parameter that is evaluated first. If its value is **nil** (i.e. false) then no new process is created; the process originally executing the **spawn** will proceed to execute *form* and **spawn** will return the resulting value. If *prop* is any non-**nil** value (i.e. true), then a new process is created to evaluate *form* and **spawn** will return a future which will eventually be realized with an actual value when the new process finishes computing *form*.

All of the constructs in Qlisp that can be used to create new processes make use of a similar propositional parameter to give the programmer a way to limit the degree of parallelism during program execution.

The following computes a list that contains a series of values of the function fun:

```
(defun function-list (fun start next-arg spawn-p &optional (count 10))
   (let ((initial-list (list nil))
         (arg start)
         val)
     (let ((point initial-list)) ; local variable for use in next-value
       (labels
         ((next-value (&optional (count 1))
            (dotimes (i count)
              (let ((tmp arg)) ;private value for use by spawned process
                (setf val (spawn (spawn-p) (funcall fun tmp))))
              (setf arg (funcall next-arg arg))
              (setf (car point) val)
              (setf (cdr point) (list #'next-value))
              (setf point (cdr point)))
            val))
         (next-value count)
         initial-list)))))
```

Note that **labels** is a Common Lisp construct used to define locally named, mutually recursive functions, in this case one called **next-value**. Also notice that the definition of next-value includes the definition-time environment, in this case the local variables fun, next-arg, spawn-p, arg, point, and val. This combination of code plus environment is called a *closure*. When a closure is invoked, the definition-time environment is reestablished. When a new process is created by **spawn** or any other Qlisp construct, a closure is created to evaluate the spawned forms. This ensures that the new task will share the environment that existed when it was created. This environment includes the values of any special (dynamic) variables that are currently bound.[1] A subsequent change to one of these variables will be seen by all those processes sharing that binding. Note that even if the parent process goes away, the spawned process can still access and modify the values of variables captured in the closure.

The above example is also interesting because the function will produce a list of length count, and the list ends with a continuation function which when invoked extends the list. The list will be of the following form:

$$((f\ x_1)\ldots(f\ x_n)\ldots C)$$

where $f =$ fun, $x_1 =$ start, and $x_{i+1} =$ (next-arg x_i). C is the continuation function and takes an optional argument, which is the number of elements by which to extend the list.

The following function is useful when traversing a list produced by **function-list**:

```
(defun force (object)
  (get-future-value
    (if (typep object 'function)
      (funcall object)
      object)))
```

2.3 QLET

The primary means of introducing parallelism into a Qlisp program is the **qlet** construct, which is used to evaluate a number of arguments to a let-form in parallel. Its form is:

```
(qlet prop ((x₁ arg₁)...(xₙ argₙ)) . body)
```

The form *prop* is again a propositional parameter that is evaluated first. If its value is **nil**, then the **qlet** behaves like an ordinary **let** in Common Lisp: The arguments

---

[1] Qlisp uses a deep-binding scheme: a stack of variable name/value pairs.

$arg_1 \ldots arg_n$ are evaluated, their values bound to $x_1 \ldots x_n$, and the statements in *body* are evaluated.

If *prop* evaluates to any non-**nil** value, then the **qlet** will spawn a number of new processes, one for each arg_i, and add them to the queue of processes waiting to run. If the value of *prop* is not the special keyword **:eager** then the process evaluating the **qlet** will wait until all of its newly created child processes have finished. When the values for $arg_1 \ldots arg_n$ are available, the parent process will be awakened, the values bound to $x_1 \ldots x_n$, and the statements in *body* evaluated.

The following is an example of one way to write parallel factorial using **qlet**:

```
(defun pfact (n depth)
  (labels
    ((prod (m n depth)
       (if (= m n)
           m
           (let ((h (floor (+ m n) 2)))
             (qlet (> depth 0)
                   ((x (prod m h (- depth 1)))
                    (y (prod (+ h 1) n (- depth 1))))
               (* x y))))))
    (prod 1 n depth)))
```

The internal function **prod** computes the product of integers from m to n inclusive. It does this by dividing the interval m–n into two approximately equal parts, recursively computing the products of the integers in those two intervals, and then multiplying the two results.

The cutoff **depth** is used to control the number of processes created. Because two are created for every recursive call in **prod**, at most $2^{depth+1} - 2$ processes will be spawned. Notice that the propositional parameter to **qlet** simply looks at the value of **depth**.

In the case that *prop* evaluates to the special keyword **:eager** then the process evaluating the **qlet** will not wait for the processes it has just spawned to complete the evaluation of the arguments $arg_1 \ldots arg_n$. Instead, it will bind each **qlet** variable, $x_1 \ldots x_n$, to a future and then proceed to evaluate the forms in *body*. If in evaluating *body* the value of one of the **qlet** variables x_i is required, the process evaluating the **qlet** will wait for the spawned process computing arg_i to finish. If the value has already been computed, no waiting is necessary.

The following is an example of the eager form of **qlet**. Suppose we need to compute very many values of several computationally expensive functions, but suppose we store selected values in a table on secondary storage. Suppose that the lookup procedure, lookup-stored-fun, takes a function and its arguments, and returns a location descriptor which may contain the value of the function and which can be used to store the value. Then we might wish to optimize the use of such functions as follows:

```
(defun function-cache (fun &rest arguments)
  (qlet :eager ((value (apply fun arguments)))
    (let ((loc-desc (lookup-stored-fun fun arguments)))
      (if (value-stored-p loc-desc)
          (progn
            (kill-process value)
            (setf value (loc-desc-value loc-desc)))
          (setf (loc-desc-value loc-desc)
                (get-future-value value)))))
    value))
```

The predicate value-stored-p is assumed to indicate whether the desired value of the function already exists in the cache. The setf method for loc-desc-value is assumed to cause the supplied value to be stored in secondary storage. The primitive **kill-process** kills the process computing the value of the future value if it is not needed.

The function function-cache overlaps the computation of the expensive function fun with the possibly lengthy search in secondary storage for the pre-computed value of fun.

2.4 Excessive Parallelism

Because Lisp programs (and symbolic computations in general) are highly recursive, they can very easily generate a large number of parallel tasks—the opportunities leap out. Because any real multiprocessor will have only a finite number of processors, and because the cost of creating and maintaining a new process is non-zero, the use of *prop* during runtime to limit the degree of multiprocessing is quite important. We need only enough parallelism to keep all the available processors busy. The **qlet** propositional parameter *prop* is a direct consequence of our design goal of limiting the number of processes created.

The following function is a frequent target of parallel benchmarking:[2]

---

[2] The discussion here is based on various experiments [3] done to test different ways to limit parallelism. Running the various Qlisp programs was quite educational as the results often did not correspond to our intuitions.

```
(defun fibonacci (n)
  (if (< n 2)
      1
      (qlet t ((x (fibonacci (- n 1)))
               (y (fibonacci (- n 2))))
        (+ x y))))
```

Even though there are vastly better ways to write this function, it is illustrative. It is pointless to use mindless parallelism as is shown above because the cost to create and maintain a process for small values of n is much greater than the computation of (fib n). It is better to use a depth cutoff as follows:

```
(defun fibonacci (n depth)
  (if (< n 2)
      1
      (qlet (> depth 0)
            ((x (fibonacci (- n 1) (- depth 1)))
             (y (fibonacci (- n 2) (- depth 1))))
        (+ x y))))
```

Here processes to compute the recursive calls are spawned down to some depth. The number of processes created is at most $2^{depth+1} - 2$. The use of such depth cutoffs is typical in Qlisp programming: a recursively defined function spawns processes to compute recursive calls down to some predefined depth.

One important aspect of the treatment of parallelism is the amount of computation required per task as compared with the amount of work needed to create a task and combine its results with those of other tasks. If the **qlet** propositional parameter is true then the parent fibonacci process will not have much work to do, though for large arguments, the addition can be a significant amount of work because Common Lisp supports arbitrary precision integer arithmetic. The **qlet** propositional parameter serves to increase the amount of computation per task.

If the above code was to be run on a system with four processors then one might expect that the best performance could be achieved by using a depth of two. However this is not the case as the amount of work required by each process will vary considerably. Three of the processes will finish well before the last, and those three processors will then be idle for the rest of the computation. By increasing the depth of the tree of processes created, the granularity of the computations done by the final nodes becomes smaller, and when a processor finishes one task, it can get another one. The result of this is to balance the work load more evenly among all of the processors, keeping them all busy and finishing the entire computation sooner. As the depth is increased beyond the optimum point, then the additional time needed to create more processes starts to slow the computation down as expected.

A better measure of when to spawn processes then is the amount of computation that each process has to do. After several runs, a programmer may have determined typical usage patterns and might be able to estimate the amount of computation for each process. Another approximation to the amount of work for each process can be based on the size of the data structures on which the processes will operate. When operating on tree structures, this approximation is essentially the number of nodes below a certain point in the tree. Note that a depth cutoff can depend only on the size above a certain point.

For a function like fibonacci the amount of computation is directly related to the argument n. This can be used to spawn additional processes whenever n is greater than some predetermined cutoff value. Beneath that cutoff no additional parallelism would occur.

Another predicate to use for the propositional parameter is qemptyp. This returns true if there are no tasks in the queue. Therefore, if progress is good as measured by this predicate, it usually is reasonable to spawn an extra task:

```
(defun fibonacci (n)
  (if (< n 2)
      1
      (qlet (qemptyp)
            ((x (fibonacci (- n 1)))
             (y (fibonacci (- n 2))))
        (+ x y))))
```

Using a predicate like qemptyp results in behavior that is quite different then that of using a cutoff, since it depends very strongly on the interactions of all the running processes. This can sometimes be quite desirable, but for a function like fibonacci it is a disaster—since most of the calls to fibonacci are for very small values of n, it will be these trivial calculations that will first detect when the run queue becomes empty, and so they will spawn most of the new processes. For fibonacci, combining qemptyp with a cutoff based on the argument value eliminates this problem.[3]

Many recursive programs share the property that each recursive call requires less total computation than the local computation of its parent. Local computation is the computation expressed directly in a function; local computation includes the computation necessary to invoke functions but excludes the computation performed by invoked functions; total computation includes the computation in invoked functions. From our point of view this has serious implications when the amount of computation at a level

---

[3] Another approach being investigated by Weening and Pehoushek (c.f. their papers elsewhere in this proceedings) makes use of a separate run queue per processor, which decouples the parallel computations so that a predicate like qemptyp works well.

is comparable to the amount of overhead required to create and maintain processes. If process creation is eliminated below the point at which process overhead dominates, the effectiveness of a parallel program depends on how closely the actual scheduling of processes to processors approximates ideal scheduling. Note that the actual scheduling can depend on which processors suffer page faults and when. The use of a fixed depth as a control on process spawning approximates the ideal of not spawning too-small tasks only for a small range of argument values. The use of a cutoff based on argument values directly implements the ideal, but the knowledge of the cutoff is not adaptively obtained, and the exact value to use as a cutoff can vary depending on the details of scheduling. Therefore, the adaptive policies of checking for idle processors or an empty run queue coupled with a cutoff is probably a close approximation to the ideal, assuming that the cost of running the policy is not too large.

2.5 AND/OR-parallelism

The construct **qlet** is an example of AND-parallelism—where there is a set of tasks to do and all of them must be completed. We also need a way to specify OR-parallelism—where there is again a set of tasks, but now when the first task is successfully completed, the other tasks can be abandoned. The initial design of Qlisp proposed to do OR-parallelism by combining **qlet** with the explicit killing of processes. This will work, but the resulting code often seems unnecessarily awkward and unclear. We now feel that providing Qlisp constructs to directly express AND/OR-parallelism will result in higher quality Qlisp programs that will be easier to write and will more clearly communicate the programmer's intent.

To do this we generalize the notion of a future to allow several processes to be associated with it, along with a combining function. As each process finishes, it calls the combining function with the value of the form it has just finished computing. When all of the processes have completed, the future will be realized. For example if the combining function is +, then the sum of all the values computed by the associated processes will be the value of the future; if it is **max**, then the maximum value returned by the processes will be the future's value. OR-parallelism is accomplished by also associating an end test predicate with the future: When the value computed by a process satisfies this end test, then the future will be realized immediately, and any processes associated with the future that have not yet finished will be killed. We distinguish between a simple *lightweight* future whose value is computed by one process, and the more complex *heavyweight* future where several processes are involved in computing the value of the future.

Heavyweight futures are created by using an extended definition of **spawn**, which accepts arguments to specify a combining function, an end test, and multiple forms to be evaluated. Additional processes can be added to a heavyweight future by passing the same future to several calls to **spawn**. The following illustrates this. The problem is to find the minimum for a function of one real variable within a given interval. The strategy is to break up the interval into n equal subintervals and to have each process search its subinterval for a local minimum. The mesh should not be any finer than the value supplied by the parameter **delta**.

```
(defun minimum-function (f lower upper delta n)
  (let ((f-min (spawn (t :combine
                      #'(lambda (report1 report2)
                          (if (< (min-value report1)
                                 (min-value report2))
                              report1
                              report2))))))
    (let ((dx (/ (- upper lower) n)))
      (dotimes (i n)
        (let ((subinterval lower))
          (spawn (t :future f-min)
                 (minf f subinterval (+ subinterval dx) delta)))
        (incf lower dx))
      (get-future-value f-min))))
```

The function **minf** does the actual search within a subinterval. It returns a data structure that includes the minimum value found for **f** within the interval and the argument for which that minimum is attained. The form (**min-value x**) extracts the minimum value from the data structure.

A new heavyweight future, **f-min**, is created that will find the data structure which represents the overall minimum. Initially no processes are associated with the future. Then n processes are added to the future using **spawn**. When all the processes finish, the future is realized and the data structure representing the location of the minimum for the function **f** is returned.

2.6 QLAMBDA

The parallel constructs described above are primarily intended to create a new process that will perform a specific task and then go away when the task is completed. We also need to provide for another class of parallel operations: where a task is repeated many times, usually at the request of other processes. Monitors are an example of this class. The characteristics are (1) that the process can be shared by many other processes, (2) that the requests to the process are sent via messages and stored in a queue, and (3) that the process fully completes the work requested of it by one process before starting on the next request. The way to do this in Qlisp is with the **qlambda** construct:

(qlambda *prop* (*lambda-list*) . *body*)

which is used to create a closure for the code in *body* similarly to an ordinary **lambda**. The form *prop* is again evaluated first, and if its value is **nil** then no new process is created; when the **qlambda** is subsequently invoked it is treated much like a normal function call. The difference in this case between **qlambda** and a regular function defined with **lambda** is that if two processes call the same **qlambda** function, the first call to it will be completed before the second call is commenced—the second process calling it must wait for the first call to complete. The body of the **qlambda** constitutes a critical region. We will use the term *integrity* to refer to this property of **qlambda**. Process closures can thus be used to restrict access to various system resources and data structures.

If *prop* evaluates to non-**nil**, then a new process is created and associated with the closure. When the closure is later invoked, the calling process will evaluate the arguments and send them in a message to the process closure. A future will be returned to the calling process as the value of the call on the **qlambda**. The process associated with the closure will then do the appropriate lambda-binding, evaluate *body*, and then return the result to the calling process by realizing the future. If the evaluation of the **qlambda** body makes any use of special (dynamic) variables, these variables are looked up in the environment of the calling process, rather than the environment where the qlambda was defined. This is in keeping with the function calling nature of **qlambda**. The process closure has a queue of requests associated with it, and when it is invoked the arguments and calling process are added to the end of this queue. The body of the process closure is fully evaluated before the next set of arguments at the head of the queue is processed. Multiple invocations of the same process closure will not create multiple copies of it.

If *prop* evaluates to **:eager**, the new process closure will immediately begin the evaluation of its body. Any arguments are bound to unrealized futures and, if one is needed, the process will block unless the future has been realized by a call on the **qlambda**. Similarly, if the evaluation of *body* completes before the **qlambda** has been called, the process again needs to block.

Note that a call to **qlambda** returns a closure as its value. This closure can then be passed to functions as an argument, returned from functions as a value, or stored in a data structure. The closure can then be invoked to execute the body of the **qlambda**. This allows us to treat processes as first-class data objects. Also note that because a closure is created, **qlambda** captures the local environment in effect when it was defined. This can be used to create variables that can only be referenced in the body of the **qlambda**.

Locally named functions can be defined in Common Lisp with **flet** and **labels**. Qlisp extends these constructs to define local process closures with **qflet** and **qlabels**.

Here is an example of the use of **qlambda** using **qflet**:

```
(defun print-leaves (trans tree stream)
  (qflet t ((print-leaf (string)
              (dotimes (i (length string))
                (output (funcall trans (elt string i)) stream))))
    (labels
      ((worker (tree)
         (cond ((null tree) nil)
               ((atom tree) (print-leaf (coerce tree 'string)))
               (t (spawn (t) (worker (car tree)))
                  (worker (cdr tree))))))
      (worker tree))))
```

This function is used to traverse a tree in some order, outputting all of the leaves to a stream. A transformation function, trans, is passed as an argument and is used to map characters in the strings associated with each leaf; these transformed characters are output to the stream stream. The qlambda is created by the form qflet. We have used a qlambda for two reasons. One is to guarantee that the transformed characters from the strings aren't mixed up. The other reason, which is not apparent from the code, is that we want to get the traversal over with so that the tree can be modified while the process that is outputting the strings moves ahead at its own pace. The integrity property of qlambda accomplishes the first goal, and the use of a separate process accomplishes the second.

The original design of Qlisp had calls on a process closure explicitly wait for the body of the qlambda to process the calling arguments. To get the full benefit of process closures, the additional constructs, wait and no-wait, had to be added. By changing the design such that when a process closure is called a future is immediately returned, these additional constructs are no longer necessary.

2.7 Locks

Another way to interlock critical code sections is to explicitly use a lock. Qlisp provides basic functions to create, acquire, release, and test locks. When created, a lock can be specified to be either a spin or a sleep lock. When a process waits on a spin lock, it will busy wait, continually checking the lock until it becomes free. A process waiting on a sleep lock will block and not consume computing resources while it waits. When the lock becomes available the process will be given ownership of the lock and added to the queue of runnable processes. Spin locks are intended for use by critical regions that need to be locked for only a very small amount of time, for example to safely update a counter or to get the next element of a queue. Sleep locks require more overhead and are intended for use when the code that is being interlocked will take an arbitrary amount of time to execute.

It is hoped that the higher-level Qlisp constructs will obviate the need for programmers to use these low-level locking functions.

2.8 Process Synchronization

A construct to simplify process synchronization is the event. Qlisp provides basic functions to create, test, wait for, signal, and reset events. When waiting for an event the default is to wait for the event to be signaled once. If the event is signaled before the call to wait on it, then no actual waiting takes place. Otherwise the process is put to sleep until another process signals the event. When the event is signaled all of the processes waiting on it are awakened. After an event has been signaled, it must be reset before any process will need to wait on it again. It is also possible to request that a process wait until the event has been signaled a specified number of times.

With futures and process closures it becomes possible to spawn a large number of tasks, and not be able to easily determine when they have all completed. The construct

$$(\texttt{qwait } form)$$

will cause *form* to be evaluated and return its value. If the evaluation of *form* causes any new processes to be created or makes any calls to process closures, then **qwait** will wait for them to finish before it returns the value of *form*. This can be useful for process synchronization and for guaranteeing that returned data structures contain only realized futures.

In the original Qlisp design a variation of this functionality was provided by **qcatch**. We now feel that the ability to wait for processes to finish is important enough to warrant a separate construct, hence the addition of **qwait**. This also allows us to reserve **qcatch** for a use that is more like the standard Common Lisp construct **catch**.

2.9 Killing Processes

So far we have described a number of constructs to create processes, but we have not yet said much about how to get rid of these processes when they are no longer useful. Each process we create consumes system resources and for efficiency we would like to eliminate a process as soon as it is no longer contributing to the overall computation. However determining when a process is superfluous is non-trivial.

The traditional way that Lisp reclaims resources that are no longer being used is via garbage collection. When it can be determined that no pointers exist to an object in memory, then that memory can be reclaimed for later use. Similarly when no pointers exist to a future, then the value of that future is no longer accessible and there is no point in continuing to work on computing it, so any processes associated with the future can be killed. A process closure can likewise be killed when there are no longer any pointers to it, provided that it has completed all of the previous calls to it. There are several problems with relying on garbage collection to kill no longer needed processes. First, garbage collection does not occur frequently (one hopes), so the interval can be quite long between when a future is no longer pointed to and when the process computing it is actually killed so that it is no longer using system resources. Second, if a task was spawned for effect no pointer to the associated future may ever be retained, as the value will never be used.[4]

Qlisp provides two explicit ways to kill a process. The simplest way is to call the Qlisp construct **kill-process** which takes as its argument a future or a pointer to a process closure. This future is used as a handle to refer to the process associated with the future. That process is then killed. If there are several processes associated with the future then they are all killed. If the future is associated with an invocation of a **qlambda** process closure, then that set of arguments is removed from the process closure's queue, or, if they were currently being processed by the process closure, then it will abort the computation and proceed to the next set of arguments. Only the specific invocation of the process closure that is associated with the future is aborted; the process closure itself is not killed. Attempting to get the value of a future whose associated process has been killed is an error.

The other way to explicitly kill a process is to do a non-local exit from the process. In Common Lisp if a computation is surrounded by a **catch**, then a **throw** to that **catch** will force a return with the specified value, terminating any intermediate computations. In Qlisp **throw** can be used to kill other processes. For example, here is a function to determine if two binary trees are equivalent:

```
(defun tree-equal (x y)
  (labels
   ((equal-aux (x y)
      (cond ((eq x y) 't)
            ((or (atom x) (atom y))
             (return-from tree-equal 'nil))
            (t
             (qprogn t
               (equal-aux (car x) (car y))
               (equal-aux (cdr x) (cdr y)))))))
   (equal-aux x y)))
```

---

[4] We are investigating ways of allowing the programmer to specify the dynamic extent of a process so that it is not necessary to maintain lists of all those processes performing useful work, but that will not be returning a value.

Processes are spawned to compare corresponding branches of the two trees. If a process finds that two leaves are different, then the **return-from** returns **nil** and causes all of the other processes examining the tree to be killed. Note that **return-from** is equivalent to **throw**, except that block names are lexically scoped while **catch** tags are dynamically scoped. If the trees are equal then no **throw** will be done, and **tree-equal** will return **t** after all of the spawned processes have finished. The construct **qprogn** spawns a new process for each form in its body, evaluating them in parallel.

Normally when a process is killed, any processes that it spawned will not be affected. In cases like the example above where the parent process has spawned child processes via a **qprogn** or **qlet** and is waiting for them to finish, if the parent is killed or if a **throw** causes control to leave the parallel construct, we can safely kill all of the child processes.

When a process is created it inherits the chain of catch frames being used by its parent. During the execution of the child process, a **throw** to a catch frame defined by the parent will result in the child process being killed and the parent process continuing the processing of the **throw**, interrupting whatever it had been doing. If the parent process exits the scope of a given catch frame, then it is no longer possible for any child process to throw to that catch frame. Also any catch frames established after a child process has been spawned are not part of the child process's chain of catch frames. If the body of a **qlambda** process closure does a **throw**, the catch frames of the process that called the **qlambda** are searched rather than those in the process that created the **qlambda**.

The various constructs for AND/OR-parallelism provide additional opportunities to kill processes because of a **throw**. If one of the processes associated with a heavyweight future is killed by a throw, then all of the other processes associated with the future may also be killed. One of the reasons for adding heavyweight futures to Qlisp is that they define a set of processes having similar lifetimes.

As an aside, sometimes it is useful to place a process in a suspended state, so that it does not compete for computing resources, and possibly resume it later. Qlisp does this with the primitives **suspend-process** and **resume-process** which also use a future or a process closure to point to the processes to suspend or resume. When suspending a process care must be taken that the process does not currently own some system resource such as a lock. A deadlock situation can occur if a process tries to acquire a lock that is owned by a suspended process. A similar problem arises if a process needs the value of a future that is associated with a suspended process. A simple solution to avoid these two types of deadlock that we are considering is to automatically resume the suspended process in such a case.[5]

3. Need for Higher-Level Constructs

One important aspect of the initial experience with Qlisp has been doing a preliminary analysis of how well Qlisp constructs model the program structures needed for parallel programming. In many ways the **qlet** construct models quite well an important class of programs.

It was thought that **catch/throw** and **qlambda** would be important in modeling two other important classes of programs: one class involving killing processes and the other class involving autonomous agents. However, we have seen that there is some inadequacy here, even though our experience has been limited. One aspect of the inadequacy can be seen when we look at one particular problem which would seem to be well-suited to the **qlambda** approach.

The problem is exemplified by the samefringe problem. The samefringe problem is to determine whether two trees have the same leaves when looking at them in left to right order. The intuitive solution is to set up two processes, one to traverse each tree in a preorder treewalk. As each process finds the next leaf, the pair of leaves, one from each process, is compared. If they differ, the processes are terminated and the result is false, and if they are the same, the processes continue until they both finish after finding the same number of leaves.

One difficulty with this solution is to be able to use an ordinary binary comparison function to do the pairwise comparisons, all within a functional style. That is, a two-argument comparison function must be able to receive input from two separate processes without an excessive amount of explicit synchronization.

3.1 Partially, Multiply Invoked Functions

We have been exploring a solution to this class of problems. Our solution is termed *partially, multiply invoked functions* or *PMI* functions. The basic idea is to separate the process of coordinating the arrival of arguments from the actual processing of arguments by the function. A related approach can be found in [5]. We prefer a functional approach rather than a stream-based approach in order to retain the performance benefits of stream-based programming without introducing this unnecessary paradigm.

---

[5] This also allows us to do demand-driven evaluation in a manner similar to the **delay** primitive in Multilisp [4].

In Common Lisp parameters can specify how arguments are to be passed and whether they are required. Required arguments must be passed by position, and optional arguments may be passed by position or by name. If an optional argument is not passed, a default value is supplied. In all cases all supplied arguments must come from the same source.

We are experimenting with a technique in which all arguments to a function are passed by position to the function by an *interface* to the function. The interface accepts only named arguments, provides for all defaulting, and coordinates the arrival of arguments from multiple sources for the function.

Here is a simple example of the technique:

```
(pmi-defun add-up (x y) (:summand :summand) (+ x y))
```

This function adds up a pair of arguments, called x and y. The interface to this function names both of these arguments :summand, because there is no particular need to have different names for them.

The expression:

```
(add-up :summand 1 :summand 2)
```

simply produces the answer 3. However, one can partially invoke the function as follows:

$$(\text{add-up } :\text{summand } 1) \rightarrow \textit{future}$$

In this case the interface remembers the supplied argument and returns a future. A second call will complete the invocation and supply a value to the previously returned future:

$$(\text{add-up } :\text{summand } 2) \rightarrow \textit{future} = 3$$

This technique, then, is not unlike currying functions, but because all arguments to the interface are named, one does not need to curry in any particular order. All calls to a PMI function that supply arguments to the same invocation receive the same future as their value. A future is returned whenever some required arguments to the function have not been supplied to the interface by a function call. The futures returned for all partial invocations of the same execution of a PMI function will, when realized, have the same (**eql**) values.

When the names of the arguments to a PMI function are different, it is possible to stream arguments to it from different sources. For example, we can produce a list of the sums from two streams supplied by two processes as follows:

```
(let ((answer (make-queue)))
  (pmi-qflet t
      ((add-stream (x y) (:summand1 :summand2)
          (add-queue (+ x y) answer)))
    (qprogn t
      (loop ...
        (add-stream :summand1 computation)...)
      (loop ...
        (add-stream :summand2 computation)...))
    answer))
```

The **pmi-qflet** expression creates a local PMI function in a process closure. The details of queue management are elided.

Sometimes the elements of a stream of arguments will get out of order. In this case we can exploit a further wrinkle on PMI functions. What we would like to do is associate a secondary tag with each argument, so that arguments with matching secondary tags are paired. This would correspond to the tagged token architectures used by dataflow. For our experiments we have substituted the concept of *colored* arguments, where the color of a set of arguments is explicitly passed as follows:

$$
\begin{aligned}
&\text{(add-up :color 1 :summand 1)} \rightarrow \textit{future1} \\
&\text{(add-up :color 2 :summand 2)} \rightarrow \textit{future2} \\
&\text{(add-up :color 2 :summand 3)} \rightarrow \textit{future2} = 5 \\
&\text{(add-up :color 1 :summand 5)} \rightarrow \textit{future1} = 6
\end{aligned}
$$

All PMI functions accept colored arguments. When a color is not supplied, a default, private color is used for that invocation.

Another reason for colored arguments is to insulate invocations from separate parts of the overall computation from each other.

At present we are not sure how well the mechanisms of partially, multiply invoked functions help programmers to understand and program in parallel effectively. But it seems clear that constructs that allow a programmer to ignore the details of synchronization are essential.

3.2 Stream-based Programming versus PMI Functions

Most stream-based approaches require programmers who use them to become aware of a different model of computation, usually by having to do one of the following: defining and creating a stream, writing code to inject and/or extract information from a stream, or arranging for information to be passed back from the receiving end of the stream.

PMI functions, on the other hand, are a small variant on ordinary function-calling, and function-calling semantics are unaltered. The caller of a PMI function passes arguments to a function and gets back a result. The fact that not all arguments are supplied changes the performance of programs written using PMI functions, and the mismatch of arguments supplied and arguments expected can be viewed as syntactic sugar.

Streams are a mechanism for achieving distributed behavior, and could be used to implement PMI functions. PMI functions allow programmers to reason about the temporal characteristics of a program, namely that the execution of a particular program will contain a sequence of function calls. Such a sequence could be viewed as a stream, but it seems simpler to use the function calling model where possible.

4. Summary

Qlisp has been proposed as a language for programming multiprocessors. An initial implementation of it has been done, and various experiments performed. Results to date indicate that the performance of Qlisp programs is good. The more interesting set of results concern how well Qlisp captures the intuition programmers have about parallel programs. Here we have found that our original conception of Qlisp requires modification. Some constructs, such as **qlambda** and **throw**, might be too low level to be easily used. To address this concern, our current strategy is to examine problems with natural parallel solutions and to find parallel constructs that express those solutions well.

References

[1] Henry G. Baker, Jr. and Carl Hewitt, *The Incremental Garbage Collection of Processes*, Proceedings of the ACM Symposium on Artificial Intelligence and Programming Languages, August 1977.

[2] Richard P. Gabriel and John McCarthy, *Qlisp* in **Parallel Computation and Computers for Artificial Intelligence** edited by Janusz S. Kowalik, Kluwer Academic Publishers, 1988.

[3] Ron Goldman and Richard P. Gabriel, *Preliminary Results with the Initial Implementation of Qlisp*, Proceedings of the 1988 ACM Symposium on Lisp and Functional Programming, July 1988.

[4] Robert H. Halstead, Jr., *Multilisp: A Language for Concurrent Symbolic Computation*, ACM Transactions on Programming Languages and Systems, Vol 7, No. 4, October 1985, pp 501-538.

[5] John Lamping, *A Unified System of Parameterization for Programming Languages*, Proceedings of the 1988 ACM Symposium on Lisp and Functional Programming, July 1988.

[6] James S. Miller, **MultiScheme: A Parallel Processing System Based on MIT Scheme**, PhD thesis, MIT, August 1987.

[7] Guy L. Steele Jr. et. al. **Common Lisp Reference Manual**, Digital Press, 1984.

[8] Mark R. Swanson, Robert R. Kessler, and Gary Lindstrom, *An Implementation of Portable Standard Lisp on the BBN Butterfly*, Proceedings of the 1988 ACM Symposium on Lisp and Functional Programming, July 1988.

Low-cost process creation
and dynamic partitioning in Qlisp

Joseph D. Pehoushek
Joseph S. Weening

Stanford University
Stanford, California

Abstract

Our experiments with Qlisp have led to two ways of improving the performance of parallel Lisp programs. One is to reduce the cost of process creation and scheduling; the other is to use a dynamic partitioning and scheduling method. We describe these techniques and present the results of several experiments that use them. We also present an analysis of the dynamic partitioning method to explain the reasons for its success.

1   Introduction

Efficient execution of programs is one of the primary goals of parallel programming. This paper discusses two techniques that we have found useful in speeding up programs written in Qlisp [3]. The first of these is an alternative implementation of process creation operations that requires much less overhead than those provided by the current implementation of Qlisp. The other is a technique we call *dynamic partitioning*, which reduces the number of processes created in many programs, and is simpler to use than the cutoff-based partitioning methods previously advocated for Qlisp [2].

In both cases, our goal is to reduce the overhead of parallel computation. Overhead can be defined as work done by the processors that would not be done in a sequential execution of the program. The main components of overhead in Qlisp are (1) process creation; (2) scheduling; (3) idle time; and (4) synchronization and other work done by a parallel program that is not needed in a sequential version. The extent to which each of these is significant depends on both the program under consideration, and the way in which basic operations of the system are implemented.

Sections 2 and 3 present these two aspects of our approach to lowering the overhead cost of parallel Lisp. The application of these methods to several programs is described in section 4. The dynamic partitioning method is analyzed in a more theoretical framework in section 5. Section 6 presents our conclusions and discusses topics for future research.

2   Low-cost process creation

Process creation (sometimes called process spawning) is a significant source of overhead in programs that make use of "fine-grained" parallelism. Reducing the cost of process creation will have increasing benefits as the average size of the processes created by a program decreases. Stated another way, as we reduce the cost of process creation, the programmer needs to worry less about the size of processes, and can thus be more liberal in his use of parallelism. This will often result in a more highly parallel program or at least a reduction of effort needed to achieve a desired degree of efficiency.

We found a number of ways to fine-tune the existing implementation of Qlisp primitives for process creation, that sped them up without any change in their observable behavior. But the largest savings in overhead cost were obtained by making a major change to the way in which processes are created. We will explain this change and then show that it actually does not affect the language significantly, but does allow more efficient process creation in many cases.

Consider the following fragment of a Qlisp program:

```
(qlet (prop) ((x (f a b))
              (y (g (car a) (cdr b))))
   ...)
```

If the proposition (prop) returns true, then new processes are created to evaluate the forms (f a b) and (g (car a) (cdr b)). The processes return the values from these function calls, which are then bound to x and y in the parent process while the body of the qlet form is executed.

The first of the child processes performs a function call to f with the values currently bound to a and b; a variety of techniques can be used to implement this correctly. The activity of the second process depends on whether the subforms (car a) and (cdr b) are to be evaluated in the parent process, or whether the entire form (g (car a) (cdr b)) is evaluated in the child process.

Qlisp chooses the second of these interpretations, because it allows a greater amount of work to be done in the child process, and thus potentially increases the parallelism in the program. In the case of car and cdr, the difference is not great, but in other cases there might be forms that take a long time to execute.

In expanding qlet, which is a macro, into code that can be compiled, Qlisp wraps a lambda-expression around each of the forms to be evaluated in a child process, and then arranges to have these functions called at runtime. In the example above, the child processes call the functions

```
(lambda () (f a b))
```

and

```
(lambda () (g (car a) (cdr b)))
```

each with no arguments.

In general, as in this case, these lambda-expressions contain free variables; this is how data is passed from parent to child processes. The runtime representations of these expressions are therefore closures, which encapsulate the bindings of lexical variables.

The use of closures also ensures the correct behavior when there are side effects to variables that are shared by processes, i.e., each process will see the side effects to shared variables made by other processes. (Synchronization is generally needed to use side effects correctly, but that is beyond the scope of this paper.)

The creation of these closures, and their eventual garbage collection, adds a significant amount of overhead to the parallel program that would not occur in a sequential version. This overhead is avoidable in many cases. In the code shown above, there are no side effects to the variables a and b. Therefore their values, instead of the environment containing their bindings, can be passed to the child processes by an ordinary function-call protocol, which uses a stack instead of dynamic memory allocation and is thus much more efficient.

Our major change to the implementation of process creation is that we arrange to have each child process call a function that has no free (lexical) variables. Data is passed from the parent process to the children by supplying arguments to these functions.

We now return to the question of whether argument forms, such as (car a) and (cdr b) in our example, should be computed in the parent or in the child process. If (car a) and (cdr b) are computed by the parent, then their values can simply be passed as arguments to the child process, which will evaluate the function g with these arguments. To compute them in the child, on the other hand, we must perform lexical analysis to determine that a and b are the free variables in the argument forms; then we call

```
(lambda (a b) (g (car a) (cdr b)))
```

in the child process, with the values of a and b supplied as arguments by the parent. Note that while this has the benefit of performing less work in the parent process, the child process now evaluates an extra function call (the call to the lambda-expression, as well as the call to g) that was not present in the original program.

Our alternative implementation of qlet, which we call qlet&, evaluates argument forms in the parent process, in order to have the simplest possible interface between parent and child and cause the least additional overhead. If this is not what a programmer wants in a particular instance, then appropriate uses of lambda-expressions can produce a different behavior. Using our example:

- To evaluate argument forms in the parent:

```
(qlet& (prop) ((x (f a b))
               (y (g (car a) (cdr b))))
   ...)
```

- To evaluate argument forms in the child:

```
(qlet& (prop) ((x ((lambda (a b) (f a b)) a b))
               (y ((lambda (a b) (g (car a) (cdr b))) a b)))
   ...)
```

Note that a smart compiler could optimize the form for x, eliminating the call to the lambda-expression, and calling the function f directly in the child process.

- To get the behavior of Qlisp's `qlet` (with closures):

```
(qlet& (prop) ((x ((lambda () (f a b)))
               (y ((lambda () (g (car a) (cdr b)))))))
 ...)
```

We can therefore define `qlet` and other forms of parallelism using macros based on `qlet&`. It is not, however, possible to go the other way and define our `qlet&` in terms of Qlisp's `qlet` without the creation of closures, which we are trying to avoid.

3 Dynamic partitioning

One of the problems faced in parallel Lisp is controlling the amount of parallelism in a program. Many programs have opportunities for parallel execution at various levels, and finding the appropriate granularity of processes is not always easy [5]. We have found that *dynamic partitioning*, which uses the state of the system at runtime to decide when to create processes, often results in near-optimal efficiency with less work for the programmer than the cutoff-based partitioning methods that were originally proposed for Qlisp.

Dynamic partitioning is not a new idea; it has been tried in Multilisp [4] and probably in other systems. After describing the basic idea in this section we will discuss an efficient way to implement it, and in a later section we will analyze its behavior in order to understand why it works well.

Qlisp originally proposed using a single, global queue in shared memory to hold information about processes that were ready to run. Forms that create processes, such as `qlet`, add work to this queue; whenever a processor is idle, it will try to remove a process from the queue and execute it. Management of the queue is first-in, first-out (FIFO), with a global lock needed to ensure correct synchronization. This is the scheduling algorithm; the partitioning method (i.e., the decision of whether or not to create a process) is based on properties of the program or the data it is processing, and does not depend on the current state of the queue.

We found that use of a global queue leads to contention problems on more than a small number of processors; that the FIFO scheduling order often leads to excessive use of memory and is not the best way to keep processors busy most of the time, and that partitioning decisions are not easy to make without knowledge of the runtime state of the system. To address all of these problems, we investigated a combined partitioning and scheduling method, dynamic partitioning, which works as follows.

There is a separate queue of processes for each processor. Processes may be added or removed from either the head or tail of this queue, so it is actually a *deque* (double-ended queue). When a process is created, it is added to the head of the deque of the processor on which its parent is running. When a processor is idle, it removes the process at the head of its own deque, if that deque is not empty. The deque is therefore used as a stack when accesses from only a single processor are considered. This results in the "unfair scheduling" method that Halstead found worked well in Multilisp.

When a processor becomes idle and its own deque is empty, it cycles among the other processors, trying to remove a process from a non-empty deque. It does this from the tail of the deque, the hope being that this will transfer a larger chunk of work and minimize the overall number of transfers from one processor to another. As we will see later, this should result in less process creation in general.

What we observed when using dynamic partitioning was that in the vast majority of cases, a process runs on the same processor as its parent. Furthermore, the lifetime of the parent completely encompasses the lifetime of its children, in the case of qlet or qlet& not using the "eager" feature (which allows the body of the qlet form to execute before the child processes finish). The execution of most processes is thus the same as ordinary function calls, and there is the potential for making a process creation almost as cheap as a function call.

By avoiding the eager form of qlet, and other Qlisp primitives that allow a parent to continue (and possibly terminate) before its child processes have finished, we are restricting our computations to a "fork/join" style of parallelism. (The "fork" is when the parent creates multiple child processes that can run in parallel, and the "join" results from the parent waiting for all of its children to finish, before continuing.) Not all parallel computations can be easily expressed in this style, but many can, so there is a benefit to making such programs run faster.

We concentrate on optimizing the creation of processes that execute on the same processor as their parent. This is done by using the following techniques:

- All data describing the state of a process is allocated as local variables in the parent, and we are careful not to use these variables in Lisp forms that would cause the creation of closures. These variables are therefore stack-allocated by the compiler.

- The scheduler data structures, i.e., the deque for each processor, are also implemented as stack-allocated variables. The alternative is to use cons cells or structures and let them be garbage-collected, but in our method we take advantage of knowing the lifetime of these cells and save this overhead.

- When a processor removes a process from the head of its own deque, it makes an ordinary function call to the code that this process is supposed to execute. There is no need to use a separate control stack or perform various other context-switching operations that Qlisp normally does whenever a process is started.

- It is still possible for a process to be transferred to another processor, but the work needed to do this is only performed when it actually happens.

The result of these optimizations, on Alliant FX/8 Qlisp, is that most process creations have an overhead of about 22 microseconds. An ordinary function call takes 10 to 12 microseconds. When a process is transferred to another processor, the additional overhead is about 25 microseconds, and when this causes the parent process to suspend and later resume, there is about 30 microseconds of overhead.

In our experiments the partitioning decision, i.e., the qlet proposition that determines whether or not to create child processes, is based on the length of the current processor's deque, rather than any property of the program itself or the input data. While it may seem counterintuitive to ignore information that could be used to avoid creating small processes, we found that this partitioning method works quite well in practice. Section 5 of this paper is devoted to explaining the reasons for this.

A benefit of this partitioning method is that it is quite simple. On a machine with a small number of processors (ours has just eight), most subcomputations are not performed in separate processes, so the the overhead of parallelism can easily be dominated by the cost of the partitioning decisions. A test of the queue size is very fast; just 2 microseconds in our implementation.

4 Experimental results

We have implemented the qlet& primitive for process creation, and the support for dynamic partitioning described above, as a set of extensions to Qlisp. In the code below, we use the following Common Lisp reader macros as abbreviations for commonly-occurring constructs.

- #!(fun arg1 ... argn) expands into

  ```
  (qlet& t ((v1 arg1) ... (vn argn))
    (fun v1 ... vn))
  ```

- #d?(fun arg1 ... argn), where d is a constant integer, expands into

  ```
  (qlet& (< (deque-size) d) ((v1 arg1) ... (vn argn))
    (fun v1 ... vn))
  ```

We sometimes call d the "depth" of the queue.

The two forms above convert an ordinary functional expression into one in which the arguments are evaluated in parallel. For #! the parallelism is unconditional, i.e., processes are always created at runtime; while #d? implements the dynamic partitioning test that we described above. The (deque-size) function returns the current length of the queue on whatever processor it is called on.

The use of #! is equivalent to #d? with an "infinite" depth d, so we will use "∞" in tables of results when comparing the #d? and #! versions of programs.

All of our experiments were run on an Alliant FX/8 multiprocessor with eight processors. Because of way in which the Alliant concurrency hardware works, the best speedup one can expect on eight processors is about 7.8. Qlisp does not yet have a parallel garbage collector, so all of the results were for runs of programs that did not invoke the garbage collector.

The tables of results for the tak and boyer programs show speedup over a sequential version of the program (not a parallel version running on one processor); the number of processes spawned; the number of processes transferred to a different processor from the one on which they were created; and an estimate of the idle time. The number of transfers is generally much less than the number of spawns, as stated previously, and will be seen to be important in the analysis of dynamic partitioning.

4.1 Fibonacci numbers

The following program to compute Fibonacci numbers contains some interesting challenges.

```
(defun fib (n)
  (if (< n 2)
      n
      (+ (fib (- n 2))
         (fib (- n 1))))))
```

There are, of course, much better ways to compute Fibonacci numbers. We are using this program as an example of "embarassingly parallel" code, in which the main challenges are to create processes of the right granularity and to balance the workload among the processors.

A version of fib that creates all possible processes is:

```
(defun pfib (n)
  (if (< n 2)
      n
      #!(+ (pfib (- n 2))
           (pfib (- n 1))))))
```

Running this program on the eight-processor Alliant, the speedup approaches 3.5 for values of n higher than 20. This is actually quite good, considering the small amount of work done by most of the processes, and indicates the benefits of low-cost process creation. However, dynamic partitioning lets us do much better.

```
(defun dfib (n)
  (if (< n 2)
      n
      #1?(+ (dfib (- n 2))
            (dfib (- n 1))))))
```

dfib creates processes only when the queue on the local processor contains fewer than one process, i.e., only when the queue is empty. This is the opposite extreme from pfib, but it turns out to be sufficient parallelism to achieve a speedup of 7.15 on eight processors for $n > 20$.

Increasing the queue depth parameter in dfib does not improve the speedup; it only results in more creation of processes than are necessary for this program. This is not always the case, as we will see in the next example. The difference between the speedup of 7.15 that we were able to obtain, and the 7.8 that we might hope for, can be attributed to the cost of the partitioning decisions, i.e., the check of the queue depth each time the function dfib is called.

4.2 Takeuchi function

Another "embarrassingly parallel" program is the original version of the Takeuchi function (not the modified version used in the Gabriel benchmarks). For appropriate

Depth	Speedup	Average # Spawns	Average # Transfers	Idle Time
1	3.52	1050694	790324	43025
2	5.11	609462	316419	14527
3	6.58	218232	76683	3225
4	6.75	240026	61181	2261
5	7.15	118155	20645	803
6	7.14	141648	18247	676
7	7.22	128031	10378	341
8	7.18	144586	8131	259
9	7.08	164284	5887	159
10	7.15	187349	4580	122
11	7.12	205628	2734	76
12	6.98	262533	2726	63
13	6.97	308028	1610	35
14	6.90	361849	1247	32
15	6.75	459889	1029	25
16	6.60	539618	579	13
17	6.43	680381	523	14
18	6.22	817782	466	12
19	6.03	1005172	490	13
20	5.85	1169371	459	13
21	5.60	1374645	500	15
22	5.44	1562194	468	12
23	5.16	1821357	462	11
24	5.01	2048918	499	14
25	4.83	2273060	448	13
26	4.71	2460059	499	14
27	4.52	2711817	477	12
28	4.27	2982362	448	12
29	4.21	3232200	426	11
30	3.97	3454729	455	12
⋮				
∞	2.90	6302431	539	15

Table 1: Takeuchi function results on 8 processors

values of the argument x, y and z, it runs for a long time without using much stack space. The function is the following:

```
(defun tak (x y z)
  (declare (fixnum x y z))
  (if (not (< y x))
      y
      (tak (tak (1- x) y z)
           (tak (1- y) z x)
           (tak (1- z) x y))))
```

Our parallel version of this function is:

```
(defun dtak (x y z)
  (declare (fixnum x y z))
  (if (not (< y x))
      y
      #!(dtak (dtak (1- x) y z)
              (dtak (1- y) z x)
              (dtak (1- z) x y))))
```

The use of #! allows unbounded process creation, as before. We also tried #d? for values of d from 1 to 30, shown in the "depth" column of table 1. The row labeled '∞' is for the use of #!.

T_s, the time to serially compute (tak 18 12 6), was 102.1 seconds. T_p is the parallel time for the same computation, on 8 processors. T_s/T_p is the speedup. For each dynamic partition depth, five trials were performed. The number of spawns, transfers, and milliseconds of idle time was averaged.

4.3 Boyer benchmark

We next look at the application of dynamic partitioning to the Boyer benchmark, a small theorem-proving program from [1]. It has two main components, a rewriter and a tautology checker, both of which can be parallelized. The tautology checker is easier to parallelize, but runtime profiling shows that the program spends most of its time in the rewriter, so that is the part we concentrate on.

Without dynamic partitioning, parallel versions of Boyer may experience a "saturation/starvation" problem, in which many needless processes are created during a period when all processors already have significant work to do (saturation), and too few are created when many processors are idle (starvation). When we tried to control process creation by cutting off parallelism based on the height or depth of the computation tree, we were not able to achieve a good speedup. Even with deep cutoffs that caused a lot of spawns, the amount of idle time was still quite large. The reason that rigid partitioning cutoffs are not very useful is that the input to the rewriter can cause the shape of the computation tree to be unbalanced for some subexpressions, and balanced for others.

However, when we used dynamic partitioning, the saturation/starvation problem virtually disappeared, because dynamic partioning only requires a roughly balanced computation tree. With dynamic partioning, during a computation, excess idle cycles tend to cause more processes to be spawned, which in turn tends to cause fewer idle cycles. This dynamic interplay between idleness and process creation is one of the most interesting features of the method.

Our modifications to the Boyer code in [1] were fairly minimal, and are shown in figure 1. One special variable, temp-temp, was made lexical, because it was only used locally. This avoided the problems caused by possible sharing of a global variable, and sped up the program's execution in Qlisp, in which special variable access is slower than lexical variable access, due to deep binding. The other special variable in the program, unify-subst, should probably be made an argument to the functions that use it. However, to make the changes as small as possible, we rebound it to nil in rewrite-with-lemmas. This makes its uses correct in a deep binding system.

```
(defun rewrite-args (lst)
  (cond ((null lst)
         nil)
        ((null (cdr lst)) (cons (rewrite (car lst)) nil))
        ;; Dynamic partitioning
        (t #3?(cons (rewrite (car lst))
                    (rewrite-args (cdr lst))))))


(defun rewrite-with-lemmas (term lst)
  (cond ((null lst)
         term)
        (t (let ((unify-subst nil))
             (declare (special unify-subst))
             (cond ((one-way-unify term (cadr (car lst)))
                    (rewrite (apply-subst unify-subst (caddr (car lst)))))
                   (t (rewrite-with-lemmas term (cdr lst)))))))))

;;;; Tautology is a fairly small part of the computation.
(defun tautologyp (x true-lst false-lst)
  (cond ((truep x true-lst)
         t)
        ((falsep x false-lst) nil)
        ((atom x)
         nil)
        ((eq (car x) (quote if))
         (cond ((truep (cadr x) true-lst)
                (tautologyp (caddr x) true-lst false-lst))
               ((falsep (cadr x) false-lst)
                (tautologyp (cadddr x) true-lst false-lst))
               ;; Always create processes
               (t #!(and (tautologyp (caddr x)
                                      (cons (cadr x)
                                            true-lst)
                                      false-lst)
                         (tautologyp (cadddr x)
                                     true-lst
                                     (cons (cadr x)
                                           false-lst)))))))
        (t nil)))
```

Figure 1: Changes to Boyer benchmark

Depth	Speedup	Average # Spawns	Average # Transfers	Idle Time
1	6.76	7737	2235	1118
2	6.96	9898	1473	631
3	6.91	14832	1270	561
4	6.77	20312	1280	562
5	6.81	27775	1280	558
6	6.68	33990	1237	546
7	6.67	41237	1255	562
8	6.57	46958	1246	542
⋮				
∞	6.38	53774	1253	547

Table 2: Boyer benchmark results on 8 processors

Processes are created at two points: in `rewrite-with-lemmas`, where the figure shows dynamic partitioning with a queue depth of 3, and in `tautologyp`, where we create all possible processes. (As mentioned above, `tautologyp` is not a major part of the overall runtime, but it is enough that we don't want it be run sequentially.)

We used the testing function provided with the Boyer benchmark, which has a sequential running time of 16.7 seconds. The results of our parallel version are shown in table 2. We varied the dynamic spawning depth from 1 to 8 (after which the results started to flatten out), and performed three trials at each depth.

These results are fairly encouraging. Increasing the queue depth from 1 to 2 made a small improvement in performance; after that, the additional overhead due to extra spawning slows us down.

5 Analysis of dynamic partitioning

The behavior of the programs that we tested led us to investigate the dynamic partitioning method in more detail, in order to determine whether the reduced amount of process creation could be predicted. For a somewhat limited class of programs, we have succeeded in explaining the behavior of dynamic partitioning.

5.1 Process creation behavior

We will analyze program executions represented by computation trees. This is not a fully general programming model, but it is what we understand at this point. Computation trees correspond to programs where each potential process has at most one point at which it can create child processes. Furthermore, for now we assume that these process creation points are binary, i.e., the parent process creates two children and waits for them to finish; or, equivalently, the parent creates one child, does a second computation on its own, and then waits for the child to finish.

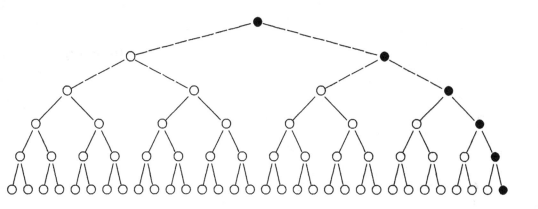

Figure 2: $O(h)$ partitioning when there is no interference

The tree corresponding to such a computation contains a node for each potential process. Its children are the processes that it can create. Several examples of trees appear as figures later in this paper.

As mentioned, each processor has a separate queue into which it adds processes that it creates, and from which it removes processes when it is idle. If an idle processor's own queue is empty, it cycles among the queues of other processors and will remove a process from one of those.

At each partitioning decision, a processor checks to see if its own queue is empty. If so, it creates the two subprocesses, putting one in the queue and running one itself, as described above. If the queue is non-empty, however, it does not create the new processes. Because of our assumption of binary computation trees, this implies that the queue will never have more than one process in it.

Suppose we are given a computation tree of height h satisfying the above assumptions, and execute it using our dynamic partitioning method on p processors. The computation starts with all queues empty and all processors idle, except for one processor that is executing the topmost node of the tree.

Consider a processor that is idle at some point in the computation. It removes a process from either its own queue or the queue of another processor. This process is either a subtree of the original computation tree, or it is the continuation of a process that was suspended waiting for one of its children to finish. For now, let us just consider the first case; later we will account for the resumption of suspended processes.

When the execution of this process begins, the processor's queue will be empty, because we assumed the processor was previously idle. (If its queue was not empty when the processor became idle, we will have made it empty by removing the process that was there—recall that there is never more than one process on a processor's queue.) Therefore, the partitioning test in the topmost node of the tree will be true, and that node will create subprocesses for its children. Let us assume without loss of generality that whenever a node creates subprocesses, it puts its right child tree onto its queue and the processor continues with the evaluation of its left child.

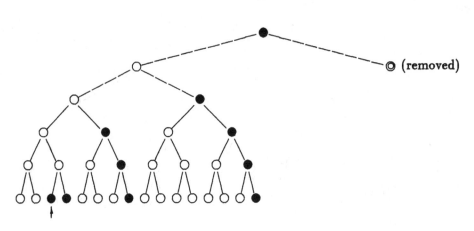

Figure 3: $O(h^2)$ partitioning when there is interference

As long as all of the processors are busy, the processes that they create are all added to and removed from their own queues; none are taken from other processors' queues. This bounds the number of processes created as shown in the following lemma.

Lemma 5.1 *If a tree of height h is executed entirely on one processor, then $O(h)$ processes are created during its execution.*

Figure 2 shows the top part of a computation tree. Let h be the height of this tree. The processor that executes the root node of this tree will execute the entire tree, as long as no other processor removes processes from its queue during the computation. In this case, the dark circles indicate those processes that decide to create subprocesses for their children, and light circles mark those that do not. No processes are created while the left child of the root node is evaluated, because the right child of the root remains on the queue. When the processor finishes with the left child of the root and becomes idle, it removes this process from its queue, and creates its right child process because the queue is now empty. Continuing in this way, it creates one process for each level in the tree, for $O(h)$ process creations altogether. $\square$

The rate of process creation can be higher when processors remove processes from each others' queues. For this case we show the following.

Lemma 5.2 *While a processor is executing a tree of height h, each time a process is removed from its queue $O(h^2)$ processes are created.*

Figure 3 shows what happens if another processor removes a process from the queue while a processor is evaluating a tree. In this example, the right child of the root node has been removed before the evaluation of the left half of the tree is finished. The arrow points to the next node that will make a partitioning decision. Since the queue is now empty, a process is created, and (assuming this process is not removed by another processor) it will be executed on the original processor at its normal time. When it finishes, however, the queue is again empty and the next partitioning decision creates a process. The darkened nodes in the figure indicate the "cascade" of processes that is created as a result of the original right child's removal.

The cascade consists of a number of "branches," each of which starts one level higher in the tree than the previous branch, and extends down the right side of a subtree. When all of the work in such a subtree is finished, the program returns to the parent node of the subtree, which has now finished its left child and begins work on its right child. At this point the processor's queue is empty, so $O(h)$ processes are created during the execution of the right child. There may be as many as h branches, leading to the $O(h^2)$ bound. $\square$

The removal of a process from the queue by another processor will be called a "transfer," to distinguish it from a processor removing a process from its own queue.

We will now derive an asymptotic upper bound on the total number of processes created during the execution of a tree of height h. All subtrees of this tree have height less than h, so using h in place of the actual height of any subtree will still give an upper bound. Each tree that causes $O(h)$ process creations as described in Lemma 5.1 must at some time have been transferred from another processor's queue, and thus causes $O(h^2)$ additional process creations. The $O(h^2)$ term dominates the $O(h)$ term, so the total number of processes created is just $O(h^2)$ multiplied by the number of transfers. We now compute an upper bound for this quantity.

At any point during the computation, various subtrees of the original computation tree are unevaluated. These must all have height less than h, the height of the original tree. Let H be the maximum height of any potential process that may still be created in the remainder of the computation. H will decrease as the computation progresses and will be 0 at the end.

For each processor i, let H_i be the maximum height of any process that processor i can create before becoming idle. (By "becoming idle," we mean finishing its current process and any process on its queue.) Clearly $H_i < H$ for each i, and $H = \max H_i$, since all potential processes are part of a computation tree being executed or on the the queue of some processor. In order to reduce H by 1, we must reduce H_i by 1 in each processor i for which $H_i = H$.

To illustrate using figure 2, if the bottom level shown has height 1, then $H_i = 4$ after the process at the root node has created its children, because those children (whose height is 5) can create processes of height 4. During the evaluation of the left half of the tree, H_i remains 4. If a process is transferred as in figure 3, then H_i becomes 3 since this is now the largest height of any process that can be created. This is one way in which H_i can be reduced by 1 in a processor.

However, not every transfer causes H_i to be reduced by 1. A processor in the cascade situation shown in figure 3 is creating many small processes, and if one of these is transferred, H_i will not change. We need to determine how often this can occur before H_i is guaranteed to be reduced.

Lemma 5.3 *At most p^2h transfers are required to reduce the quantity $H = \max H_i$ by 1.*

Figure 4 shows what happens when some of the processes in the "cascade" are transferred. At most one process along each branch of the cascade can be transferred, because for each branch, the first process to be transferred carries with it all of the processes

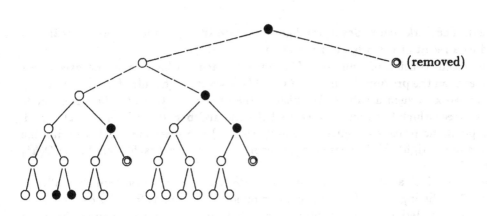

Figure 4: Multiple transfers

that remain to be created along that branch. Therefore, after at most h transfers, we can be sure that H_i has been reduced by 1 in the processor under consideration.

There are at most p processors for which $H_i = H$, and H_i must be reduced by 1 in each of them. Let us call these the "significant" processors. There are also at most p processors removing processes from them. Each of these cycles among the other processors whenever it becomes idle. Therefore, at least one out every p^2 transfers takes place from one of the significant processors. Furthermore, at least one out of every h of these reduces H_i in a significant processor, as explained above. □

Suspension and resumption of processes can be handled in a way does not affect the amount of process creation. Under the assumptions we have made, a process will only suspend its execution when it has created processes for its children, finished execution of the left child, and cannot run the right child because it has been transferred to some other processor. The parent process is then suspended, and resumed when the child has finished execution. Meanwhile, the processor on which the parent was running becomes idle and tries to transfer a process from another processor's queue.

When the child finishes execution, the parent process is resumed. Rather than try to continue it on the processor that it originally ran on (which may now be running some other process), it can be resumed on the processor that was running the child, since this processor is now idle. This results in runtime behavior that is essentially the same as if the original processor had continued running the parent process. In each case, the processor's queue is in the same state (empty) after the child process has finished.

We can now tie the lemmas we have proved into the following result.

Theorem 5.4 *Under the assumptions made thus far, the total number of processes created, in executing a tree of height h, is $O(h^4 p^2)$.*

Since the initial value of H is h, and H is reduced by 1 after every $p^2 h$ transfers, the total number of transfers is bounded by $p^2 h^2$ since then H will be 0 and the computation will be done.

And since each transfer can cause $O(h^2)$ processes to be created, the total number of processes created is $O(h^4 p^2)$. □

5.2   Extending the basic result

Theorem 5.4 is based on several assumptions, which we will now show can be removed with little or no change in the conclusion.

We first consider a generalization of the partitioning method. Instead of creating a process only when the current processor's queue is empty, which results in the queue always having either 0 or 1 processes in it, let us consider having a higher bound on the number of processes in the queue.

Lemma 5.5 *If a tree of height h is executed entirely on one processor, with processes created whenever the length of the queue is less than c, for some constant c, then the number of processes created is $O(h^c)$.*

The case $c = 1$ corresponds to lemma 5.1. For larger values of c, after the root node has spawned its right child, the execution of the left half of the original computation tree behaves just as a tree of height at most $h - 1$ with a bound of $c - 1$ on the queue length. Then the right child is removed from the queue and executed, so the right half of the tree, whose height is at most $h - 1$, is executed with a bound of c on the queue size. If $S(c, h)$ is the maximum number of processes created for any c and h, then

$$
\begin{aligned}
S(c, 0) &= 0 \\
S(0, h) &= 0 \\
S(c, h) &= 1 + S(c - 1, h - 1) + S(c, h - 1)
\end{aligned}
$$

The solution to this recurrence is the sum

$$
S(c, h) = \binom{h}{c} + \binom{h}{c - 1} + \cdots + \binom{h}{1},
$$

which implies $S(c, h) = O(h^c)$. □

Lemma 5.2 is also affected when up to c processes can be present in each processor's queue. If d of these processes are removed by other processors, then the processor in question can create a "cascade" of $O(h^{d+1})$ new processes. The worst case, therefore, is when $d = c$ and $O(h^{c+1})$ processes can be created.

Theorem 5.6 *If processes are created whenever the current size of the queue is less than c, then the total number of processes created in executing a tree of size h is $O(h^{c+3} p^2)$.*

As in the proof of theorem 5.4, at most $p^2 h^2$ processes are transferred altogether. Each of these causes $O(h^{c+1})$ other processes to be created, and the product of these factors is the desired bound. As in theorem 5.4, this term dominates the $O(h^c)$ processes that are created even if no processes are transferred. □

We have also assumed that child processes are created just two at a time. Suppose that, instead, a program creates up to k processes at a time. The quantity k is constant for any program, because the language constructs we are considering, such as qlet,

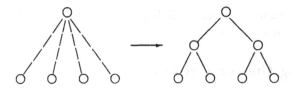

Figure 5: Transforming the creation of multiple processes

do not provide a way of creating a variable number of processes at one time. Such a program therefore corresponds to a computation tree in which each node has at most k children.

The analysis of this situation depends on whether a single partitioning decision is made once to create all k child processes or none; or if a separate decision is made for each child process. The first of these situations is difficult to deal with, because if we create the children whenever the queue size is less than a constant c, we may end up with $c + k - 1$ processes in the queue, whereas our analysis assumed that there are never more than c.

The second situation fits into the framework we have developed, however. If each a node in the computation tree with k children is transformed into a binary tree with the k children as leaf nodes, as illustrated in figure 5, then the new tree satisfies our assumptions. The height of this tree is bounded by a constant factor times the height h of the original tree. If we use balanced binary trees as in the figure, the new height is at most $h \lceil \log_2 k \rceil$.

5.3   Making use of dynamic partitioning

We have shown an upper bound of $O(h^{c+3} p^2)$ process creations when the dynamic partitioning method is used, in a certain restricted class of programs. (Binary computation trees, with at most one partitioning decision in each potential process.) For the method to be effective, the time T_{create} spent creating processes should grow more slowly than the sequential execution time T_{seq}.

Our examples accomplished this by making h, the height of the computation tree, be logarithmic in T_{seq}. This resulted from having balanced or nearly balanced trees. In this case, any polynomial in h will grow more slowly than T_{seq} as the problem size n increases. For any given value of p, the performance of the dynamic partitioning method will approach perfect speedup.

To make use of this result in implementing parallel language constructs, care should be taken to make computation trees balanced whenever possible. This strategy can be built into high-level language constructs that map over elements of a set or sequence, for instance.

6 Conclusions and future work

Low-cost process creation and dynamic partitioning are both useful techniques for improving the performance of parallel programs. We found that a change to the basic process-creation primitive of Qlisp, to avoid the creation of closures, resulted in a greatly reduced cost for process creation, allowing more fine-grained parallelism to be used. Minimizing the number of processes created is still necessary in order to reduce memory usage as well as overhead time, and the dynamic partitioning method accomplishes this for many programs.

Our analysis of dynamic partitioning still only applies to a subset of the programs with which we know the technique is successful, and needs to be extended to more programs. Doing the analysis was useful for more reasons than just to gain an understanding of the method; that understanding has led us to further optimizations of the techniques and we expect it will lead to ways to speed up programs that are currently difficult to parallelize.

An unsolved question is how to choose the dynamic spawning depth appropriately for a given problem. We have found that a maximum depth of just 1 is enough for many programs, but sometimes it does not work well, as in the Takeuchi function. Increasing the maximum queue depth to a small constant solves this problem, but we do not have a good understanding of how to choose this constant, other than by experiment.

Acknowledgements

This work was conducted as part of the Qlisp project, headed by Prof. John McCarthy at Stanford University and Dr. Richard P. Gabriel at Lucid, Inc. Support for this project has come from the Defense Advanced Research Projects Agency under contract N00039-84-C-0211. The second author's research was also supported by a fellowship from the Fannie and John Hertz Foundation.

References

[1] Richard P. Gabriel. *Performance and Evaluation of Lisp Systems*. Computer Systems Series. MIT Press, Cambridge, Massachusetts, 1985.

[2] Richard P. Gabriel and John McCarthy. Queue-based multiprocessing Lisp. In *Conference Record of the 1984 ACM Symposium on Lisp and Functional Programming*, pages 25–44, Austin, Texas, August 1984.

[3] Ron Goldman, Richard P. Gabriel, and Carol Sexton. Qlisp: Parallel processing in Lisp. In *Proceedings of the US/Japan Workshop on Parallel Lisp*, June 1989.

[4] Robert H. Halstead, Jr. Multilisp: A language for concurrent symbolic computation. *ACM Transactions on Programming Languages and Systems*, 7(4):501–538, October 1985.

[5] Joseph S. Weening. Parallel execution of Lisp programs. Technical Report STAN-CS-89-1265, Stanford University, Stanford, California, June 1989.

CONCURRENT SCHEME

Robert R. Kessler and Mark R. Swanson*

Utah Portable A.I. Support Systems Project, Department of Computer Science

University of Utah, Salt Lake City, Utah 84112

Abstract

This paper describes an evolution of the Scheme language to support parallelism with tight coupling of control and data. Mechanisms are presented to address the difficult and related problems of mutual exclusion and data sharing which arise in concurrent language systems. The mechanisms are tailored to preserve Scheme semantics as much as possible while allowing for efficient implementation. Prototype implementations of the resulting language are described which have been completed. A third implementation is underway for the Mayfly, a distributed memory, twisted-torus communication topology, parallel processor, under development at the Hewlett-Packard Research Laboratories. The language model is particularly well suited for the Mayfly processor, as will be·shown.

1 Introduction

The intent in developing Concurrent Scheme (CS) has been to provide an efficient concurrent Lisp for distributed memory multiprocessors, in particular for the Mayfly architecture, a descendent of the FAIM-1 Symbolic Multiprocessing System[DR85]. The approach adopted has been to minimize the addition of new syntax and mechanism and to limit

---

*Work supported by Hewlett-Packard Research Labs - Palo Alto.

changes in familiar Lisp semantics to a few well-defined areas. CS itself is based on Scheme, as defined in *The Revised³ Report on the Algorithmic Language Scheme* (R3RS)[RC86].

The design of the language has been driven by three forces:

1. the expected nature of the computations to be supported;

2. the characteristics of the underlying architecture;

3. a pragmatic requirement of real, demonstrable performance through concurrency.

The structure of a computation in the original FAIM-1, and in the current Mayfly system, is an object-oriented one. The design envisions multiple objects, each completely encapsulating its state, communicating via messages. The design also envisions the existence of multiple threads of control and a sufficiently large population of objects, so that at any one time evaluation can be occurring within multiple objects. This model of computation was chosen both for its desirable programming characteristics of modularity, encapsulation, abstraction, etc. and for its promise of potential concurrency that arises from the relative independence of objects.

The design of the architecture and the design of the programming model are closely intertwined. The distributed nature of the Mayfly system constrains the universe of efficiently implementable mechanisms. For example, a monolithic shared address space across all processors is not practical. On the other hand, we shall see that message passing and its inherent data copying may be quite acceptable.

Finally, the Mayfly is more than an exercise in building a distributed multi-computer. A real goal exists of producing a system that outperforms existing sequential systems utilizing similar technology.[1] Scheme was the Lisp dialect selected because its compactness and constrained set of language features provide the potential for an efficient uniprocessor implementation and for a distributed implementation. Also to this end, certain language features have been included in or excluded from Concurrent Scheme largely because of their effects on global efficiency of the language implementation.

---

[1] Actually, the goal is to outperform uniprocessors using faster/more expensive circuit technology with a Mayfly system constructed from a large number of less-costly/slower components.

In the first section, Concurrent Scheme's reliance on closures is discussed. In the following section, new mechanisms are described and motivated and the deviations from standard Scheme semantics are likewise described and motivated. The next section discusses specification of concurrency and synchronization. The fourth section addresses the existing implementations, their particular strengths and weaknesses. In the final section, the Mayfly architecture and its suitability for supporting Concurrent Scheme are described.

2 Threads and Closures

CS provides for the creation of multiple threads of control; the procedure make-thread, given a function object as an argument, will create a new thread that will apply that function to the rest of its arguments. Make-thread is similar to the *future* construct[BH77, HJ85]. The new thread is not necessarily run immediately, so make-thread returns an object called a placeholder[Mil87] as soon as the new thread is created. The creating process can then continue, using the placeholder *in place of* the value that make-thread will eventually return. Unlike *future*, make-thread cannot be wrapped around any arbitrary form, but rather functions like apply. The reason for this difference will become clear later in this section.

Concurrent Scheme relies on the *closure* as its primitive for object-oriented programming. A closure exhibits those features of an object that we deem most important: pairing of computational methods with an associated instance of state (the closure's environment) and encapsulation of that state by the lexical scoping of the environment variables. These features do not present what is commonly thought of as a complete object system, but do provide the core upon which an object system can be built.

A further consideration in concentrating upon closures as a key mechanism in Concurrent Scheme is that closures would have to be supported in a consistent manner in any event. In a language such as Scheme, environments can be nested to arbitrary depths, with sharing occurring at different depths. The lifetimes of these environments is, however, are determined dynamically rather than statically, due to the existence of closures. Introducing the ability to create new threads of control at arbitrary levels in these environments introduces an expanded need to preserve and share environments.

```
(define foo
  (lambda (n)
    (let ((m nil))
      (touch (future (set-! m (bar n))))
      m)))
```

Consider the function foo; note that the future construct, rather than make-thread has been used. When foo creates a new thread to evaluate (set! m (bar n)), the environment defining m must be captured in order for the set! to produce the correct side effect, for bar to receive the proper argument, and for the function to return the correct value.[2] In effect, an implicit closure has been generated to capture this environment.

Concurrent Scheme limits the specification of concurrency to function application. A legal formulation of foo in CS would be:

```
(define foo
  (lambda (n)
    (let ((m nil))
      (set! m (touch (make-thread bar n)))
      m)))
```

No closure need be produced in this formulation, since the arguments to make-thread are evaluated in the existing environment before make-thread is invoked. Thus, the problem of environment preservation for concurrency is removed. Real programs are more complex than this simple example. Should the new thread need to share an environment with an existing thread, using explicitly created closures as the functional argument to make-thread can achieve the desired effect, as in the following version of foo[3].

---

[2] Touch is a system function that blocks the current thread until the thread created by future completes. The value of touch is the value of its argument.

[3] This example also results in deadlock in CS, as will be shown in the next section.

```
(define foo
  (lambda (n)
    (let ((m nil))
      (touch (make-thread (lambda () (set! m (bar n)))))
      m)))
```

We have taken *implicit* instances of closures and made them explicit. As the following section will show, considerable effort has been expended to rationalize closure behavior in a distributed, concurrent environment. Having spent this effort on an object-like mechanism, introducing and supporting a competing object mechanism would be both redundant and wasteful.

3   Domains

Any concurrent programming system with shared, mutable data must offer mechanisms for mutual exclusion. Earlier parallel Lisps, such as MultiLisp[HJ85] and MultiScheme[Mil87] depend on explicit specification and use of locks by the applications programmer. Qlisp [GM84] provides both locks and closures with queues. While locks provides the programmer with almost unlimited flexibility and precision in specifying mutual exclusion, three factors motivate against using this model for CS. First, the commonly used technique of sharing of structure within Lisp data objects is highly dynamic — so much so that Lisp programmers rarely think about it. This sharing can obscure the true boundaries of mutually exclusive operations and may make it impossible to actually utilize the precise control which user-specified locks appear to offer. Second, on general purpose architectures, even a highly tuned implementation of locks will result in an operation that is quite costly, relative to other constructs in the language such as function call or constructing a simple data object like a cons cell. Thus, use of locks to provide fine-grained mutual exclusion is likely to provide only the illusion of fine control. Third, we wished to provide a programming environment that was largely similar to the sequential environments programmers are familiar with. The need to specify locks around accesses to shared data is a direct violation of this goal.

3.1 Mutual Exclusion

A domain is an entity containing mutable data, specifically in the form of closure environments. It has the property that at most one thread of control can execute within ("occupy") it at any time. The name derives from the domain construct in Hybrid [Nie87]. The mechanism is also very similar to Hoare's monitor [Hoa74], but with modifications to address the needs of a highly dynamic language operating in a truly concurrent environment. It provides a guarantee of *mutual exclusion*. Other threads needing to execute within an *occupied* domain are queued outside the domain by the runtime system. In a CS program, *all* computation occurs within these monitor-like objects; i.e., mutual exclusion is the norm.

```
(define foo
  (lambda (n)
    (let ((m nil))
      (touch (make-thread (lambda () (set! m (bar n)))))
      m)))
```

This example from the previous section was noted as resulting in deadlock. The behavior responsible for this outcome is easily explained. The initial thread creates a new thread and proceeds immediately to wait for that thread's completion. In waiting, the initial thread continues to "occupy" the current domain. The new thread, which must also execute in that domain, cannot gain entry and can never begin execution, let alone complete.

A domain is created by calling the procedure make-domain. Make-domain requires at least one argument, a function object. It creates a new domain, *enters* that domain, and applies the function object to the remaining arguments, if any. The value of that application is the value returned by make-domain. Note in particular that domains are not hierarchical; the new domain is in no sense "contained" within the domain that caused its creation.

This behavior is also similar to that of the qlambda construct of Qlisp, which creates a closure with an associated queue and a guarantee of mutual exclusion. A domain's specification of mutual exclusion is more complete than that of qlambda, because the mutual exclusion is a characteristic of entire environments contained within the domain rather than just being an attribute of a particular closure.

```
(define (foo x)
  (let ((state (list x)))
    (cons (qlambda t (arg)
            (set! state (cons arg state)))
          (qlambda t (arg)
            (set-car! state arg)))))
```

In this example[4], the pair of closures resulting from the qlambda's each has its own queue, but since they both access the same environment variable, state, the consistency of that variable is not protected by the qlambda construct.

```
(define (foo x)
  (let ((state (list x)))
    (cons (lambda (arg)
            (set! state (cons arg state)))
          (lambda (arg)
            (set-car! state arg)))))
```

This version of foo is simply standard Scheme syntax. The domain discipline of CS guarantees mutual exclusion for both closures, since they *must* exist in the same domain and only one thread can execute in that domain at any given time.

---

[4] Qlisp is actually based on Common Lisp; the example uses Scheme syntax. The first argument of qlambda is a concurrency control device which can be ignored for our purposes here.

In addition, the domain "operationally" encapsulates data; data that "enters" or "leaves" a domain is *copied*, not passed by reference. When a domain is created by calling the procedure **make-domain**, the first argument, the function object, is applied in the new domain to *copies* of the remaining arguments, if any. A *copy* of the value of that application is the value returned by **make-domain**.

3.2 Closures

Domains are not first-class objects; references to them are indirect. A program can create domains and can invoke a closure existing within a domain. To maintain a domain as "reachable" or "live," a program must maintain a live pointer to a closure in that domain. This in turn implies that the function object supplied to **make-domain** must return a closure if the domain is to remain reachable.

```
(define (make-collection)
  (let ((state ()))
    (lambda (method-name . args)
      (cond ((eq? method-name 'add)
             (set! state (cons (car args) state))
             '())
            ((eq? method-name 'contents)
             state)))))

(set! a-collection
  (make-domain make-collection))
```

Here an invocation of **make-domain** returns a closure existing within a newly created domain. As long as a-collection, or some other reachable location, retains the value returned by **make-domain**, that new domain will remain "live." When no reachable location contains that object, the domain itself is no longer reachable and will be garbage collected.

This close interaction between closures and domains is entirely intentional. In CS, all closures exist within domains. A stronger condition exists: a closure's entire environment exists within some specific domain. An implication of this is that closures that share an environment, even if the sharing is partial, must exist in the same domain. This implication is transitive. The mutual exclusion provided by the domain is sufficient to provide exclusive access to environment variables shared by multiple closures. Since closures represent the "methods" for primitive "objects" in CS, this encapsulation of closures within domains makes invocation of methods in CS atomic by default.

3.3 Copying Semantics

CS's domain mechanism goes beyond simple monitors, `qlambda`'s, and Hybrid's domains in that domain boundaries are also the boundaries at which copying semantics is specified to hold. This congruence is reasonable, considering that mutual exclusion is normally specified to ensure consistent access to and modification of data objects. Exporting pointers to the structured data of a domain would void the utility of the mutual exclusion provided by the domain.

In the `collection` object of the example above, the `contents` method returns the list which contains the object's state. Were the expression (a–collection 'contents) evaluated immediately after the expression that created the `collection` object, the result of that expression would be a copy, in the current domain, of the list contained in the `collection` object.

This use of copying semantics for interactions between domains is the most far-reaching divergence of CS semantics from those of Scheme. A domain interacts with another domain by invoking, as a normal function call, a gateway object that corresponds to a closure in the other domain. The arguments passed to the gateway and the results returned through it are *copied* from one domain to the other. Unless otherwise specified, copying preserves structure sharing. Closures, however, are not really copied. Instead we create and pass gateway objects. There are three motivations for this use of copying semantics, one at the language level and the other an implementation consideration:

Encapsulation – At the language level, we view the closure as a form of object. An object here is simply some state, or data, with related behavior and an exported interface. One "virtue" of these objects is the encapsulation of the state of the object. This encapsulation is an artifact of the lexical scoping of the closure's environment variables. Complete encapsulation can only be guaranteed by ensuring that not only names, but the structure of the closure's component objects be contained. Placing these objects (closures) within domains ensures this complete encapsulation, since only *copies* of the state variables can leave the domain (and hence the closure).

Distributed Systems – Since our target architecture falls into the class of distributed systems, a choice arises between managing external data pointers or copying data between processors. For a variety of complexity and performance reasons, we have chosen to copy data between processors. Physical placement of objects onto particular processors may differ between different executions of an application. As a result, copying that was simply an artifact of the placement of interacting objects would potentially yield different results with different placement strategies. Hence we chose to impose copying semantics as a language feature at the domain level.

Predictability – Interactions between separate domains entail possible scheduling activities. The scheduling characteristics are generally not part of the language definition. It is not possible, in the general case, for a programmer to predict the order of evaluation of independent threads. This means that between the time the invocation of a closure in a different domain is initiated and the time that evaluation actually occurs, the state of the invoking domain could have changed. This could occur if the invocation was the result of `make-thread` or by use of `delegate` (see Section 3.8). If pointers to structured data were passed as arguments, this unpredicatbility of actual time of use of the arguments would, without explicit synchronization by the programmer, lead to unpredictable results. *Copying* the arguments preserves their values at the time of closure invocation. A similar argument can be made regarding return values.

Although we have introduced copying semantics at the inter-domain level, CS is not intended to be a purely functional language, even at that level. The objects themselves can be, and are, shared, albeit in a mutually exclusive manner. This sharing is accomplished through the exported interface, which in CS is defined in terms of closures. Thus, when a closure is transmitted from one domain to another, it cannot be copied, since this would be tantamount to copying the entire object and would preclude sharing of objects. Rather, the closure is transformed into a gateway, which is an executable object that implements monitor-like access to the shared closure. There is a further operational characteristic of gateways: in determining the domain in which to evaluate a form, they ensure that control travels to the location of data, so that control never acts upon remote data.

As a result of the imposition of copying semantics on inter-domain transactions, it can be guaranteed that no pointers to a domain's mutable structured data exist outside of that domain. Likewise, if a pointer to mutable data is found within a domain, it points to that domain's data. These "invariants" have significant impacts on other language features, notably global variables and storage management.

3.4   Global Values

Another major divergence from standard Lisp semantics involves CS's treatment of global values. The combined effects of copying semantics and a distributed implementation result in severe constraints on the use of globals.

As with all other structured data items, the values of globals must exist within some domain. A distinguished domain exists that contains all global values. The language supports only single assignment of global values.[5] The language does not *enforce* the single-assignment discipline; i.e., subsequent assignments can be performed, but the language does not define the results for such assignments. The language also specifies, and again does not enforce, that global values should not be destructively modified.

These restrictions are necessary to maintain the invariant stated at the end of the

---

[5] At the time the assignment is performed, the value is copied into the distinguished domain, maintaining the invariant of the last section.

previous section, that a domain completely encapsulates pointers to its mutable data. Since globals are not mutable, it is acceptable to have pointers to global data within a domain; likewise, the immutability of globals guarantees that a global value cannot be changed to contain a pointer to some domain's private data.

The distributed nature of CS also serves to motivate against multiple assignments to global variables. Current implementations employ broadcast of global values to replicated symbol tables on each of the physical processors. Thus, for shared, read-only data structures, fast local references are provided.[6] A correct implementation of multiple assignments would require serialization of "simultaneous" assignments to the same variable. This would require global synchronization mechanisms that the design of CS has purposely avoided.

3.5 Storage Allocation and Reclamation

A side effect of the complete encapsulation of mutable data is that storage allocation and garbage collection can be limited to the scope of individual domains. This reduces the size, scope, and latency of garbage collections, since collections become strictly local to the current domain. The roots of the collection are limited to the stacks of any threads that might contain pointers into the domain[7] and the list of potentially live closures that have been exported to other domains. Global synchronization for allocation and garbage collection of normal Scheme data structures is unnecessary.

Garbage collection must address exported closures, of course. Export information is kept externally to the domain and is managed on a reference count basis. Therefore, although garbage collection does not entail any global synchronization, it often results in message passing to maintain the reference count of other domains' exported objects.

---

[6] Read access time to globals in CS is identical to that in sequential Scheme.

[7] Note the use of the plural for threads; this apparent violation of the rule of mutual exclusion is addressed in Section 3.8.

3.6 Open Semantic Issues

Standard Scheme does not include dynamic, or "special," variable bindings. CS, with its previously mentioned constraints on global variables, provides no support whatever for dynamic variables.

One major facility that is not yet provided is fully general continuations. The distributed nature of CS implies that the representation of a continuation is distributed. At a minimum, the continuation includes the stack(s) associated with a thread, portions of which exist on each node visited by a thread. Full continuations, while not conceptually difficult, promises to be an expensive facility.

The current error handling facilities are rudimentary at best. Scheme specifies little in this respect, so we have turned to Common Lisp for a mechanism. Limited forms of *catch* and *throw* are supported. A special error value is provided to communicate an error termination of a remote procedure invocation. No facilities currently exist for pruning task trees descended from error-producing branches.

3.7 Concurrency

The potential for concurrency exists when multiple threads of control exist and those threads are executing in *different* domains. Other factors must be considered to determine whether physical concurrency will actually be realized. One factor is the physical placement of the domains on nodes within the system; this is discussed in Section 5. Another factor is the interaction of the various threads and their "footprint" within the space of domains. When a thread executing in one domain invokes a closure residing in another domain, the thread will execute in (and "occupy") that other domain if it is not currently occupied; otherwise it will wait to enter that domain. What about the invoking closure's domain? That domain will remain occupied while the thread is executing, and while it is waiting to execute, if that case occurs, in the other domain. The thread's "footprint" covers all of the domains that it simultaneously occupies.

```
(define (first-fn-maker)
  (let ((other-domain (make-domain second-fn-maker 'second-fn)))
    (lambda (x)
      (other-domain x))))


(define (second-fn-maker name)
  (lambda (x)
    (display name)
    (newline)
    (display x)
    (newline)))


(let ((first-fn (make-domain first-fn-maker)))
  (first-fn 'some-argument))
```

In this example, we start by creating a new domain that contains and returns just
one closure. This closure is saved in the variable first-fn. Within that closure the
variable other-domain is bound to another closure residing in another newly created
domain. When first-fn is invoked, the current thread of control enters the domain
containing first-fn. This domain is now *occupied*; until the call on first-fn returns,
no other thread can enter that domain. Now, in the body of first-fn, the closure stored
in other-domain is invoked. The current thread enters the domain in which this second
closure resides, occupying it, too. After displaying the variable name and the argument
x, the second closure returns. Its domain is now "unoccupied." The first closure likewise
returns, rendering its domain unoccupied, too.

Pairs (or groups) of threads interacting in the same domains must take care to avoid
deadlock. Delegate (see Section 3.8 is one way minimize this situation). A single thread
executing in several domains generally can not cause deadlock; an exception is described
in Section 6. The constraint that only a single thread may occupy a domain does not
preclude a thread from re-entering a domain multiple times without intervening exits
from the domain. At creation, a thread is assigned a unique, system-wide identifier. Using

this identifier, the runtime system determines whether a thread attempting to enter an occupied domain is actually the thread currently occupying it. In that case, the thread is allowed to enter, even if other threads are queued waiting to enter.

3.8 Delegation

There are times when maintaining the regimen of a thread occupying a domain from closure invocation until return from that closure is too restrictive. The function delegate provides a way for a thread to leave the current domain without exiting the procedure through the normal return-unwinding route. Delegate takes at least one argument, a function object, and applies it to the rest of the arguments, if any. Before the application occurs, however, the thread "leaves" the current domain, causing it to be unoccupied, so that some other thread may enter the domain. The thread then performs the application, observing the normal rules for entering new domains (or the original domain, if the function object specifies that domain); Section 4.1 describes how a thread's new location is determined. When the function object returns, the thread must re-enter the original domain; this re-entry once again observes the rules of exclusive access to the domain. The thread may well be queued waiting to re-enter the domain. The return value of delegate is the value returned by the function object.

```
(define (manager workers)
  (let ((jobcount 0))
    (do ((w workers (cdr w)))
        ((null? (cdr w)) (set! (cdr w) workers)))
    (lambda (job)
      (let ((worker (car workers))
            res)
        (set! workers (cdr workers))
        (set! res (delegate worker job jobcount))
        (set! jobcount (+ jobcount 1))
        res)))))
```

The **manager** procedure, when called with a list of "worker" closures, circularizes the list and returns a closure that, given a "job" to be done, assigns that "job" in a round-robin fashion to the next worker. The "manager" uses **delegate** to make the assignment, so that it is immediately available to respond to another request to assign another job. Note that the manager has been constructed in such a way that its state is consistent at the point **delegate** is used, since another thread may enter the manager before the delegated one returns. Also note that jobcount is only incremented after the delegated thread re-enters the domain. Suppose that **worker** returns as its value its third argument, in this example jobcount. It is not necessarily the case that **res** and jobcount will be equal after the return from **delegate**, since other threads may have entered and completely transmitted the procedure in the meantime.

4 Specifying Concurrency and Synchronization

In CS, concurrency is *explicitly* specified by the programmer through the action of creating a new thread of control to evaluate some function. The related syntax is (**make-thread** <procedure> . <args>), which is similar to **apply**, except that the application occurs in a new thread. Make-thread was introduced earlier, but its behavior is somewhat more complex than indicated by that simple exposition. The actual activities it performs are as follows:

- determine from the function object the initial domain of execution for the new thread;

- perform a structure-preserving copy of the arguments, if any, for the function object;

- initiate creation and subsequent scheduling of a new thread;

- create a placeholder to receive the value of the thread's evaluation and return that placeholder.

Each of these activities is explained in more detail in the following sections.

4.1   Initial Thread Location

The domain within which a newly created thread initially executes is determined by the nature of the function argument to make-thread. If the function is not a closure, then the thread will be started in the current domain. The new thread must obey the usual rule of exclusive access, of course, so, in the latter case, it will not start until the thread that created it causes the current domain to become unoccupied (either by returning out of it or by performing a delegate).

If the function is a closure, the new thread will start in the domain that contains the closure. Were every thread to start in the current domain, a new thread would not actually start until its creator left the current domain, severely limiting realizable concurrency.

```
(define (thread-maker closure-list)
  (let ((results #f))
    (do ((c closure-list (cdr c)))
        ((null? c))
      (set! results (cons (make-thread (car c)))))
    (do ((r results (cdr r))
         (ans 0))
        ((null? r) ans)
      (set! ans (+ ans (car r))))))
```

Assume that closure-list is a list of closures in domains other the one where thread-maker is invoked. Further assume that each of these closures will return some integer of interest. After creating the threads and collecting the resulting placeholders, thread-maker proceeds to sum the results. Since + is strict in its arguments, it will block if any of the threads have not completed and returned a value by the time + needs that value. Now consider what would happen if the threads did not start in the other domains, but rather started in the current domain. The computation would deadlock, since the main thread will not leave the thread-maker function (and therefore will obviously not leave thread-maker's domain) until all of the new threads have finished. But the new threads would not start until the main thread left the domain.

4.2   Argument Copying

Make-thread always copies the arguments provided (beyond the first one, the function object). In the case where the function object is a closure residing in another domain, the arguments are copied into that domain in keeping with the copying semantics discussion in Section 3.3. In the case of a non-closure function object, or a closure that resides in the current domain, the arguments are still copied, even though there is no crossing of a domain boundary. This behavior ensures that when the thread starts, its arguments will be unchanged from their values at the time the thread was created. If the actions of the function are intended to produce side-effects to structured data shared with other threads, such data must be accessible in the function's environment rather than being passed as arguments.

4.3   Thread Creation and Scheduling

Make-thread initiates the creation of a new thread. This does not imply anything about when the thread will actually be started, or even when it will be created. It is not necessarily the case that the thread has been created when make-thread has returned, especially in a multi-node system where the thread may actually be created on a different physical node. There is, in fact, no guarantee that the threads created by sequential calls on make-thread will be created or scheduled in that same sequence. Occasionally, some guarantees about *relative* scheduling are useful. Make-acked-thread guarantees that the thread it creates will be scheduled before other threads created in the same target domain by subsequent calls to make-thread by the same originating thread. Suppose two threads called A and B, executing concurrently (necessarily in different domains), both start a number of threads in a third domain using make-acked-thread. The threads started by A will start in the same order that A created them; likewise for those created by B. Nothing, however, is implied or guaranteed about the order of A's children with respect to B's and vice versa.

4.4 Return Value

Since make-thread may return before the new thread has a chance to return a result, a placeholder is "attached" to a thread and this placeholder is returned by make-thread. An alternative procedure, make-orphaned-thread, is provided for use when no result is expected and the thread is created for the side-effects it will produce. The return value of make-orphaned-thread is simply #f and no placeholder is created. This form can be an important optimization tool. Not only are the costs associated with creation and later reclamation of the placeholder saved, but a return of control by the thread is avoided.

4.5 Placeholders

A placeholder is a first class object in CS that can be allocated independently of creation a new thread. The standard procedure make-placeholder will return a new, unresolved placeholder. An unresolved placeholder is one that has not yet been given a value. Attempting to use the value of an unresolved placeholder in a strict operation causes the current thread to block. The blocked thread will wait until the placeholder receives a value, at which time the thread will be allowed to proceed.

Placeholders can receive values in two ways. First, the placeholder associated with a thread by make-thread will receive a value when the thread completes execution. In this case the value of the placeholder is the value returned by the thread. Second, a placeholder may be explicitly given a value by the determine function, which takes two arguments, an unresolved placeholder and the value it is to be given. If the placeholder already has a value, determine signals an error. The programmer can test whether a placeholder has a value using the function determined?. This function takes a single argument, which should be a placeholder. It returns #t if the placeholder has a value or #f if it does not. Note that it is possible to use determine explicitly to set the value of a placeholder associated with a thread. In this case, the thread will cause an error when it completes and an attempt is made to place the return value in the placeholder.

Because they can be separately allocated and explicitly determined and tested, placeholders provide a mechanism for explicit synchronization in CS programs. There is an additional function, touch which explicitly synchronizes on a placeholder. Given a single argument which is an unresolved placeholder, touch causes the current thread to block until the placeholder receives a value. If the argument is a resolved placeholder, touch returns the placeholder's value; if it is any other data type, touch simply returns its argument. Touch is analogous to Common Lisp's identity function, except that it is *strict* in its argument.

```
(define (make-worker obj go-ph done-ph)
  (lambda ()
    (touch go-ph)
    (munge obj)
    (determine done-ph 'done)))


(define (worker-mgr obj-lst)
  (let ((go-ph (make-placeholder))
        (done-phs '()))
    (do ((objs obj-lst (cdr objs)))
        ((null? objs) #f)
      (set! done-phs (cons (make-placeholder) done-phs))
      (make-thread
        (make-domain
          make-worker (car objs) go-ph (car done-phs))))
    (do-managerial-stuff obj-list)
    (determine go-ph 'go)
    (do ((done done-phs (cdr done)))
        ((null? done) #f)
      (touch (car done)))))
```

In this example, make-worker returns a closure that will perform some task after its creator frees it to do so. This delay is achieved by touching the argument go-ph, which should be an undetermined placeholder. After it performs the munge task, it signals completion of the task by (determine done-ph 'done). Worker-mgr creates one worker object for each object in the list passed to it. Each of these workers exists in its own domain (and so can potentially run concurrently with the other workers). In addition, it starts threads for running each of the worker objects. Then it performs some unspecified administrative tasks with the list of objects and finally frees the workers to perform their individual tasks by (determine go-ph 'go). The manager function waits for all the workers to finish by touching the list of placeholders associated with the workers.

Touch has an optional second argument. If this second argument is missing or is #f, then touch behaves as previously described. If the second argument is given and is not #f, then touch will *leave* the current domain unoccupied if it is blocked because the first argument (the placeholder) is unresolved. The motivation for this behavior is similar to that for delegate: the programmer may wish to allow multiple threads to begin some potentially blocking activity within a domain, without excluding other threads. This is an exception to the mutual exclusion rule; hence the syntax requires explicit specification of the exception. As with *delegate*, the programmer is responsible for ensuring the consistency of shared data.

5 Nodes and Generators

CS is designed to run on systems of physically distributed processors or nodes. Several global variables are available to provide the program with information about the configuration of the system. *Pe-self* contains the zero-relative logical node number; it will, of course, differ depending on which node a thread is running on. *Maxpes* is the number of nodes in the system; it will always be greater than zero.

At system startup, each node has (at least) one domain. The function ith-gen, given a non-negative integer argument n, will return a closure residing in the initial domain on node (mod n *maxpes*). This closure is a *generator*. Its purpose is to initiate evaluation on that other node. The generator closure takes its first argument, a function object, and applies it to the rest of the arguments. Its result is the value returned by the application.

Since the generator is a closure, it will enter the domain it resides in *on whatever node the domain exists* just as any other closure. It is usually the case that the function object passed to the generator should not be a closure, since invoking that closure within the generator will entail entering the closure's domain. This is not usually the intended use of a generator. Generators are usually used either to distribute "pure" computations or to create new domains on other nodes.

```
(let ((i (+ *pe-self* 1)))
  (set! a ((ith-gen i) fact 99)))
```

Assume that fact is not a closure, that *maxpes* is greater than 1, and that *pe-self* is 0. This sequence will result in the evaluation of (fact 99) on node 1 within the domain that contains node 1's generator closure. We have here an example of distribution of computation *with no concurrency*, since only one thread is involved. Note that the first assumption is crucial. If fact were a closure, then evaluation of (fact 99) within the generator (and its domain) would in fact entail entry into the domain containing fact, as noted above.

```
(set! i (+ *pe-self* 1))
(set! a (make-thread (ith-gen i) fact 99))
(do-something-else)
(print a)
```

With the same assumptions as before, this sequence not only distributes the computation but contains potential concurrency, since a new thread has been introduced. Do-something-else may execute concurrently with fact provided that node 1 is not busy, node 1's generator is not currently "occupied," and do-something-else takes long enough for fact to be invoked on node 1.

In normal practice, the function argument to the generator is often make-domain. The new domain created by make-domain resides on the node where make-domain is invoked. Thus, generators can be used to spread domains and the closures they contain across the available nodes.

```
(define (worker-mgr obj-lst)
  (let ((go-ph (make-placeholder))
        (done-phs '()))
    (do ((objs obj-lst (cdr objs))
         (node 0 (+ node 1)))
        ((null? objs) #f)
      (set! done-phs (cons (make-placeholder) done-phs))
      (make-thread
        ((ith-gen node)
          make-domain
          make-worker (car objs) go-ph (car done-phs))))
    (do-managerial-stuff obj-list)
    (determine go-ph 'go)
    (do ((done done-phs (cdr done)))
        ((null? done) #f)
      (touch (car done)))))
```

Worker-mgr is the same function used in Section 4.5 except that it now produces potential concurrency. The do-variable node is used in conjunction with ith-gen to spread the workers across the available nodes in a round-robin fashion. The sequence of events for each invocation of make-thread is as follows:

1. the argument to make-thread is evaluated; this results in the next four events;

2. (ith-gen node) returns a closure which is the generator for some node;

3. the generator closure, which resides in its own domain, applies make-domain to the arguments make-worker, (car objs), etc.;

4. make-domain creates a new domain on the same node as the generator, enters that domain, and applies make-worker to the remaining arguments;

5. make-worker returns a closure to make-domain, which returns it to the generator which also returns it; this is the argument to make-thread;

6. **make-thread** creates a thread with initial domain determined by the its argument and which may well be on another node;

7. **make-thread** returns a placeholder.

6   Delay Queues

Although placeholders provide a powerful synchronization device, they are not always appropriate. For instance, it is sometimes desirable that the interacting objects not contain specific synchronization which would limit the generality of their use. Another mechanism, the delay queue[Nie87], is provided that allows methods within an object to control the availability of its methods. A delay queue is similar to a condition variable in the monitor construct[Hoa74]. The function make-delay-queue, given a closure, creates a delay queue and associates it with that closure. The delay queue can be either "open" or "closed." A thread invoking a delay-queue associated closure from outside the closure's domain can only proceed, i.e., enter the domain, if the delay queue is "open." This constraint is *in addition to* the mutual exclusion property of domains. If the delay queue is "closed," the thread will wait *outside the domain* until the delay queue is opened. The thread does not, therefore, occupy the domain, which would prevent other threads from entering it. This is necessary, since a closed delay queue can only be opened by some other closure (method) which contains the closed delay queue in its environment. That is, a thread must be able to enter a domain in order to open a delay queue belonging to that domain.

```
(define (bounded-buffer)
  (letrec
    ((buffer #f)
     (full? #f)
     (get-method
       (make-delay-queue
         (lambda ()
           (set! full? #f)
```

```
                (dqopen put-method)

                (dqclose get-method)

                buffer)))

          (put-method

            (make-delay-queue

              (lambda (val)

                (set! full? #t)

                (set! buffer val)

                (dqclose put-method)

                (dqopen get-method)))))


        (dqclose get-method)

        (dqopen put-method)

        (lambda (m)

          (if (eq? m 'get-method)

            get-method

            (if (eq? m 'put-method)

              put-method

              (error "bounded-buffer: no such method"))))))


(define (producer sink)

  (do () ()

    (sink (produce-a-datum))))


(define (consumer source)

  (do () ()

    (consume-a-datum (source))))


(define (manager)

  (let* ((buf (bounded-buffer))

         (p (make-thread

              (ith-gen 1) producer (buf 'put-method))))
```

```
(c (make-thread

    (ith-gen 2) consumer (buf 'get-method)))))))
```

In this example, the manager function creates a bounded buffer (which, for simplicity's sake is of size one) and two other objects, a producer and a consumer. The manager connects the producer and consumer by passing them the bounded buffer put and get methods, respectively. The buffer performs the necessary synchronization without any "knowledge" of this synchronization in either the producer or consumer. It uses make-delay-queue to cause the two methods (closures) that it exports to be associated with delay queues. It then opens and closes the delay queues as its internal state dictates.

6.1 Delay Queues and Domains

Delay queues are attributes of a domain; this has a number of implications for their use. Their scheduling characteristics are only enforced at domain boundaries. This means that a thread already executing within a domain can invoke a "closed" delay queue/closure and it will not block. Were it to block, the domain would be permanently deadlocked, since the occupying thread would be blocked and no other thread could enter the domain to open the delay queue. If it is necessary for such a thread to observe the delay queue regimen, it should use delegate to leave the domain. before trying to enter the delay queue.

The delay queue primitives (those already mentioned, plus dq-open?) are only valid within the domain containing the closure and associated delay queue. Calling any of these functions with a closure residing in another domain is an error. One implication of this is that control of delay queues can only occur within the domain containing the associated closure. Further, it is not possible to determine the state of a delay queue from outside the domain it resides in; in fact, it is not even possible to find out if it is a delay queue.

7   A Short Example

The following simple example computes factorial in a distributed manner.

```
(define grain-size 10)


;;; Compute a partial range for the factorial.


(define (partial-fact start end product)
  (if (= start end)
    (* end product)
    (partial-fact (- start 1) end (* start product))))


;;; Portion out the work in grain-size chunks


(define fact-aux
  (lambda (low high)
    (if (> (- high low) grain-size)
    (let ((rest
            (make-thread (ith-gen (+ *pe-self* 1))
                          fact-aux low (- high grain-size))))
      (* (partial-fact high (- high (- grain-size 1)) 1)
        (touch rest #t)))
    (partial-fact high low 1)))))


(define (fact n)
  (fact-aux 1 n))
```

The function partial-fact recursively computes the product of the integers in the range start through end (inclusive). Fact-aux is the actual agent of distribution. It partitions the range of (assumed positive) integers passed as arguments: one portion to be passed to partial fact *within the current thread* and the rest to be processed by a new thread on another node (by means of ith-gen). Note the use of touch with its optional second argument; for a sufficiently large range of integers, ith-gen's modulo calculation will eventually wrap around to a node already in use. To avoid deadlock, the domain is left unoccupied so that subsequent threads, whose values will be needed to complete earlier threads, will be available.

8 The Prototype Implementations

8.1 Architectural Support

The decision to avoid implementing external data pointers was based in part on the expectation that concurrent Lisp would always be run on general-purpose processors; that is, on processors with no integral support for runtime detection and resolution of external references. It was expected, however, that support *external to the processor* would be available to absorb some of the cost of communications. This, in fact, is the case with the Mayfly architecture and to a lesser extent with the BBN GP1000.

To date, three different implementations of CS have been produced. They vary in how they utilize the Mayfly model in which each processing element is really a shared memory parallel processor with an Evaluation Processor (EP) which executes the current task and a Message Processor (MP) which is responsible for task management, inter-node message traffic, and message preparation. The first of these is a uniprocessor implementation, which served as a testbed for the basic mechanisms of multiple threads, mutual exclusion, and copying semantics. It remains as a baseline implementation on which initial development and debugging of CS programs can be performed, free from the effects of "true" concurrency. The other two implementations, the BBN GP1000 multiprocessor version and the networked workstation version, both deliver true concurrency but at widely separated points in the spectrum of multiple/cooperating computers. Each implementation has made different contributions to the ongoing development of the CS model.

8.2 The GP1000 Implementation

The GP1000 is a shared memory multiprocessor of the NUMA (non-uniform memory access) variety. As a shared memory machine, it offered the opportunity to experiment with the Mayfly model in which message transmission and reception time, including copying time necessitated by copying semantics, could be overlapped with evaluation of application code. Therefore, we implemented individual PEs as asymmetric pairs of GP1000 nodes, sharing memory. Message passing communication between the MPs was straightforward to implement using shared memory.

Using the GP1000, it has been possible to develop and test the kernel mechanisms for creating, managing, and scheduling threads and performing communications tasks on an MP while concurrently running application code on an EP sharing the same physical memory. We have a high degree of confidence that the large portion of CS support code comprising these mechanisms will perform correctly on the Mayfly architecture when it becomes available, which was the initial motivation for the GP1000 implementation.

While GP1000 is a NUMA machine, the Mayfly PE is an Uniform Memory Access (UMA) machine, and the CS support code is currently tailored for the UMA architecture. As a result, the performance of the current GP1000 implementation is poor and its primary value is as a prototype.

8.3   The Network Implementation

A networked implementation is used for debugging the CS runtime system and to develop parallel application programs in a truly concurrent environment. Although the majority of the software is identical for all of the implementations, the networked version differs markedly from the Mayfly model since we use only one physical processor for each PE. The single processor divides its time between MP tasks and applications code. Communication between PEs is implemented as point-to-point UDP links [FJSW85], with a minimal reliability protocol provided by the CS kernel.

The communication characteristics of the networked version differ from the Mayfly model. Not only is message overhead not offloaded to an MP, but message latency is much higher than in either the GP1000 or the Mayfly architecture. In addition to these direct effects, there are indirect effects. For instance, message passing activity involves a switch to the kernel's context, and potentially can result in another process being run while CS waits. Such context switches will not occur on the Mayfly, and on the GP1000 will never occur *as a side-effect of message passing.* This difference in communications costs has an effect on the granularity of tasks that can be usefully run in parallel.

One useful capability available with the network implementation is the ability to start fully interactive Lisp sessions on each of the remote processors. This allows the application programmer to use the debugging tools provided by Lisp such as trace, backtrace, etc., on each node. Interaction is provided using optional "xterm"[8] windows which are "connected" to each Lisp session using TCP sockets. When xterm windows are not used, only the "root" node is interactive, and output from remote nodes is displayed by sending normal CS messages to the root node. In this way, the remote nodes function more like Mayfly processing elements, waiting for messages to arrive to initiate work. The value of the networked version is in prototyping applications. Its advantages are the common availability of networked workstations and the debugging environment of separate toploops for each physical processor.

9　The Mayfly Architecture

To provide high performance support of Concurrent Scheme, an architecture needs at least the following characteristics:

- low latency, high-bandwidth inter-node communications;

- fast (or overlapped) message preparation, transmission, and receipt;

- fast (or overlapped) task scheduling;

- fast (or overlapped) context switch;

- sufficient memory to hold a reasonable population of tasks;

- sufficient memory bandwidth to support concurrent evaluation and message passing activities.

---

[8] Xterm is the terminal emulator for the X Window System.

The Mayfly architecture[Dav89] is a distributed memory machine consisting of a number of nodes or PEs. Each PE is connected to six of its neighbors in a twisted torus via fast serial lines. Fully configured Mayfly "surfaces" come in a selection of sizes; the first version will be a nineteen PE surface. The Mayfly is scalable in terms of these surfaces; i.e., one could imagine tiling a plane with these nineteen PE surfaces. The Mayfly nodes and interconnect are designed to display the characteristics listed above. Each node is comprised of 9 subsystems:

1. a Post Office chip;

2. a message processor (MP);

3. an evaluation processor (EP);

4. a floating-point coprocessor;

5. a dual-ported data cache;

6. separate instruction caches for each of the two processors;

7. a moderately-sized (8 megabytes) main memory;

8. a custom context cache device.

The Post Office chip[SRD86] is the communications engine connecting each individual PE with six of its neighbors. Together with the topology, it provides the low latency and high-bandwidth necessary to support many distributed, message-passing objects. It provides packet buffering, flow control, and routing services, so the task of message-passing as seen by the rest of the PE consists largely of address calculation (which can be table driven) and packetization/de-packetization.

Each PE is actually an asymmetric shared memory parallel processor with an EP and an MP; both of which are one chip implementations of the HP Precision Architecture. The EP evaluates application code. A task on the EP runs to completion, times out, or requests a service from the MP, such as invocation of a gateway procedure. When the EP cannot continue execution of the current thread for any of these reasons, it performs a context switch and starts another available thread from a queue of threads maintained by the MP. The MP performs system services such as task scheduling, message preparation (including copying) and reception, and driving packets to/from the Post Office chip.

Message preparation includes the overhead of copying values between domains. This is true even for intra-PE domain interactions, so that on a Mayfly system the costs of copying semantics will be absorbed by the MP through the overlap of its execution with that of the EP. The same approach is used to absorb the cost of scheduling.

Achieving fast context switch using general purpose processors is more difficult. Early designs of the Mayfly actually included a second EP; it was intended that the two EP's could alternate roles, one actively processing while the other performed a context switch. This design was considerably more complex, requiring a third instruction cache, a third port to the data cache, switching logic for FP the coprocessor, and inter-EP interrupt logic. The second EP was abandoned in favor of a *context cache*. The context cache (CC) is actually a separate memory module divided into a fixed number of caches. The CC also has a co-processor interface to each of the EP and MP. Through these interfaces, each of the EP and MP can select a particular module which will respond to memory requests lying within a pre-defined context cache address range. Values comprising a task descriptor are assigned addresses in this range. A context switch then reduces to selecting the number of a new context module (presumably from a queue of ready contexts) and making that the current context via the CC coprocessor interface. The CC also implements a cache for the top 128 entries of the control stack.

Adequate memory bandwidth is provided by the combination of caches: separate instruction caches for the EP and MP, the shared data cache, and the CC. In addition to speeding up context switches, the CC serves to diminish demands on data cache and main memory bandwidth, since references to values in the task descriptor and the control stack are serviced by the CC. Furthermore, since contexts need not be saved to/restored from main memory (except in the case of context cache overflow), main memory bandwidth demand is further reduced.

10   Recent Changes

Since the time the workshop was held, Concurrent Scheme has matured. One major area of change has been scheduling and synchronization. The introduction of delay queues was the primary development, with the addition of a version of touch that left the domain unoccupied was a pragmatic addition motivated by certain areas of application (notably non-object oriented applications). The other major development lay in coalescing the two major functions of domains. Originally two kinds of domains were specified: temporal and spatial, which, respectively, addressed the issues of mutual exclusion and copying semantics. Experience in developing applications indicated that copying semantics was generally not specified except in the presence of mutual exclusion; hence, the two kinds of domains are presented as one to users. At the implementation level, spatial domains remain a useful device.

11   Conclusion and Future Work

Make-thread's similarity to *future* make it the least interesting mechanism added in creating Concurrent Scheme. The more pervasive change of copying semantics and the fundamental mechanisms of domains and gateways are the contributions that set Concurrent Scheme apart from previous efforts.

Our main parallel constructs, domains, are small, dynamically-created, monitor-like objects, which provide the basic mutual exclusion mechanism. We are currently tuning the existing implementations and preparing to transport the system to a two PE Mayfly in May 1990.

We have handled the problem of data in a distributed system by specifying mutual exclusion between threads and by copying data sent across domain boundaries. Aside from the major impact of copying semantics, the language supported is standard Scheme.

The most problematic part of our current system is that it requires an understanding of closures and an appreciation for the subtle issues of what syntax leads to creation of closures. It is easy for an application programmers to produce a closed procedure unwittingly by macro expansion (our Scheme does have compile-time macros). Conversely, not all parallelism fits into our model; programmers needing to distribute computation of a non-closed function are forced either to use the generator functions, or to create closed functions based on unused environment's.[9] We are investigating making domains a first-class data type, but the problem remains open.

As noted earlier, the cost of fully-general, structure-preserving copying can be substantial. We are exploring methods to decrease this cost in two ways:

- by providing syntax to specify that structure preservation is not required;

- by providing copiers tailored to types of the arguments and/or result values specific to a particular gateway.

In the longer term, implementation of an object system is envisioned which implicitly uses the CS mechanisms, thereby hiding them from the programmer. Eventually, we plan to create a parallel Utah Common Lisp, but the size of Common Lisp persuades us not to divert our efforts in this direction at the current time.

References

[BH77]   H. Baker and C. Hewitt. *The Incremental Garbage Collection of Processes.* AI Memo AIM-454, MIT AI Laboratory, Cambridge MA, December 1977.

[Dav89]   A. Davis. *The Mayfly Parallel Processing System.* Technical Report HPL-SAL-89-22, Hewlett-Packard Research Laboratory, March 1989.

[DR85]   A. L. Davis and S. V Robison. The Architecture of the FAIM-1 Symbolic Multiprocessing System. In *Proc. IJCAI-85*, pages 32–38, 1985.

[FJSW85] E.J. Feinler, O.J. Jacobsen, M.K. Stahl, and C.A. Ward. *DDN Protocol Handbook, Volume Two, DARPA Internet Protocols.* Sri International, 1985.

[GM84]   R.P. Gabriel and J. McCarthy. Queue-based Multi-processing Lisp. In *Conference Record of the 1984 ACM Symposium on Lisp and Functional Programming*, pages 25–44, August 1984.

---

[9]This practice is suspect, since compiler technology can sometimes optimize away the unneeded environments.

[HJ85]   R.H. Halstead Jr. Multilisp: A Language for Concurrent Symbolic Compu-
           tation. *Transactions of Programming Languages and Systems*, 7(4):501–538,
           October 1985.

[Hoa74]   C.A.R. Hoare. Monitors: An Operating System Structuring Concept. *Com-
           munications of the ACM*, 17(10):549–557, October 1974.

[Mil87]   J. S. Miller. *MultiScheme, A Parallel Processing System Based on MIT
           Scheme*. PhD thesis, Department of Electrical Engineering and Computer
           Science, MIT, August 1987.

[Nie87]   O. M. Nierstrasz. Active Objects in Hybrid. In *Object-Oriented Program-
           ming Systems, Languages, and Applications 1987 Conference Proceedings*,
           pages 243–253, 1987.

[RC86]   J. Rees and W. Clinger. Revised[3] Report on the Algorithmic Language Scheme.
           SIGPLAN Notices, 21(12):37–79, December 1986.

[SRD86]   K. Stevens, S. Robison, and A. L. Davis. The Post Office: Communications
           Support for Distributed Ensemble Architectures. In *Proceedings of the 6th
           International Conference on Distributed Computing Systems*, pages 160–166,
           May 1986.

The Design of Automatic Parallelizers for Symbolic and Numeric Programs*

Williams Ludwell Harrison III and Zahira Ammarguellat

1 Introduction

Parcel is a compiler and run-time system that automatically parallelizes a Scheme program for execution on a shared-memory multiprocessor; it is described at length in [Har89]. Parcel was a success in several respects: its interprocedural analysis makes it capable of extracting high-level parallelism from complex applications; it introduced a number of program transformations that are especially useful in parallelizing symbolic computations; and its run-time system makes good use of multiple procedure versions to achieve parallelism without undue inefficiency. However, Parcel suffers from a software engineering defect common to parallelizing compilers: its intermediate form is complex, and is specific to the source language it accepts, making it impossible to adapt the compiler to a new source language, and difficult to add new passes. This defect, along with the desire to extend the power of Parcel's interprocedural analysis, and to apply the techniques of Parcel to a broad class of programming languages (rather than to a single source language), have motivated the design of Miprac. Miprac is an interprocedural, parallelizing compiler that operates upon a semantically-oriented intermediate form. It attempts to fuse the techniques of Parcel (for symbolic programs) with those developed for Fortran (for numeric programs) in a single compilation system. Programs from a variety of source languages, including Scheme, Common Lisp, C, and Fortran have a straightforward translation to Miprac's intermediate form. Moreover, the intermediate form obeys a number of simple theorems that make it easy to analyze and transform. In this paper we will describe the strengths and weaknesses of Parcel, and outline the design of Miprac in light of our experience with Parcel.

*This work was supported in part by the National Science Foundation under Grant No. NSF MIP-8410110, the U.S. Department of Energy under Grant No. DE-FG02-85ER25001, the Office of Naval Research under Grant No. ONR N00014-88-K-0686, the U.S. Air Force Office of Scientific Research under Grant No. AFOSR-F49620-86-C-0136, and by a donation from the IBM Corportation.

2 Parcel

The input to the Parcel compiler is a sequential Scheme program, and its output is an object code for the Alliant FX/8 or Cedar multiprocessor. The compiler operates in four phases: interprocedural analysis, standard transformations, parallelizing transformations, and code generation. From every procedure of the input program, Parcel produces two code versions, one sequential, one parallel. The Parcel run-time system selects between these versions during execution. The parallel versions are executed when the processors of the target machine are underutilized, and the sequential versions are used when the machine is saturated.

2.1 Strengths

2.1.1 Interprocedural analysis

The technology of automatic parallelization originated with vectorizing Fortran compilers, which were concerned principally with innermost loops, or with loops nested but a few levels deep, and where the nesting was static (that is, where the nesting did not arise because of procedure calling). Interprocedural analysis, if performed at all, was ordinarily done to strengthen dependence analysis of loops, to infer aliasing among parameters, and to fold constants across procedure boundaries, but seldom with the goal of extracting high-level parallelism from a Fortran program. (There are exceptions; see [Tri84, BC86].) For this reason, such compilers are typically quite capable of extracting fine-grained parallelism, but do less well in extracting large-grained, high-level parallelism.

A typical Lisp program contains many more, and much smaller, procedures than its Fortran counterpart, and while it is sensible to extract parallelism from innermost iterative or recursive constructs, it is also apparent that in many an application, the richest source of parallelism is not the innermost level, but intermediate or even outermost layers in the program's control flow. In the presence of side-effects (and both the Scheme and Common Lisp standards permit every variety of side-effect, both upon variables and upon compound data), to extract such parallelism requires an understanding of the interprocedural visibility of side-effects. That is, given a procedure f that directly accesses (uses or modifies) a memory location, we must ascertain to which procedures that call f this access is visible, in order to correctly construct dependence graphs of those calling procedures, so that their control-flow structures can be parallelized.

In Parcel, this is accomplished by an abstract interpretation that monitors the interprocedural movements made by objects, from their points of creation, to the points at which they are used and modified. On the basis of these movements, the analysis reveals to which procedures every (direct) side-effect within a program is visible. In essence, the observation applied by this analysis is the following: the visibility of a side-effect is restricted to the subtree of

```
(define list-of-sums (lambda (1)
   (if (null 1) '()
       (cons (sum (car 1) (counter 0))
             (list-of-sums (cdr 1)))))))
(define sum (lambda (1 ctr)
   (if (null 1) 0
       (begin (sum (cdr 1) ctr)
              (ctr)))))
(define counter (lambda (x)
   (lambda () (set! x (1+ x)) x)))
```

Figure 1: An example of Parcel's interprocedural analysis

computation that contains the lifetime of the object affected. (The interested reader will find this analysis described and proven correct in [Har89].) From this information, Parcel constructs dependence graphs of individual procedures, and thereafter parallelizes their control-flow structures regardless of whether they are "outermost" or "innermost" procedures (indeed, such a characterization may be meaningless, as a procedure may be invoked in many different contexts, as well as recursively).

Parcel's analysis is also used in memory management. In the simplest application, the analysis decides for every dynamically instantiated object (lexical variable, cons cell, etc.) whether the object can be stack-allocated, or whether it must be heap-allocated. This lifetime information can also be used to guide the placement of objects in the hierarchical shared memory of a machine like Cedar. These ideas are developed in detail in [Har89].

As an example of this analysis, consider the program in Figure 1. The procedure counter returns an object (a closure that increments a free variable x and returns its updated value). The analysis reveals that the procedure sum has a side-effect upon (an instance of) x as result of using such a counter. However, the analysis also reveals that list-of-sums has no such side-effect, despite that it calls sum. Therefore, there is no dependence between the expressions

```
(sum (car 1) (counter))
```

and

```
(list-of-sums (cdr 1))
```

even though the former has a side-effect. Therefore, the compiler is justified in rewriting the procedure list-of-sums as in Figure 2. The construct plet is identical to let, except that it evaluates in parallel the forms (sum (car 1) (counter)) and (list-of-sums (cdr 1)), rather than sequentially as let would do.

```
(define list-of-sums (lambda (l)
   (if (null l) '()
       (plet ((a (sum (car l) (counter)))
              (b (list-of-sums (cdr l))))
          (cons a b)))))
```

Figure 2: A parallelized version of list-of-sums

2.1.2   Automatic parallelization of control structures

Just as the role of interprocedural analysis in vectorizing compilers was dictated by the objective of those compilers (generate vector code from innermost loops) and their input programs (loop-laden numeric code), so were the types of transformations they performed dictated by these considerations. Consequently, parallelizing compilation has been largely a synonym for loop transformations; to name a few, we have loop distribution, loop fusion, loop interchange, loop unrolling, loop blocking, etc. And for good reason: if the iterations of a substantial loop are independent, an enormous source of parallelism is latent.

These loop transformations were much the easier because of the regular structure of Fortran's DO loop, where the number of iterations is computed prior to entrance to the loop, and is not infrequently a constant. Lisp programs differ markedly from Fortran ones in this respect: there is no iterative construct so simple in Lisp as Fortran's DO; rather, a typical iterative computation is expressed using tail-recursion, or a generalized iterative facility that resembles a WHILE or REPEAT loop. The number of iterations of such a construction is not available prior to its entrance, but rather the termination condition is computed, along with other quantities, during the iterations themselves.

Indeed, many Lisp computations are not iterative at all, but are described by recursive procedures (not tail-recursive ones). These must be, to a parallelizing Lisp compiler, what DO loops are to a parallelizing Fortran compiler, if the principal parallelism within applications is to be discovered automatically.

For these reasons, Parcel makes use of two transformations called "exit-loop parallelization" and "recursion splitting." The former parallelizes iterative structures (control-flow cycles with exits) that may have no simple translation to DO loop form; the latter translates a self-recursive procedure into two loops, the first of which performs the "downward" portion of the procedure (that portion of the procedure body between the entrance to the procedure and the self-recursive calls), the second of which performs the "upward" portion (between the return from the self-recursive calls and the exits from the procedure). These loops are, in turn, parallelized by exit-loop parallelization and other loop parallelization techniques.

Exit-loop parallelization and recursion splitting require that the compiler be able to recognize the recurrence relations that govern the exit of an iterative or recursive computation, and to transform such a recurrence into parallel code.

For this reason, Parcel is equipped to recognize and solve a variety of symbolic and numeric recurrences, including recurrences over s-expressions.

2.1.3   Run-time support for automatically parallelized codes

An object code produced by the Parcel compiler has directives for parallelism (parallel loops and calls to parallel recurrence solvers), and invocations of Scheme's intrinsic procedures (car, cons, call/cc, etc.), in addition to assembly language instructions. It is linked to the Parcel run-time system to produce an executable object.

As mentioned above, the object code contains two versions of every compiled procedure, one sequential and one parallel. These versions have quite different purposes, and therefore result from quite different restructuring processes. The sequential version creates no additional threads of activity, but rather is intended to complete its computation as quickly as possible on a single processor, with a minimum of disturbance to the shared memory of the computer. The parallel version is intended to create additional threads of activity, and makes less efficient use of memory than the sequential version, in order to do so (see the example below). As the program executes, parallel threads of activity are created, and these in turn may create parallel threads of activity, and so forth. When the nesting of these parallel threads is judged to be sufficient to saturate the machine (this judgement is made according to one of several experimental strategies; see [Cho90]), the sequential versions of procedures are invoked, so that no further creation of parallel activity will occur beyond that nesting depth.

A traditional microtasking environment [Cra82, EHJP90] associates a stack with every processor. When a processor initiates a parallel loop, the continuation of that loop is on its stack; it must wait for all iterations of the initiated loop to terminate, before it executes the continuation.

We observed, however, first that the parallel loops in Parcel's object codes often have very few iterations (2 or 3 being common), and second that the running times of these iterations may vary radically one from another. The latter is likely precisely because Parcel often creates parallel loops that are quite "high" in a program's calling graph, so that the computation that is performed in each iteration may entail many procedure calls and conditional branches. To address this irregularity in the execution time of its parallel loops, we broke the traditional binding between processors and stacks. The Parcel run-time system has more stacks than processors. When the processor that initiates a parallel loop finds that others are still executing iterations of the loop (but that there are no further iterations to begin), it relinquishes its stack, allocates another, and turns to the microtask queue to find available work. The last processor to finish work on the parallel loop will return its stack to the pool, seize the stack abandoned by the initiating processor, and execute the continuation of the loop. This scheme is described in [Cho90].

```
(define copy-integer
  (lambda (n) (copy-integer-aux 1 n)))
(define copy-integer-aux
  (lambda (i s)
    (if (>= i s)
        i
        (copy-integer-aux (1+ i) s))))
(define copy
  (lambda (x)
    (if (atom? x) (if (integer? x) (copy-integer x) nil)
        (cons (copy (car x)) (copy (cdr x))))))
(write (copy (read)))
```

Figure 3: The procedure copy and its auxiliary procedures

As an example of the transformations performed in Parcel, consider the program in Figure 3. The procedure copy is defined, to copy a tree of cons cells. When the procedure finds an integer at a leaf of the tree, it copies it by calling copy-integer, which counts from 1 until an integer is reached that is greater than or equal to the leaf. Else, when the procedure finds an atomic leaf that is not an integer, it returns nil, and finally when it finds a cons cell it recursively copies the car and cdr of the cell into a fresh cell.

From this definition of copy, Parcel arrives by a sequence of transformations to the version in Figure 4. The syntax of this figure requires explanation. First, the list of variables

<i t-33 t-36 t-37 t-38 t-39 t-40 t-41 t-42>

are the local variables bound by the procedure. They are uninitialized until assigned. The syntax

```
(exit-block EXPR
    (l1: EXPR1)
    (l2: EXPR2)
        . . .
    (ln: EXPRn))
```

denotes a loop that runs until it is exited by a branch (go form) to one of the labels l1: to ln:. The symbol #self-closure# denotes the innermost closure (procedure + environment) in which the symbol appears. A return form exits the innermost procedure that contains the form, and provides its argument as the return value of the procedure.

We can see from this figure that all of the procedures from Figure 3 are merged into a single procedure body. Also note that the values of all subexpressions are captured in temporary variables; this gives the compiler maximum flexibility in code motion, common subexpression elimination, and so on.

```
(lambda nil
  <copy t-43 t-44 t-45>
  (set!
    copy
    (lambda (x)
      <i t-33 t-36 t-37 t-38 t-39 t-40 t-41 t-42>
      (set! t-37 (atom? x))
      (cond
        ( t-37
          (set! t-38 (integer? x))
          (cond
            ( t-38
              (set! i 1)
              (exit-block (repeat (set! t-33 (>= i x))
                                  (if t-33 (go 1-210:)
                                           (set! i (1+ i)))))
                          (1-210: (set! t-36 i))) )
            ( else
              (set! t-36 #f) ) ) )
        ( else
          (set! t-41 (car x))
          (set! t-39 (#self-closure# t-41))
          (set! t-42 (cdr x))
          (set! t-40 (#self-closure# t-42))
          (set! t-36 (cons t-39 t-40)) ) )
      (return t-36) ))
  (set! t-45 (read))
  (set! t-44 (copy t-45))
  (set! t-43 (write t-44))
  (return t-43) )
```

Figure 4: The sequential version of copy

```
(lambda nil
  <copy t-43 t-44 t-45>
  (set!
    copy
    (lambda (x)
      <i t-33 t-36 t-37 t-38 t-39 t-40 t-41 t-42 t-47
       i-48 i-49 i-50 i-51 i-52 t-53 t-54 i-55 t-56>
      (set! t-47 (length x))
      (set! x (allocate x t-47))
      (set! t-39 (allocate #f t-47))
      (set! t-41 (allocate #f t-47))
      (do (i-51 t-47) (set! x[i-51.1] (cdr x[i-51.0])))
      (doall (i-49 t-47)
             (set! t-41[i-49.1] (car x[i-49.0]))
             (set! t-39[i-49.1] (#self-closure# t-41[i-49.1])))
      (set! x (restore x t-47))
      (set! t-38 (integer? x))
      (cond
        ( t-38
          (set! i 1)
          (exit-block (repeat (set! t-33 (>= i x))
                              (if t-33 (go l-210:)
                                       (set! i (1+ i))))
                      (l-210: (set! t-36 i))) )
        ( else
          (set! t-36 #f) ) )
      (set! t-56 (allocate-r #f t-47))
      (do (i-55 t-47)
          (set! t-56[i-55.1] (cons t-39[[i-55.1]] t-56[i-55.0])))
      (set! t-56 (restore-r t-56 t-47))
      (set! t-36 (append2 t-56 t-36))
      (return t-36) ))
  (set! t-45 (read))
  (set! t-44 (copy t-45))
  (set! t-43 (write t-44))
  (return t-43) )
```

Figure 5: copy after Recursion Splitting

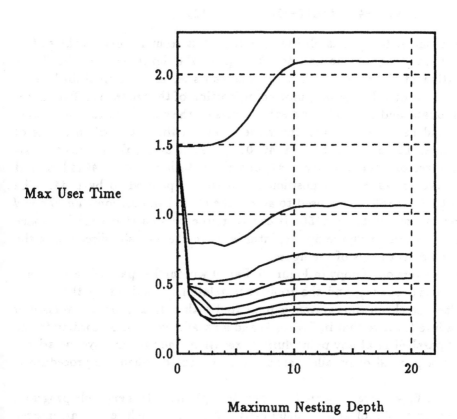

Maximum Nesting Depth

Figure 6: Execution profile for copying a tree of 10000 cons cells

In Figure 5 we have illustrated the program after a single transformation, recursion splitting, has been performed on the program of Figure 4. This transformation breaks the definition of copy into two halves. The first half contains all of the code from the entrance to the procedure, until the recursive call

```
(set! t-40 (#self-closure# t-42)),
```

and the second half contains all the code from this recursive call to the exit of the procedure. The first do and doall loops of the figure perform the *downward* portion of the recursion through this call site, and the final do loop of the figure performs the *upward*, unwinding portion of the recursion. The procedures allocate and allocate-r create vectors on the stack, and the procedures restore and restore-r return the value stored in the last position of one of these vectors. The notation t-41[i-49.0] is used to access the (i-49)'th position of the vector pointed to by t-41, and the notation t-41[i-49.1] is used to access the (i-49 + 1)'th position of the vector pointed to by t-41. The notation t-39[[i-55.0]] is used to access the (i-55)'th position *from the end* of the vector pointed to by t-56. It can therefore be seen that iteration space of the final do loop of Figure 5 runs, intuitively, in the opposite direction of the first do and doall loops of the figure.

From the version of copy in Figure 5, Parcel will further parallelize the inner loop (the exit-block), and the recurrence relations described by the two do loops. The Parcel run-time system is presented with both a sequential version of the procedure (near to that in Figure 4) and a parallel version. According to the degree of parallelism at any point during execution, the run-time system selects either the sequential or parallel version to be executed, when the procedure is called.

In Figure 6, we have presented an execution profile of this example program, when copying a tree of about 10000 cons cells, where each leaf is an integer with an (average) value of 50. The program was executed on an eight-processor Alliant FX/8; there is one curve in the figure for each value of the number of active processors, from one to eight. (When two processors are active, the others are in the idle state, not accessing the memory of the machine.) On the horizontal axis is shown the nesting depth of parallelism that is achieved before the sequential version of copy is invoked. If, for example, the nesting depth is 10, then the doall loop of Figure 5 is nested (by recursive procedure calls) ten levels deep, before the sequential version of copy is invoked. On the vertical axis is given the user cpu time (the maximum of the user cpu times over all of the processors of the machine). The program achieves a maximum speedup of around 6.5, at a nesting depth of about 4, with 8 processors active. We are experimenting with a number of strategies for automatically selecting between the parallel and sequential procedure versions during execution; the results of these experiments are reported in [Cho90].

2.2   Shortcomings

While Parcel was successful in a number of respects, including those mentioned above, it also has a number of shortcomings, in its interprocedural analysis, its parallelizing transformations, and its run-time system.

2.2.1   Interprocedural analysis

Intrinsic procedures   Scheme has a fairly large collection of built-in (intrinsic) procedures, including car, cons, putprop, equal?, etc. Some of these have side-effects, and virtually all are restricted in the types of objects they accept or return. The properties of an intrinsic procedure are important in several ways during automatic parallelization and compilation. First, during interprocedural analysis, we must take into account any side-effects performed by the built-in procedure for the sake of correctness. Second, any type restrictions upon parameters or return value can be used to sharpen the analysis. Third, we would like to generate in-line code from an invocation of an intrinsic procedure, whenever such an invocation is discovered by the interprocedural analysis (such an analysis is necessary to discover that, for example, the expression (foo x) is really an invocation of the procedure car, and whereas the expression (cdr x) is *not* an invocation of the intrinsic procedure cdr, because the program has modified the global variable cdr.

In Parcel, special knowledge concerning each built-in procedure was built into the interprocedural analysis. This made the analysis sharp: the types accepted and returned by each intrinsic procedure, as well as any side-effects it might perform, were written directly into the analysis. This unfortunately meant that many thousands of lines of code were dedicated to the treatment of intrinsic procedures, and therefore that the analysis could not be retargeted to another input language without rewriting most of the analysis, despite that the analysis is essentially language-independent. Thus, for example, Parcel cannot be easily adapted for the interprocedural analysis of Common Lisp programs, much less of C or SmallTalk programs.

This difficulty would have been largely alleviated if the intrinsic procedures had been written in Scheme itself, where possible, and presented to the compiler in this form, along with the user-defined procedures. To do so, however, would have reduced the sharpness of the interprocedural analysis slightly (not a major problem). More significantly, a number of the intrinsic procedures have no straightforward representation in Scheme. These include, for example, putprop, vector-ref, and a number of intrinsic procedures added to Parcel for the support of parallelism. The difficulty here is that Scheme is too high-level a language for the direct expression of such procedures. As a consequence, the dependence consequences of these procedures were treated specially and directly by the interprocedural analysis.

```
(define house (lambda (color owner)
   (lambda (x y)
      (cond ((eq? x 'color!) (set! color y))
            ((eq? x 'owner!) (set! owner y))
            ((eq? x 'color) color)
            ((eq? x 'owner) owner)))))
(define house-color (lambda (x) (x 'color #f)))
(define house-color! (lambda (x y) (x 'color! y)))
(define house-owner (lambda (x) (x 'owner #f)))
(define house-owner! (lambda (x y) (x 'owner! y)))
```

Figure 7: The structure house represented using closures

Compound objects A second problem with Parcel's analysis is that it treats
all mutable, compound data objects (vectors, user structures, etc.) as though
they were lexical closures over free variables. For example, a two-element structure called house, expressed in terms of nested lexical contours, is illustrated in
Figure 7. An instance of house is represented as an instance of the inner procedure in this figure; it is applied to a symbol (one of color!, owner!, color,
or owner), and a value. If the symbol is color! or owner!, then the color
or owner field of the structure is assigned the value, otherwise the value of one
of these fields is simply returned (with no update occurring). The procedure
house-owner is used when reading a field of a house, and an expression like
(set! (house-owner x) y) is macro-expanded to the form (house-owner!
x y).

   While this analogy (between structures and closures) is quite correct, it leads
to a number of difficulties. First, the interprocedural analysis must be highly
sensitive to correctly notice that house-owner! uses and modifies an instance
of the variable owner, whereas house-owner only uses this variable (does not
modify it). Second, the representation (within the interprocedural analysis) of
closures contains much information that could be compressed or eliminated,
if one were to represent structures like house directly. These two facts make
the analysis considerably more costly to perform than need be. Finally, while
structures can be represented quite precisely as closures, the representation
given to vectors for the purpose of analysis is much less precise; consequently, the
analysis is much less sharp concerning side-effects upon vectors than upon user
structures or lexical variables. In particular, the analysis cannot benefit from
even the simplest test for independence among subscript expressions [Ban76,
Ban79].

Connectivity Analysis Finally, Parcel's anlaysis allows one to build a dependence graph of each procedure based upon the side-effects attributed to the
expressions of that procedure; this was illustrated in the example of Figure 1

above, where it was found that there are no dependences between

(sum (car l) (counter))

and

(list-of-sums (cdr l))

because the intersection of their visible side-effects is empty. In short, the observation employed here is that *the visibility of side-effects upon an object is restricted to the subcomputation that contains the lifetime of the object*. This observation is effective in identifying coarse-grained parallelism from the program, but is not generally effective in extracting medium- and fine-grained parallelism from traversals that modify data structures, because it does not make use of information concerning the connectivity of pointers between objects (even though such information is provided by the anlaysis), but simply characterizes side-effects by the lifetimes of the objects involved.

2.2.2 Automatic parallelization of intermediate form

Unstructured intermediate form   Parcel represented its input programs as control-flow graphs for the purpose of transformations, and because these graphs were transformed rather radically from their original form, they were often less structured than a Scheme program would be. For example, in the example of Figure 4, we see an exit-block form. This is a printed representation of a sequential loop as Parcel views it. Such a loop is simply a cycle of control flow, with a single entrance and (possibly) many exits. In the case of Figure 4, there is but one exit, a branch to the label 1-210. In general, such an exit might simultaneously escape from several, nested loops. Parcel's loop-parallelization algorithms accept as input a sequential loop in this form, and attempt to render it as a do loop, before further parallelizing it. This process is somewhat ad-hoc, and in any event is very complex, owing to the generality of form of input loop it treats. The representation given to the program is likewise quite complex, as it is dictated by the generality of structure of the loops.

Intrinsic procedures and dependences   In all phases of Parcel, Scheme's intrinsic procedures (including those added to the run-time system for support of parallelism) proved to be a nagging difficulty. During program transformation, Parcel had to account for the particular dependence consequences of a number of intrinsic procedures. As in the case of interprocedural analysis, this difficulty would have been alleviated had the intrinsic procedures been written in Scheme itself and presented to the compiler along with the user-defined procedures; but as mentioned above, a number of the intrinsic procedures, including many added to Parcel for support of parallelism, have no straightforward representation in Scheme.

2.2.3 Code Generator and Run-time system

Parcel's code generation was, in most respects, quite successful. The compiler produces a high-level assembly program, that contains macro invocations for data movement, for invocations of intrinsic procedures, for accessing lexical variables, for entering and exiting lexical contours, etc. To target Parcel for a particular machine means to expand these macros into the assembly language of the target machine. The only difficulty here is, once again, that the intrinsic procedures must be hand-crafted for each target machine. Moreover, the compiler requires several versions of each intrinsic procedure, according to whether its arguments will arrive in registers or in memory, and according to where its return value is to be placed. Like the other problems caused by the intrinsic procedures, this would have been solved had they been written in Scheme itself, which proved impossible for many of the low-level intrinsics.[1]

3   Miprac

If we publicly enumerate the shortcomings of Parcel, it is only by way of announcing a new compiler project that is intended, first, to extend the techniques of Parcel and apply them to a broad class of procedural programming languages, and second to correct the shortcomings we have found in Parcel. This project is called Miprac. The details of the design of Miprac will be presented elsewhere; our intention here is simply to give the reader a feel for the direction of our research.

3.1   Intermediate form

Miprac is intended to bring automatic parallelization to programs that perform both numeric and symbolic computations. Miprac compiles a simple intermediate form in which one there are three types of forms: those concerning *control*, those concerning *memory*, and those concerning *numbers*. In terms of program semantics, these three types of constructs manipulate the domains of *continuations*, *stores*, and *values* respectively. A number of simple theorems concerning control and data dependence apply to this language, and make it particularly easy to transform and analyze. A program arrives to this form by three phases of rewriting. First, the program is translated from a source language (Scheme, C, Fortran) into an unstructured dialect of the intermediate form. From here, a radical control-flow normalization [Amm90] leaves only properly nested ifs, single-entry, single-exit while loops, and begin forms as the control structures within a procedure. Finally, these while structures are rewritten as tail-recursive procedures so that there is no cyclic control-flow

---

[1] By the time code generation is reached in Parcel, the program has calls to a number of parallel recurrence solvers, and procedures that manipulate the stack; these procedures simply have no natural expression in Scheme.

within a procedure. In this form, the only control structures in the program are begins, properly nested ifs, and procedure calls.

Recent work on intermediate forms for parallelizing compilers has put forth several, similar graph-based representations that incorporate control and data dependences in a single representation of the program. See [FOW87, CF89]. These representations have the advantage that updates to the program representation automatically update the control and dependence graphs. The disadvantages are that one must take care when adding dependence arcs to the program, not to arrive to a program graph for which there is no corresponding program (by contrast, one may add edges willy-nilly to a conventional dependence graph and preserve its correctness), and that transformations must be conceived and executed in terms of the program graph, rather than in (the arguably more natural) terms of the objects in a language described by a grammar. In Miprac, we have opted in favor of an intermediate form which is described by a simple grammar. While simple theorems describe the data dependences of programs in this form, the data dependences themselves are not represented directly in the intermediate form; we view the dependence graph as a constraint upon program transformation, and not as a representation of the program itself. Control dependences are so simplified by the control-flow normalization of Miprac that they are manifest in the syntax of the normalized programs, and require no separate representation.

3.2   Generalized interprocedural analysis

Miprac attempts to parallelize by a deep, interprocedural semantic analysis (abstract interpretation). Like Parcel, this analysis accounts for the lifetimes and interprocedural movements made by objects, but it extends Parcel's analysis in several important ways.

First, compound data objects are represented directly in the abstract semantics. This makes the analysis both less expensive to perform, and more accurate concerning side-effects upon structures, vectors, etc.

Second, it characterizes the connections (pointers) between objects in memory according to the relative time at which the objects are instantiated. This "relative time" is described in terms of the interprocedural movements that take place between the instantiation of the objects, and is used to infer "linearity" (freedom from cycles) in the links of a data structure. This allows one to extract medium- and fine-grained parallelism from a traversal of a data structure that modifies its constituent objects, when the traversal follows a linear path through the structure.

Third, it employs a gcd test [Ban76, Ban79] to establish the independence of references that fall within a single block of storage.

What results is a three-level analysis of side-effects and dependences. At the highest level, the visibility of side-effects is characterized in terms of the lifetimes of the objects affected, and in terms of the gross attributes of the objects involved. For example, two side-effects do not interfere if they affect objects that arise from distinct points in the program text. At the next level, connectivity analysis reveals independence between side-effects that affect distinct instances of objects that arise from a single point in the program. At the lowest level, analysis of pointer arithmetic is used to discover independence between references that fall within a single object.

3.3 Procedure-based parallelization

In Parcel, every effort was made to coerce the program into the form traditionally treated by parallelizing / vectorizing compilers: nested do loops. From this form, transformations like scalar expansion, loop distribution, recurrence recognition and replacement, etc., could be applied. In Miprac, we are experimenting with the opposite strategy: programs are driven into a form in which procedure invocation is the principal control mechanism, and traditional parallelization techniques are being recast to treat programs in this form. This appears to have several advantages. First, it accords well with the interprocedural analysis technique we are applying, for the reason that the analysis expresses the visibility of side-effects, and the lifetimes of dynamically allocated objects, in terms of the crossing of procedure boundaries (that is, in terms of calls to and returns from procedures). When advancing from one iteration of a loop to the next is expressed as crossing a procedure boundary, the analysis is able to reason directly about the independence of loop iterations. Second, a number of transformations, like variable privatization, invariant floating, etc., are quite neatly expressed in terms of nested lexical contours. Finally, since to successfully parallelize Lisp and C programs entails, in any event, the parallelization of computations that involve procedure invocations, it may simplify matters to coerce all control structures into the form of procedure invocations and concentrate upon the latter.

3.4 Source-language independence

There are two ways in which the intermediate form treated by Miprac helps to make the compiler easy to retarget to new source languages. First, programs from many popular procedural languages (notably Scheme, Common Lisp, C, and Fortran) have a straightforward translation into the intermediate form. (We have, at present, parsers from Scheme, ANSI C and Fortran 77 into the intermediate form.) Second, the intermediate form is designed to allow us to express the intrinsic procedures provided by these languages in a form that is both clear (for the sake of accuracy in interprocedural analysis) and efficient (in that the form can be compiled into efficient code for a target machine). In particular, the intermediate form allows one to perform arithmetic on pointer variables, and to write and read values of various sizes to and from the memory. Tags on data items are *not* built into the intermediate form, but are rather implemented in the translation from source language (Scheme or Common Lisp) to the intermediate form. This has been done to allow the compiler to optimize the extraction and insertion of tags, and to allow one to implement a variety of tagging mechanisms without rewriting major portions of the compiler.

3.5 Modularity

A significant shortcoming of Parcel, and several other parallelizing compilers with which the authors are familiar, is that the language accepted by one pass of the compiler might not include the language produced by the pass. For example, a pass that produces parallelized code might not accept parallelized input programs; one that produces programs with recurrences recognized might not accept programs in which there are calls to recurrence solution routines. In general, we might say that there are restrictions imposed upon the input programs to a pass that are not satisfied by its output. In such a compiler, composing passes is a tricky business, one that must take into account the pre- and post-conditions of each pass.

A goal of the intermediate form of Miprac is to accommodate both the input and output programs in a single language whose formal semantics are built into the compiler. This means that input programs may contain the parallel construct provided in the intermediate language (there is only one such construct); the semantics of this construct are specified formally, and are a legitimate part of the language accepted by the compiler. Likewise, any manipulations of storage that are necessary in performing advanced transformations (like scalar expansion) can be expressed in the intermediate language, and could be found in an input program. In this way, the transformations provided in Miprac may be composed arbitrarily (though not always profitably).

4 Conclusion

Parcel was arguably the first complete system for the automatic parallelization of Lisp programs. It was quite successful in several respects: it introduced a sharp interprocedural semantic analysis that computes the interprocedural visibility of side-effects, and allows the placement of objects in memory according to their lifetimes; it introduced several restructuring techniques tailored to the iterative and recursive control structures that arise in Lisp programs; and it made use of multiple procedure versions with a flexible microtasking mechanism for efficient parallelism at run-time. Parcel had several shortcomings however: the intrinsic procedures of Scheme, and those added to Parcel for support of parallelism, were embedded in its interprocedural analysis, transformations, code generation and run-time system, making the system difficult to adapt for other source languages; its interprocedural analysis handled compound, mutable data only indirectly (by analogy to closures), making it less accurate and more expensive than necessary; and its representation of programs as general control-flow graphs made the implementation of complex transformations difficult.

Miprac is a successor to Parcel, in which we are extending the techniques of Parcel, and applying them to a broad class of procedural languages. Miprac's interprocedural analysis includes a gcd test for independence among memory accesses that fall within a single block of storage; consequently, it may be used to analyze programs that create blocks of storage (structures, vectors) dynamically, and access them either by constant or computed offsets. Like Parcel's, this analysis computes the lifetimes of objects and the visibility of side-effects upon them, but also discerns properties of their structure.

Miprac's intermediate form is a compact language in which the concerns of control, memory, and values are made orthogonal. By a radical control-flow normalization, programs in the intermediate form are made highly structured so that transformations may be simply conceived and executed. The intrinsic procedures of the source language being compiled are expressed in this intermediate form, which allows the interprocedural analysis, transformations, and code generation to be written in a language-independent manner, so that retargeting the system to another source language or target machine entails only the implementation of the intermediate form itself.

References

[Amm90] Zahira Ammarguellat. Normalization of program control flow. Technical Report 885, Center for Supercomputing Research and Development, University of Illinois at Urbana-Champaign, 1990.

[Ban76] Uptal D. Banerjee. Data dependence in ordinary programs. Master's thesis, University of Illinois at Urbana-Champaign, November 1976.

[Ban79] Uptal D. Banerjee. *Speedup of Ordinary Programs*. PhD thesis, University of Illinois at Urbana-Champaign, October 1979.

[BC86] Michael Burke and Ronald G. Cytron. Interprocedural dependence analysis and parallelization. In *Proceedings of the SIGPLAN 1986 Symposium on Compiler Construction*, pages 162–175. Association for Computing Machinery, July 1986.

[CF89] R. Cartwright and M. Felleisen. The semantics of program dependence. In *Proceedings of the 1989 ACM SIGPLAN Conference on Programming Language Design and Implementation*. ACM, ACM Press, jun 1989.

[Cho90] Jhy-Herng Chow. Run-time support for automatically parallelized lisp programs. Master's thesis, University of Illinois at Urbana-Champaign, 1990.

[Cra82] Cray Research, Mendota Heights, MN. *Cray X-MP Series Mainframe Reference Manual (HR-0032)*, 1982.

[EHJP90] R. Eigenmann, J. Hoeflinger, G. Jaxon, and D. Padua. Cedar fortran and its compiler. Technical Report 966, Center for Supercomputing Research and Development, University of Illinois at Urbana-Champaign, jan 1990.

[FOW87] J. Ferrante, K. J. Ottenstein, and J. D. Warren. The program dependence graph and its use in optimization. *ACM Transactions on Programming Languages and Systems*, 9(3):319–349, 1987.

[Har89] Williams Ludwell Harrison III. The interprocedural analysis and automatic parallelization of scheme programs. *Lisp and Symbolic Computation: an International Journal*, 2(3), 1989.

[Tri84] Remi Triolet. *Contributions to Automatic Parallelization of Fortran Programs with Procedure Calls*. PhD thesis, University of Paris VI (I.P.), 1984.

A Reflective Object Oriented Concurrent Language ABCL/R

(Summary)

Akinori Yonezawa

Department of Information Science

Faculty of Science, University of Tokyo

7-3-1 Hongo, Bunkyo-ku, Tokyo 113, Japan

Abstract

Reflection is the process of reasoning about and acting upon itself. A reflective computational system is a computational system which exhibits reflective behavior. ABCL/R is an extension of our previously proposed language ABCL/1. This paper is a summary of the author's talk at the workshop. More details on ABCL/1 and ABCL/R will be found in a collection of papers edited by the author — "ABCL: An Object-Oriented Concurrent System (MIT Press, 1990)".

1 ABCL/1

ABCL/1 is a programming language designed for describing distributed algorithms and modelling various types of distributed systems. The semantics of ABCL/1 is based on an object oriented model for parallel computaion, in which computations are represented in terms of concurrent message passing among abstract entities called *objects*.

ABCL/1 is intended to serve as an experimental programming language to construct software in the framework of object-based concurrent programming. It is also intended to serve as an executable language for the modelling and designing various parallel and/or real time systems such as operating systems, office information systems, and factory automation systems. Thus ABCL/1 also serves as a language for rapid prototyping.

The primary design principles of this language are:

1. Clear semantics of Message Passing
   The semantics of message passing among objects should be transparent and faithful to the underlying computation model.

2. Practicality
   Intentionally, we do not pursue the approach that every single concept in computation should be represented purely in terms of objects and message passing. In describing the object's behavior, basic values, data structures (such as numbers, strings, lists), and invocations of operations manipulating them may be assumed to exist as they are, not necessarily as objects or message passing. And also control

structures (such as *if-then-else* and looping) used in the description of the behavior of an object are not necessarily based upon message passing.

In ABCL/1, *inter*-object message passing is entirely based on the underlying object oriented computation model, but the representation of the behavior (script) of an object may contain converntional *applicative* and *imperative* features, which we believe makes ABCL/1 programs easier to read and write from the viewpoint of conventional programmers. Since we are trying to grasp and exploit a complicated phenomenon, namely *parallelism*, a rather conservative approach is taken in describing the internal behavior of individual objects. Various imperative features in the current version of ABCL/1 are expressed in terms of Lisp-like parenthesized prefix notations.

2 ABCL/R

ABCL/R is an extension of ABCL/1 with reflective architecture based on the notions of meta-objects. The following is the summary of ABCL/R:

- Each object is represented/implemented by its *meta-object*. The meta-object incorporates the meta-level representations of structural and computational aspects of the object in a meta circular way. A meta-object is also an object of ABCL/R. This implies the infinite tower of meta-objects. (For its implementation, see below.) An evaluator (interpreter) of the language is also an object. In our computation system, a number of such objects may work in parallel.

- Reflective computation is performed by *message transmissions to meta-objects* and such message transmissions take place concurrently. Reflective computation can be performed in meta-objects of any level because of the infinite tower of meta-objects. Sending messages to a meta-object makes it possible to inquire and modify the structure and behavior of the object. It is possible to send messages to the meta-object of an object while the object is performing its tasks. Thus, a concurrent system can gradually modify itself in the way that objects and (their) meta-objects in the system send messages each other.

- The dynamic modification of running objects in a concurrent system can be described by using reflective language constructs of ABCL/R. Typical examples are: dynamic (concurrent) modification such as acquiring (or inheriting) scripts from other objects, and monitoring a running object by modifying its meta-object through the meta-object of the meta-object.

- Enhancement of program modularity can be attained by using meta-objects. The example of simple Time Warp mechanism[1] demonstrates this. In a simulation program using this mechanism, the meta-level part is separated from the object-level part by specifying a non-default meta-object for each simulation object.

[Current Status of ABCL/R]

Currently, we have built a prototype implementation of ABCL/R written in ABCL/1 (written in Kyoto Common Lisp on Unix and Symbolics Common Lisp on Symbolics Lisp Machines).

The primary concern of implementation is how to represent the infinite tower of meta-objects. In our implementation, meta-objects are created in the lazy way. A meta-object ↑x of an object x is actually created when the access to ↑x takes place — when the evaluator first evaluates an expression [meta x].

References

[1] T. Watanabe and A. Yonezawa, *Reflection in an object-oriented concurrent language*, Proceedings of Object Oriented Programming System: Languages and Applications, 306-315(1988)

[2] A. Yonezawa (ed), *ABCL: An Object-Oriented Concurrent System* (MIT Press, 1990)

Optimistic and Pessimistic Synchronization
in
Distributed Computing

Etsuya Shibayama

Department of Information Science, Tokyo Institute of Technology
etsuya@is.titech.ac.jp

Akinori Yonezawa

Department of Information Science, University of Tokyo
yonezawa@is.s.u-tokyo.ac.jp

Abstract

This short article presents a part of our research results in object-based distributed computing: simulation results of optimistic and pessimistic synchronization mechanisms in distributed computing environments, where communication latency is not small. We show, for some difficult problems in distributed computing, e.g., distributed simulation of systems with tight feed back loops, any approach based on either sole optimistic synchronization or sole pessimistic synchronization does not work efficiently. For the purposes of highly efficient execution, we have to predict the degree of communication latency and the average behavior of the system and combine both synchronization mechanisms in an proper manner based on the prediction.

1 Why Distributed Processing?

One aim of this short article is to introduce a part of our research activities in object-based concurrent/distributed computing. Strictly speaking, our target language ABCL/1[Yon89] is not a parallel lisp, but an object-based language for concurrent/distributed computing. Though parallel lisps and ABCL/1 share the same goals (e.g., high speed symbolic computations), our approach and parallel lisp approaches are different. We compare these approaches in this section.

Recently, a lot of parallel lisp dialects are implemented on commercial multi-processor systems (See papers in this book and [Hal85, GG88, KRHHM89]). Most parallel lisp dialects heavily depend on the existence of a central shared memory system. In other words, they assume more or less a universal single address space. In contrast, our approach does not assume any universal address space but assumes a distributed memory system. Though it is obvious that shared memory models are more expressive than distributed memory models, a shared memory system with a large number of processors seems infeasible (If the desired degree of parallelism is at most eight or ten, a multi-processor approach is promising, of course). Our target is not multi-*processor* systems but multi-*computer* systems[AS88] consisting of hundreds to thousands of small computers with high speed communication links. It is hard (or at least inefficient) to maintain a single universal address space on a loosely coupled multi-computer system.

We therefore take an approach to cope with a multiple address space model. Fortunately, most lisp dialects (and other symbolic computation languages) do not depend so much on a mechanism mapping addresses to their contents. Instead, what we need is a mechanism which

---

A car wash system consists of an *attendant* and *car washers*. Cars arrive at the attendant one by one at random intervals and each car washer has its own wash speed. The attendant allocates car washers to cars according to the following rule:

1. Cars must be washed in their arrival order.
2. When a car is arriving at the attendant,
   - if some washers are idle, the car must be washed by the one that has been idle for the longest duration.
   - otherwise (i.e., every washer is washing a car), the car must be washed by the one that will become idle earliest.

If more than one washer finished (or, will finish) washing a car at the same time, they can start their next jobs in an arbitrary order. It takes no time for the attendant to allocate a car washer to a car.

Figure 1: Specifications of the Car Wash Problem

chases (possibly remote) references efficiently. With an appropriate abstraction mechanism such as the one provided by the notion of object-orientation, the number of remote references can be kept small (at lease much smaller than the number of the addresses) and a reasonably efficient implementation on loosely coupled multi-computer systems may become possible. Anyhow, a large number of concurrently accessible global addresses will cause trouble in programming, and thus we need a good abstraction mechanism, which we consider is provided by our approach.

2 A Hard Problem

Since we choose a distributed computing approach, we can rely on neither on universal shared memory nor on global time. In a distributed computing environment, it is hard to maintain a global time in a precise manner because of communication latency. For instance, considering near future technologies, a 10GHz clock will be feasible and so even 30 cm distance requires at least 10 clock delay for communication.

Lack of the notion of global time makes it difficult to solve distributed discrete event simulation problems. Even though object-oriented programming can provide a natural modeling for simulation, it is difficult to maintain *temporal relationships* among events.

As a hard example, we consider the *car wash problem*[Mis86] whose specifications are given in Figure 1. The latter part of these specifications refer to temporal relationships among events. Suppose, for instance, that there are three washers, say W_a, W_b, and W_c, and that they need 10, 5, and 8 time units, respectively, to wash a car. Suppose also that five cars, say C_1, C_2, C_3, C_4, and C_5, arrive at the attendant at times 0, 2, 6, 8, and 9, respectively. A simulation result is a possible sequence of events such as:

Time 0: C_1 arrives at the attendant and W_a starts washing it.
Time 2: C_2 arrives at the attendant and W_b starts washing it.
Time 6: C_3 arrives at the attendant and W_c starts washing it.
Time 7: W_b finishes washing C_2.
Time 8: C_4 arrives at the attendant and W_b starts washing it.
Time 9: C_5 arrives at the attendant.
Time 10: W_a finishes washing C_1 and starts washing C_5.

Time 13: W_b finishes washing C_4.
Time 14: W_c finishes washing C_3.
Time 20: W_a finishes washing C_5.

3 Pessimism and Optimism

To maintain temporal orders among events, several techniques have been proposed (e.g., [CM81, Jef85]). Roughly speaking, there are two kinds of approaches. In one approach (e.g., [CM81]), a *block-resume* mechanism or something similar to it is used so that the execution of each object (or process) is *blocked* while *time conflicts* may occur and *resumed* after it is guaranteed that no time conflicts can occur. This approach is based on *pessimism*. It is cautious and sacrifices a high degree of concurrency for consistency. In the other approach (e.g., taken by [Jef85]), a *rollback* mechanism is used: as long as no time conflicts are detected, the object executes its script without any consideration of temporal relationships; unfortunately, if some object detects a time conflict, this object and those which receive its messages, directly and/or indirectly *rollback* as much as necessary in a distributed manner and re-execute their scripts so as to avoid the conflict. This approach is based on *optimism* and concurrency is exploited as long as no conflicts are detected. If, unfortunately, a conflict is detected, it is resolved at the sacrifice of efficiency. Generally, safe execution and a high degree of concurrency are conflicting goals.

In design of a distributed program which solves the car wash problem, the essential part is an allocation algorithm of car washers to cars. Unfortunately, however, any approach without optimism cannot exploit parallelism. Suppose, for instance, the case in the previous section, where three washers W_a, W_b, and W_c wash five cars C_1, C_2, C_3, C_4, and C_5. With the pessimistic approach, the attendant cannot assign W_b to C_4 until the time when all the washers physically finish their first jobs. Therefore, we need some degree of optimism.

4 Evaluation of Simulation Strategies

In this section, we evaluate the efficiency of the simulation programs For the purposes, we simulate the simulation programs (*higher order simulation!!*) under the following assumptions:

1. Latency of every message passing is the same.
2. All the washers have the same physical computing power.
3. The attendant processes all the messages for allocation and undoing in the same physical period.

These assumptions are introduced for simplicity. On evaluation of the programs, we vary the parameters such as the physical speeds of washers, communication latency, and the degree of optimism.

From the simulation results[Yon89, Chapter 9], we conclude that the optimistic allocation strategy is efficient at least under the following conditions:

- latency of message passing is small;
- the attendant is fast enough so that it is not a bottleneck;
- washers can perform an undo operation quickly.

For instance, when the optimal degree of parallelism might be 2.4, 4.9, and 11.7, the optimistic algorithm is about 2, 4, and 7.5 times faster than the sequential algorithm.

We also have simulation results under the conditions that message passing latency is not small and/or undo speeds of washers are slow. When the number of the washers is small (e.g., 3), latency of message passing directly influences the efficiency of the optimistic allocation algorithm. In contrast, the undo speeds of washers do not influence so much. However, if the number of washers increases, the optimistic allocation cannot get any good results. Moreover, when undo speeds are slow, smaller communication latency may decrease the execution efficiency (Chaotic situation!!).

In such cases, an appropriate degree of pessimism is a great help to efficient execution. When the number of washers is not small and undo operations are heavy jobs, without helps of pessimism, we cannot finish simulation in a reasonable amount of physical time. The combinations of optimism and just a low degree of pessimism make allocation algorithms much efficient.

5 Future Works

For efficient managements of temporal relationships on a distributed environment, we have to know the trade-off point between *pessimism* and *optimism*. Unfortunately, we have not yet had any universally applicable solutions concerning this problem. Our future works will be to analyse as many problem domains as possible and establish a methodology to estimate the trade-off point between *pessimism* and *optimism*.

References

[AS88]   William C. Athas and Charles L. Seitz. Multicomputers: Message-passing concurrent computers. *IEEE Computer*, 21(8):9–24, 1988.

[CM81]   K. M. Chandy and J. Misra. Asynchronous distributed simulation via a sequence of parallel computations. *Communications of the ACM*, 24(11):198–206, 1981.

[GG88]   Ron Goldman and Richard P. Gabriel. Qlisp: Experience and new directions. In *ACM/SIGPLAN PPEALS*, pages 111–121, 1988.

[Hal85]   R. H. Halstead. Multilisp: A language for concurrent symbolic computation. *ACM Transactions on Programming Languages and Systems*, 7(4):37–79, 1985.

[Jef85]   David R. Jefferson. Virtual time. *ACM Transactions on Programming Languages and Systems*, 7(3):404–425, 1985.

[KRHHM89] David A. Kranz, Jr. Robert H. Halstead, and Eric Mohr. Mul-t : A high-prefomance parallel lisp. In *SIGPLAN '89 Conference on Programing Design and Implemantation*, pages 81–90, 1989.

[Mis86]   Jayadev Misra. Distributed discrete-event simulation. *ACM Computing Surveys*, 18(1):39–65, March 1986.

[Yon89]   Akinori Yonezawa, editor. *ABCL: An Object-Oriented Concurrent System — Theory, Language, Programming, Implementation and Application*. The MIT Press, 1989.

Toward a New Computing Model for an Open Distributed Environment

Mario Tokoro*

Department of Computer Science, Keio University

3-14-1 Hiyoshi, Yokohama 223 JAPAN

Abstract

This paper proposes a new computing model called *computational field model*, or *CFM* for short, for solving a problem in an object-oriented open distributed environment. In this model, we envisage an open-ended distributed environment as a continuous computational field. We introduce the notions of distance between objects and the mass of an object to the model. Thus, solving a problem can be seen as a mutual effect between the computational field and the problem.

1 Introduction

Recent demands on computer systems can be summarized as:

1. to solve larger and more complex problems,
2. to realize more reliable real time processing, and
3. to provide better user interfaces.

We have realized the necessity of following software-related items to answer these demands based on the advancement of hardware technology: raising the level of abstraction in describing problems, employing inherent parallelism of problems, accepting the notion of *Open Systems* [Hewitt 84], and introducing the notion of atomic transaction, time, and so forth.

In this paper, we pick up the first demand as our primary concern and propose a new computing model called *computational field model*, or *CFM* for short. CFM is a computing model for solving a large complex problem on an object-oriented open-ended distributed environment. In this model, we envisage an open-ended distributed environment as a continuous computational field. We introduce the notions of distance between objects and the mass of an object to the model. Thus, solving a problem can be seen as mutual effects between the computational field and the problem.

---

*also with Sony Computer Science Laboratory Inc., Takanawa Muse Building, 3-14-13 Higashi Gotanda, Shinagawa-ku, Tokyo, 141 JAPAN. Tel: +81-3-448-4380, Telefax: +81-3-448-4273, E-mail: mario@csl.sony.co.jp

2 Object-oriented Computing

The adjective *object-oriented* emerged in early 1970's at almost the same time in the fields of programming languages, operating systems, artificial intelligence, databases, and graphics. The commonness and difference in the usages were realized in 1980's. The most common and important feature in those is that object-orientation is a technique of modularization or abstraction in programming and knowledge representation, where modularization is performed in analogy to objects in the real world, so that computation is modeled as a simulation of the world.

We define *object* and *object-oriented computing* as follows:

> An **object** is a physical or logical entity that is self-contained and provided with a unified communication protocol.

> **Object-oriented computing** is a method of computing in which objects request computation and receive answers from each other in terms of the unified communication protocol.

A unified communication protocol means that an object can communicate with *any* other objects through the communication protocol when it knows the addresses (or id's) of the objects. An object possesses a set of procedures which correspond to computable requests and a local storage to keep its state.

Object-oriented computing can be understood as the departure from the microscopic view of computing where computation proceeds by executing an algorithm of a procedure to the macroscopic view where computation proceeds as mutual effects among objects.

3 Concurrent Objects

A concurrent object [Tokoro 88] possesses a (virtual) processor in addition to its local storage and a set of procedures. By incorporating a processor in an object, we can eliminate the notion of the *locus of execution* or *allocation of a processor to an object* from object-oriented computing. Thus, we can employ concurrent objects as a simpler unit for concurrent and distributed computing. Hewitt has been advocating this notion as the theory of Actor [Hewitt 73]. Orient84/K [Tokoro 84], ConcurrentSmalltalk [Yokote 86] [Yokote 87], also employ this notion. As a result, those languages have the following very important advantages:

- Objects in the real world exist in parallel and execute in parallel. By using concurrent objects, it becomes very easy and natural to model computation in analogy to the real world.
- The allocation of processors to objects becomes an implementation issue rather than language issue. Therefore, a program becomes independent from the executing system architecture (i.e., shared/distributed memory system, the number of processors in the system, and so forth).

Most concurrent object-oriented programming languages provide a special object, usually called a *future object*, to receive an answer for an asynchronous request. The notion of future object can easily be extended so that a future object receive more than one answer. Thus, we can incorporate *stream* in object-oriented computing. On the other hand, *assignment* in conventional languages is to generate a future object and to request the destination object to return the answer to the future object.

4 Parallel Computing

Parallel computing is one of the important methods for high-speed computing. Parallel computation of a program is achieved in the following two steps taking balancing of load and reducing overhead for sharing information into account:

1. decomposing a problem into subproblems
2. allocating subproblems to parallel hardware

Sharing of information is achieved in either of the following schemes:

1. sharing a memory region, or
2. sending messages.

Sharing a memory region is advantageous when the amount of information shared among subproblems is large. We can even take this approach to a system with distributed memory by using the technique of *shared virtual memory* [Li 86]. However, there is a large possibility of processors being idle due to mutual exclusion among subproblems.

Using messages is advantageous when the amount of information shared among subproblems is small. However, there is the overhead of message transmission and reception.

That is, sharing a memory region has no overhead of message transmission and reception, while it may suffer from performance degradation due to processors being idle. Using messages has a lower probability of processors being idle, while it may suffer from the overhead of message transmission and reception.

It is difficult in general to determine the allocation of subproblems to processors/computers in advance of execution so that the load of each processor/computer balances for the entire course of execution. Thus, we need dynamic allocation of subproblems to processors/computers. In case of sharing a memory region for sharing information, it is difficult to allocate subproblems to processors/computers beyond their directly accessible regions. It becomes difficult even to write a correct program and maintain it which uses a memory region for sharing information, when the problem becomes large and complex. This is because we need a lower level of synchronization among subproblems than the object level.

Thus, sharing by message is advantageous when we need wide-range load averaging for a large problem. If we have a large amount of information to share, we make it one or more objects so that we can share the information by messages. We can employ the shared virtual memory technique as the base so that object migration can be easily achieved as well.

5 Distributed Computing

In order to perform parallel computing, we decompose a problem into subproblems and allocate them to parallel hardware. This in fact yields distance between subproblems. Distance manifests in communication delay. And, this prevents an object from knowing the current status of other objects. This is an essential characteristic of distributed systems.

We can now define *distributed computing* as computation with more than one activity (or object) where distance, or communication delay, between activities (or objects) has to be considered. In the other words, *parallel computing* can be defined as a sort of distributed computing where distance, or communication delay, between activities can be ignored.

If all the objects concerned with a computation have to have the *unique view* of an object in distributed computing, we need synchronization among all the objects for every event when the object changes its state. We call this *complete sharing* of an object. Instead, the objects concerned with a computation can give up having the unique view of an object, so that we can reduce the frequency of synchronization. We call this *incomplete sharing* of an object. In a distributed system, it is impractical to do complete sharing, especially when distance among objects is long and the amount of shared information is large. And it is not always necessary in spite of [Carriero 89][Birman 85].

6 Open Systems

We started parallel computing by decomposing a problem into subproblems. However, our recent computational environment consists of existing servers (i.e., objects or agents). The number and services of servers change from a time to time. Recent computation is thus performed in a distributed computational environment. Consequently, programming style is changing from an algorithmic/synthetic way to "try to use them" way. That is, a program is written to make maximal use of existing services at each step in the computation.

In such a programming style, it is impossible to know in advance of execution what kinds of services are available at a certain time. In addition, in order to know the available services in the course of executing a program, an object has to use time and computational power. Nevertheless, the result returned to the object might not be correct, since the state of the system could change before it takes the planned action. This is the significance of *Open Systems*[Hewitt 84]. Although this is an unavoidable drawback from the conventional viewpoint of programming methodology, we should affirmatively utilize this characteristic for efficiency and robustness of a system.

7 Computational Field Model

As the number of computers increases, and as the mesh of networks becomes finer, it would be reasonable to consider an open distributed environment as a continuous *computational field*. This is one level higher model than the model of computers connected with networks, since we can ignore the topology and capacity of networks, and kinds and performance of connected computers.

We call such a model *computational field model*, or *CFM* for short. In this model, solving a problem is envisaged as a mutual effect between the computational field and the problem. By using CFM, we can first observe the nature and behavior of a problem macroscopically and find the method to control the problem so as to maximally utilize the given resources.

One important notion in CFM is the *principle of locality*. Effect of any event is local. This is due to the distance between objects in the field, and communication delay in the field. We propose one way of controlling the mutual effect between problems and the computational field in the next three sections.

8 Distance

In distributed computing, especially in open environments, it is very important to keep the communication delay between objects short. Communication delay is a function of geographical distance, communication bandwidth, and other communication overhead. Let us define distance between objects as communication delay between the objects[1].

In open systems where computation proceeds utilizing existing objects (servers), we should use closer objects if the same services are provided, and we should ask objects to move closer for higher performance.

However, an open system is a multiuser system. Thus, an object which is used by n users (or n objects) should be placed at (or migrated to) a location where those users can efficiently use it. In order to decide such an ideal location, it is rational to define *gravitational force* between objects by the frequency of communication between the two objects.

If we want to define the locations of objects only by gravitational forces, all of the objects get together at one single point. In such a case, although communication delay is minimum, the execution speed of each object is slowed, because all the loads are gathered into one computer. Thus, we should introduce *repulsive force*, which can be defined by the load of a processor.

By knowing the distance and communication frequency between objects in CFM, it is possible to determine the optimum position of objects for each event in the course of execution. However, it should also be noted that observing distance requires time and computing power, and the measured distance may already incorrect when we take action to the object.

9 Mass

Assume that at a certain time in the course of computing the objects are all placed at their optimum locations. Also assume that we can know their optimum locations at the next time. It is not always true that migration should take place. This is because we have to pay a cost for migration.

The cost for migration is a function of the distance and the *mass* of the migrating object. The mass can be defined by the size of the object. We may also have to take the *inertia* of an object into consideration, which is interpreted as the overhead for migration. According to the above consideration, the location of the objects at the next time should be determined by the cost and the effect of migration.

---

[1]This definition is reasonable since ultimate communication delay between objects is determined by geographical distance.

10 MD-based Computing

We now define *MD-based computing* as a method of computing in CFM where computation proceeds by trying to maximally utilize existing objects and determining the optimal location of objects at the next timing taking cost and effect of migration into account. Determination of the optimal locations is performed by using the notions of distance, mass, gravitation force and repulsive force, where distance is a function of communication delay between objects, mass is the size or inertia of an object, gravitation force is a function of frequency of communication between objects, and repulsive force is a function of additional load to a computer.

Thus, MD-based computing is a computational method in which each user (or each object) does locally a best effort to achieve satisfactory allocation of objects using the notion of distance and mass. Conflict between users for their satisfactory object allocations should be solved by negotiation between users to find sub-satisfactory object allocations for them. This is viewing computation as transforming a part of the huge computational field into its adequate shape. That is to say, in MD-based computing, solving a problem is considered as mutual effects between the computational field and the problem.

Figure 1 illustrates MD-based computing in CFM. There are two tasks (Task A and Task B) being executed in a open distributed computational field. If you want to start a new task, you will put the task to the field through your interface computer. The load of the computer becomes very high so that repulsive forces appear among the objects consisting the task. At the same time, gravitational forces appear between these objects and some existing objects on the computational field, as these objects communicate with the existing objects. Thus, the task starts to diffuse, that is, objects consisting the task migrate. Some of the existing objects may move to their new locations, being attracted by the new task. Negotiations among objects may be necessary for finding satisfactory locations. Please note that all the existing computations in the computational field form the environment for the new task, and the new task changes the environment.

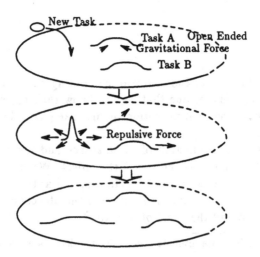

Figure 1: MD-based computing in a computational field

11 Conclusion

In this paper, we proposed a new computing model called *computational field model* for solving a problem in an open distributed environment. In this model, we view an open distributed computing environment as a continuous computational field, as opposed to conventional view of a computing system being a discrete computational field. We also proposed the method of MD-based computing to give a concrete idea of how to perform computation in the computational field model. We introduced the notions of distance and mass in MD-based computing, and we envisage solving a problem as mutual effects between the computational field and the problem.

Based on the notion of the computational field model and MD-based computing, we have been developing a new operating system called MUSE[Yokote 89] which supports object migration. We are also developing a programming language called MUSIC[Watari 90] to describe wide variety of application programs on the MUSE operating system.

Acknowledgment

The author is indebted to Professor Carl E. Hewitt, who is currently an IBM Chair Visiting Adjunct Professor at Keio University, for giving him an insight of Open Systems. The author wishes to thank Shinji Kono, Chisato Numaoka, Eiichi Osawa, Rik Smoody, Shigeru Watari, and Yasuhiko Yokote for their critical comments and discussion.

References

[Birman 85] Kenneth P. Birman. Replication and Fault-Tolerance in the ISIS System. In *Proceedings of the 10th ACM Symposium on Operating System Principles*, ACM, December 1985.

[Carriero 89] Nicholas Carriero and David Gelernter. Linda in context. *Communications of the ACM*, Vol.32, No.4, 1989.

[Hewitt 73] C. Hewitt, P. Bishop, and R. Steiger. A Universal Modular ACTOR Formalism for Artificial Intelligence. In *Proceedings of the 3rd International Joint Conference on Artificial Intelligence*, August 1973.

[Hewitt 84] Carl Hewitt and Peter de Jong. Open Systems. In J. Mylopoulos and J. W. Schmidt M. L. Brodie, editors, *On Conceptual Modeling*, Springer-Verlag, 1984.

[Li 86] Kai Li. *Shared Virtual Memory on Loosely Coupled Multiprocessors*. Technical Report, Yale University, December 1986.

[Tokoro 84] Mario Tokoro and Yutaka Ishikawa. Object-Oriented Approach to Knowledge Systems. In *Proceedings of the International Conference on Fifth Generation Computer Systems 1984*, November 1984.

[Tokoro 88] Mario Tokoro. Issues in Object-Oriented Concurrent Computing. In *Proceedings of 4th Conference of Japan Society for Software Science and Technology*, September 1988. (in Japanese).

[Watari 90] Shigeru Watari, Ei-ichi Osawa, Yasuaki Honda, and Mike Reeve. *Towards Music: A Description Language for the Muse Object Model.* Technical Report SCSL-TM-90-001, Sony Computer Science Laboratory Inc., February 1990.

[Yokote 86] Yasuhiko Yokote and Mario Tokoro. Design and Implementation of ConcurrentSmalltalk. In *Proceedings of Object-Oriented Programming Systems, Languages and Applications in 1986*, ACM, September–October 1986.

[Yokote 87] Yasuhiko Yokote and Mario Tokoro. Concurrent Programming in Concurrent-Smalltalk. In Akinori Yonezawa and Mario Tokoro, editors, *Object-Oriented Concurrent Programming*, pp.129–158, The MIT Press, 1987.

[Yokote 89] Yasuhiko Yokote, Fumio Teraoka, and Mario Tokoro. A Reflective Architecture for an Object-Oriented Distributed Operating System. In *Proceedings of European Conference on Object-Oriented Programming*, July 1989. also appeared in SCSL-TR-89-001 of Sony Computer Science Laboratory Inc.

PART II

Parallel Lisp

Systems and Architectures

Concurrent Programming in TAO — Practice and Experience

Ikuo Takeuchi

NTT Basic Research Laboratories

3-9-11, Midori-cho, Musashino-shi, Tokyo, 180 Japan

E-Mail: nue%ntt-20.ntt.jp@relay.cs.net (CSNET)

Abstract

This paper describes various aspects of the concurrent programming in the Lisp language and related problems, based on our practice and experience with a concurrent Lisp dialect TAO. TAO realizes a multiple process and multiple user environment of practical performance and significance on a single ELIS processor by its powerful concurrent primitives.

Topics described in this paper include: a Lisp-style process management, sharing Lisp programs among processes and users, name space problems around symbol packages, concurrent primitives, concurrent program debugging, and some performance figures. Further extension of TAO towards to a multiple ELIS processor system is also discussed briefly.

1 Introduction

TAO is a Lisp dialect with multiple paradigms on the ELIS Lisp machine [Watanabe 88], which fuses the traditional procedural, or more precisely, Lisp paradigm, object-oriented paradigm, and logic paradigm into one language [Takeuchi 86]. TAO also provides a set of powerful concurrent programming primitives which can serve as a basis for some higher level concurrent programming languages embedded in TAO. Using these primitives, TAO realizes a practical multiple process and multiple user environment on the ELIS Lisp machine. In fact, TAO/ELIS is the first Lisp machine which realizes such a multiple user environment of practical performance. We are now designing the extension of the TAO concurrent primitives for a multiple ELIS processor system. Since the concurrency of the TAO processes is coarse grained, the parallelism aimed at by the multiple ELIS processor system will also be coarse grained.

In this paper, we describe the practice and experience of the TAO concurrent programming, which might not be apparent in other systems than TAO/ELIS, in which we had to control all the system behaviors only by TAO itself. In this sense, we think of TAO as an operating system as well as a Lisp language. Such simple concurrent primitives as semaphore and mailbox come to have some peculiar characteristics in TAO. We also describe a big problem, the name space problem, which arises when we use a Lisp language as an operating system for multiple processes and multiple users. Some other related topics: concurrent program debugging, performance evaluation, research direction towards the parallel programming on a multiple ELIS processor system will also be discussed in this paper.

2 Design Principles

The concurrent programming features of TAO are based on the following design principles:

(1) TAO should be able to describe the operating system for multiple processes and multiple users. We believe that there would be still cases in which multiple users on a single Lisp machine are desirable. Or, even if it is not the case, the techniques to cope with multiple user environment will be useful to really complicated multi-processor applications connected mutually by network, where name space problems will be vital.

(2) Programs should be able to be shared among processes and users as far as possible. This requirement is crucial if a number of programs and users run the same big program package on the same machine. Lisp's most intrinsic principle "program as data" implies that data space should also be able to be shared. That is, data space should be uniform, not separated among processes and users. For example, there should be only one "next cons pointer" for all processes and users. This principle will, however, be valid only under the assumption that the users are not malicious but only careless sometimes, of course.

(3) TAO should be self-contained to control the system behavior even when some system malfunction has happened. For example, if a user happens to be trapped in a trouble by some unhappy reason, there should be a means for another user to be able to help him out of the trouble.

(4) The concurrency in TAO should bear real-time applications as far as possible. Since our starting point in 1980 was a single ELIS processor, the granularity of the concurrency is coarse, and hence the speed of the process switching is more significant than the speed of process creation and destruction.

(5) TAO should provide an ample set of low-level powerful concurrent primitives rather than prematurely designed, strongly disciplined concurrent language constructs. Thereby we can have a free hand to experiment a variety of new concurrent languages on it.

(6) Finally, in conjunction with multiple ELIS processors, TAO should provide a way of highly modular parallel programming instead of massively parallel programming. That is, each ELIS processor should do significant amount of job in a unit without overly dispatching it to other processors. In other word, each ELIS processor should

be a highly integrated intelligent agent. A rather loosely coupled cooperation of
them does a big job as a whole. This is a natural consequence of (4) and it is quite
unlike other medium-grain or fine-grain parallel Lisp systems such as EVLIS Lisp
[Saito 83], Qlisp [Gabriel 84], Multilisp [Halstead 86], PaiLisp [Kon 86], Connection
Machine LISP [Steel 86], and Paralation Lisp [Sabot 88]. This point will be discussed
further in the Section 9.

On designing the concurrent primitives of TAO, we have been much influenced by
ZetaLisp on Symbolic 3600 and Lambda [Weinreb 83], especially in their naming. Many
functions have the same names or similar names, but their meanings and implementation
may be different.

We think, as we said in (5), that the time is not ripe yet to settle the concurrent
programming disciplines and constructs into the final shape. Our experience in TAO/ELIS
would, however, make them more clearly in sight after we will get and experience the
multiple ELIS processors, called MacELIS II.

3 Processes, Logins, Users and Process Management

In this section, we introduce the basic concepts around the TAO processes for the convenience of later sections.

3.1 Processes

TAO has only one notion, process, which represents the course and environment of computation. Processes are defined as a user defined object under the class **process** in TAO.
Here, the word "object" means exactly the same thing as typical object-oriented programming languages such as Smalltalk-80 [Goldberg 83] means. We call the user defined
object a udo (pronounced as "you-daw") for short. Figure 1 shows the structure of a
process udo.

Like other systems, processes can be either inactive (or dormant) or active. When a
process is active, it may be either running, or runnable (queued in the runnable process
queue), or waiting for some event. Figure 2 shows the state transition graph between
them.

To create an inactive process, we write, instead of using the low level **make-instance**,

```
(make-process NAME ...)
```

where ... stands for some keyword arguments. To activate an inactive process, we write

```
(process-preset PROCESS INITIAL-FN INITIAL-ARG-LIST)
```

sys:priority	2
sys:quantum♡	5
sys:default-sysmode	#4
sys:status	#10
sys:whostate	running
sys:job	"current-process in ZEN"
sys:wait-for-what	(10)
sys:semi-globals♡	{vector}676600(bas:semi-global-variables . 172)
sys:variable-cache♡	{vector}7169343(sys:variable-cache . 256)
sys:name	univ:tak
sys:login♡	{udo}7169421[login]
sys:interprocess-closure♡	nil
sys:initial-function♡	my-top
sys:initial-argument-list♡	({udo}39952[fundamental-stream] {udo}39967[fundamental-stream])
sys:interrupt-fn-args♡	()
sys:semaphores	nil
sys:io	({udo}6572368[net:telnet-client-stream] {udo}39952[fundamental-stream] {udo}39967[fundamental-stream])
sys:plist	(sys:workbuf2 {memblk}4152474(#!8b-memblk . 1024) sys:workbuf1 {memblk}4152604(#!8b-memblk . 1024) :login-time 2819424884 :keyboard-idle 0)
sys:cpu-time	2834
sys:subsecond	4732
sys:error♡	zen:zerror
sys:backtrace♡	((illegal-argument car foo) vanilla-error backtrace-stopper)
sys:package	{package}7169429[tak]
sys:package-use-list♡	({package}42039[net] {package}56291[spell] {package}42075[jpro] {package}42063[zen])
sys:readtable	{vector}40051(readtable . 128)
sys:readtable-sp	{stkpt}#73400
sys:sp	{stkpt}#72376
sys:sbr	#176402
sys:bottom-stack-block#	14
sys:prestk-memblk-list	()
sys:pool	{dnil}1074
sys:base-vector	nil

Figure 1. A Process Udo

A process udo is represented internally as a vector. Instance variables and their values are paired as shown. In this figure, the order of the instance variables are rearranged for the reader's convenience. The actual order is determined by the microcode efficiency. Instance variables marked with ♡ are explained somewhere in the paper. Some of them without ♡ are, however, worth brief explanation here. **sys:status** is a bit table which represents the process's status. **sys:wait-for-what** represents what the process is waiting for. **sys:semaphores** keeps a list of semaphores the process currently occupies, by virtue of which all the semaphores can be forced to be released when the process is reset. Instance variables below **sys:readtable** can be ignored since they are for system internal use.

which orders PROCESS to apply INITIAL-FN to INITIAL-ARG-LIST. If one wants to reuse the initial function and initial argument list already stored in the process udo, it is enough to write

```
(process-reset PROCESS)
```

Note that process-preset and process-reset. are applicable to even active processes. An active process holds its computational environment in its udo and in its associated environment stack (designated by sys:sp and related instance variables in the process udo shown in Figure 1). Inactive processes are not associated with an environment stack, since the stack of ELIS is implemented with a very high speed dedicated memory and it is an important and precious system resource.

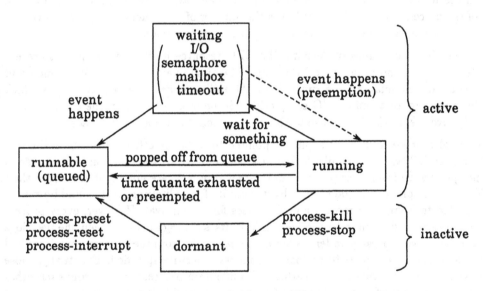

Figure 2. State Transition of a Process

3.2 Logins and Users

When a user logs in to the ELIS machine, a udo of the class login is created. The user's process for the top-level Lisp listener, called main process of the login, will be stored in sys:process slot (i.e., stored as the value of the instance variable sys:process) of the login udo, and it is the only process of the user which is pointed to from the login udo. There are no direct pointers from the login udo to other processes which the user creates in his login session.

If the same user logs in more than once at the same time, different login udo's will be created, since they should be absolutely distinguished. Login udo's will be collected as garbage if they are not pointed to from anywhere, i.e., if it is logged out.

There is a class user which represents the user registered to a particular ELIS machine. It contains the information specific to the user, such as user name, password, default file directory, etc.

3.3 Process Management

The scheduling of the processes is based on a simple round-robin method with priority and preemption. (Though the runnable process queue is represented by a list, it is carefully coded to reuse the cons cells in the queue in order to circumvent the garbage collection problem in the monitor kernel. The same implementation techniques are commonly used elsewhere in the microprogrammed monitor kernel.)

All the active processes are registered in the system table called the process pool. The size of the process pool is 128 and it limits the number of the concurrent active processes. Note that any active process is accessible from the process pool.

A running process goes on keeping the CPU resource until its time quanta are exhausted if there is no interrupt on the way. The time quantum is 20 milliseconds and the defaulted time quanta for a run is 5, or 100 milliseconds. However, a process which has been waiting for terminal I/O completion will be preempted upon the completion in order to give the quickest response to the user keyboard and mouse interface.

Generally, processes are not explicitly pointed to from any other processes on the system's responsibility. For example, forked processes created by the function process-fork are not pointed to from their parents, and parent processes are not pointed to from their children. Every process should survive by its activity for its lifetime, or it should be explicitly pointed to from other more stable processes for its survival. However, every process under the same login points to the login udo in its sys:login slot. When the user logs out, all the active processes under his login will be sought from the process pool described above, and killed (i.e., made to be inactive) unless otherwise specified. Eventually, those inactive processes are collected as garbage. To maintain processes apart from each other is suitable for a sort of Lisp-style process management and it is a natural way to prevent the user from being annoyed by unexpected memory waste by garbage processes created by him, especially when or after some accident has happened. This principle is also justified by the fact that if processes are mutually dependent, they have only to use primitives such as mailbox to communicate with each other, and there is no need to point to other processes directly. A similar principle will be applied to the future inter-processor process management in a multiple ELIS processor system, as will be discussed in the Section 9.

4 Variables

As we said in (2) in the Section 2, we have to make programs sharable as far as possible among processes and users. In this section, we describe various problems about variables which arise in conjunction with the program sharing.

4.1 Deep Binding

First of all, we decided to use the deep binding in TAO. As can be easily seen, the deep binding is apparently superior to the shallow binding with respect to the multi-processing, because the deep binding has much less overhead for process switching than the shallow binding. A disadvantage of the deep binding is the relatively slow speed of variable search. However, it can be more or less alleviated by using cache techniques extensively. In fact, the non-local variable cache table attached to each process (sys:variable-cache slot in Figure 1) speeds up accesses to special variables in the deep binding to be nearly comparable with those in the shallow binding.

4.2 Sharing Variables

It is one of the main problems in the design of TAO to decide how variable sharing among processes and users should be nicely controlled. Unlike other languages, Lisp keeps variable names as data at run time and it inherently raises the problem of sharing data, since variable names themselves are a kind of data in Lisp.

There are two ways of classifying how variables are shared. The first classification is based on what part of information of a variable is shared. A variable can be shared either only in its name, or both in its name and in its value. We call the latter case a variable being shared in binding.

In most cases of sharing a program, only variable names are shared among processes. The deep binding is the best choice for these cases. However, if processes want to control the use of some common resources cooperatively or to communicate with each other, such primitives as semaphores and mailboxes have to be able to be seen by those processes in common. Sharing variables in bindings is obviously the easiest and most natural way to realize it, though it is possible to share those through different variable names from each process.

The second classification is based on to what extent variables are shared among processes. Some variables may be shared by all processes in the system, for example, a system global variable such as *features*. Some are shared among the processes under a user's login. For example, a global variable in the user's symbol package can be accessed by all his processes if their default symbol packages are the same. Some variables are required to be more subtly shared by a specific subset of the user's processes.

A typical device to make variables be shared by a specific subset of processes is the inter-process closure. To make an inter-process closure of variables VAR1, VAR2, ..., we evaluate the form

```
(interprocess-closure VAR1 VAR2 ...)
```

and give the value to the processes with the keyword :interprocess-closure upon creating them by make-process. The macro interprocess-closure is simply defined as follows:

```
(defmacro interprocess-closure (&rest vars)
  '(closure ',vars #'(lambda (fn args) (apply fn args))) )
```

The process which is given this closure will apply this closure to its initial function and initial argument list when the process gets started by process-reset or process-preset. Hence they will have VAR1, VAR2, ... in common at the bottom of the environment stack. Note that TAO has a function which makes a function closure explicitly and, unlike Common Lisp [Steel 84], special variables can be enclosed in a closure as well as lexical variables. Thus, VAR1, VAR2, ... may be special variables. An example of the usage of inter-process closures will be shown in Section 6.8.

It is the user's responsibility to resolve the problem of mutual exclusion and synchronization in the access to the binding-shared variables. From this viewpoint, an interesting usage of binding-shared variables is to share a logical variable between processes. The logical variable is a different kind of the TAO variable whose value is instantiated (or bound) by the unification. As far as the unification concerns, a logical variable behaves just like a variable in "single assignment" languages. So if it is shared in binding, it can be used as a synchronization primitive since the unification of a logical variable is an inseparable operation, i.e., a kind of test-and-set operation.

4.3 Semi-global Variables

It is often desirable to have process-wide global variables which are local to a process and can be declared (or undeclared) dynamically after the process has been started. Special variables in the Common Lisp sense cannot cope with the requirement, since the extent of a special variable corresponds to the static nesting of program structures in the process, not to the process itself, or otherwise it becomes suddenly global to all the processes which use the same symbol package in common, that is, it will suddenly be package-wide global. Moreover, in TAO, there are cases that processes are reset explicitly by process-reset or by accident (caused by some bugs), and still are desired to continue the computation somehow[1]. For example, the main process of a login (the top-level TAO listener) can be aborted to the top-level loop in the course of lengthy or buggy computation by hitting a control backslash from the keyboard. However, there may be rare cases the abort action does not work. The last means to get back control again is to force the process to be reset. Even in such a case, users want to keep the values of important variables such as the conversation history. That is, a stable process-specific global variables are desired. Similarly, a sort of login-wide global variables are also desired.

Semi-global variables are variables global within a process or a login. The former is called process semi-global and the latter is called login semi-global. Each kind of semi-global variables can be declared, respectively, as follows:

```
(semi-globals :process goo choki pah)
(semi-globals :login tit tat)
```

---

[1]When a process is reset, its corresponding environment stack is entirely cleared. Thus, nothing in the stack is expected to survive.

To make process semi-global variables undeclared, evaluate

```
(undeclare-semi-globals goo pah)
```

It is not allowed to make login semi-global variables undeclared, because it is dangerous in most cases. Since the process (or login) semi-global variables are attached to the process (or login) udo permanently, they are stable against process resetting.

These semi-global variables are extensively and crucially used in the TAO concurrent programming. For example, a number of important variables for the screen editor called ZEN (an Emacs [Stallman 87] clone written by Yoshiji Amagai [Amagai 87], which uses the TAO object-oriented paradigm extensively) are declared to be process semi-global. These variables cannot be special variables declared within the ZEN program, since if it were, such important information as editor buffer contents would be lost if the user once exits ZEN. These variables cannot be either login semi-global or package-wide global, since there may be more than one ZEN activation instances under the same login, for example, when a user opens multiple windows in some of which he invokes ZEN independently. Similarly, a number of important variables for the TCP/IP network system are declared to be process semi-global.

Examples of login semi-global variables are *standard-output*, *error-output* and such. If a process spawned with a minimum variable environment causes an error, the error report should come out to the stream which is the value of the semi-global variable *error-output*. If the variable is not declared as a login semi-global variable, it will be output to the stream which is the value of the system global variable *error-output*, namely, to the main console terminal. That would not be a good practice. Another example of a login semi-global variable is that for Japanese word processor's dictionary. The user's dictionary is customized for each user, and continually updated according to the reference statistics. The dictionary should obviously be common to all the processes under the same login, and generally, final update into the disk is desired to take place only once at logout. Hence, it is appropriate to be represented as a login semi-global variable. It cannot be a package-wide global variable in the user's symbol package, because the variable name belongs to a global symbol package jpro for the Japanese word processor, and is shared by many other users.

Here, we should briefly explain the order of the variable search, since there are so complicated hierarchies in the TAO variables. First, variables within the lexical scope are searched. Second, instance variables are searched if the lexical scope limit corresponds to a method for a class's message. Third, special variables which are declared in some program constructs are searched. Fourth, process semi-global and then login semi-global variables are searched. Finally, the value field of the variable name is checked. Of course, such a fuss is considerably sped up by an extensive use of cache techniques.

4.4 Bindings

To cope with various requirements about variable sharing, we define the concept of variable binding as an explicit data type, which can be manipulated, at least, at the system programming level. It makes various experiments on variable sharing easy. Binding is a simple data type of the following cons cell structure:

```
(VALUE . VARIABLE-NAME)
```

which is pointed to with a binding tag (By a historical reason, the actual tag name is splvar instead of binding). Binding is a kind of invisible pointer, only whose car is visible in ordinary list operations. That is, usually a pointer with binding tag is automatically converted, or peeled out to the car of what the pointer points to, when it is actually needed.

Special variables, enclosed variables in a closure, and semi-global variables use bindings for their internal representation. Even instance variables and global variables can be manipulated as being represented in bindings, by pointing to the inside of udo or symbol with the tag binding, since the internal structure in the corresponding word (or cell) is similar to a binding (See Figure 1).

5 Name Space

Symbol packages in Common Lisp have resolved a number of name space problems in Lisp. However, it seems to be far from an ideal solution in conjunction with multiple processes and multiple users. In this section, we describe some of the problems we have encountered and their tentative solutions.

5.1 Hacking Other Symbol Packages

The first problem is raised by the fact that symbol packages can be shared by more than one users in the multiple user environment. If a user redefines system functions such as mapcar and sort, then all the other users suffers from unexpected behavior of the system. It can be easily understood that similar disasters happen if a user clobbers symbols in a shared symbol package.

Our simple solution to this problem is incomplete but seems to be enough for our current usage. We put a simple check that will signal a hack-other-package error when someone is going to redefine, or reassign a symbol globally without the privilege, which does not belong to his own packages. This check is also useful when someone makes a program package sharable by other users. If he forgets to declare a variable within his program constructs and therefore the variable is interpreted as a package-wide global variable, the hack-other-package error will be readily caused when the package is released to other users, even though the error must not occur in the test in his environment. On the contrary, he can leave it intentionally as a package-wide global variable, if he wants the variable to be almost immutable.

We does not, however, implement the similar check to the functions related to the property list, since we expect that the object-oriented paradigm will reduce the signifi-cance and usefulness of the symbol's property list. (Of course, there might be such radical solutions as making the property list "relative" to the users. But we don't think of it as a right direction.) The lack of the check may occasionally cause a collision of property names, especially when programs are ported from other Lisp systems. Even in such cases, the collision does not seem to be so often, since property names tend to be separated among users even if they have the same print name. (However, it may be disastrous if a user clobbers a symbol's property list as a whole.) Anyway, users are discouraged from using property lists in TAO.

5.2   Visibility between Symbol Packages

The second problem is the scope of a symbol package, that is, the problem about to what extent the symbol package can be seen. It is undesirable that a user can see symbol packages of other users. Hence, it is natural to realize the entire symbol package system in a tree structure. Figure 3 shows the current hierarchical structure of the symbol packages in TAO. Unlike Common Lisp, there may be a parent-child relationship between symbol packages. (ZetaLisp has a similar tree structure.) A symbol is sought first in the parent package chain and then in the packages used by the current package.

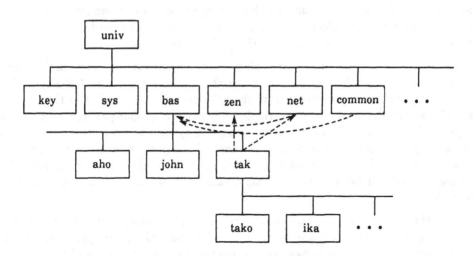

Figure 3.   Structure of the Symbol Packages
(Dashed lives indicate package-use relationship)

When a user logs in, his home package, namely, a symbol package with his name is created under the bas package (akin to the lisp package in Common Lisp). In this case, unlike other cases, the parent-child link between them is one way; only an upward link from the user's home package to the bas package is established, in order to make users' packages unreachable from each other by following the links up and down, and to make them immediately collectable as garbage when users log out. It follows the principle that things should survive by their own activities against the garbage collection as described in Section 3.3.

Under a login, tree structured nesting of the user's symbol packages are not expected to be so deep. In general, such functions like `in-package` and `make-package` create a new symbol package just under the user's home package.

5.3 Lifetime of Symbol Packages

The third problem is that symbols of users who had already logged out may remain uncollected by the garbage collector. For example, if a user puts something which contains his package's symbols in it in the property list on a system's symbol and then logs out, those symbols cannot be collected as garbage, and hence the symbol package pointed to from the symbol's package pointer, all the symbols in the package and all things which are referred directly or indirectly from those symbols are uncollectable! That is, if a user does such a thing, the user's ghost will survive as if he had not logged out, at least, with respect to the memory consumption. In fact, this sort of ghost had been often wandering around in the TAO/ELIS system of the early development stage. We had occasionally to shut down the system for cleaning up the memory!

Our current solution is as follows. When a user logs out, his login udo is removed from the system variable which maintains all the current login udo's in a list. All of his processes are killed immediately, unless otherwise specified. Now, there must be no links from the system to what is relevant to the user's login session. The outdated symbols are collected by two successive occurrences of the garbage collection.

In the first occurrence of the garbage collection, when collecting symbols in the collection phase, the garbage collector rewrites the symbol package pointer field of a symbol to nil if the symbol package pointed to from the field has not been marked in the marking phase. (Note that the marking is not rippled beyond the symbol package pointer field of a symbol in the marking phase.) That is, such a symbol is forced to be uninterned by the garbage collector. In the next occurrence of the garbage collection, uninterned and unmarked symbols are collected as garbage. (Note that when an interned symbol is not marked, it will not be collected if it has a value or function definition or non-empty property list.)

Besides this general mechanism, however, we also implemented explicit ways of getting rid of such symbols. For example, when a user logs out, all the property lists of the system's symbol such as those in `bas` package are thoroughly examined and any property name in the logged out user's packages are removed.

Similar caution is needed in conjunction with the object-oriented paradigm. For example, if a user wants to define his own subclass of a system defined class such as one of those in the ZEN editor. In our implementation of the object-oriented paradigm, super-classes keep their subclasses in the `component-of-what` slot (again in ZetaLisp or Flavors terminology) in order to propagate their change to their subclasses properly when they are redefined somehow. However, if such links are unconditionally established, it is obvious that a similar lifetime problem arises. So TAO does not establish the downward link from a superclass defined in a symbol package to a subclass defined in a different symbol package. It will be justified by the fact that the system defined classes are relatively stable and the change propagation is hardly needed.

5.4 Special Symbol Packages

The last problem concerns the discrepancy between the static nature of the symbol package linkage and the dynamic nature of using symbol packages within processes. Each symbol package is usually associated with a program package, a set of functions and variables which does some useful work collectively. Symbol packages guarantee the uniqueness of symbols in I/O operations. However, in general, program packages should guarantee the integration and encapsulation of the programs at run time. This difference between symbol packages and program packages raises a number of problems in conjunction with multiple processes and users.

For example, the ZEN editor which is written in the zen symbol package provides a set of useful functions, classes and message interfaces for the user. When a user wants to use ZEN, it is not sufficient only to establish a link from the current package to the zen package, which is meant by use-package in Common Lisp, since a number of semi-global variables have to be declared before using ZEN as described in Section 4.3. Hence, we made it possible to attach some eval-when-use actions to symbol packages. If a symbol package is attached with eval-when-use actions, they are evaluated when the package is to be used. Symbol packages attached with eval-when-use actions are called special. For example, the zen package is attached with declaration of a number of semi-global variables and creation of some udo instances.

However, this rather simple-minded solution will not work if the user creates a process in which the symbol package is the same as the parent process. Though, say, the zen package is used by the both processes in the Common Lisp sense, the eval-when-use actions have not been fulfilled yet in the child process and hence ZEN does not work there correctly. Similar contradictory problems also happen when a process issue unuse-package of some special symbol package which is now used commonly by a set of processes. This illustrates in what point symbol packages and program packages differ from each other. The use-used relationship between symbol packages are thought of static, but using program packages is dynamic for each process.

Our current solution to these problems is as follows. We put sys:package-use-list slot in the process udo to maintain the usage of special symbol packages. Special symbol packages are registered to this slot only after eval-when-use actions are performed. In the I/O operations, a symbol which belongs to a special symbol package which can be seen through the static links of symbol packages is made invisible, if the special symbol package is not registered in the sys:package-use-list slot of the current process. If a process unuses a special symbol package, the corresponding eval-when-unuse actions are performed and the package is removed only from the sys:package-use-list slot of the process.

We need, however, to put a small check function check-usedness at the entry point of each interfaced (exported) function of the special symbol package in many cases. The function check-usedness examines whether the package is actually used by the process and performs the eval-when-use actions if necessary. This is because we want a sort of auto-loading function facilities for everyday convenience. For example, it is desirable that if the user call the function z, the zen package is automatically used and then invokes zen:z, the main entry function of ZEN. To do so, the first z should be interned to the user's home package, which is defined so as to replace its body by an appropriate new body when being called for the first time. After the z's body has been replaced, the symbol z is still in the user's home package and hence visible and callable by all his processes, most of which may not have put the zen package in their sys:package-use-list slot yet. This is the reason why check-usedness is needed at the entry point of ZEN.

However, we confess that these solutions seem to be far from elegant and satisfactory. We need more experience on the matter and may need to consider a radical reformulation of the symbol package concept.

6 Concurrent Primitives

In this section, we describe some unique concurrent primitives of TAO and related topics. These include such popular semaphores and mailboxes. However, even those have unique features in TAO. At the end of this section, we show some illustrative examples.

6.1 Waiting for Event and Allowing Schedule

An active process can come into a waiting state in one of the following cases:

- I/O wait.

- Semaphore wait.

- Mailbox wait.

- Timeout wait.

- Multiple wait, that is, waiting for one of a combination of the events: I/O, mailboxes, and timeout.

- FEP (Front End Processor) wait such as that for responses for file opening.

To wait for a timeout, the function wait-until-timeout is used.

```
(wait-until-timeout TICKS)
```

where TICKS is the number of ticks to wait and one tick is 20 milliseconds. Some event waiting functions can be supplemented by with-timeout to overlap the waiting event with a timeout event. For examples,

```
(read-char-with-timeout TICKS &optional STREAM)
(tyi-with-timeout TICKS &optional STREAM)
(tyo-with-timeout TICKS CODE &optional STREAM)
```

where `tyi` and `tyo` are almost equivalent to `read-byte` and `write-byte` of Common Lisp, respectively. This type of overlapping is more efficient than that of `multiple-wait` which will be described in Section 6.4.

To make a process release the CPU resource and get queued in the runnable process queue explicitly, we evaluate

```
(process-allow-schedule)
```

just like ZetaLisp.

6.2 Semaphores

Semaphores of TAO are the simplest ones. However, it is implemented as a udo. It can have a name itself. It has a slot to keep the process which currently occupies it, which is very useful when something wrong happens mainly by a bug. Functions related to semaphores are[2]:

```
(p-sem SEMAPHORE)
(p-sem-with-timeout TICKS SEMAPHORE)
(v-sem SEMAPHORE)
(sys:v-sem SEMAPHORE)
```

The function `p-sem-with-timeout` may be useful to detect a semaphore deadlock in the debugging stage. It may also be useful for some real-time applications. The function `sys:v-sem` can force the semaphore to be released even it has been occupied by another process. (The function `v-sem` will signal an error if a process is going to release the semaphore which has been occupied by another process.) It is needed to recover the resource when, for example, a process goes out of control holding the semaphore. Such an operation may not be sound but it is needed if one wants to write and control everything in a single language. On the contrary, `sys:v-sem` can be positively used with care in some cases.

It is not a good practice, of course, to use such primitive P-V operations on semaphores. However, one can easily define a macro which makes programs more structured and readable as follows:

```
(defmacro critical-section (semaphore &rest body)
   '(without-interrupts
     (unwind-protect
      (progn (p-sem ,semaphore) ,@body)
      (v-sem ,semaphore) )))
```

It is not, however, the main objective of this paper to discuss such a sort of discipline.

---

[2]Corresponding message passing forms can be easily defined of course.

6.3 Mailboxes and Pipe Streams

Mailboxes are the most general means for processes to communicate with each other. Since TAO is a Lisp, it is easy and natural to realize a mailbox with indefinitely long mail queue and process queue, and to make arbitrary Lisp data be able to be passed through the mailbox (except for nil!). Mailboxes are also implemented as a udo.

There are also a rich variety of functions related to mailboxes:

```
(send-mail MAILBOX DATA)
(signal-mail MAILBOX DATA)
(send-active-mail MAILBOX FN ARGS)
(signal-active-mail MAILBOX FN ARGS)
(receive-mail MAILBOX)
(receive-mail-with-timeout TICKS MAILBOX)
(receive-mail-no-hang MAILBOX)
(peep-mail MAILBOX)
```

The function send-mail sends DATA to MAILBOX and the process which sends the mail will go on running. DATA should not be nil. The value of send-mail is DATA. The function signal-mail sends DATA only when at least one process is waiting in the mailbox's process queue. If no processes are waiting, it returns nil indicating the failure.

The function send-active-mail as well as signal-active-mail does not send data but a pair of function and its argument. If a process receives such a pair other than ordinary data, it applies the function to its argument to get the value of receive-mail. The advantage of sending an active mail is to be able to leave the final evaluation of the required value to the receiver process. However, its origin was to make it possible to pass an error to the parent process which are waiting for the result to be posted in a mailbox by his child process. If the child process finds an error, it can simply send an error reporting active mail to the parent, which may cause an error in the parent process. If this mechanism is not provided, the parent process should always check the value according to some protocol, or the error is disposed of by such asynchronous a mechanism as process-interrupt, by which the parent may be interrupted even when he does not wait for the result any longer.

The function receive-mail will receive a mail from the mailbox if there is one, otherwise the process will be queued to the mailbox's process queue. The function receive-mail-with-timeout overlaps the mail wait and timeout wait. It is extensively used in the TCP/IP network system in TAO/ELIS [Murakami 88]. The function receive-mail-no-hang will return the mail (a non-nil value by definition) only when there has been posted at least one mail in the mailbox, otherwise returns nil. The function peep-mail returns t or nil, according to the existence of the mail in the mailbox.

Note that mails are not copied by sending mail. It is user's responsibility to take care in sharing data structures between the sender and receiver.

A pipe stream is one of the I/O streams in TAO, by which two processes can communicate one way concurrently. It can be thought of as an efficient mailbox specially tuned to pass sequences of bytes or characters between the processes. If the user once open a pipe stream by `open-pipe-stream`, it can be used completely in the same manner as other I/O streams. It is easy to make a pipe command like that of Unix by using pipe streams.

6.4 Multiple Event Wait

It often happens to be necessary to be able to wait for multiple events in OR, that is, wait until one of the waited events takes lace. For example, in the experiment of cooperative multiple ELIS processors connected by the TCP/IP network, a process may want information from any one of the processors he communicate with by various kinds of communication channels. In that case, without a multiple event wait mechanism, the user has to prepare as many processes as the waited events and make them pass each event through a single common mailbox to the main waiting process as shown in Figure 4. It is obviously cumbersome.

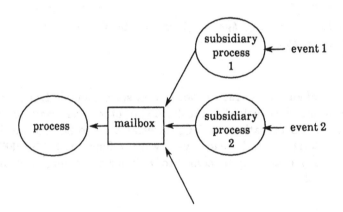

Figure 4. Multiple event wait without a
multiple-wait mechanism

The special form (in fact, a macro) `multiple-wait` alleviates the problem. It is written in the following form:

```
(multiple-wait VAR
   (WAIT-EVENT-1 ACTION-1 ...)
   (WAIT-EVENT-2 ACTION-2 ...)
   ...
   (WAIT-EVENT-n ACTION-n ...) )
```

where `WAIT-EVENT` is one of the following:

```
(tyi &optional STREAM)
```

```
(tyo CODE &optional STREAM)
(receive-mail MAILBOX)
(timeout TICKS)
```

where timeout wait is allowed only for the last WAIT-EVENT-n.

If this form is evaluated, the first occurring event, or more precisely, the value of the first returned WAIT-EVENT (nil for timeout) is setq'ed to VAR, the corresponding sequence of ACTION is evaluated and its last value will be returned as the value.

The following illustrates a typical usage of multiple-wait in ZEN.

```
(multiple-wait ch
  ((tyi) (if (eq (int-char ch) #\bell)
             (progn (write-line "Talk canceled.")
                    (cancel-talk him) ))
         nil )
  ((receive-mail r-mbox) ch)
  ((timeout 1600)
   (write-line "Ringing Again. Canceled by Control-G")
   (ring him r-mbox)
   nil ))
```

The implementation of multiple-wait is not trivial, since a simple I/O operation on a certain special stream may be eventually transformed to other event wait, for example, a mailbox wait. In fact, I/O operations on TCP streams tend to become waiting for a mailbox. So multiple-wait has to let each event waiting function WAIT-EVENT to run through until it eventually gets value or comes to wait for something, still under the control of multiple-wait!

6.5   Process Interrupts

The process interrupt is, as ZetaLisp, the means to make another process execute a given function asynchronously with its current computation being suspended for a while. It is unlike other systems in that it does not only signal an interrupt, but the interrupt signal itself indicates the action to be executed upon interrupt.

To signal an interrupt, the function process-interrupt is used:

```
(process-interrupt PROCESS FN ARGS FLAG)
```

where FN and ARGS denote the function and arguments to be executed upon interrupt. The last argument FLAG is a Boolean which indicates the degree of urgency of the interrupt. When a process is signaled an interrupt, the interrupt signal is queued in its sys:interrupt-fn-args slot (Figure 1). They are popped off from the queue and executed one by one, just before the interrupted process is going to run, or to get the CPU resource. The values of those executions are all discarded. Then, in general, the process will resume running as if nothing had happened.

If FLAG is nil, the execution of the interrupt signals is postponed until the interrupted process comes to run eventually. Otherwise, even if the interrupted process is waiting for something for a long time, the process is forced to be queued to the process runnable queue and the interrupt will have an effect as soon as possible, and after the interrupt it will wait for the same event again unless the interrupt affects the process's status somehow. (In that case, however, timeout wait will be canceled in the current implementation.)

Process interrupts are useful not only in rescuing a malfunctioning process but also in making the program's behavior more dynamic, even though a certain amount of care is needed to regulate the asynchronism. For example, cooperative problem solvers will need the process interrupt capability to control overall system behaviors in such cases as detecting and recovering from a deadlock, propagating a global strategy change to processes, etc [Onai 88].

Indeed, process interrupts are extensively used in TAO/ELIS. For example, the user's keyboard interrupts such as aborting back to the top level or resetting the main process are directly represented by a process interrupt. Another important concrete usage will be shown in the section 7.

There are two kinds of process interrupt inhibition. One is the absolute inhibition of the process switching, which is written in the special form:

```
(sys:without-interrupts FORM ...)
```

As can be easily imagined, this is an indispensable mechanism to write truly critical sections in TAO, since the process switching may occur at any timing between Lisp instructions, for example, at any fetch of LAP byte code. (For safety, however, the inhibition is automatically canceled if the process happens to come into a waiting state.)

The other is a process specific inhibition written in the macro:

```
(without-interrupts FORM ...)
```

Within this macro, process interrupt signals are only registered to the signal queue of the process. Their execution will be postponed until the inhibition is taken off. This mechanism is also indispensable to make sure of a critical code sequence of a program to be uninterrupted. Note that semaphores do not work for this purpose.

6.6   Auto-flush Streams

It happens for us to recognize it needs tedious or inelegant programming to write a sort of action which is to be performed when nothing more happens at that time. For example, the TELNET terminal stream in the TCP/IP network system should flush out its buffer contents when it becomes full (it's easy to detect), or there seems to be no more input to the buffer for some short interval of, say, 60 milliseconds. Of course, it is stupid to flush out the buffer contents every time something comes into the buffer, considering the overhead to make a transmission packet only for small amount of information.

The event that nothing has happened for a while is a sort of negative event. So it is difficult to detect it by the process itself since it does nothing too for that interval! To circumvent this problem, the former TELNET program created a daemon process which continually watches the TELNET server process whether or not there is some increment to the buffer since the last watch. If there is no increment, the buffer contents, if any, will be flushed out. Though it worked quite well, it was tedious and inelegant.

Auto-flush streams are introduced to give a final solution to this problem. The idea is simple enough. A buffered output stream can be designated to be an auto-flush stream, which is represented by a single bit in the status bit table of the stream. When a process is going to release the CPU resource, the message :flush will be sent to the auto-flush streams to which something is output during the last running quanta. Besides that, at every tick, it is checked if there is no increment to the buffer of the auto-flush streams after the last output. If there is no increment, the same message :flush is sent to the auto-flush streams during the clock tick interrupt. The user should take care not causing confusion between possible successive :flush messages to the same auto-flush stream.

Note that the automatic :flush message sending can be thought of as another kind of process interrupt which will be executed just before a process releases the CPU resource or at every clock tick. It is contrastive to the process interrupt described in Section 6.5 which is executed just before the process gets the CPU resource. We could have generalized this "afterward process interrupt" notion, not being limited to the auto-flush stream, but we hardly feel the necessity of such things for the present.

Auto-flush streams are used for TELNET server streams, X-window streams [Takada 89], and ZEN-shell streams to enhance the real-time efficiency of TAO/ELIS. For example, The ZEN-shell stream is used as a redirected output stream to the ZEN buffer from any application program. In this case, it is inefficient to flush out the output from the application program to the input to the ZEN buffer every time some output comes, since ZEN has to do some amount of work for redisplay every time input comes. So it is desirable to group the input into as big chunks as possible.

6.7 Sideward Funarg Problem

There had been the so-called funarg problem since the birth of Lisp and it seems to have been resolved in Common Lisp at the cost of the interpreter inefficiency. However, a new kind of funarg problem comes up in conjunction with the concurrent programming, which can be called a sideward funarg problem. For example, consider the case in which a lambda function closure is conveyed to another process than that which has created it and it is going to exit a lexically closed named block from inside, which is still alive in the original process. Is it sound to allow the control transfer across the process in such a case? Or, if so, in what way is it possible?

However, we decided to invalidate the lexical scope rule with respect to the control structure when a function closure is conveyed "sideward" to another process, since such kind of inter-process lexical control transfer is considered to be mostly unexpected for the user. Invalidating those, however, makes some amount of check in the function closure's execution necessary in order to be able to signal an error if such a transfer is going to take place.

We have to have another kind of lambda expression to cope with the problem. In fact, surprisingly enough, we have four kinds of lambda expressions in TAO! Lambda expressions can be made by either one of `bas:lambda`, `common:lambda`, `sys:lambda`, and `bas:expr`. The TAO native `bas:lambda` is for the lambda expression which can be used only in the downward (or inward) direction. The `common:lambda` makes a strict lexical closure for the compatibility with Common Lisp. The `sys:lambda` does not care to keep the environment where it stands. Its free variables may access to local variables declared where it is actually applied. So it is thought of as the most naive lambda in the Lisp 1.5 sense [McCarthy 65]. The following `bas:expr` makes a lambda expression with no lexical environment outside it as well as `sys:lambda`.

```
(expr (VAR ...) ...)
```

However, its free variables should access to non-local variables, i.e., special, semi-global, and global variables, since it limits the lexical scope within itself.

A lambda expression made by `bas:lambda` causes an error if it is conveyed upward or sideward and is to be applied. A lambda expression made by `common:lambda` will not cause an error even if is conveyed sideward. However, only when a lexical control transfer out of it is going to take place, an error is signaled. As can be easily imagined, `bas:lambda` is much more efficient than `common:lambda`. A lambda expression made by `sys:lambda` or `expr` does not cause an error wherever it is conveyed and applied. And they, especially `bas:expr`, are more efficient than `bas:lambda`. An explicitly created function closure by the function `closure` in the form:

```
(closure '(VAR1 VAR2 ...) #'(lambda ...))
```

keeps the enclosed variables in a list of bindings described in Section 4.4, and does not keep the lexical control structure with it. So it can also be conveyed and applied anywhere if one is careful of possible concurrent accesses to the enclosed and thereby binding-shared variables.

It may be confusing for the user that there are so many kinds of lambda expressions which are only subtly different from each other. It is, however, partly because of a historical reason, and partly because of the trade-off problem between generality and efficiency. From our experience, `bas:lambda` and `bas:expr` are enough in most cases. It is strongly recommended to use `bas:expr` to write a lambda expression for an initial function to be given to a spawned process.

6.8 An Illustrative Example

The following trivial example illustrates the use of an inter-process closure and how variables can be shared by a specific subset of processes.

```
(defun p-c (seeds rate)
  (let (p c ipc mbox)
    (declare (special mbox rate))
    (!mbox (make-instance 'mailbox :name 'p-c-channel))
    (!ipc (interprocess-closure mbox rate))
    (!p (make-process 'foo :initial-function 'produce
                  :initial-argument-list (list seeds)
                  :interprocess-closure ipc ))
    (!c (make-process 'bar :initial-function 'consume
                  :initial-argument-list ()
                  :interprocess-closure ipc ))
    (process-reset p)
    (process-reset c) ))
```

where an exclamation mark just after an opening parenthesis means a general assignment like setf of Common Lisp. If one calls p-c, two processes named foo and bar are spawned and start cooperating together through the mailbox designated by the shared variable mbox. Note that each process does not know the other process directly since the variables p and c are not passed to them. The variable rate is a variable denoting a fixnum which somehow represents a transportation rate between the two processes and is occasionally changed by either of them. Of course, mbox and rate are referred to from produce and consume as special variables. Now, assume that one calls p-c again. Then the same variables mbox and rate have two binding instances, respectively, each of which is shared by each pair of producer and consumer independently.

7   Concurrent Program Debugging

Generally, it is not easy to debug a program which creates a number of concurrently running processes. We have not yet integrated debugging tools especially tuned for the concurrent program debugging. However, TAO provides some basic mechanisms on which one can make and experiment a good disciplined, integrated debugging system.

Those mechanisms are mainly concerned with the error disposal. A process udo has two slots for the error disposal: sys:error and sys:backtrace shown in Figure 1. The sys:error slot holds an error disposal function which is particular to the process. In TAO, any error is reported with three kinds of information: error name, main information, and additional information. For example, if one is going to take the car of a symbol, say foo, these three will be illegal-argument, car and foo. The error disposal function held in the slot may be any function with three arguments. It is invoked when an error has happened. The defaulted function is vanilla-error.

The sys:backtrace slot keeps the backtrace information, or the information about the function call nesting at the time just when the most recent error has happened, if the error disposal function is specified to do so as vanilla-error is. It is crucial that the error disposal function and the most recent error backtrace information are directly attached to the process udo, not bound to some variables in the process, since there is no other means to record them once the process halts. In most cases, inspecting the error backtrace information is sufficient to detect what wrong has happened, because there is no difference in the information quality between an error in the user's main process and an error in a spawned process.

When a process seems to get wrong and it is still running somehow or waiting for something unexpected, it is convenient to use the function process-peep which is defined as follows:

```
(defun process-peep
    (process
     &optional (fn #'backtrace) (args ())
     &aux mailbox )
    (!mailbox (make-instance 'mailbox :name 'peeper))
    (process-interrupt process
            #'(expr (m fn args)
                    (send-mail m (catch 'error (apply fn args))) )
            (list mailbox fn args)
            t )
    (receive-mail mailbox) )
```

A call of process-peep without optional arguments will return a backtrace information of the running process just at the time it is interrupted without affecting it. Of course, one can supply a more intelligent function for the functional argument of process-peep. However, such simple one proves to be superbly useful from our experience, since the returned backtrace information is provided with both lexical and special variable names appearing just where they are declared in the function call nesting even when the program is compiled.

For example, if the ninth line in the function fib shown in Section 8

```
(list (1- n) m)
```

is carelessly written as

```
(list m (1- n))
```

then (fib 9) will cause an error in its spawned subprocesses. A backtrace information kept by one of them looks like:

```
((illegal-argument < {udo}6502416[mailbox])
 vanilla-error
 (n {udo}6502416[mailbox]) fib
 send-mail
 (m 8) (n {udo}6502416[mailbox]) #!expr-simple)
```

even if **fib** is compiled. The information is an alternating list of function names and their variables (if any) from near to far, headed by the error information. Here, one can easily see the bug that the argument of **fib** is a mailbox, not a number. In fact, another seed for more readable backtrace information is embedded in the **sys:backtrace** slot behind an invisible pointer. The advantage of using such an S-expression is that it can be easily manipulated by an intelligent debugging system.

In addition, a process udo can be inspected just like other objects as can be seen in Figure 1. (To inspect an actively running process however, one should not forget to apply **sys:without-interrupts**, since portions of the process udo may change in the course of the inspection.) TAO is inherently suitable for debugging whether the program is concurrent or not. Nevertheless, bugs related to the process asynchronism are still difficult to discover and remove, of course.

8   Performance Figures

In this section, we sketch some performance figures and "feeling" of the TAO concurrent programming on the ELIS Lisp machine. We omit the implementation technique issue since it will be too tedious to describe here, though we admit that if one wants to describe the performance evaluation of a system, he has also to describe the implementation of the system in a certain detail.

As described above, there can be at most 128 concurrently active processes. They share the high speed hardware stack memory for their environment representation. So there happens to take place a swapping in and out between the stack and the main memory if processes are to collide on the stack memory. By the limitation of the current ELIS machine's architecture, the amount of maximal usable stack memory for each process varies from only 2K words to 28K words. But we scarcely feel inconvenience by this limitation, except when we run a sort of toy program which simply recurs to itself, for example, calculation of the factorial of 2000.

It was one of our main objectives to make the process switching as fast as possible. If a process switching involves no stack swapping, it takes only about 40 microseconds. Even if stack swapping is necessary, it takes typically within 1 or 2 milliseconds. However, the possible worst case takes 22 milliseconds, though it is never expected to happen. Anyway, this delay is hardly noticeable to users in the conversational use.

It takes 13 milliseconds to make a process and start it running in a simplest manner. However, it takes 23 milliseconds to fork a process by the function **process-fork** since it does much more work to copy the parent's environment.

The following is a trivial and stupid program which calculates the Fibonacci number of n by creating subprocesses instead of recurring to itself.

```
(defun fib (n)
    (if (< n 2) 1
        (let ((p1 (make-process (string-append (pname n) "-1")))
              (p2 (make-process (string-append (pname n) "-2")))
```

```
      (m1 (make-instance 'mailbox))
      (m2 (make-instance 'mailbox)) )
  (process-preset p1
      #'(expr (n m) (send-mail m (fib n)))
      (list (1- n) m1) )
  (process-preset p2
      #'(expr (n m) (send-mail m (fib n)))
      (list (- n 2) m2) )
  (+ (receive-mail m1) (receive-mail m2)) )))
```

By the limitation mentioned above, Fibonacci of up to 9 can be calculated by this program. The elapse time to get the value of (fib 9) which spawns totally 108 processes is about 1.6 second. (Speaking for a ridiculous comparison, an ordinary recursive Fibonacci function gets the value of (fib 9) in 1.2 millisecond in the compiled run, and in 4.2 milliseconds in the interpreted run.)

As a matter of fact, the performance of the TAO concurrent programming can bear 5 or more users concurrently using the same ELIS machine. Typically, over a dozen of processes are running on the ELIS machine, about half of which are such system processes for the TCP/IP network system, for the ZEN editor (called "ZEN-basso-continuo" process), and for the window system. However, of course, most of them are in a waiting state.

Another rather surprising evidence of the performance of the TAO concurrent programming is the TCP/IP network system written by Ken'ichiro Murakami. It is an about 15K line TAO program written in the object-oriented paradigm (excluding such application layers as NFS and X-window). It spawns 6 or more processes: ether, arp, tcp-in, tcp-out, udp, ftp-server, etc. It can work even if all of the code runs in the interpreter! Hence, Murakami could debug the system in a conversational mode while the network system is running in the actual environment. We have never heard one could test and debug the TCP/IP network system in the interpreter of some language.

The high performance of the TAO concurrent programming is mostly due to the fact that almost all the key primitives are written in microcode. The amount of the microcode dedicated to the concurrency is estimated to be about 3K steps among over 50K step microcode. Thus, the TAO/ELIS system can be considered as a specially tuned Lisp machine for the concurrent programming. It is quite a simple secret!

9 Extension Towards Multiprocessor System

In this section, we discuss the future direction of the TAO concurrent programming for the multiple ELIS processor system whose prototype called MacELIS II is now being developed by Hirohide Mikami and his colleagues. Unlike most parallel Lisp machines or parallel Lisp implementations, its component processor is itself a rather big Lisp machine which can, in turn, run multiple processes inside. This would drive our research to somewhat different direction from others.

First of all, we have to make our starting point clear. It can be summarized as follows.

(1) Each processor is big enough and capable of running over a hundred processes concurrently as described above. Hence, the aimed parallelism must not be fine grained. It is the most urgent problem for us to find an ample variety of applications on such coarse-grained multiprocessor systems. However, some simple examples easily come to mind. For example, one of the processors may be (of course, maybe partly) dedicated to jobs related to a sort of intelligent Japanese word processing, thereby only one copy of a big common dictionary need be maintained in the entire system. The amount of information to be passed to utilize such big a unit of computation is sufficiently small but the communication speed is required as high as possible, even though. We will call this type of parallelism a highly modularized parallelism, in contrast with a sort of massive parallelism aimed at by most parallel Lisp systems.

(2) Processors in our multiprocessor system can share memory in somewhat a limited manner. That is, it is only possible to share the latter half of its main memory (latter half of the 128 megabyte address space at maximum[3]). The other half memory of each processor can be accessed in a special manner from other process. That is, an object in another processor can be accessed by its 32 bit byte-address but not directly by its Lisp pointer. We will call the shared memory of the former type is a symmetric shared memory, and the other an asymmetric shared memory. It is a problem how to accommodate this asymmetric shared memory in the programming concept.

(3) We do not want the garbage collection to be global to all the processors, which would make the garbage collection not real-time even if each processor has a real-time garbage collector. (This problem was once discussed by Robert Halstead [Halstead 84]. Indeed, we are now developing a real-time garbage collector based on a simple mark-and-sweep method for the single ELIS machine.) This implies a principle similar to that described in the former sections that any object in a processor should survive by its own responsibility if it is *conscious* that it is referred to from other processors. If it can be assumed, each processor can run each real-time garbage collector asynchronously and independently from each other. Though this principle seems to be unsound and make programming a little difficult, we think this approach would be more promising in a practical sense.

(4) As was suggested in (1), we will not, or we cannot aim at the full transparency about the processor multiplicity such as the parallelism transparency (making the user unconscious to whether or not his program is running on a single machine in a pseudo-parallel manner), the processor multitude transparency (making the user unconscious how many processors are running for his program), and the process migration transparency (making the user unconscious on what processor some of his function is running [Tanaka 89]). We can at most aimed at network connection transparency (making the user unconscious to whether a processor is connected via a shared memory or via a network [Murakami 89]). However, we want to design the language as near to be parallelism-transparent as possible. That is, if one has a

---

[3] ELIS is a 32 bit machine, and 8 of 32 bits are used as a tag. However, since 24 bit address part represents a cell address, the maximum address space is 128 megabytes.

correct concurrent program on a single processor, the modification needed to get it run on a multiprocessor system efficiently should be as little as possible. (Still the modification would be necessary.)

Those points should be directly reflected to our principles on designing the parallel processing primitives in TAO. It is easy to make semaphores and communication channels between processors, since ELIS has a basic mechanism to lock the memory access. However, it is not trivial how to represent an object on another processor and how to associate the representation with the object efficiently in the actual implementation. There remain still many controversial points on these matters. So we will not go further about the concrete design issue in this paper for the present.

10   Conclusion

We described the concurrent programming features of TAO and a variety of related topics based on our practice and experience. Some of them may be useful to the designers and implementors of similar systems. Though the TAO concurrent programming has rather a long history since the middle of 1980's, we think it is far from the final accomplishment as well as other language aspects such as the true integration of the multiple paradigms incorporated in TAO. However, we have been continually encouraged by the famous saying by LaoTze:

> The TAO that is named the TAO is not the true TAO.

We are continually changing TAO, especially with respect to the concurrent programming, since its ever widening usage continually reveals out new problems. And now, the pressure of MacELIS II may bring in a drastic reformulation of the TAO concurrent programming. But we will be ready to admit it. That is *the TAO*.

Nevertheless, TAO/ELIS seems to succeed to prove that a concurrent system based on Lisp can have practical performance and significance. If we can say only one thing about the TAO concurrent programming, this is the very one. We believe that it would encourage many Lisp lovers in the world.

Acknowledgment

We would like to express thanks to many colleagues and users for their patience with, suggesting improvements on, and making complaints with the TAO concurrent programming features. Some of them may have sometimes suffered from the catastrophe caused by careless system bugs. We would like to express special thanks to Rikio Onai, Ken'ichiro Murakami and Yoshiji Amagai for their "pioneer spirit" to exploit new features of the concurrency and their extensive utilization of them. And we would also like to express special thanks to Hirohide Mikami who is now going to give a new horizon to the TAO concurrent programming by conducting the MacELIS project.

References

[Amagai 87] Amagai, Y., An Object-oriented Implementation of a Display Editor Making the Modules Reusable, Proceeding of the 1987 Programming Symposium of IPSJ, 1987 (in Japanese).

[Gabriel 84] Gabriel, R. and McCarthy, J., Queue-based Multiprocessor Lisp, Proceedings of the 1984 ACM Symposium on Lisp and Functional Programming, August 1984.

[Goldberg 83] Goldberg, A. and Robson, D., *Smalltalk-80: The Language and Its Implementation*, Reading, Massachusetts, Addison-Wesley, 1983.

[Goldman 88] Goldman, R. and Gabriel, R., Qlisp: Experience and New Direction, Proceedings of the ACM/SIGPLAN PPEALS 1988, July, 1988.

[Halstead 86] Halstead, R., Loaiza, Juan. and Ma, M., *The Multilisp Manual*, MIT, 1986.

[Halstead 84] Halstead, R., Implementation of Multilisp: Lisp on a Multiprocessor, Proceedings of the 1984 ACM Symposium on Lisp and Functional Programming, August 1984.

[Kon 86] Kon, A., Matsuyama, T. and Ito, T., Parallel Evaluation of Lisp Programs — Design and Implementation, IPSJ SIG Notes 86-SYM-37, 1986 (in Japanese).

[McCarthy 65] McCarthy, J., Abrahams, P. W., Edwards, D. J., Hart, T. P., and Levin, M. I., *Lisp 1.5 Programmer's Manual, second edition*, MIT Press, 1965.

[Murakami 88] Murakami, K., Connection Oriented Implementation Model for Network and its TCP/IP Implementation in Object-oriented Programming, Computer Software, Vol. 6, No. 1, 1988 (in Japanese).

[Murakami 89] Murakami, K., A Pseudo Network Approach to Inter-processor Communication on Shared-memory Multi-processor MacELIS, Proceedings of the 1989 US-Japan Workshop on Parallel Lisp, 1989.

[Onai 88] Onai, R., Tsuruoka, Y., Proposal and Evaluation of Dynamic Object-Oriented Programming, Transactions of IEICE (D), Vol. J17-D, No. 12, 1988 (in Japanese).

[Sabot 88] Sabot, G., *The Paralation Model*, MIT Press, 1988.

[Saito 83] Saito, T., Doi, T., Nishikawa, T., Maegawa, H. and Yasui, H., Fast Lisp Machine and List-Evaluation Processor EVAL II — Machine Evaluation on Interpreter, Transactions of IPSJ Vol. 24, No. 10, 1983 (in Japanese).

[Stallman 87] Stallman, R., *GNU Emacs Manual, Fifth Edition Version 18*, Free Software Foundation, 1987.

[Steel 84] Steel, G. ed., *Common Lisp*, Digital Press, 1984.

[Steel 86] Steel, G., Hillis, D., Connection Machine LISP: Fine-Grained Parallel Symbolic Processing, Proceedings of the 1986 ACM Conference on Lisp and Functional Programming, August, 1986.

[Takada 89] Takada, T., NueX: An Implementation of X-window System Interface in Object-Oriented Programming, JSSST SIG Notes of 1989 WOOC, 1989 (in Japanese).

[Takeuchi 86] Takeuchi, I., Okuno, H. and Ohsato, N., A List Processing Language TAO with Multiple Programming Paradigms, New Generation Computing, Vol 4, No. 4, Ohmusha and Springer, 1986.

[Tanaka 89] Tanaka, Y. and Nakanishi, M., An Implementation of a Distributed Processing Environment by the Lisp Machine SYNAPSE, IPSJ SIG Notes 89-SYM-50, 1989 (in Japanese).

[Watanabe 88] Watanabe, K., Ishikawa, A., Yamada, Y. and Hibino, Y., The Architecture of 32 bit AI Chip ELIS, IPSJ SIG Note 69-ARC-10, 1988 (in Japanese).

[Weinreb 83] Weinreb, D., Moon, D. and Stallman, R., *Lisp Machine Manual, Fifth Edition, System Version 92*, LMI, January, 1983.

A Pseudo Network Approach to Inter-processor Communication on A Shared-memory Multi-processor MacELIS

Ken-ichiro Murakami

NTT Electrical Communications Laboratories

3-9-11, Midori-cho, Musashino-shi, Tokyo, 180 Japan

Phone: +81 422 59 3589

E-Mail: murakami%ntt–20.ntt.jp@relay.cs.net (CSNET)

Abstract

MacELIS is a workbench for experimental distributed parallel list processing under development at NTT ECL (Electrical Communications Laboratories). It provides a coherent processor abstraction mechanism by a *Pseudo Network Model*. In this model, the shared-memory in MacELIS appears as a network medium and the same network access methods can be used for inter-processor communication between any processors independently of location and network hardware. This paper describes the design of the MacELIS network system. It concentrates on the three topics: in-core pseudo network, implementation in object oriented programming, and data transparency on the network.

1 Introduction

MacELIS is an experimental distributed list processing system currently under development at NTT ECL. It consists of a Macintosh II and several built-in VLSI ELIS (Electrical Communications Laboratories List processor) processor cards. Although the initial purpose of the MacELIS is to provide a workbench for distributed processing, it also provides a primitive function for parallel processing. MacELIS hardware is carefully designed to be compatible with the conventional single ELIS processor system [1] with respect to microcode, the kernel language TAO [2], the TCP/IP network [3], and other software modules. Each ELIS processor and MC68020 in Macintosh II has its unique main memory address in 4Gbyte NuBUS space. Therefore, all the ELIS processors can share the main memory and access it directly as a sequence of 8bit-wide memory. However, ELIS cannot access the higher memory address space as 64bit-wide cell, because of the narrow cell address space of the conventional VLSI ELIS processor. To cope with this constraint, each ELIS processor regards the shared memory as a network medium. This network is called *In-core Pseudo Network*. One of the processors in the in-core pseudo network works as a transparent gateway, and forwards packets between the pseudo network and external networks. This provides a simple and coherent access method to inter-processor communication.

This paper describes the design of MacELIS network system. First, this paper explains requirements and constraints for the MacELIS multiprocessor system. Next, it focuses on in-core pseudo network protocol and object oriented network implementation. Finally, data representation and remote procedure call protocol are discussed.

2 MacELIS architecture and constraints

Figure 1 shows an overview of the MacELIS hardware. Unlike the conventional single ELIS processor, it has some new features such as shared memory and one board compact CPU card. Each ELIS CPU card has a 16Mbyte main memory and up to 5cards can be attached to Macintosh II NuBUS slots. MC68020 processor in Macintosh II works as a FEP and handles file I/O requests, terminal I/O requests and network I/O requests. Although MacELIS is designed as a multiprocessor system, it is also required to work in a single processor configuration like the conventional ELIS system. Therefore, the basic requirement for MacELIS is compatibility with the conventional hardware, microcode and software. However, it gives rise to the following constraints;

(1) The conventional microcode requires a main memory in each ELIS CPU board to start at address 0 for the basic symbols. For fundamental functions such as CAR, CDR, etc, the address for each symbol is equated with the corresponding WCS entry address. Since no more than the symbol addresses are required to get the WCS entry address, high speed execution is obtained. NuBUS allocates two address blocks to each NuBUS card, that is, ELIS card. However, no block starts at 0.

(2) The ELIS VLSI CPU is designed to allow a 24bit cell address, providing 128MByte cell space. This is called cell addressing. Another addressing mode, byte addressing, is also provided. In this mode, ELIS can access in a 32bit byte address, 4Gbyte. Unfortunately, it cannot handle the memory as cell in the byte addressing mode. This means ELIS CPUs in Macintosh II cannot share the entire memory as a single cell space.

Memory address translation on local X-bus partially solves the former problem. NuBUS address for each main memory in the ELIS processor board is mapped onto the local X-bus address space in the range 0 through 0FFF FFFF (in Hexadecimal) only for the local ELIS processor. However, the memory is also accessible in the original NuBUS address. The latter problem is not only true for MacELIS. Interworking in a networked environment imposes the same problem, since physically distributed processors cannot share main memory at all. Therefore, this constraint strongly suggests a common network approach to inter-processor communication both for shared-memory multi-processor and physically distributed multi-processor system. For this purpose, shared-memory should be regarded not as memory but as network medium. This network is called an in-core pseudo network.

3 In-core pseudo network

The features of the in-core pseudo network are (1) high speed and low overhead, (2) broadcast and multicast support and (3) multiple protocol support. The packet format is shown in Figure 2. The first byte is used for a flag. This indicates the buffer ownership between the source and destination processors. The second and third bytes represent the destination and source processor address, respectively. The address is equal to the NuBUS slot number. Two byte field, in-core data length, follows these address fields. The next two bytes indicate the protocol type. This enables multiple higher level protocols to share the same in-core pseudo network without conflict.

After a source processor completes the in-core header, it interrupts a destination processor to pass the buffer memory address. For broadcast and multicast, the source ELIS processor interrupts all the rest processors on the in-core pseudo network. All the processors which received the broadcast packet share the packet. Since memory is a highly reliable device, neither retransmission nor error detection is required. In addition, packet transfer needs no buffer copying by DMA, unlike ordinary network media such as Ethernet. Instead, the packet is shared by source and destination processors. This realizes high speed and low CPU overhead network.

4 Object oriented network implementation

In MacELIS, TCP/IP(Transmission Control Protocol/Internet Protocol) protocol suite [4] is employed to utilize conventional internetworking technology for both memory-shared MacELIS and physically distributed single ELIS processors. Figure 3 shows the network protocol layers. IP protocol is employed on top of the in-core pseudo network to forward packets between the in-core pseudo network and external networks such as Ethernet. Since it controls routing automatically and absorbs media dependency, a coherent inter-processor communication model is provided for programmers independently of processor configuration, as shown in Figure 4. Two lisp oriented protocols are designed for MacELIS. SuperBEX protocol ensures data transparency over network and superRPC protocol provides a remote function call capability.

The network system is implemented in the object oriented programming. This provides flexibility in the protocol combination as well as a high speed buffer access facility. Figure 5 shows the class hierarchy. There are two kinds of classes: the connection class and the layer class. The layer class is an abstract class, each one corresponding to a protocol at a layer. It defines a collection of specific operations and services for the corresponding protocol. For example, IP-mixin and TCP-mixin are layer classes and define operations and services for IP protocol and TCP protocol, respectively. The connection class inherits required layer classes and provides network users with a standard network interface, that is, stream. In TAO, streams provide generic input/output access methods and are implemented as an object. To create a virtual connection, the network user instantiates a connection class.

The class fundamental-stream in TAO defines a data structure including a buffer memory and methods of accessing them. These accessing methods, such as TYI and TYO, are fully implemented in microcode. Since all the network streams inherit `fundamental-stream` microcoded `TYI` and `TYO` can be applied to the streams. These methods allow the network users to access the buffer memory directly. This realizes as fast access to communication buffers as conventional file streams and terminal streams in TAO.

5 Network transparency

SuperBEX protocol provides data transparency over network. In MacELIS, UDP is adopted as the fundamental transport service. SuperBEX is a superset of the conventional BEX protocol which is mainly used for high speed access to Lisp data stored in TAO/ELIS file system. BEX stands for Binary Expression and it is contrasted with Symbolic Expression. As shown in Figure 6, superBEX transfer syntax consists of (1) data type identifier (2) data length in bytes and (3) data field. This enables the receiving end to completely decode the incoming data unlike XDR (eXternal Data Representation) [5] protocol. Data type identifiers can be dynamically defined and bound with encoding and decoding methods by the superRPC function. Therefore, it allows an interactive protocol development. This feature is very important in developing a new protocol.

SuperPRC provides network programmers with functions to execute a remote function based on a server/client model. Unlike RPC (Remote Procedure Call) [6], superRPC has a self extension facility and it can modify and extend its protocol by recursively invoking superRPC function. This allows effective, dynamic and incremental protocol extension. The process is shown in Figure 7. First, the client in CPU_1 requests a remote function call through the client stab. If the receiving server stab in CPU_2 finds an unknown function identifier in the request packet, it requests the binding information to CPU_1 through the client stab in the same processor. Then, the receiving server stab in CPU_1 returns with the information to CPU_2. After execution, CPU_2 replies the result to CPU_1.

The usage of superRPC is a topic for further investigation. On top of superRPC, users can implement any inter-processor communication model and parallel programming style by writing server and client. SuperBEX and superRPC are simple and kept as small as possible, since they allow for users to extend or modify the protocol interactively.

6 Summary

This paper proposed an in-core pseudo network approach to inter-processor communication and described the design of the MacELIS network system. In conjunction with IP protocol, the in-core pseudo network provides coherency in inter-processor communication models independent of communication hardware and location. On top of the in-core pseudo network, a TCP/IP protocol suite is implemented. This provides co-operative work with widely distributed ELIS processors and MacELISes. The network is implemented in the object oriented programming. It provides a high speed buffer access facility. To ensure network transparency, superBEX protocol is designed. Unlike XDR, it decodes original data without type specification. For interactive protocol expansion, superRPC protocol is designed. SuperRPC provides recursive superRPC and allows dynamic binding of newly defined methods and its identifiers.

On top of the network system, we plan to built a cooperative LAN diagnostic and observation Expert system [7]. The performance evaluation of the in-core pseudo network is also a topic for the further investigation.

Acknowledgment

The author wishes to acknowledge the contributions and thoughtful suggestions made in this study by I.Takeuchi, Chief of the programming environment research group, Software Laboratories.

References

[1] K. Watanabe, A. Ishikawa, Y. Yamada and Y. Hibino. "The ELIS Interpreter-Oriented Lisp-Bases Workstation," *Proc. of the 2nd IEEE conference on Computer Workstations*, 1988, pp70–79.

[2] I. Takeuchi, H. Okuno, and N.Ohsato. "A List Processing Language TAO with Multiple Programming Paradigms," *New Generation Computing*, Vol. 4, No. 4, 1986, pp.401-444.

[3] K. Murakami. "Connection Oriented Implementation Model for Network and its TCP/IP Implementation in Object Oriented Programming (In Japanese)," *Computer Software*, Vol. 6, No. 1, 1989, pp.30-40.

[4] D. Comer. "Internetworking with TCP/IP ," Prentice Hall, 1988.

[5] Sun Microsystems, "XDR: External Data Representation standard ," RFC-1014, 1987.

[6] Sun Microsystems, "RPC: Remote Procedure Call protocol specification ," RFC-1050, 1988.

[7] T. Sugawara. "A Cooperative LAN Diagnostic and Observation Expert System ," in preparation.

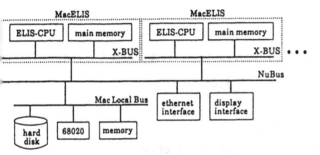

Figure 1. Configuration of MacELIS Hardware

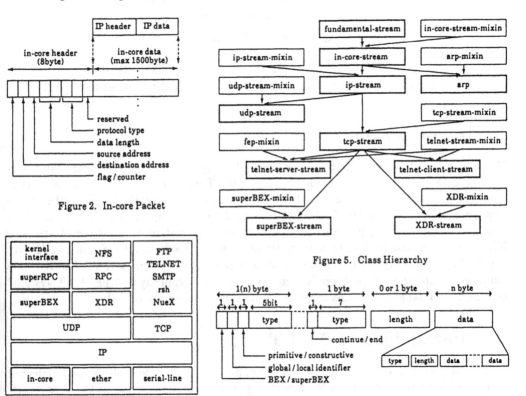

Figure 2. In-core Packet

Figure 3. MacELIS TCP/IP layer

Figure 5. Class Hierarchy

Figure 6. superBEX Transfer Syntax

Figure 4. Users View of MacELIS Cluster

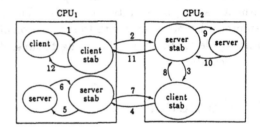

Figure 7. superPRC

Mul-T: A High-Performance Parallel Lisp (Extended Abstract)

David A. Kranz
Laboratory for Computer Science
Massachusetts Instutue of Technology
545 Technology Square
Cambridge, Ma 02139

Robert H. Halstead, Jr.   Eric Mohr
DEC Cambridge Research Lab   Yale University

1   Introduction

Mul-T is a parallel Lisp system that has been developed to run on an Encore Multimax multiprocessor. Mul-T is an extended version of the T version 3 (or "T3") system[17] that supports parallel processing using Multilisp's `future` construct[10, 11, 12]. Multilisp's implementation uses a layer of interpretation that limits its speed, but Mul-T uses T3's ORBIT compiler[13, 14] (suitably modified) to generate native code for the Multimax's NS32332 processors, leading to a dramatic increase in speed (about a factor of 100 over the Multilisp system). Mul-T names both a parallel Lisp system and the parallel Lisp language it supports; where there is ambiguity, we refer explicitly to "the Mul-T system" or "the Mul-T language." This extended abstract is a summary of [15].

2   Parallelism in Mul-T

Mul-T (like Multilisp) is an extended version of Scheme[1, 18], a lexically scoped dialect of Lisp. Mul-T's basic mechanism for generating concurrent tasks is the `future` construct. The expression (`future` X), where X is an arbitrary expression, creates a task to evaluate X and also creates an object known as a *future* to eventually hold the value of X. Concurrency arises because the expression (`future` X) returns the future as its value without waiting for the future to resolve. Thus, the computation containing (`future` X) can proceed concurrently with the evaluation of X. When execution of a Mul-T program is not made explicitly parallel using `future`, it is sequential. See [15] for details of the implementation .

3   Compiler

Two features of Mul-T required significant changes to the ORBIT compiler:

1. Support for a large number of very lightweight tasks.

2. Implicit touches performed by strict operations.

Supporting these features means introducing overhead even in programs that don't make use of them. To a large extent, the effectiveness of Mul-T as a general purpose environment will depend on how small this overhead can be made.

Under Unix, a large number of stacks can be handled only by explicitly checking for overflow. The check need not be done on every push but must be done by every procedure that needs space on the stack. This check will involve at least a compare and a conditional branch.

Having strict operations such as + and car implicitly touch their operands means that a type test must be performed on each operand to make sure it is not a future. The cost of both this test and the stack overflow check could be absorbed by well known hardware technology, but they are a real problem on conventional hardware like the Encore Multimax which uses National Semiconductor NS32000 series processors.

Many of these touch operations can be eliminated by having the compiler perform a simple first-order type analysis. For example, if a value has been tested once, it doesn't need to be tested the next time it is referenced. In several benchmarks the overhead without these optimizations was about 100%; with the optimizations it ranges from under 20% to nearly 100%; however, 65% seems to be a fairly typical number for programs that do not heavily emphasize iterative loops, such as the Boyer and **compiler** benchmarks (see Section 6 and the data in Table 3).

4 User Interface

Sequential Lisp systems are known for their strong program development environment. Extending this environment to handle multiple tasks gracefully presents some problems, which other parallel Lisp systems have been only partially successful in solving. Mul-T's solutions are based on the *group*, a collection of tasks resulting from the evaluation of a single expression typed by the user. Groups can be started, stopped, resumed, and killed independently of other groups of tasks. An important departure from conventional sequential Lisp implementation strategy is required to support groups well—the Mul-T runtime system uses distinguished tasks to control exception handling and access to terminal I/O.

Groups in Mul-T allow a natural parallel extension of the stopped computation idea. All tasks created during evaluation of an expression typed by the user belong to the same group G. If an exception occurs the group G is stopped, suspending all of its constituent tasks. At this point the user regains control and may examine and alter the state of any of the stopped tasks. Even though several tasks may be stopped, the computation is represented by a single stopped group. There may be several stopped groups at a given time, analogous to the nested breakloops of sequential Lisps. The most recently stopped group is called the *current group*, and the task in which the exception occurred is called the *current task*. The usual Lisp debugging commands apply by default to the current task of the current group, so using Mul-T feels just like using T. But the commands also allow referring to other tasks or other stopped groups.

T3	14.5 sec
Mul-T, no touch optimizations	29
Mul-T plus touch optimizations	24

Table 1: Performance of cleaned-up, sequential Boyer benchmark

5 Optimization of future

An opportunity to optimize the implementation of future arises out of the observation that, in the expression (future X), execution of the parent task concurrently with the evaluation of X is *permissible* but is not *required*. It is thus permissible for an implementation to evaluate X fully before proceeding with execution of the parent task: in other words, to treat future as an identity operator. We refer to this treatment as *inlining* because the expression X is effectively evaluated "in line" as a subroutine, rather than concurrently as a separate task.

Identifying suitable places to apply inlining is the real challenge in applying inlining effectively. A simple strategy is for a processor to apply inlining to all futures encountered when the number of tasks on that processor's queues is greater than or equal to some threshold T. If $T = 0$, then *all* futures are inlined and no parallel tasks are created; if $T = 1$, then the existence of a single queued task will be enough to suppress task creation; and so on.

6 Performance of Mul-T

To evaluate Mul-T's performance, we ran a modified version of the Boyer theorem-proving benchmark from the Gabriel book of Lisp benchmarks[6]. As Table 1 shows, the sequential Boyer benchmark takes 14.5 seconds to run on the unmodified, sequential T3 system. Since the performance of compiled code in the T3 system is about as good as that of any other compiled code on the same hardware[13], we view this as a good estimate of top speed for this application on the Multimax's NS32332 processor. The same sequential code, when run under Mul-T with touch optimizations disabled, takes twice as long to run. Since this code contains no futures, the increase in running time is attributable solely to implicit touches. Although every one of these touches reveals that no action is necessary, they occur frequently enough to double the execution time of the program. When the touch optimizations discussed in Section 3 are enabled, the time for the cleaned-up, sequential Boyer benchmark is reduced to 24 seconds, representing a reduction in the overhead due to touch checks from 100% of the execution time on T3 to 65%.

Table 2 shows the performance of the parallel Boyer benchmark for different numbers of processors and different settings of the inlining threshold. Touch optimizations were enabled during these measurements. Without inlining (*i.e.*, when the inlining threshold $T = \infty$) the execution time on one processor was 44 seconds—20 seconds more than the corresponding time in Table 1. This represents the extra overhead introduced by the use of future in the parallel benchmark. The execution times given in Table 2 for 2, 4, and 8 processors, however, clearly indicate that Mul-T has successfully exploited a substantial

Number of processors:	1	2	4	8
Without inlining ($T = \infty$)	44	23	12	7.5 sec
With inlining ($T = 1$)	25	13	7	4

Table 2: Performance of parallel Boyer benchmark

n	permute	queens	compiler	mergesort measured	mergesort theoretical
seq	8520	27.8	98	.99	
1	11554	33.2	159	1.82	(1.82)
2	5823	16.6	94	.99	.98
4	2995	8.5	64	.57	.60
8	1598	4.3	53	.45	.42
12	1293	3.0	54	.43	

Table 3: Execution time (in seconds) for Mul-T benchmarks

amount of parallelism in the benchmark, so that the execution time on 4 and 8 processors is less than that of the sequential benchmark on T3.

The second line of Table 2, which was obtained by setting the inlining threshold $T = 1$, offers further encouragement. Inlining is seen to be an extremely effective optimization for the Boyer benchmark, reducing the extra execution time on one processor due to introducing future from 20 seconds to one second. Moreover, the execution times given for 2, 4, and 8 processors show that Mul-T has continued to be successful in exploiting parallelism, bettering the T3 performance even when only two processors are used.

Table 3 shows timings of four other Mul-T programs. The first line ("seq") shows the time of a sequential version of each program in T3; subsequent lines show Mul-T times for increasing numbers of processors. Our timings were somewhat variable because Mul-T's "processors" are really Unix processes, subject to interruptions by the UMAX (Unix) scheduler. The figures shown are averaged over 5 or 10 successive trials; typically variation did not exceed 5%.

These programs are described in [15].

7   Related Projects

The Mul-T project builds on the results of several other projects. Aside from the obvious debts to the developers of T3 and Multilisp, Mul-T borrows from the work of Carl Hewitt and Henry Baker, who first articulated the concept of futures[3]. Another early parallel Lisp system, which was developed for the BBN Butterfly Machine[5], is MultiScheme[16]. Like Multilisp, MultiScheme used a layer of interpretation in its implementation (although there have been plans to add a compiler) and thus was not fast in absolute terms.

We are aware of three other parallel Lisp systems that have been implemented using a compiler for high performance: Butterfly Lisp[2], implemented for the Butterfly Machine; Qlisp[7, 8, 9], implemented for the Alliant FX-8; and a parallel version of Portable Standard Lisp[19] (let us call this "PPSL"), also for the Butterfly Machine. Butterfly Lisp and PPSL, like Multilisp and Mul-T, rely primarily on **future** as a concurrency mechanism. Qlisp supports futures but also provides several other concurrency constructs.

Butterfly Lisp, like Multilisp and Mul-T, includes implicit touches for strict operations, but Qlisp and PPSL require programmers to insert explicit **touch** operations whenever a future might appear as an operand to a strict operation (the implementors of Qlisp are in the process of incorporating implicit touches). As Section 6 shows, implicit touches are expensive on stock hardware, but inserting explicit touches will be tedious and error-prone for programs that use futures heavily.

8 Conclusion

The development of Mul-T has been valuable in several ways. First, Mul-T is a complete, working parallel Lisp system, publicly available to interested users. Second, its single-processor performance is competitive with that of "production quality" sequential Lisp implementations, and therefore a parallel program running under Mul-T can show absolute speedups over the best sequential implementation of the same algorithm. This is attractive to application users whose primary interest is raw speed rather than the abstract gratification of having demonstrated speedup via a time-consuming simulation. Finally, implementing Mul-T has allowed us to experiment with and evaluate implementation strategies such as inlining. The Mul-T experience has also allowed us to probe the limits of implementing futures on stock multiprocessors, and has suggested (for example) that hardware assistance for tag management may be a more significant benefit in a machine for parallel Lisp (where it can eliminate the 65% overhead of implicit touches) than it has ever proven to be in machines for sequential Lisps.

References

[1] Abelson, H., and G.J. Sussman with J. Sussman, *Structure and Interpretation of Computer Programs*, MIT Press, Cambridge, 1985.

[2] Allen, D., S. Steinberg, and L. Stabile, "Recent developments in Butterfly Lisp," *AAAI 87*, July 1987, Seattle, pp. 2-6.

[3] Baker, H., and C. Hewitt, "The Incremental Garbage Collection of Processes," M.I.T. Artificial Intelligence Laboratory Memo 454, Cambridge, Mass., Dec. 1977.

[4] Clark, D.W., "An efficient list-moving algorithm using constant workspace," *Communications of the ACM 19(6)*, pages 352-354, June 1976.

[5] Crowther, W., et al., "Performance Measurements on a 128-Node Butterfly Parallel Processor," *1985 Int'l. Conf. on Parallel Processing*, St. Charles, Ill., Aug. 1985, pp. 531–540.

[6] Gabriel, R., *Performance and Evaluation of Lisp Systems*, M.I.T. Press, Cambridge, Mass., 1985.

[7] Gabriel, R.P., and J. McCarthy, "Queue-based Multi-processing Lisp," *1984 ACM Symp. on Lisp and Functional Programming*, Austin, Tex., Aug. 1984, pp. 25–44.

[8] Gabriel, R.P., and J. McCarthy, "Qlisp," in J. Kowalik, ed., *Parallel Computation and Computers for Artificial Intelligence*, Kluwer Academic Publishers, Boston, 1988, pp. 63–89.

[9] Goldman, R., and R.P. Gabriel, "Preliminary Results with the Initial Implementation of Qlisp," *1988 ACM Symp. on Lisp and Functional Programming*, Snowbird, Utah, July 1988, pp. 143–152.

[10] Halstead, R., "Multilisp: A Language for Concurrent Symbolic Computation," *ACM Trans. on Prog. Languages and Systems 7:4*, October 1985, pp. 501–538.

[11] Halstead, R., "Parallel Symbolic Computing," *IEEE Computer 19:8*, August 1986, pp. 35–43.

[12] Halstead, R., "An Assessment of Multilisp: Lessons from Experience," *Int'l. J. of Parallel Programming 15:6*, Dec. 1986, pp. 459–501.

[13] Kranz, D., *et al.*, "Orbit: An Optimizing Compiler for Scheme," *Proc. SIGPLAN '86 Symp. on Compiler Construction*, June 1986, pp. 219–233.

[14] Kranz, D., "ORBIT: An Optimizing Compiler for Scheme," Yale University Technical Report YALEU/DCS/RR-632, February 1988.

[15] Kranz, D., R. Halstead, and E. Mohr, "Mul-T, A High-Performance Parallel Lisp", *ACM SIGPLAN '89 Conference on Programming Language Design and Implementation*, Portland, OR, June 1989, pp. 81–90.

[16] Miller, J., *MultiScheme: A Parallel Processing System Based on MIT Scheme*, Ph.D. thesis, M.I.T. E.E.C.S. Dept., Cambridge, Mass., August 1987.

[17] Rees, J., N. Adams, and J. Meehan, *The T Manual*, fourth edition, Yale University Computer Science Department, January 1984.

[18] Rees, J., and W. Clinger, eds., "Revised[3] Report on the Algorithmic Language Scheme," *ACM SIGPLAN Notices 21:12*, Dec. 1986, pp. 37–79.

[19] Swanson, M.R., R.R. Kessler, and G. Lindstrom, "An Implementation of Portable Standard Lisp on the BBN Butterfly," *1988 ACM Symp. on Lisp and Functional Programming*, Snowbird, Utah, July 1988, pp. 132–142.

INTEGRATING PARALLEL LISP WITH MODERN UNIX-BASED OPERATING SYSTEMS

Dan L. Pierson
Encore Computer Corporation
Marlborough, MA, USA

Recent advances in shared-memory parallel Lisp implementations, affordable, off-the-shelf shared-memory parallel computers, and Unix-based Operating System support for parallel computation are rapidly converging. Several organizations are actively working on standard interfaces to Unix or Unix-like parallel processing. The Mach Operating System from CMU and Encore Computer Corporation serves both as a candidate standard in its own right (e.g. as the basis for OSF/1) and as a model for other proposals such as the Pthreads proposal being developed by the Posix 1003.4 Real Time Extensions group.

At Encore we are developing a shared-memory parallel Common Lisp system based on Qlisp [1]. This system is intended to develop into a parallel Lisp product with full attention to support of multiprocessing user interfaces, parallel debugging and performance evaluation, and inter-parallel-language operability. While common in product level serial Common Lisp implementations, all of these are significant extensions to most existing parallel Lisps. Together they pose a new, more complex problem of how best to integrate parallel Lisp with underlying operating system services and standards.

While our initial implementation is targeted for Mach, we would like to retain the option of supporting our parallel System V operating system (UMAXV) as well.

Processes

While traditional Unix processes have acceptable performance characteristics for interactive human use, they are well known to be rather large, slow objects from the viewpoint of a parallel language. Consequently, most existing parallel language implementations multiplex their own underlying process structure onto a smaller set of Unix processes. This multiplexing is unpleasant for several reasons including: implementation difficulties caused by mismatches between Unix process semantics and the languages' resource sharing requirements, lack of flexibility caused by the expense of process creation, and unavoidable performance costs associated with process context switching and scheduling.

Mach is one of several Unix-compatible operating systems that provide cheaper, more convenient mechanisms for parallel processing. In Mach, the Unix concept of process is separated into a *task*, which owns resources such as virtual memory and IO descriptors, and one or more *threads*, which are the actual execution engines. Encore's Nunix extension to Unix System V provides an analogous, but more flexible facility by using a resource sharing mask to control the precise characteristics of a forked process. The draft Posix Pthreads standard is expected to provide a portable facility similar in many ways to the Mach Cthreads library interface to Mach threads.

It appears simple, and initially very tempting to remove all the process and multiplexing code from a parallel Lisp and let one Lisp process equal one thread (or whatever). Unfortunately, this is not a good solution for highly parallel Lisp dialects. because thread creation costs, kernel thread scheduling, and kernel context switching are still ill suited to computational processes that may execute as few as 100 instructions before returning a value. However, larger-grained Lisp processes, such as those used to implement user interface tasks, may well be most effectively implemented as threads.

Scheduling

Most current parallel Lisp implementations have focused on providing basic parallel programming facilities. As the experience and user base of these systems has grown the limits of the initial process scheduling support have become more apparent. Initial systems had simple schedulers designed to optimize the overall performance of a large number of programmed processes each of which needed to run to completion in order to finish the overall computation. Recent work has concentrated on adding support for speculative parallelism, i.e. sets of parallel processes in which not all processes must or should run to completion. As the features of modern serial Lisp implementations and programming environments are incorporated in parallel Lisp systems, other process types become important. Modern Lisp user interfaces depend on serial multitasking facilities such as the Lisp Machine stack groups. Advanced parallel programming environments such as Encore's Parasight [3] require support for parallel debugger processes.

We now have four types of parallel processes: computational, speculative, user interface, and debugger. Each of these requires a different kind and level of scheduler support as shown below:

Process Type	Requirements
Computational	Fast, low-overhead, small grain size
Speculative	Fast, low-overhead, controllable, small-medium grain size
User Interface	Fair, responsive, large grain size
Debugger	Non-intrusive, continuous, medium-large grain size

Requirements for Process Types

Simple, unfair schedulers as used in Multilisp, MulT, and Qlisp seem to work quite well for computational processes. Scheduling and controlling speculative parallel processes is currently an interesting research area [2]. Researchers in this area need either access to the full scheduler sources or powerful and flexible support for user written schedulers. Both of these types of schedulers are probably best implemented as part of the parallel Lisp system. Further, the speculative scheduling support will be easiest to use if it is implemented in Lisp code which interested researchers can inspect and modify or replace as needed.

The needs of user interface and debugger processes are quite similar to the needs of timesharing users. Since Unix process scheduling is already optimized for this purpose, there is little to be gained by imposing an additional layer of Lisp code over it.

This leads to a process mapping in which the Lisp system directly controls and schedules a number of virtual processors that are dedicated to computational and speculative processes. The user interface and debugger processes can be implemented as individual Mach threads (or minimal Nunix processes, or Pthreads).

Signals and Exceptions

Mach currently provides two overlapping signalling mechanisms: BSD4.3 Unix Signals, and task and thread exception ports. Unix signals are task oriented. Any thread can specify signal handling for the entire task, but signals will be delivered at random to the first convenient thread. There is no simple way to determine which thread caused a synchronous error signal (e.g. illegal memory reference). Mach exception ports are synchronous and thread oriented. An interested thread obtains exceptions by waiting to read the first message on one or more ports.

Since Unix signals cannot be dispensed with, there has to be a signal handler function capable of running in any process to receive and handle or dispatch such signals. Despite this, most common error conditions can better be handled as Mach exceptions. The parallel Lisp system will create one or more threads that are dedicated to reading exception ports and handling errors appropriately. Unix signals will be converted to messages and serviced by one of these dedicated threads whenever possible.

Conclusions

We intend to eventually support both Mach and System V with Encore's Nunix extensions. Both Mach and Nunix provide equally good support for processes and scheduling (Pthreads may also provide satisfactory support). While Mach exception ports are clearly superior to Unix signals for parallel Lisp systems, there is currently no way to escape from the need to handle some signals. When parallel signal handling in the System V environment is finally resolved, the result may prove easier to use than the troublesome mixture currently provided by Mach.

Mach's other main advantage is the additional flexibility offered by its virtual memory systems. We have yet to explore the possibilities offered by a large sparse address space and external pagers.

1. R. Goldman, R. Gabriel, C. Sexton, *Qlisp: Parallel Processing in Lisp*, US/Japan Workshop on Parallel Lisp, Sendai, Japan.
2. R. Osborne, *Speculative Computation in Multilisp*, US/Japan Workshop on Parallel Lisp, Sendai, Japan
3. Z. Aral, I. Gertner, Parasight: *A High-Level Debugger/Profiler Architecture for Shared-Memory Multiprocessors*, 1989 ACM International Conference on Supercomputing, Saint Malo, France

mUtilisp: a Lisp Dialect for Parallel Processing

Hideya Iwasaki

Department of Mathematical Engineering
Faculty of Engineering, University of Tokyo
7-3-1 Hongo, Bunkyo-ku, Tokyo 113, Japan

1. Introduction

The mUtilisp (multiprocessing Utilisp) language [3,4,5] is a Lisp dialect which allows multiprocessing computation. Since it is an extension of the Utilisp [6] (University of Tokyo Interactive Lisp) system, almost all functions of Utilisp are implemented with the same meaning in the mUtilisp system. Like Utilisp, the scope rule of mUtilisp is the dynamic one, which is different from that of Common Lisp.

The mUtilisp system is now available on a uniprocessor Unix machine, whose CPU is a MC68000 series microprocessor such as Sun3. Each parallel computation within mUtilisp is, therefore, executed in pseudo parallel manner.

This paper proposes an approach to the multiprocessing carried out in the mUtilisp system. The term "process" is used as a parallel computation within the mUtilisp system, not as a usual "process" in the Unix operating system.

2. Main Features

The main features of mUtilisp are as follows:
1. Exclusion of shared Lisp objects and environment.
2. Explicit parallelism.
3. Access to a process through its name.

The system that allows shared Lisp objects and environment must provide constructs for mutual exclusion. In most cases, however, the use of these constructs is bothersome, and shared Lisp objects may cause subtle bugs which are difficult to find out and fix. Exclusion of shared Lisp objects (especially shared environment) can avoid unpredicted interferences between processes. Moreover, this feature matches with the distributed and multiprocessor environments.

Since mUtilisp processes share no Lisp objects in common, they must communicate to each other by means of sending messages. In mUtilisp, a process must be named when created, by which it can be designated from other processes. The process name is used in various process related functions including interprocess communication, and enables the user to handle processes explicitly.

3. Inheritance and Translation

In mUtilisp, a process is created dynamically by calling a process creating function. By the parent-child relationship between processes, all processes constitute a single tree

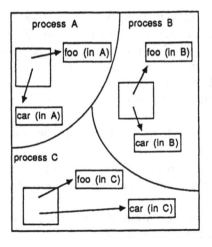

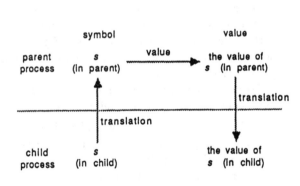

Figure 1. Division of Symbol Space   Figure 2. Inheritance and Translation

structure. The process which stands at the root of the tree is called the *root process*. The tree structure plays an essential role in constructing the environment of a process.

An *environment* is a set of associations from a symbol to its value, definition and property. Each process of mUtilisp has a separate, distinct environment based on the division of symbol space. The division of symbol space means that any two symbols with the same name pointed from different processes are not assumed to be eq (the same pointer) even if they can be considered to correspond to each other (Figure 1). This feature is extended to all data types (cons cells, etc). Processes in mUtilisp are, therefore, assumed to share no Lisp objects. According to this feature, interprocess communication is achieved by message passing.

The environment of a process is constructed depending on the following rules:

- Initially, a process inherits the environment of its parent process for its "inherent" environment. This mechanism is called the *inheritance* of the environment.
- Establishing an association (value, definition or property) of a symbol changes the environment about this symbol within the process, and shadows the "inherent" environment about it.

Inheritance may take place across more than two generations. That is, a process inherits all the environments of its ancestor processes, but an environment of the "younger" ancestor has preference to those of the "older" ones.

Note that a process only inherits, *not shares* the environment of its parent. The inherited environment is reconstructed into another Lisp object not to be shared within two processes. In addition, a change of the process environment may affect only the environments of its descendant processes, and it never affects those of the others. This means that the parent can transmit information to its descendants by the inheritance mechanism, but it is the initial environment for its descendants.

All predefined values and definitions are kept in the symbols owned by the root process (that is, the environment of the root process). All processes can inherit them unless an intermediate process redefines the environment about the predefined symbols.

The inheritance mechanism needs two kinds of correspondence between Lisp objects. One is to make identity between symbols owned by the child and by the parent. The other is, as described before, to convert a Lisp object, which is the environment of the parent process, into a Lisp object accessible by the child process. mUtilisp unifies them into the mechanism called *translation* (Figure 2). The translation from a process into another process is a mechanism to make the correspondence between "similar" Lisp objects to avoid sharing.

We define the translation of a Lisp object x from a process *proc1* into another process *proc2*, especially for symbols and cons cells, as follows:

- If x is a symbol, the symbol which is registered in the symbol table of *proc2* with the print name of x by the algorithm of the built-in function `intern` is the translation of x.
- If x is a cons, another cons cell whose car is the translation of the car of x and whose cdr is the translation of the cdr of x is the translation of x.

Although the inheritance (and message passing described later) needs a reconstruction of a Lisp object by the translation, mUtilisp hides this fact into the language specification so that a user usually need not be worried about it.

4. Basic Constructs

In this section, we show the syntax and semantics of some basic constructs provided by mUtilisp. In mUtilisp, a process itself is a Lisp object which has a unique name (string). The designation of a process as an argument of the basic constructs accepts both the process itself and the process name (string).

The primitive function to create a process is `create-process`, whose form is:

```
(create-process name fn arglist)
```

It resembles `apply` except that the name string of the child process is given by its first argument. This function creates and returns a child process, allocating its symbol table and stack region. Initially the child process is in "suspended" state, and the `resume` construct starts its computation. The computation executed by the child is to apply the function *fn* to the set of arguments list given by *arglist* with the environment inherited from the parent. Of course, *fn* and *arglist* are translated into the child process. The child process does not return the result (value) to its parent automatically even if it finishes its computation. When the value is required, the `send` and `receive` constructs must be used explicitly.

Interprocess communication is based on message passing, which meets the design features described before. As the case of inheritance, a message is translated from the sender into the receiver.

```
(send receiver message)
(receive)
(receive sender)
```

`send` sends *message* (any Lisp object) to the process *receiver* asynchronously (send no-wait). It means that the call of this function never causes a delay of the sender process whether the receiver process is in the "blocked" state (by the call of `receive`) or not.

To receive a message, the function `receive` is used. With no argument, `receive` can receive a message from any process, so it is used for many to one communication. `receive` with a single argument, which is either a process or a list of processes, specifies the sender process, and the communication is one to one or many to one, respectively. The process which has called `receive` becomes "blocked" if there is no message to receive. Two processes are synchronized by the blocking mechanism of `receive`. `receive` returns a cons cell whose car is the sender process and whose cdr is the message.

mUtilisp provides other constructs, but they are not described here.

5. Process Management

There are two levels of process management in the mUtilisp system. One is the interpreter level, and the other is the scheduler level. The former is coded within the mUtilisp interpreter and protected from the user. On the other hand, the latter is a Lisp program level executed by a special process called the *scheduler*, which can be customized by the user.

The interpreter level switchs the executing process at an appropriate interval. The scheduling on this level is preemptive except the scheduler, and the scheduler can assign arbitrary time-slice to each process.

The mUtilisp interpreter level also detects external and internal events (interruption from the keyboard, a need for scheduling etc.), and transmits them to the scheduler in the form of messages. These messages are an interface between the interpreter and the scheduler levels.

At the scheduler level, the scheduler selects the next process to run by its scheduling strategy. The user has the means to extend the work of the scheduler by attaching Lisp functions to the scheduler, and to replace the system scheduler by his own scheduler process. These features enable the user to realize his process management including the scheduling and handling of various events, and to customize the entire mUtilisp system. For example, process priority specifiable by the user, step execution of a particular process and so forth are easily implemented by the user.

6. Extension to the Network Environment

We are now trying to extend mUtilisp to the network (distributed) environment. There are two main purposes and motivations for this extension. The first is to provide an experimental multiprocessor environment. The second is to give mUtilisp the power for constructing network-based software such as a server of a window system.

We define the term *task* as a collection of processes managed by the same scheduler. Tasks may exist on the same host machine, and similar to a process, a task is named uniquely within its host. The basic constructs described before are extended by allowing a process designation (string) whose contents is '*hostname:taskname:processname*.'

To achieve the network extension, two basic functions for remote message passing, task-send and task-receive are provided to the original mUtilisp system. Remote messages are encoded into a string and transferred to a remote task by task-send.

Messages from other tasks (remote messages) are handled by a process called *taskd* (task daemon). When the taskd receives a remote message by task-receive, it decodes the received string to a Lisp object and re-distributes it to the real receiver process. Like the scheduler, the user can extend its work or replace it with another process.

The "remote child" mechanism (child process in another task) is an example of the extended work of the taskd. The "remote child" means a process which is logically a child of the parent process in the same task, but whose entity (execution) is in another task. For example, if a parent creates a process in another task, it becomes a remote child of the parent. The taskd process is designed to accept a request for process creation by a remote message between taskds, assign an appropriate name (within the same task) and create a process with this name which executes the computation of the remote child. In addition, the taskd maintains a mapping table between parent processes and their remote children.

The extended mUtilisp unifies both local and remote message passing into the same constructs send and receive. Since most parts of the network extension are implemented in the mUtilisp program and process level, the entire system becomes very flexible.

7. Discussions

One of the new ideas of mUtilisp is, first, as described before, the exclusion of shared Lisp objects. It contrasts with the shared memory policy in Multilisp [2] and Qlisp [1]. By the benefit of this idea, the mUtilisp system was extended to the network environment with a few modifications to the original mUtilisp. Also, it is easy to develop a process in mUtilisp without affecting the other processes. One demerit of our policy is the overhead of the translation. In our implementation, the child process caches a translated (inherent) environment within its symbol space and reuses it to decrease this overhead accompanied with the inheritance.

Second, mUtilisp introduces the inheritance mechanism, which has two aspects of information transmission. One is information publication, and the other is information hiding. If a process registers a symbol in its symbol table by the built-in function intern, the environment about the symbol becomes public to its descendant processes. On the other hand, a process may hide some parts of its environment by registering a symbol into its symbol table by its own algorithm.

Third, mUtilisp emphasizes on the procedural aspects of the Lisp language more than the functional aspects. It means that mUtilisp needs some function-calls to control processes. For example, Multilisp and Qlisp have a synchronization mechanism by referring to a shared "future" value which will be determined by another process, while mUtilisp must call send or receive to synchronize with another process. However, it may be easy to understand the transition of process status from the program written in mUtilisp.

8. Conclusions

This paper has proposed mUtilisp as a multiprocessing Lisp language. Our implementation is flexible so that users can customize his own system for various purposes by the system processes (the scheduler and taskd). The execution within each process is almost the same as Utilisp except the process related parts, and various utilities written in Utilisp can run in mUtilisp without modification. This feature helps the user to debug a program for each process by Utilisp.

Since a parallel processing environment of the mUtilisp system is easy to use, we think that it can be a description language for various applications [7]. After the workshop, a multiprocessor machine was installed in our laboratory, and we are implementing the mUtilisp system on it to provide a "real" parallel environment.

Acknowledgements

I would like to thank Minoru Terada who gave me helpful comments and implemented the first version of the network extension. I am also grateful to Prof. Eiiti Wada for his comments and encouragement.

References

[1] Gabriel, R.P. and J. McCarthy: Qlisp, J. Kowalik, ed., *Parallel Computation and Computers for Artificial Intelligence*, Kluwer Academic Publishers, Boston, pp.63–89 (1988).

[2] Halstead, R.H.: Multilisp: A language for Concurrent Symbolic Computation, *ACM Trans. Program. Lang. Syst.*, Vol.7, No.4, pp.501–538 (1985).

[3] Iwasaki, H.: Programming and Implementation of a Multi-processing Lisp, *Trans. IPS Japan*, Vol.28, No.5, pp.465–470 (1987) (in Japanese).

[4] Iwasaki, H.: *mUtilisp Manual*, METR 88-11, Department of Mathematical Engineering and Information Physics, University of Tokyo (1988).

[5] Iwasaki, H., Terada, M. and Yuasa, K: mUtilisp on the UNIX Operating System, Preprints of WGSYM Meeting, IPS Japan, 88-48 (1988) (in Japanese).

[6] Kaneko, K. and Yuasa, K.: A New Implementation Technique for the Utilisp System, Preprints of WGSYM Meeting, IPS Japan, 87-41 (1987).

[7] Terada, M: Implementation of Full GHC by Communicating Processes, *Proc. of Logic Programming Conference '88*, ICOT, Tokyo, pp.169–176 (1988).

PM1 and PMLisp:
An Experimental Machine and Its Lisp System for Research on MIMD Massively Parallel Computation

Taiichi YUASA and Takafumi KAWANA

Department of Information and Computer Sciences

Toyohashi University of Technology, Toyohashi 440, Japan

Abstract

The PMLisp system is a collection of Lisp drivers, which can communicate with each other via message passing. The whole PMLisp system is running on an experimental parallel machine PM1 which currently has only 24 processors but can be upgraded to become an MIMD massively parallel computer. The PMLisp system is intended to provide an interactive environment for quick prototyping of parallel algorithms and for building higher-level parallel mechanisms on the PM1. This paper overviews the PM1, and then explains the message passing mechanisms of the PMLisp system in a certain detail, along with some example programs and implementation discussions.

1 Introduction

The P-Machine project of Toyohashi University of Technology (TUT) is working for massively parallel computation. Its research area includes:

- fundamental architecture

- communication mechanisms among processor elements (PEs)

- programming languages and tools

- massively parallel algorithms

By "massively parallel computation", we mean that the computation is proceeded by thousands or tens of thousands processors running in parallel and communicating each other. Although we are interested in both SIMD (Single Instruction, Multiple Data) and MIMD (Multiple Instruction, Multiple Data) architecture, our current target is MIMD massively parallel computation. This is mainly because we regard SIMD as a special case of MIMD computation, where processors are synchronized more often than usual.

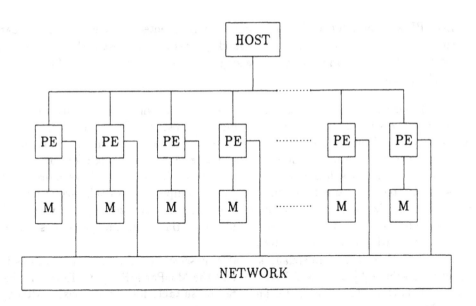

Figure 1: An outline of PM1

In order to provide an environment for experiments on massively parallel computation with a reasonable cost, we began by developing an experimental machine PM1 [11], which has the following features (see Figure 1).

- This machine has an MIMD architecture. As an experimentation tool, we prefer an MIMD machine rather than an SIMD machine, because MIMD machines can simulate SIMD machines.

- Each PE has its own local memory in which programs executed by the PE are stored. The local memory of a PE is not accessed by the host or by other PEs.

- Host-PE and PE-PE communications are the only means to exchange information among PEs and the host.

- The architecture is scalable. Although the current configuration of PM1 consists of only twenty-four PEs, the architecture is designed so that it can be extended to much larger configurations. To enlarge the configuration, we only need to add devises between PEs to resolve the fun-in/fun-out problem that may arise when a single communication line is shared by a large number of PEs. We do not need to change the PEs, however large configuration we want.

- The topology of PE-PE communication network is a butterfly rather than the popular hyper cube [15]. As we will explain shortly, the butterfly connection requires a fixed number of communication lines per PE, while the hyper cube requires n lines per PE for the configuration of 2^n PEs. This feature helps assure the scalability of the machine.

- Each PE and the associated local memory is implemented as a low-cost single board computer. If the machine has ten thousands processors, the cost of the machine is at least ten thousands times the cost of a single processor. Thus the cost of a processor is a large concern to us.

As for the cost of a processor, as the price of CPUs is going down rapidly, the size of the local memory is the major factor to determine the cost. On the other hand, too small local memory would limit application areas. The size of each local memory we chose is 64K bytes. Currently, we are not sure whether this size is large enough for our purpose. Our future experiments will answer to this question. However, we have already seen many sophisticated programs that run on personal computers with this size of memory. Even though the size of each local memory is small, the total size is quite large. If the application program and data are distributed appropriately among processors, even a large-scale application might be executable.

Now a days, there are commercially available massively parallel machines such as the Connection Machine [9], the AMT DAP [3], and the MasPar MP-1 [13]. However, these machines all have SIMD architecture and are not suitable for our purpose. Although many MIMD parallel computers have been proposed and constructed, many of these machines assume shared-memory architecture and thus cannot be extended to be a massively parallel computer. Some MIMD machines, e.g. the Cosmic Cube [15], have been designed for massively parallel computation, but they are still experimental machines and are not available to the public. Thus we ought to have built our own machine for experimentation on massively parallel computation.

In order to provide an interactive programming environment for PM1, a Scheme dialect called PMLisp [19] has been designed and implemented. Programs in PMLisp is intended to run on each PE of PM1. That is, each PE has its own PMLisp driver running on it, and the whole computation is proceeded by programs running in parallel on these drivers and communicating with each other. The key feature of PMLisp is that any data object can be passed between PEs. This implies that even expressions, procedures, and continuations can be passed between PEs because these are first class data objects in Scheme. This simple feature of PMLisp provides a flexible and powerful tool for experimentation.

The design of PMLisp is not finished yet. This paper reports the key features of PMLisp so far designed and implemented for PM1. The next section quickly overviews the PM1 architecture. Section 3 introduces the PMLisp language by focusing on its fundamental features, and Section 4 provides an example of the use of PMLisp. Section 5 shows how we can build higher-level language mechanisms on top of PMLisp, by providing an example mechanism which abstracts the network connection of the PM1. Some implementation issues are discussed in Section 6.

2 The PM1 Architecture

The processor element of PM1 is implemented as a single-board micro computer system (see Figure 2). Each PE board (approximately 10cm by 10cm) consists of an 8-bit micro processor Z80, communication devices for communications with the host machine and with other PEs, 8K bytes of ROM, 64K bytes of static RAM. Each PE has two communication

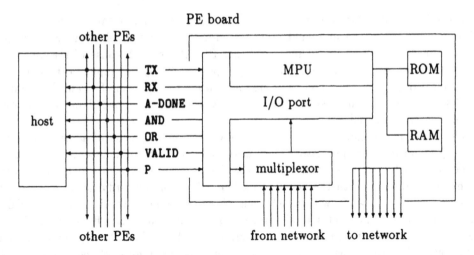

PE board

other PEs

TX
RX
A-DONE
AND
OR
VALID
P

host

MPU

I/O port

multiplexor

ROM

RAM

other PEs   from network   to network

Figure 2: The processor element of PM1

lines (RX and TX) for host-PE communications, and five synchronization lines (A-DONE, AND, OR, VALID, and P). Each of these lines is connected together with the lines from other PEs to form a wired-OR logic. Commands from the host are broadcast to all PEs via the TX line. It is up to each PE whether to execute a command or to ignore it. When a PE gets ready to receive another command from the host, it switches its own A-DONE line from 1 to 0. Since all the A-DONE lines are connected together to form an OR logic, the host knows that all PEs are ready to receive the next command, by checking the A-DONE line. On the other hand, messages from the PEs to the host are passed via the RX line. Since the RX line is shared by all PEs, only one PE can send a message to the host at a time. In order to avoid collision in the RX line, PEs can send a message only when the host requests so. Such a request is passed via the TX line in terms of a command from the host.

AND, OR, and VALID are general-purpose synchronization lines. Use of these lines depends on the application. Consider, for example, an application which requests all PEs to look for a solution in parallel. It may use one of the synchronization lines, say OR, in order for the host to know that one of the PEs has found a solution. To do this, each PE first sets its own OR line to 0. As soon as a PE finds a solution, it switches its own OR line from 0 to 1. By looking at the OR line, the host knows at least one of the PEs has found a solution. Either AND or VALID can be used instead of OR, since the logic of these two lines is exactly the same as that of OR. (These lines are named as they are, for historical reasons.)

In order for the host to receive the solution, another line ATTN (which does not appear in Figure 2) is used. The role of the ATTN line is to notify the host which PE has found the solution. For this, all ATTN lines from PEs are connected to a so-called priority encoder, whose output is the physical number of the PE which turns its own ATTN line to 1. If more than two PEs have turned the ATTN line to 1, then only one of them will be selected. The host then sends a request to the selected PE to send the solution to the host via the RX line.

The P line is used for synchronization of the network communication. In PM1, each PE has eight output lines and eight input lines for PE-PE communication. Each output line is connected with an input line of another PE. However, because of the limitation of the hardware, each PE has only one output port and only one input port for PE-PE communications. Thus these I/O ports are multiplexed to implement 8-channel I/O ports. The P line is used to send a signal from the host to switch from one channel to another synchronously among all PEs.

The physical communication network of PM1 is a combination of a mesh (which is typically found in image-processing machines) and a butterfly. The intention is that, for applications such as image-processing, we use the mesh network with which each PE can communicate directly with the neighboring four PEs. The butterfly network is used as a general-purpose network, with which each PE can communicate with any other PE in time at most logarithmic to the total number of PEs. To form a butterfly network of PM1, the PEs are divided into n rows, each consisting of 2^n PEs. Each PE is given its address in the butterfly network as $< i, b_n \cdots b_1 >$, where i is the number of the row where the PE resides and $b_n \cdots b_1$ is the binary representation of the column number. The butterfly network of PM1 connects this PE directly with the four PEs whose addresses are:

$$< i - 1, b_n \cdots b_i \tilde{b}_{i-1} \cdots b_1 >$$
$$< i - 1, b_n \cdots b_i b_{i-1} \cdots b_1 >$$
$$< i + 1, b_n \cdots b_i b_{i-1} \cdots b_1 >$$
$$< i + 1, b_n \cdots \tilde{b}_i b_{i-1} \cdots b_1 >$$

where $\tilde{b}$ indicates logical negation of b, i.e., $\tilde{b} = 0$ if $b = 1$ and $\tilde{b} = 1$ if $b = 0$. In the current implementation of PM1, $n = 3$ and the total number of PEs is $3 \times 2^3 = 24$.

The butterfly network is adapted in PM1 for the following reasons.

1. The number of communication channels per PE is always four, without respect to the total number of PEs. Thus the same PE board can be used for any configuration of the system. In contrast, the butterfly network which is popularly used as general-purpose network requires each PE to have n lines for the configuration of 2^n PEs.

2. The network enables modularization of PEs and provides scalability of the PM1 system. That is, a PM1 system with $n2^n$ PEs can be used to build an upgraded system with $(n + 1) \cdot 2^{n+1}$ PEs with only minor changes to the network connection. To do this, we can use two PM1 systems with $n2^n$ PEs each, and additional 2^{n+1} PEs. The two PM1 systems form the left half and the right half, respectively, of the first n rows of the upgraded system. The additional 2^{n+1} PEs form the last $(n+1)st$ row of the upgraded system. The networks of the two PM1 system are used without modification, except for the PEs at the boundary. This property, together with the above property, makes it easy to upgrade the PM1 system, and thus is highly useful for building an experimental MIMD massively parallel computer like PM1.

3. The butterfly network contains a nearly-balanced tree with an arbitrary PE as the root. This property is highly useful when almost all PEs try to send a message to a particular PE, because the intermediate PEs can reduce the number of messages by combining two or more messages into a single message as required by the application.

For example, when the destination PE (i.e., the root PE of the tree) requires the sum of the values in all messages, each non-root PE can make a partial sum and send it towards the root in a single message. The property is also useful when a PE wants to send a same message to many other PEs. Rather than sending messages to one PE after another, the source PE may send a message to two neighbors, so that the message can be forwarded down through the tree whose root is the source PE.

4. Each PE can send a message to any PE at most in time $2n$, for the PM1 system with $n2^n$ PEs. This is comparable with other "faster" networks such as hyper cube where each PE can send a message to any PE at most in time n for a system with 2^n PEs.

Since we chose the butterfly network, the total number of PEs should be $n2^n$ for some n. Thus the mesh network does not always allocate PEs in a square matrix. In general, the mesh network of PM1 allocates PEs in r by s matrix, where r and s are whole numbers such that $rs = n2^n$ and $|r - s|$ is as small as possible. For example, a system with 24 PEs are allocated in 4 by 6 matrix, and a system with 64 PEs are allocated in 8 by 8 square matrix to form a mesh network. Figure 3 and Figure 4 illustrate the mesh connection and the butterfly connection, respectively, of the current configuration of PM1 with 24 PEs.

A small program, called *Agent*, runs on each PE. This program plays as the "operating system" in each PE. The major role of the Agent in each PE is to take care of the lowest level communication with the host and with other PEs. This program is stored in the ROM of each PE board and is copied into the RAM when PM1 begins to run. Currently available programming languages are the Z80 assembly language, C, and a Lisp. Programs in C and the assembly language are cross-compiled (or cross-assembled) by the host, and the object modules are down-loaded to all or some PEs by using the host-PE communication. On the other hand, Lisp users interact with the host Lisp system, which down-loads the Lisp driver to all PEs, sends Lisp programs to each PE, and receives the results of execution.

3 PMLisp and Its Primitive Operations

PMLisp is a compact interpreter-based Lisp system that runs on the Z80 micro processor, i.e., the CPU of the processor element of PM1. In order to provide powerful control mechanisms in a small Lisp language that fits the small memory size of Z80 (64K bytes), we chose Scheme [10] as the base language, which is characterized by the following features.

- first-class continuations

- tail-recursive implementation

- lexical scoping and lexical closures

- single name space for both functions and variables

- delayed evaluation

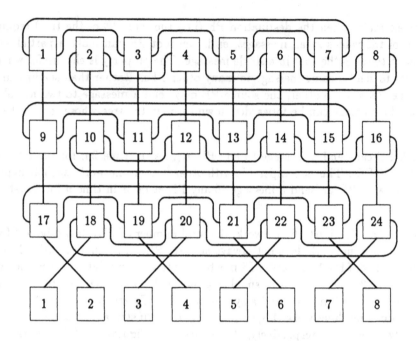

Figure 3: The mesh subnetwork that constitutes the PM1 network for 24 PEs

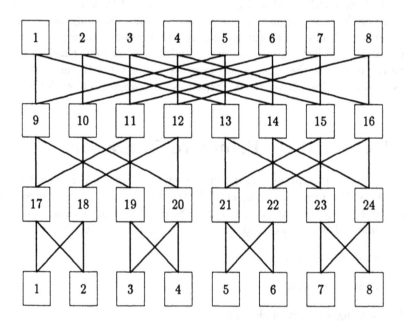

Figure 4: The butterfly subnetwork that constitutes the PM1 network for 24 PEs

Let us explain why these features are desirable for our purpose.

First-class continuations allows programmers to write multi-tasking programs on top of Lisp. If the number of PEs is smaller than required by an application, each PE has to act as multiple "virtual processors". In that situation, each physical PE runs several tasks, each corresponding to the task of a single virtual processor. Although it is desirable that the operating system distributes tasks among PEs automatically, we need to do some experiments to fix the algorithm for task distribution among PEs and task scheduling within each PE. First-class continuations are convenient for such experiments. As will be described shortly, any data object can be sent from one PE to another. If tasks are represented as first-class continuations, they can be moved from one PE to another in order to balance the load of each PE. Although continuations are large data structures and it takes time to move continuations among PEs, the mechanism of such automatic load balancing among PEs is an interesting research topic in the future.

The tail-recursive implementation saves the stack space to a great extent. Efficient use of the stack is important not only for the small size of the local memory but also for the possibility of passing continuations among PEs. When a continuation is captured, the whole stack will be saved in the continuation. The tail-recursive implementation reduces the stack size and thus reduces the size of the continuation, making the continuation passing faster.

Lexical closures can also be passed among PEs, since they are first-class objects. By passing a lexical closure, the sender PE can send its lexical environment to another PE, which in turn executes a function in the same environment of the sender. Note that the two environments (one in the sender and the other in the receiver) are the same but not identical. As we will describe later, when a data object is sent from one PE to another, the receiver constructs a copy of the object in its local memory, and thus there is no data-sharing among PEs.

The single name space of Scheme enables programming in an object-oriented style. We believe that object-oriented programming will give a solution to ease programming in MIMD massively-parallel computers. In object-oriented programming, a program consists of several objects that communicate each other via message passing. This computation model matches well with our image of MIMD massively-parallel computers. By mapping each object to a single PE (or a single virtual processor), programs written in object-oriented style will be executed straightforwardly and efficiently. Incidentally, the *network models* in PMLisp which will be described later have flavors of object-oriented programming and are implemented on top of PMLisp, by making use of the single name space.

The mechanism of delayed evaluation in Scheme allows the possibility of building a high-level construct for synchronization among PEs. Several parallel Lisp languages such as Multilisp [8], MultiScheme [12], and Qlisp [6] use the so-called *future* objects as the communication and synchronization devices between two processes. Future objects can be regarded as a sort of *promises* that sequential Scheme creates when the evaluation of an expression is delayed. The only semantic difference is that the evaluation of the expression for a future object is proceeded concurrently, while the evaluation of the delayed expression begins only when the value is required. Although these parallel Lisp languages are intended for shared-memory architecture, the same idea may be used for parallel Lisp languages on loosely-coupled architecture.

special forms:	and	cond	define	delay	if	lambda
	letrec	or	progn	quote	setq	
control functions:	apply	call/cc	eval	force		
type predicates:	atom	codep	consp	integerp	null	symbolp
equality predicates:	eq	equal				
list functions:	append	assoc	car	cdr	cons	list
	nth	rplaca	rplacd			
integer functions:	*	+	-	/	1+	1-
	2*	2+	2-	mod		
integer predicates:	=	<	>	<=	>=	
	plusp	minusp	zerop			
bit manipulation:	logand	logior	lognot	logrol	logror	logshl
	logshr	logxor				
communication:	init*	send*	send?	recv*	recv?	
	print	print?	read	read?		
miscellaneous:	not	syscall	my-address			

Table 1: List of PMLisp functions

The language of PMLisp is a small Lisp dialect with the above five features of the Scheme family. In order to provide large memory space for user programs, PMLisp supports minimal functionality. The available data objects are:

- conses

- symbols

- fixnums of 14 bits long

- compiled code objects (for built-in functions)

- the empty list (which is used also as the false value in conditional expressions such as if expressions)

The current set of the built-in functions are listed in Table 1. Note that we follow the Common Lisp language [16] for the namings of built-in functions. For instance, the Scheme function set-car! is given the corresponding name rplaca of Common Lisp. This is simply because the authors were (and many Lisp programmers are) more familiar with programming in Common Lisp than in Scheme. Essentially, PMLisp is more like a Scheme language than Common Lisp. Those functions that have no counterparts in Common Lisp are given Scheme names such as call/cc and letrec.

PMLisp does not have special data types for continuations, promises, and lexical closures. These objects are represented by lists whose first elements are special symbols #continuation, #promise, and #closure, respectively. These symbols are special in the sense that the user cannot input these symbols directly, because of the prefix '#'. This simple-minded representation not only simplifies the type system of the language, but also simplifies the message passing mechanism of PMLisp among PEs as we will describe later.

The model of parallel computation with PMLisp is to have a huge number of Lisp programs running in parallel, communicating with each other by passing PMLisp forms as messages. The receiver of a message understands the intention of the sender by evaluating the form. In general, several sorts of messages are required for parallel computation on loosely-coupled MIMD machines. Possible sorts of messages include:

- just a datum which the receiver knows how to treat,

- a simple command such as setting a value to a variable of the receiver,

- a request to forward a message to another PE, and

- a program to be executed later by the receiver.

By passing Lisp forms and evaluating them, any of these sorts of messages can be implemented. Thus this model of parallel computation is highly flexible and is suitable for experiments on loosely-coupled MIMD computers.

As the most primitive mechanisms for communication, PMLisp is provided with the following built-in functions.

(init* *function*)
Initializes the communication buffers, and invokes the *function* with the PE number as the only argument. The value of the *function* must be a list of fixnum pairs

$$((s_0 \ r_0) \ (s_1 \ r_1) \ \cdots \ (s_k \ r_k))$$

This list is used to set up the *index table* which controls the multiplexor for PE-PE communication channels. Not all applications of PMLisp need to use all of the eight communication channels. For example, image-processing applications may need only those channels that form the mesh network, and conventional MIMD algorithms may need only the channels for the butterfly network. In addition, we would like to use the physical network of PM1 for experiments on other networks such as hyper cubes and full shuffle networks. By allowing the programmer to selectively use the communication channels, the physical network of PM1 will be used flexibly and efficiently. For this purpose, each PE of PM1 has its own *index table* to control the multiplexor. Each entry of the index table consists of the numbers of the output channel and the input channel to be selected at each time slice. These channels are selected from one to another in the order of entries in the index table. Given the above value of the *function*, the output channels and input channels will be selected in the following order

Output: $s_0 \rightarrow s_1 \rightarrow \cdots \rightarrow s_k \rightarrow s_0 \rightarrow s_1 \rightarrow \cdots$
Input: $\quad r_0 \rightarrow r_1 \rightarrow \cdots \rightarrow r_k \rightarrow r_0 \rightarrow r_1 \rightarrow \cdots$

There are four primitive functions for message sending/receiving in PMLisp. In these functions, *index* specifies the input/output channels stored as the *index*-th entry of the index table.

(**send*** *index object*)
Sends the *object* to the *index*-th output channel.

(**recv*** *index*)
Receives an object from the *index*-th input channel.

(**send?** *index*)
Tests if the object sent to the *index*-th output channel has already been sent to the receiver. That is, returns true if the output buffer of the channel is empty, and returns false otherwise.

(**recv?** *index*)
Test if some object has arrived at the *index*-th input channel. That is, returns false if the input buffer of the channel is empty, and returns true otherwise.

These primitive operations are general enough and it is up to the programmer how to use them for PE-PE communication. The typical way of using these operations is to define a hook function which takes care of all PE-PE communication independently of the main task of the program running in a PE. For example, the following form defines a hook function which evaluates the message if one has arrived at an input channel.

```
(setq *eval-hook*
  ((lambda (next)
     (lambda ()
       (if (recv? next)
           (eval (recv* next)))
       (setq next (mod (1+ next) k))))
   0))
```

The PMLisp interpreter **eval** checks the value of the system variable *eval-hook* each time it evaluates a form. If the value is a function, **eval** invokes the function (the current hook function) with no argument. On return from the hook function, **eval** resumes its execution. In this example, the hook function is a lexical closure that is created by the inner **lambda** form. In the closure is enclosed the parameter **next** of the function that is defined by the outer **lambda** form. Since the argument to this function is 0, the initial value of **next** is also 0. Each time the hook function is called by **eval**, it checks if a message has arrived at the **next**-th channel. If one has arrived, it evaluates the message. Then the hook function increments **next** by one (in modulo k) and returns. When the hook function is invoked again, it checks the next channel and evaluates the message if one has arrived. In this way, the hook function checks input channels in turn, one at each call, and evaluates the message if one has arrived at the channel.

The hook function is "atomic" in that **eval** does not call the hook function while it is executing the hook function. If the user wants to program an "atomic" operation that should not be disturbed by the hook function, he can embed the body of the hook function

benchmark test	PMLisp	KCL interpreter
(hanoi 9)	3.88 (3)	1.37 (0)
(queen 8)	35.77 (26)	15.43 (5)
(tak 18 12 6)	301.88 (236)	135.93 (49)

Table 2: Benchmark results on PMLisp and the KCL interpreter (The time is in seconds. The numbers in parentheses are the numbers of garbage collection.)

into a conditional expression, so that the body is not executed during execution of user-defined atomic operations. Alternatively, he can assign an empty list to *eval-hook*.

The conventional I/O functions read and print are used for host-PE communication in PMLisp. That is, read receives a message from the host and print sends a message to the host. As in the case of PE-PE communication, a message from/to the host can be any PMLisp object. In order to check if a message has arrived from the host, read? is used with no argument. Also, in order to check if the previous message to the host has already sent to the host, print? is used with no argument. Remember that the communication line to the host is shared by all PEs. Therefore, a message from a PE to the host may remain in the output buffer of the PE for a long time.

A superset of PMLisp runs on the host machine. The programmer interacts with this host Lisp system. The communication functions of the host system are send, send?, and recv, and recv-ready?, which correspond to send*, send?, recv*, and recv?, respectively, of the PMLisp in PEs. send sends a message to a specified PE or broadcast a message to all PEs. send? is used to check if the previous message has actually sent to the destinations. recv reads a message from the specified PE. If no message has arrived from the specified PE, recv waits until one message arrives. recv-ready? is used to check if any message has arrived to the host. If true, this function returns the PE number of one of the PEs that have sent a message to the host. For example, the following expression represents a loop that waits until at least one message arrives from some PE. When this loop is exited, the arrived message will be returned as the value of the expression.

```
(do ((pe (recv-ready?) (recv-ready?)))
    (pe (recv pe)))
```

To show the performance of the PMLisp system in a single PE, we list some benchmark results on PMLisp and on a Common Lisp system KCL (Kyoto Common Lisp) [20] in Table 2. We used the KCL interpreter on the SUN3/150 with 16MHz MC68020 CPU. The benchmark programs are found in [5] and [18]. As will be clear from the Table, the performance of PMLisp is about one half of the performance of the KCL interpreter on the SUN. The KCL interpreter uses A-lists (Association lists) to keep track of the lexical environment, and thus collects list cells in those A-lists that are not used any more. The PMLisp interpreter also uses A-lists to keep track of the lexical environment. Notice that

PMLisp invokes the garbage collector much more times than KCL. This is partly because the small memory space of PMLisp, but also because PMLisp uses lists to represent its stack.

4 An Example - Finding the Shortest Path

As we mentioned earlier, the key idea of the flexibility of PMLisp as a tool for experiments is that computation can be proceeded by passing expressions that are to be evaluated by the receiver. The typical use of this idea is to run a loop that waits until a message arrives, and then evaluates the message. Thus the main program on each PE has the following control flow.

1. Initialize the program.

2. Wait until a message arrives.

3. Evaluate the message.

4. Go to 2.

Messages will be sent to other PEs or the host during the initialization and the evaluation of a message. Typically, only selected PEs send messages during the initialization to trigger the computation. The wait-and-evaluate loop terminates if some condition is established during the message evaluation.

As an example of such typical use of PMLisp, we will show a program that finds the shortest length path between two vertices in a directed graph. The problem to be solved is formulated as follows.

Suppose we are given a directed graph with vertices V and weighted edges $E \subset V \times V \times Int$, and a "starting vertex" $s \in V$. For all vertex $x \in V$, finds the path $s, v_1, v_2, \ldots, v_n, x$ such that $(s, v_1, w_0), (v_1, v_2, w_1), \ldots, (v_n, x, w_n) \in E$ and $\sum_{i=0}^{n} w_i$ is minimum.

To simplify the discussion, let us assume we have as many PEs as the vertices of the given graph. Then we can assign each vertex to a single PE, and the problem is solved by the following PMLisp program running in each PE.

```
(define distance -1)

(define (path n)
  (if (or (= distance -1)
          (< n distance))
      (progn
        (setq distance n)
        (mapc (lambda (edge)
                (send (destination edge)
                      (list 'path (+ n (weight edge)))))
              edges-from-me))))
```

The variable `distance` holds the minimum length of the paths to the vertex so far found. Its initial value is `-1`, meaning no path is found yet. The messages in this example have the form `(path n)`. Each message informs the receiver of the fact that there is another path to the receiver and its length is `n`. The function `path` defines the behavior of the receiver. It first checks if this message is the first one, or if the new path is shorter than the shortest path so far found. In both cases, the receiver sends messages to its neighbors, i.e., those PEs that represent vertices to which there are edges from the current vertex. The variable `edges-from-me` holds the information on the edges in the graph whose source vertex is the current vertex. This information is represented as a list of pairs of the destination vertex and the weight of the edge.

In order to start the computation, the PE that represents the starting vertex s invokes the following function.

```
(define (start)
  (setq distance 0)
  (mapc (lambda (edge)
          (send (destination edge)
                (list 'path (weight edge))))
        edges-from-me))
```

Then each vertex tries to find the shortest path. After a while, when there is no message in the network, each vertex has got the length of the shortest path from the starting vertex. If the programmer wants to know the shortest paths rather than the length, he can modify the program so that each message conveys the path (in terms of a list) and each PE saves the shortest path so far found.

Notice that we have used `send` rather than the built-in function `send*`. `send` is a user-defined function that sends a message to an arbitrary PE which is specified by the second argument. Since each PE is not directly connected with all PEs, this function is responsible to find the shortest route to the destination PE. Finding the "shortest" route, however, is a difficult problem, because the actual time that is required for a message to reach the destination highly depends on the traffic in the communication network. Solving this problem would be a future research topic of the P-Machine project. For this example, we define `send` so that it simply chooses the physically shortest route in the butterfly network. Incidentally, `mapc` in the above program is also a user-defined function which is equivalent to the Scheme function `for-each` which invokes the specified function as many times as the length of the specified list. Each element of the list is used as the argument to the function.

The above program does not tell when all vertices have found the shortest path. The programmer has to look at the LED indications of PM1, which display the communication status of each PE. We would rather want the host to know the end of the computation. Our algorithm to solve this problem is to send back an acknowledge when a path reaches a deadlock. When a PE receives a `path` message,

1. if the path is not shorter than the shortest path so far found, then the PE immediately returns an acknowledge message to the sender,

2. otherwise, the PE immediately sends `path` messages to its neighbors as before, and it returns an acknowledge message to the sender

(a) when it receives acknowledge messages to all the **path** messages, or

(b) when it receives another **path** message that informs of a shorter path than the previous one.

When the PE for the starting vertex receives acknowledge messages to all the **path** messages it has sent during the initialization, it sends a message to the host to notify the end of the computation.

We need three additional variables to implement this algorithm:

- **pe-to-ack** to remember to which PE the acknowledge should be returned when the current PE has received acknowledges to all the **path** messages that were sent according to the current shortest path.

- **ack-id** to identify the **path** message for the current shortest path. Since a message is sent to a neighboring PE each time a new shortest path is found, we can use the new distance to identify a message.

- **pe-to-wait** to member those neighboring PEs who have not yet returned acknowledges.

Here is the revised definition of the **path** function.

```
(define (path n from id)
  (if (or (= distance -1)
          (< n distance))
      (progn
        (if (not (= distance -1))
            (send pe-to-ack (list 'ack (my-address) ack-id)))
        (setq distance n)
        (setq pe-to-ack from)
        (setq ack-id id)
        (setq pe-to-wait '())
        (mapc (lambda (edge)
                (send (destination edge)
                  (list 'path (+ n (weight edge)) (my-address) n))
                (setq pe-to-wait (cons (destination edge)
                                       pe-to-wait)))
              edges-from-me)
        )
      (send from (list 'ack from id))))
```

Acknowledge messages are in the form (ack *sender message-id*), meaning this acknowledge is returned from *sender* for the previous message with *message-id*. The handler of acknowledge messages is very simple.

```
(define (ack from id)
  (if (= id distance)
      (progn
```

```
(setq pe-to-wait (remove from pe-to-wait))
(if (null pe-to-wait)
    (send pe-to-ack (list 'ack (my-address) ack-id))))))
```

It checks if the acknowledge is for the current shortest path. If not, it ignores the acknowledge. Otherwise, it removes the sender of the acknowledge from pe-to-wait. If pe-to-wait becomes empty, then all acknowledges have been returned and thus the current PE returns an acknowledge to the sender of the path message of the current shortest path.

For the PE that represents the starting vertex, we need a slightly different definition of ack. The only difference is that, when pe-to-wait becomes empty, the starting PE returns a message to the host to notify the end of the computation.

```
(define (ack from id)
  (if (= id distance)
      (progn
        (setq pe-to-wait (remove from pe-to-wait))
        (if (null pe-to-wait)
            (print 'end)))))
```

Figure 5 shows how each PE works during the computation of the revised version of the shortest path program. The graph we used is a perfect directed graph (i.e., every vertex has an edge to any other vertex) which has eight vertices and whose edge weights are all 1. We used the eight-vertex graph simply because PM1 could not remember the log data for perfect graphs with more vertices. Note that even if only eight PEs are used to represent vertices, all 24 PEs work to transfer messages. We randomly chose the first eight PEs as vertices and the first PE as the starting vertex. The reason why we chose the weights to be 1 is that, although we have tried several graphs with random weights, the results were almost the same.

In Figure 5, each PE has three raws: one above the first horizontal line, the second between the two horizontal lines, and the third below the second horizontal line. The first raw indicates when the PE received a message and how long the receiving process took. Similarly, the second raw is for message handling, and the third raw is for message sending. As will be expected, the first eight PEs spent some period of time to process the first few messages because they have to further send messages to other PEs. For most messages, the PEs immediately returned acknowledges. Thus the typical pattern is to receive a message, process the message, and return an acknowledge, all in a short period of time. For PEs other than the first eight, one of the three processes sometimes took a relatively long time. This is because the garbage collection occurred during the process. When the first PE received the last acknowledge, it returned a message to the host to indicate the end of the computation. The host received this message in about 32 seconds after it invoked the initialization function in the first PE.

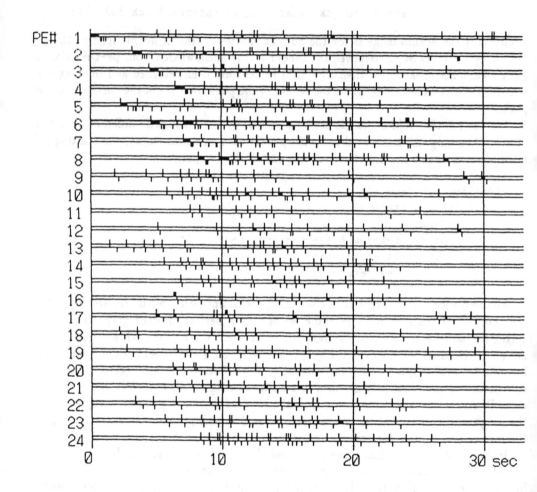

Figure 5: The behavior of PEs for the shortest path program

5 Network Models

In this section, we present an example of extending the PMLisp language by adding it high-level constructs to ease programming on PM1. This example is to build *network models* which give abstraction of physical network connections among PEs.

The physical network of PM1 contains several interesting networks as its subnetworks. Such subnetworks include:

- full shuffle networks, which are topologically equivalent to butterfly networks

- ring networks, which are subnetworks of mesh networks

- binary trees, which are subnetworks of butterfly networks

- cyclic hyper cubes, which are subnetworks of butterfly networks

In addition, if we regard PEs in each column of the butterfly network in Figure 4 as a single PE, we can obtain an hyper cube network. The programmer can develop parallel programs for these subnetworks by setting up the index table of input/output channels mentioned above. The network models are intended to make it easier for the programmer to build programs that depend on a particular network connection.

Each network model defines a *network object* and associated *PE objects*. Each PE object corresponds to a PE that joins the network model. (Note in general that not all PEs join a network model.) However, different network models may define different PE objects for a same PE (which should become clear after reading this section). These objects are implemented as Lisp functions and are used as *objects* in object-oriented programming.

Network objects are used by the host Lisp system. The most important message to network objects is `for-each-pe` which causes expressions to be evaluated in parallel.

> (*network* '`for-each-pe` *procedure*)

invokes the *procedure* once for each PE that joins the network model. The argument to the *procedure* is the PE object associated with the *network*. The return value of each invocation of *procedure* is regarded as a Lisp expression, which is sent to the PE for evaluation. The results of these expressions are returned to the host and are collected together into a list in the order defined by the network model. This list will then be returned as the value of the above expression.

Figure 6 gives a simple example of the `for-each-pe` message. This function implements the odd-even transposition sort [7] using ring network. For simplicity, we assume that the argument to this function is a list of 48 integers.

> $(a_0 \ a_1 \ \cdots \ a_{46} \ a_{47})$

`ring-model` is a system variable which holds the network object for the ring network. By passing the `for-each-pe` message to this network object, the function defined by the `lambda` expression will be invoked once for each PE and the returned value is sent to each PE for evaluation. In this example, the expression to be evaluated by the i-th PE is:

```
(define (even-odd-sort data)
  (apply append
         (ring-model 'for-each-pe
           (lambda (pe)
             (list 'even-odd-sort-on-pe
                   pe
                   (nth (- (* (pe 'index) 2) 2) data)
                   (nth (- (* (pe 'index) 2) 1) data))))))
```

Figure 6: Host program for even-odd sort

```
(define (even-odd-sort-on-pe self data1 data2)
  (letrec ((loop (lambda (n a b)
                   (if (plusp n)
                       (progn
                         (if (not (self 'leftmost)) (self 'left a))
                         (if (not (self 'rightmost)) (self 'right b))
                         (if (not (self 'leftmost))
                             (setq a (max a (self 'left))))
                         (if (not (self 'rightmost))
                             (setq b (min b (self 'right))))
                         (loop (- n 1) (min a b) (max a b)))
                       (list a b)))))
    (loop (self 'pe-count) data1 data2)))
```

Figure 7: The PE program for even-odd sort

(even-odd-sort-on-pe *i-th-PE-object* a_{2i-2} a_{2i-1})

where **even-odd-sort-on-pe** is the name of the function which is stored in all PEs and does the actual computation (see Figure 7). Each call of **even-odd-sort-on-pe** returns when the PE finds $(2i-2)$th and $(2i-1)$th integers in the sorted list. And the return value is a list of these two integers. Thus, when all calls of **even-odd-sort-on-pe** return, the host gets a list:

((0th-integer 1st-integer)
  ⋮
((2i − 2)th-integer (2i − 1)th-integer)
  ⋮
(46th-integer 47th-integer))

By appending all elements of this list, the host obtains a sorted list of integers.

PE objects are mainly used by the PEs. Usually, the host sends to a PE the PE object corresponding to the PE, at the beginning of computation, as in the example in Figure 6. Each PE object contains all information about the network model, that is necessary for each PE to proceed its own computation.

Messages to PE objects include:

(*PE-object* `'pe-count`), which returns the total number of PEs that join the network model with which the *PE-object* is associated.

(*PE-object* `'index`), which returns the index number of the PE in the network.

(*PE-object direction*), which reads an object from the neighboring PE in the *direction*. The available set of *directions* depends on the network model. For the ring model, for example, possible *directions* are `left` and `right`. For the mesh model, possible *directions* are `n`, `e`, `w`, and `s`.

(*PE-object direction object*), which sends an object to the neighboring PE in the *direction*.

There are some messages to test the location of the PE in the network. Such test messages depend on the network model. For example, in the ring model,

(*PE-object* `'leftmost`) and (*PE-object* `'rightmost`)

are available, which are used when the ring model acts as a non-cyclic sequence of PEs.

Figure 7 defines the function **even-odd-sort-on-pe**. This function calls its local function **loop** n times recursively, where n is the total number of PEs that join the ring model, i.e., the value of (**self** `'pe-count`). Each call to **loop** exchanges integers with the neighboring PEs. It sends the smaller integer a to the **left** neighbor, and the larger integer b to the **right** neighbor. Then it receives an integer from the **left** neighbor and keeps it only when it is larger than a. Also, it receives an integer from the **right** neighbor and keeps it only when it is smaller than b.

Figure 8 illustrates an implementation of the ring model, written in PMLisp. Associated with the variable **ring-model** is a function which is executed in the host PMLisp system. If the message to the ring model is **for-each-pe** (line 2), then it executes the handler of the **for-each-pe** in lines 3 - 24. The handler consists of two parts. In the first part (lines 3 - 17), the handler sends messages to start the execution of PEs. That is, for each PE, it sends a message to initialize the communication buffer (line 6), invokes the function given as the second argument to **ring-model** (lines 8 - 16), and then sends the return value to the PE (line 7). The argument to the function is a PE object (lines 9 - 16) which is implemented as a lexical closure in Figure 8. In the second part (lines 18 - 25), the handler receives results from PEs. It waits in a **do** loop (line 21) until a result value is returned from a PE (line 22). It then saves the value in the appropriate place of the temporary vector **v** (line 22). This process is repeated until all PEs return a value (line 20). Then the values in the temporary vector are put into a list, which is returned as the value of **ring-model**.

```
1    (define (ring-model msg . args)
2      (cond ((eq msg 'for-each-pe)
3             (do ((pe 1 (1+ pe))
4                 (init-table init-table-list (cdr init-table)))
5                ((> pe 24))
6               (send '(init* ,(car init-table)) pe)
7               (send
8                ((car args)
9                 (lambda (msg . args)
10                   (cond ((eq msg 'left)
11                          (if args (send* 0 (car args)) (recv* 1)))
12                         ((eq msg 'right)
13                          (if args (send* 1 (car args)) (recv* 0)))
14                         ((eq msg 'leftmost) (= pe 1))
15                         ...
16                         )))
17               pe))
18             (do ((v (make-vector 24))
19                 (count 24 (1- count)))
20                ((zerop count) (vector->list v))
21               (do ((pe (recv-ready?) (recv-ready?)))
22                  (pe (vector-set! v (1- pe) (recv pe)))
23                  )
24               )
25             )
26             ...
27             ))
```

Figure 8: Implementation of the ring model

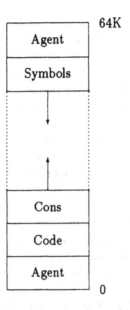

Figure 9: Memory map of PMLisp

6 Implementation

The key implementation issue of PMLisp is how to send an arbitrary PMLisp object between PEs and between a PE and the host. Since the memory associated with a PE is not accessed directly by other PEs and the contents of the memory is in general not the same as the contents of other PE's memory, we cannot send just a pointer to the object. Thus, some mechanism is necessary with which the receiver of the object can make a copy of the original object in its own memory. One possible solution would be to send a textual representation of the object. This solution, however, is not satisfactory: The length (i.e., the number of bytes) of textual representations tends to be long and the length of messages affects the total performance of the PMLisp system. Our solution is to encode the object.

Before going to the details of our encoding, let us mention about the object representation and memory allocation of PMLisp (see Figure 9). The local memory (64K bits) of each PE is divided into six areas: two areas for Agent (the operating system of PM1), the code area of PMLisp where function objects of built-in functions of PMLisp are stored, the area of cons cells, the area of symbol cells, and the free area. The sizes of the first three areas are fixed. The cons area expands towards higher addresses and the symbol area expands towards lower addresses. When the free area has been exhausted, the compactifying garbage collector is invoked, which moves all cons cells in use towards lower addresses.

While contents of the cons area of a PE may differ between PEs, contents of the symbol area are common to all PEs, so that symbols can be passed among PEs simply by their addresses. In order to satisfy this condition all the time, no PE is allowed to create its own symbol. Indeed, no function is supported in PMLisp to create a symbol.

A new symbol is created only when a message from the host contains a symbol that does not exist in the symbol area of PEs. Before sending a message, the host checks if a new symbol is included in the message, and if so, suspends execution of all PEs to create the symbol in the symbol area of all PEs. In addition to this "heavy **gensym**" mechanism, the PMLisp garbage collector never collects symbols. This is because collecting a symbol requires to check that the symbol is not used by any PEs, and thus requires network-wide garbage collection.

Each PMLisp object is represented with two bytes (i.e., 16 bits). Among the five PMLisp data types (symbol, cons, code, fixnum, and the empty list), only fixnums are represented as immediate data with their least significant bits 01. Other objects are pointers to symbol cells, cons cells, code entries and the unique empty list. These pointers are 4-byte pointers, i.e., their least significant bits are 00. The second least significant bit of each object is used as the mark bit during garbage collection.

The object encoding scheme adopted for PE-PE and PE-host communication is as follows. Objects other than conses are encoded to themselves. Lists are encoded to a sequence of encodings of the list elements followed by a 2-byte command [LIST n], where n is the number of elements in the list. Dotted lists are encoded similarly, except that another 2-byte command [LIST* n] is used. These commands are distinguished from objects by the two least significant bits. For example,

(+ 3 4) and (cdr (quote (a b . c)))

are encoded to

+ 3 4 [LIST 3]

and to

cdr quote a b c [LIST* 3] [LIST 2] [LIST 2]

respectively. The first encoding is 8 bytes long and the second encoding is 16 bytes long. Note that the gain of this encoding scheme is usually much larger than in these examples because symbols may have longer names and fixnums may have more digits. In addition, the receiver can decode the object more quickly than reading the text representation, mainly because no interning is required for symbols.

In order to encoding structured objects with shared cons cells, commands [#= n] and [## n] are used, which, roughly speaking, correspond to Common Lisp read macros #=n and #n#. Thus the following cyclic list

#0=(a b . #0#)

will be encoded to the following 10-byte sequence.

[#= 0] a b [## 0] [LIST* 3]

7   Concluding Remarks

As part of the P-Machine project for massively parallel computation, we have developed an experimental loosely-coupled MIMD machine, called PM1. In order to provide an interactive programming environment for PM1, we have designed and implemented a Lisp dialect PMLisp. The computation model of PMLisp is to have a huge number of PMLisp programs running in parallel, one on a single processor element of PM1. These programs communicate with each other by sending PMLisp objects to be evaluated by the receiver. In order to implement several interesting networks using the physical PE-PE network, the notion of *network models* have been introduced, which allows the programmer to easily build a program that depends on a particular network connection, independently of the physical network of PM1.

The performance of the current PMLisp system is not so good, partly because of the low speed of the communication devices of PM1 and partly because of the absence of compiler. However, PMLisp works well as a tool for development and experimental implementation of parallel algorithms on PM1. Our current research interest about PMLisp is to build higher-level constructs for loosely-coupled MIMD parallel computers on top of PMLisp.

So far, most successful massively parallel machines (i.e., most machines in use for realistic applications) are SIMD machines. Indeed, the three commercial machines listed in the Introduction are all SIMD machines. Some MIMD machines have been designed (see [1,2] for recent survey) for massively parallel computation, but they are still experimental machines.

There can be several reasons for the success of SIMD machines. Among them, we consider the followings as the most important reasons. One is that it is relatively easy to program for SIMD machines, since the programmer can easily imagine the situation that every processor is executing the same instruction at a time. Another reason is that synchronization of the processors is "built-in" in the architecture. All processors are synchronized at every step of the instruction sequence. Thus the programmer need not worry about the classical problem of process synchronization. Thus, as far as the application has SIMD parallelism, there is no doubt for the suitability of SIMD machines.

On the other hand, there are several applications that have MIMD parallelism, or that are expressed more naturally in MIMD fashion. One typical example is traffic system simulations which have to simulate the movement and reciprocal relation of heterogeneous objects such as pedestrians, cars, and tracks. Such applications would be naturally programmed by having each processor simulate one of the existing objects. Although it is possible to use SIMD machines for such applications, the performance of the application would be not so good as in the case of simulating homogeneous objects. Hence the need for MIMD massively parallel machines.

The major problem in MIMD massively parallel machines is the difficulty of programming. Since each processor has its own instruction stream, process synchronization must be controlled by the program directly or indirectly. There are three possible levels to describe the synchronization. At the lowest level is to require the programmer to explicitly control the synchronization in a low-level programming language. At the second level is to provide a high-level language in which the synchronization control is implicit but the programmer still needs to know the actual computation mechanism in order to obtain efficient programs. At the highest level is to develop an intelligent, sophisticated compiler that can convert programs in conventional programming languages. This third level is most desirable but we cannot expect such a compiler to appear in the very near future, as will be clear if we recall the failure of the dream of vectorizing compilers for vector processors. As for the possibility of a high-level language, there already exist several examples for SIMD massively parallel machines, such as Connection Machine Lisp [17], Paralation Lisp [14], and Fortran 8X [4]. Although several high-level languages (and high-level language constructs to be embedded in conventional languages) have been proposed for MIMD parallel computation, none of them are proved to be suitable for controlling a huge number of processors. In order to find or to develop a language that is suitable for MIMD massively parallel computation, we need more experiences in programming for MIMD massively parallel computers.

Acknowledgements

The authors would like to thank Hiroaki Waki, Tsuyoshi Obayashi, and Susumu Komae for implementation of the PMLisp kernel, and the other students at the authors' laboratory who have been working for the P-Machine project. The authors also would like to thank Shozo Takeoka who designed the processor element of PM1 and joined the design discussions of PMLisp. The authors also would like to thank Prof. Takayasu Ito and Dr. Robert Halstead for their recommendation to write this paper and for their valuable comments to the draft.

References

[1] L. S. Haynes, R. L. Lau, D. P. Sieqiorek, and D. W. Mizell: A Survey of Highly Parallel Computing. Computer, January 1982.

[2] C. G. Bell: Multis: A New Class of Multiprocessor Computers. Science 228, 1985.

[3] DAP Series Technical Overview. Active Memory Technology Ltd., 1988.

[4] Fortran 88: A Proposed Revision of Fortran 77. ISO/IEC JTC1/SC22/WG5 N357, 1989.

[5] R. P. Gabriel: Performance and Evaluation of Lisp Systems. Computer Systems Series Research Reports, MIT Press, 1985.

[6] R. P. Gabriel and J. McCarthy: Qlisp. in J. Kowalik, ed., Parallel Computation and Computers for Artificial Intelligence, Kluwer Academic Publishers, 1987.

[7] A. N. Habermann: Parallel Neighbor Sort. Technical Report, Carnegie-Mellon University, 1972.

[8] R. Halstead: Parallel Computing Using Multilisp. in J. Kowalik, ed., Parallel Computation and Computers for Artificial Intelligence, Kluwer Academic Publishers, 1987.

[9] W. D. Hillis: The Connection Machine. The MIT Press series in artificial intelligence, 1985.

347

[10] R. Jonathan, W. Clinger, et.al.: Revised Revised Revised Report on the Algorithmic Language Scheme. ACM SIGPLAN Notices 21(12), 1985.

[11] S. Komae, H. Miyoshi, M. Matsuda, S. Takeoka, and T. Yuasa: Experimental Implementation of Massively Parallel Computer PM1. Proceedings of "Fire County" mini-symposium on parallel processing, 1988 (in Japanese).

[12] J. Miller: MultiScheme: A Parallel Processing System Based on MIT Scheme. TR-402, Laboratory for Computer Science, MIT, 1987.

[13] MP-1 Family Data-Parallel Computers. MasPar Computer Corporation, 1989.

[14] G. W. Sabot: The Paralation Model. The MIT Press, 1988.

[15] C. L. Seitz: The Cosmic Cube. Comm. ACM, Vol.28, No.1, 1985.

[16] G. L. Steele: Common Lisp the Language. Digital Press, 1984.

[17] G. L. Steele and W. D. Hillis: Connection Machine LISP: Fine-Grained Parallel Symbolic Processing. Proceedings of the 1986 ACM Conference on Lisp and Functional Programming, 1986.

[18] T. Yuasa: Common Lisp Drill. Academic Press, 1987.

[19] T. Yuasa, H. Waki, T. Kawana, and S. Komae: PMLisp Manual. Technical Report, Yuasa Laboratory, Toyohashi University of Technology, 1989 (in Japanese).

[20] T. Yuasa: Design and Implementation of Kyoto Common Lisp. Journal of Information Processing, 1990 (to appear).

DESIGN OF THE SHARED MEMORY SYSTEM FOR MULTI-PROCESSOR LISP MACHINES AND ITS IMPLEMENTATION ON THE EVLIS MACHINE

Hiroshi YASUI, Toshikazu SAKAGUCHI, Kohichi KUDO & Nobuyuki HIRONISHI

Department of Applied Physics, Faculty of Engineering, OSAKA University

Abstract

This paper presents the design and implementation of a shared memory system to reduce memory interference in an environment of a multi-processor system composed of a pool of EVAL-II processors and aiming for high performance through parallel evaluation of a Lisp program.

The performance of a multi-processor system varies with many factors. We introduced several useful methods to control the granularity of the processes, and have confirmed their effect through dynamic measurement on the multi-processor Lisp machine - the EVLIS machine -. Dynamic measurement also shows that the interference of access to shared memory is a difficult problem. We show a solution for this problem in two different ways. First, we modified the form of the free cell list to reduce the interference from exclusive operation. Second, we present the design of the shared memory system which solves the memory interference on read accesses in particular, and its implementation with the use of conventional memory chips and TTL's.

1. Introduction and project history

This paper describes the design and implementation of the memory systems of the EVLIS machine, a multi-processor system of a pool of EVAL processors. The EVLIS machine project started in 1978. The proposed architecture of the machine is in the paper published in 1979[1]. As a new approach to attain higher speed with a LISP system, the EVLIS machine had been proposed[2], [3]. We built up the EVLIS machine system, and it reached essentially its present form in early 1982[4]; by that time it had successfully run a number of bench mark programs in the Lisp 1.5[5]. Because most of the Lisp users have almost no practical experience with the language of Parallel Lisp computing like Multilisp[6] or QLisp[7] and cannot achieve dynamic control of parallel lisp machine, the language and command for control of the EVLIS machine has been simplified accordingly. The EVLIS machine takes care of all the problems related with parallel execution, including the allocation of the processors, the communication among processors and the correct propagation of side effects caused by the execution of list-altering functions such as "rplaca". Consequently, the EVLIS machine executes automatically parallel processing even if the program is written in the grammar of the Lisp 1.5 which does not support parallel processing.

The EVLIS machine's lisp was designed to rapidly execute Lisp programs with an interpreter named "Parallel Lisp"[8], [9]. Parallel Lisp has the control organs for increased efficiency in parallel execution; a specifier "*" is used to specify functions which have arguments to be evaluated in parallel, and a level control command/function for the control of the level of depth in the execution of a nested task program; the regulation list in its argument list is for control of granularity according to task size. Further support for fast execution comes from a Parallel Lisp compiler that allows the above control mechanism; this is described in papers on the parallel Lisp compiler for the EVLIS machine[10].

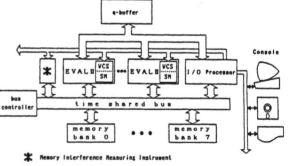

✱ Memory Interference Measuring Instrument

Figure 1. Block diagram of the EVLIS machine

2. Structure of the EVLIS machine

Figure 1 is a simplified block diagram of the EVLIS machine. The EVLIS machine consists of the EVAL-II processors[11], the Q-buffer[3], the I/O processor and the shared memory system with the hardware for measuring the memory interference (Memory Interference Measuring Instrument)[8].

2-1. EVAL-II processor

We designed the EVAL-II without commercial micro processors, using only TTL's and conventional memory chips. The EVAL-II has a micro instruction time of 100nsec, an 8K words(48-bits) writable control storage (WCS), a 4K words(21-bits) scratch pad memory (SM), CAR-CDR operation facility and diagnostic interface. The EVAL-II hardware is implemented with approximately 620 shottky TTL IC's on 10 circuit boards.

2-2. Q-buffer

The Q-buffer holds a queue of the pointers to the processes; the processes which are spawned by each processor during the execution and are not processed yet.

2-3. Main memory and time shared bus

The main memory is used for storing list cells (car portion and cdr portion; 20 bits each), atoms, the frames and the mail boxes for the communication between processors. Frames hold the environment in the parallel processing, a child frame holds the environment of each argument which is to be evaluated in parallel, and a mother frame holds the environment of the function which has arguments to be evaluated in parallel. Access between the processors and memory banks is multiplexed by the time division (50 nsec.) of the main memory bus. The competition among banks for a bus are controlled by the priority sequence (which changes at every 50 nsec.). Access is allowed to the bank by the highest priority level. The competition among the processors for a bank is controlled by the fixed priority level of each processor. Access to the car portion or cdr portion in a cell is handled separately. In section 5, you will find the hardware architecture of the new memory system in which all of the processors can read the banks of the system simultaneously.

3. Classification of the total time of execution

To make the refinements of machine architecture, we classify the total time of execution into five states and investigate each up for the sake of decrease of some factors which are obstacles for rapid execution of the Parallel Lisp[8][9].

(a) T_e : T_e is the essential time to execute any given S-expressions.

(b) T_h : Overhead time. T_h is the excess time to perform extra operations for the parallel version of any program in Parallel Lisp compared with the serial version of the programs, and consists of the following two items. One is the time to manipulate processes. The other is the time to access the shared memory, such as the exclusive operation of the "cons" function . Of course, this can be obtained in a static way. First, the time T_l is measured, which it takes only one active processor using a parallel version of a whole program. Consequently, T_l is expected not to contain any other states caused by the dynamic properties (c), (d) and (e) which follow below, then $T_h = T_l - T_e$.

(c) T_w : T_w is the time when processors are idle in the case where no processes exist in the queue which holds pointers to frames.

(d) T_i : T_i is the wait time for more than one processor accessing the shared memory simultaneously. This can be broken down further into two details. One is the wait time arising from exclusive operations for accessing certain kinds of resources, which cannot be handled exclusively at the logical level. The other is the wait time on the hardware structure which allows only one processor access at any time. This is incurred for physical reasons. To observe these phenomena, we have equipped the equipment Memory Interference Measuring Instrument (MIMI), which can measure both the interference on the time sliced bus (physical only) and one on each memory bank (both physical and logical).

(e) T_o : Others. More over, there are two kinds of the time of the whole execution. One is the time to communicate with other processors on interrupt, and the other is the time to wait as processors access the Q-buffer at the same time.

To execute the Parallel Lisp rapidly, we will concentrate on the above five states through the execution of Parallel Lisp. We must reduce T_h, T_w, T_i and T_o.

4. Controlling the granularity of processes in Parallel Lisp and its result

In this section, we present three methods which reduce T_h and T_w developed by us for this project. After that, we show the results.

4-1. Controlling the granularity of processes in Parallel Lisp

To reduce T_w, we can easily make Parallel Lisp produce finer processes. But, that grows T_h because the total number of processes grows. We hence try to optimize both T_h and T_w, and had implemented three methods on the Parallel Lisp interpreter and the Parallel Lisp compiler.

(a) specification for parallel evaluation

we must choose the kinds of functions which produce coarse granularity processes on being executed in parallel. This is supplied only by adding an "*" in front of the function name, which is done with an editor, or the like, as shown in Figure 2 below.

(b) Controlling the depth of function calling

We define the depth of function calling from a form as "level". If the magnitude of the level achieves the threshold set by the user beforehand, Parallel Lisp does not produce any child processes for any deeper level and executes sequentially. See Figure 3, where the way to set the threshold is found.

(c) the regulation list for parallel evaluation

This is developed to make the granularity of processes uniform and to spread side-effects among processes properly. An example is shown in Figure 4 . First, evaluate arg1, then produce two processes to be executed in parallel, one is made from arg2 and arg4 with priority in this sequence, another is made from arg3.

```
(fn arg1 arg2 arg3 arg4)
    ==>
            (* fn arg1 arg2 arg3 arg4)
```

Figure 2. Illustration of "*"

```
(setlimit 8)    ......    in function form
/setlimit 8     ......    in command form
```

Figure 3. Declaration of the level

```
(* (1 ((2 4) 3)) fn arg1 arg2 arg3 arg4)
```

Figure 4. Illustration of the regulation list

4-2 Dynamic measurements on Parallel Lisp

With the methods described above, we obtained dynamic measurements on the Parallel Lisp interpreter and the Parallel Lisp compiler. The experiment uses the program, called "List-Tarai-4"[12]. Against this benchmark, the EVLIS machine takes 151.7msec., 107.3msec. and 87.3msec. under the serial version of the program, the parallel version of the program with two processors and with three processors, respectively (EVAL-II's clock time was 100nsec., clock time of main memory was 61nsec.). The measurements were carried out in an environment with three EVAL-II's and its clock time was 200nsec., clock time of main memory was 100nsec., clock time of the Q-buffer was 50 nsec. And total time of the execution is normalized with the time of the sequential execution. In Figure 5, details of each execution time against control by depth for function calling for parallel evaluation, on the compiled object. The level and the regulation list were 4 and ((1 (2 3))), respectively.

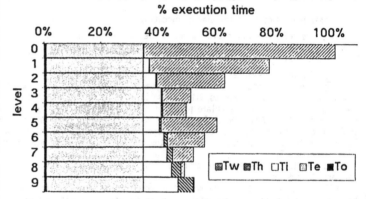

Figure 5. Detail of execution time against the level (compiler)

5. Some strategies to reduce Ti

Concerned with the shared memory system, we have confirmed the effect using the two methods described before. But to achieve greater speed on Parallel Lisp, we tried to reduce T_i, and that we had developed two approaches to do so[8].

5-1 Reduce Ti by memory management

In stead of the conventional free cell list, we proposed a structure like a bunch of bananas, which we call the free cell bunch[13]. We show this on Figure 6. Suppose that ■ is the length of a list which constructs the free

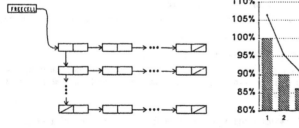

Figure 6. Structure of the free cell bunch

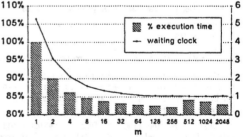

Figure 7. Execution time and waiting clock at the memory bank

cell bunch, the times of the exclusive operations becomes about $1/m$ of the time of "cons". We called this strategy "Parallel-cons".

Figure 7 shows variation of the execution time and waiting clock on a memory bank against m. The level and the regulation list are 8 and $((1\ 2\ 3))$, respectively.

5-2 Reduce T_i based on memory architecture

To make the memory read operation rapid, we tried to design a multi port memory. In Lisp machine, until now there is the only architecture of the 3 parallel read port registers on the FLATS machine[14]. But our new memory is shared, enable more than one processor to read simultaneously, and composed of conventional memory chips and TTL's. Its architecture is shown in Figure 8. A new memory bank contains $2 \times n$ sub-banks. Each processor is assigned two of them, and can access via an interface module and a read-write change over switch. One of the sub-banks is used for read access, another for write access, and they change their roles rapidly at predescribed memory alternation intervals.

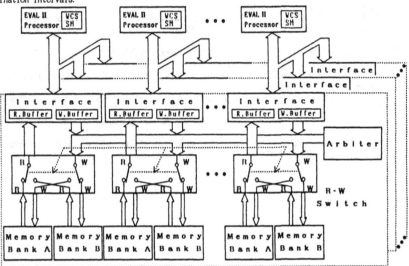

Figure 8. Block diagram of new memory system

On write access, until it has completed, the new memory bank does these three steps.

1. A processor writes data on its write buffer contained in its own particular interface module.

2. All write sub-banks are affected by this write buffer.

3. After the uses of sub-banks have been changed, i. e. all write sub-banks are affected again, they then become read sub-banks for the next cycle.

2. and 3. need arbitration. But if the write buffer of some processor is empty, the processor can write on it without any interference.

On read access, each processor can read simultaneously at any time except when one of the processors locks the new memory bank, and when operations arise from write accesses that have not been completed yet. In Figure 9, some resulting data for read access operations with this memory are shown. The function "mmread5" acts read accesses five times as many as the function "mmread" which reads lists frequently.

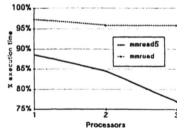

Figure 9. Execution time for a lot of read operations

6. Conclusion

In this paper, we have described some of the techniques and architectures used to improve the performance of the parallel lisp machine - EVLIS machine -. The results of the effect of the new multi port memory was affected by programs which contained many read operations. And, the results of the "parallel cons" system was affected by programs which contained many write operations. In the case of the system combined with the above hardware and software architectures, we were able to take a step forward to the rapid processing of various Lisp programs on the parallel lisp machine. After this workshop, we tried to make sure of a peak at level 5 in Figure 5, and get the fact that only one process is running and is relatively coarser than others. This is caused by the characteristic of List-Tarai-4. Furthermore, in later days on this workshop we presented the proposal and implementation of the hybrid system of the neuro engines (a engine is constructed with dataflow architecture and memory module) and the EVLIS machine[15].

References

1. YASUI, H., et al. : Architecture of EVLIS machine and Dynamic measurements of Parallel Processing in Lisp. IPSJ SIG Reports 79-SYM-10-4, 1979, (in Japanese).
2. YAMAMOTO, M. : A Survey of High level Language Machine in Japan. Computer 14, 7, 1981, 68-78.
3. YASUI, H. : A survey of LISP Machine. IPS Japan 23, 8, 1982, 757-772, (in Japanese).
4. MAEGAWA, H., et al. : Constitution of List-Evaluation Processor on EVLIS Machine, IPSJ SIG Reports 82-SYM-17-1, 1982, (in Japanese).
5. McCARTHY, J., et al. : LISP 1.5 Programmer's Manual. MIT press, Cambridge, Mass., 1962.
6. HALSTEAD, R. H. : Implementatoin of Multilisp:Lisp on a multiprocessor. Conf. record 1984 ACM Symp. Lisp and functional programming(Aug. 1984), 9-17.
7. GABRIEL, R. P. : Qucue-based Multi-processing Lisp. Conf. rocord 1984 ACM Symp. Lisp and functional programming (Aug. 1984), 25-44.
8. NISHIKAICHI, H., et al. : Dynamic Measurements and Evaluation of LISP Parallel-Processing Machine -EVLIS Machine-. IPSJ SIG Reports 85-SYM-31-9, 1985, (in Japanese).
9. OKUNO, H. G. : The Report of The Third Lisp Contest and First Prolog Contest. IPSJ SIG Reports 85-SYM-33-4, 1985.
10. YASUDA, H., et al. : Parallel Lisp Compiler for the EVLIS Machine. IPSJ SIG Reports 87-SYM-40-3, 1987, (in Japanese).
11. MAEGAWA, H., et al. : Fast LISP Machine and List-Evaluation Processor EVAL II-Processor Architecture and Hardware Configuration. J. Inf. Process. 8, 2, 1985, 121-126.
12. OKUNO, H. G. : The proposal of the benchmarks for The Third Lisp Contest and The First Prolog Contest. IPSJ SIG Reports 85-SYM-28-4, 1985, (in Japanese).
13. KUDO, K., et al. : The Management of free-storage on the EVLIS Machine. Proc. 37th Annual Convention IPS Japan(Sep. 1988), 675-676, (in Japanese).
14. GOTO, E., et al. : Disign of a LIsp Machine - FLATS. Conf. record 1982 ACM Symp. Lisp and functional programming (Aug. 1982), 208-215.
15. YASUI, H., et al. : The hybrid system of the Parallel Lisp machine -EVLIS machine- and Neuro engines. Proc. 39th Annual Convention IPS Japan(Oct. 1989), 1750-1751, (in Japanese).

TOP-1 Multiprocessor Workstation

Norihisa Suzuki

IBM Research, Tokyo Research Laboratory

5-19, Sanbancho, Chiyoda-ku, Tokyo, JAPAN 102

Abstract

IBM Tokyo Research Laboratory developed a high-performance multiprocessor workstation, TOP-1, which is currently running with a multi-threaded multiprocessor version of AIX operating system, as a research prototype to study and clarify the multiprocessor architecture design points as well as to study operating systems, compilers, and application programs for multiprocessor workstations.

The novel architectural features of TOP-1 are the 2-way interleaved dual bus for providing wider bus bandwidth, the effective message broadcasting mechanism for asynchronous communications, the mechanism to allow several different snoop protocols to coexist at a time, and the high-speed and fair arbitration mechanism. In particular, it has a statistics unit that enables us to obtain statistics on operating system and application programs running on the real machine.

Keywords: Cache coherency, Snoop cache, Shared-bus multiprocessor, Interprocessor communication, Queuing model simulation

1 Introduction

A multiprocessor workstation is a very promising solution to the continuously increasing need for personal computing power.

IBM Research, Tokyo Research Laboratory has for the last two years been working on a multiprocessor workstation. As the research vehicle we developed a high-performance multi-processor workstation, TOP-1 (Figure 1), to evaluate the multiprocessor architecture design points as well as to do research on operating systems, compilers, and applications for multiprocessor workstations. Our laboratory has been focusing on applications of the future computer systems by prototyping advanced applications such as machine translation, advanced graphics rendering, image database, formula manipulations programs, CAD tools and robot task control systems, and expert system applications for manufacturing. Al of them are highly resource intensive computation. We would like these applications to run much faster using personal supercomputers.

There are a number of reasons to believe that the future of personal supercomputing will be multiprocessing. One is that major applications of workstations can be easily parallelized and can run faster. Many of them require the displaying of excellent 3D graphics pictures and the manipulation of them on the screen at real time speed. All the pipeline stages of graphics processing can easily parallelized. There are also research results showing that the programming environments can be easily parallelized. Furthermore, the recent advance in parallelizing compiler techniques is making it easier to transport existing applications in uniprocessing language to multiprocessors.

Because of the ease of software development and porting, we decided to build a tightly-coupled, shared memory multiprocessor workstation. The workstation we built, TOP-1, is currently running with multi-threaded, multi-processor version of AIX(TM). Top-1 is a ten-way multiprocessor with Intel 80386 and Weitek 1167. Each processor has 128Kbytes of snoop cache [1][2][3][4]. Besides, it has a number of other unique architectural features. In particular, it has a statistics unit that enables us to obtain various statistics on operating systems and applications.

In this paper, important architectural features of TOP-1 will be described and be evaluated based on the running system. In Chapter 2, hardware organization of TOP-1 will be described. In Chapter 3 and Chapter 4, design considerations on the memory system and the inter-processor communication mechanisms are discussed. In Chapter 5, we will evaluate the design, especially the memory system design, based on the actually measured performance results by using a special assist hardware embedded in the cache and bus subsystem of the TOP-1 processors. And in Chapter 6, we will briefly report the current status of the software design and development.

2 System Organization

One principal objective of the project is to study hardware and software trade-off. We know very little about the behavior and characteristics of software on a shared memory multiprocessor. Therefore, we would obtain run-time statistics, analyze them, and reflect them for the design of future multiprocessor. For this purpose, hardware statistics unit was built, which can gather various statistics from the real machine without any run-time overhead.

Furthermore, we would like to change the hardware algorithms by the compiler or operating system using the statistics. We have implemented multiple snoop cache protocols and variable priority arbitration mechanisms.

2.1 Preliminary Performance Evaluation

We were most concerned with the design parameters for the memory system. In tightly-coupled multiprocessor systems with a large number of processors, bus conflicts caused by cache misses, cross cache update or invalidate, and hot-spots caused by locks implemented as shared data are known to degrade system performance in earlier experiences of tightly-coupled multiprocessors such as IBM System/370.

Therefore, we carried out extensive performance evaluation using instruction trace data of existing 80386 applications as well as queuing model simulator to determine the design parameters. The results of the performance prediction is shown in Figure 2.

2.2 Hardware Architecture Overview

As shown in Figure 3, TOP-1 is organized around a shared common bus. Attached to the bus are up to 128Mbyte system memory and up to 11 identical processing units, each of which consists of an Intel 80386 and a Weitek 1167 Floating-point coprocessor, 128Kbyte snoop cache, and the system bus interface. Also on this bus is the Micro Channel

Interface adapter to connect PS/2 Model 80 through the Micro Channel standard. By this Interface adapter, PS/2 Model 80 can directly access the TOP-1 shared bus, and therefore the shared memory. This allows users to use various standard I/O adapters as I/O devices of TOP-1. We built a special adapter for hard disk on TOP-1 bus to realize a high-performance and large capacity of hard disk subsystem. All 11 processors are completely identical, but one processor is dedicated for the hard disk management by connecting the processor to the hard disk control adapter via the local bus extension.

The unique architectural features are the 2-way interleaved dual 64-bit buses that are supported by two snoop cache controllers per processor card, communication and interruption to notify asynchronous events each other, a mechanism to allow several different snoop coherency protocols to coexist in the system at a time and also to be changed by software for each memory operation, and an efficient arbitration mechanism that allows prioritized quasi-round-robin service with a distributed control.

3 Memory System

The memory system uses like other small-scale, tightly-coupled multiprocessors snoop cache. The unique aspects are that the snoop cache supports four different protocols.

3.1 Snoop Cache

The cache controller is implemented using IBM CMOS gate array with 16,000 gates. It controls the TOP-1 snoop cache as well as the shared bus interface including the arbitration logic. It also includes a hardware unit to collect statistics such as program characteristics, snoop cache performance, and bus performance.

A number of snoop cache protocols have been proposed, but none of them is considered to be the best for all the situations[5]. Coherency protocols can be generally classified into update and invalidate protocols, each of which is suitable for different situations.

The novel aspect of TOP-1 is that it supports both update and invalidate protocols. Furthermore, each type of protocol can have two protocol modes: standard and block I/O. In total, there are four kinds of protocol combinations, all of which can coexist in the system at a time, and on each processor the protocol can be dynamically changed by programs for each memory operation.

TOP-1 update type protocol updates the cache line in other caches if the line is shared and write operation is performed on the line in the cache, which is similar to those of Xerox's Dragon[1] and DEC's Firefly[2] protocols. Taking into consideration of the difference in cycle times of the cache memory and the main memory, TOP-1 update protocol is designed to optimize the cache performance. Update protocols generally yield good performance in situations with a small number of shared blocks and high contentions for those blocks like semaphores.

Top-1 invalidate protocol invalidates all the shared lines in other caches when write occurs like Berkeley's SPUR[3]. This is suited in situations with a large number of shared lines and low contentions for them. Invalidate protocol is also preferred for the case where a process is migrated from one processor to another processor, and as the result, lines belonging to that process are shared between two caches even though the lines only include local data. In this case, it is obviously better to invalidate cache lines in the original processor when first bus write occurs for the shared block.

The block I/O mode is prepared for consecutive block data transfer to and from external devices so as not to leave lines no longer needed in the cache. Data transfer with input and output devices must be carefully designed, so as to maintain data consistency in the multicache system. In TOP-1, we solved the problem by using snoop cache also for input and output subsystem. However, the new problem with this method is the increase of shared data in the system after data transfer. The sharing will increase particularly after paging from a hard disk. The data read into the shared memory also resides in the I/O controller's cache, even after the line has been actually used by a requesting processor. Write overhead for shared lines adds extra bus traffic and makes the system performance worse. The block I/O mode of cache protocol forces the cache line of the transmitting processor to be written back to the memory and to be invalidated after the last word of the line has been written from the I/O. This mode of protocol is useful for avoiding unnecessary shared lines in the cache.

3.2 System Bus

As mentioned previously, the common shared bus is a limiting resource which degrades the system performance, even though a private cache is added to each processor to reduce the bus traffic. Therefore in the system bus design, goals are to maximize the bus bandwidth and to minimize the access latency delay with a reasonable cost and complexity of hardware.

To maximize the bus bandwidth, there are a number of design choices for the bus transfer mechanism such as ECL high-speed bus, block transferred bus, and packet controlled bus. The block transferred bus can provide higher bus bandwidth if the memory cycle time is much larger than the bus cycle time, because one memory cycle is required for the first word and only one bus cycle for each consecutive word. Actual situation of the current technology, however, shows that the memory cycle time is only a few times larger than the bus cycle (e.g., 62.5ns for the bus and 187.5ns for the memory in the case of TOP-1), because the bus cycle time has a technical limit in conjunction with buffer delays and clock skews. In that case, the data width of the bus and the shared memory should usually be as wide as the line size, since it is desirable to transmit an entire line in one transfer cycle time.

Packet controlled bus complicates snoop mechanism and increases the latency delay time for a bus access

Instead of using the block transferred bus or packet controlled bus, TOP-1 uses 2-way interleaved buses with a 64-bit data width each. The bus, the shared memory, and the cache are all interleaved in 2-way with an 8-byte boundary. Each bus is independently arbitrated. Consequently, the shared bus can provide 85Mbyte/sec effective data transfer rate both for read and write operations.

Another novel aspect of the shared bus design is the high-speed and fair-served arbitration mechanism. Using a unique high-speed arbitration mechanism which we named a modified back-off arbitration mechanism, the shared bus is arbitrated in one bus cycle or 62.5ns at 16MHz operation in a distributed manner. Instead of an encoded arbitration code which is used for a so-called back-off mechanism, each requester issues a decoded code on the bus according to the current request priority. This mechanism allows high-speed arbitration, because no feed-back loop is required for settling the arbitration bus. After somebody gets an access right of the bus as the result of the arbitration, every arbiter counts up its arbitration code, so that a quasi-round-robin service is realized. Moreover, each arbiter can set its priority range so that the arbitration code is rotated within the range specified. Since this mechanism allows processors to be classified into several groups with regard to the arbitration priority range, it is useful for process scheduling. For instance, some processors on which high priority processes are allocated can run faster by assigning high priority range.

4   Multiprocessor Synchronization

In general, multiprocessor synchronization can be implemented by shared variables on the shared memory or hardware message passing mechanisms. TOP-1 implements both mechanisms.

4.1   Inter-Processor Signaling

Although TOP-1 is a shared-memory multiprocessor, a message passing hardware mechanism is also provided to allow the processors to communicate asynchronous events or to interrupt each other. Messages are broadcasted to any processors specified as the destinations. Then, the message is received or discarded by the destination processors, according to the state of the receiver's buffer. We provide two kinds of message passing protocols. One is Everybody messaging and the other is Anybody messaging.

In the Everybody messaging, all receivers receive the message and generate an interrupt to the processor only when all the specified receivers can receive the message. If any one of the receivers cannot receive the message, no interrupt is generated. The sender can detect whether the message was received or not with no overhead. This mechanism is important for an operating system to maintain TLB consistency and also for multiprocessing programming languages to interrupt executions of other processors.

In the Anybody messaging, each receiver receives the message and generates an interrupt only when it can receive the message. The sender detects that the message was successfully received only when one or more receivers can receive the message. This mechanism is useful for asking some service to any processor that is ready to serve.

4.2   Bus Locking

We made 80386 locked-instructions, which correspond to 'test-and-set', to work correctly. Namely when 80386 issues a locked-instruction like XCHG, the bus is locked with no regard to the cache hit or miss, and the effects of the memory modification is broadcasted instantaneously. This enables us to implement spin lock. A process which enters a critical region makes a spin lock on a semaphore by read loop. When the contents of the semaphore is changed, then the process issues a locked-instruction to make sure that nobody is in the critical region.

We also support Lock and Unlock instructions that locks and unlocks the bus respectively. Higher level synchronization operations such as enqueue and dequeue can be easily implemented by a sequence of few instructions, if the sequence can be treated as an atomic operation. In order to assure the atomicity, the bus has to be locked while such an instruction sequence is being executed.

5 Design Evaluation

The cache behavior of uniprocessor has been extensively analyzed so far in the literature, and some papers have reported cache performance of tightly coupled multiprocessors [5][6][7]. However, most of them were using software simulators driven by statistical parameters or traces like as our preliminary performance evaluation described in Sec. 2.1.

We, however, used the hardware statistics unit built in the TOP-1 cache/bus controller to evaluate the actual performance of the cache and bus.

Using the statistics unit, we can gather the statistical data from the real machine without any overheads. Furthermore, we can accurately count the number of fetches including instructions which are prefetched but are not actually executed due to the prefetch queue flush. When a program has a tight loop which is intensively executed, normal software simulations should give an incorrect result, because the effect of the prefetch queue can not be taken into account. The statistical events captured by this unit are:

1. number of memory access (instruction fetch, data read, and data write, separately),

2. cache hit ratio,

3. number of write access to the private data and to the shared data,

4. number of write back for dirty lines,

5. number of cache updated/invalidated by snoop,

6. number of dirty data reply to the requester, and

7. number of processors waiting for the bus.

In addition to that, we can dynamically specify the address range (page base) in which the statistics unit counts the numbers shown above. Thus, if the program mapping is previously known or can be controlled by the operating system, we can selectively gather the various statistics corresponding to the high-level language source code. For example, we can get the cache hit ratio only for the kernel, only for the synchronization variables, or only for processing data.

We used Dhrystone and a matrix multiplication as the standard benchmark program to evaluate TOP-1 hardware performance. We compiles C Dhrystone using MetaWare High C compiler. TOP-1 executed 5710 Dhrystones/sec by one processor and 57000 Dhrystones/sec by ten processors independently. Therefore, there was no performance degradation even when ten processors were running in parallel. It's because the working set of Dhrystone is quite small and the processors can run completely independently with each other in this case, since TOP-1 has 128K byte cache on each processor. Matrix multiplication could be a good example to evaluate the shared memory multiprocessor operating system. We have obtained preliminary results by running UNIX 'make', an image edge detection program, and a ray tracing program on TOP-1. TOP-1 configuration for this evaluation was: one kernel processor, five user processors and one special processor dedicated to statistics gathering. The results by running those three programs showed that the cache miss ratio was very low. Cache miss ratio of all these programs are less than 3%, and moreover, most of then are less than 1%.

6 Software Systems

6.1 Operating System

We created a multiprocessor, multi-threaded operating system based on UNIX. We modified uniprocessor UNIX by adding locks and process dispatcher for multiple processors. The kernel runs on one processor, the processor which controls disks. There is one ready process queue and one free processor queue so that whenever a processor becomes free, the first ready process will run on it.

Thread is an independent flow of control that shares the address space with other threads belonging to the same process. We have implemented two kinds of threads: kernel-controlled thread and user-controlled thread. Kernel-controlled thread, like thread of Mach, is implemented in the kernel so all the operations on the thread are kernel calls . Therefore, they are safe but slow. On the other hand, user-controlled threads are like coroutines and the dispatch routines run at the user level. Therefore, it is unsafe but fast.

6.2 Compilers

We are supporting C and FORTRAN on TOP-1. Calls to the subroutines in the thread package can be added to C programs, and the programs will run in parallel. The version of FORTRAN running on TOP-1 is IBM PARALLEL FORTRAN with parallel constructs such as DOALL. PARALLEL FORTRAN programs are put through a preprocessor called PREFACE which transforms input to ordinary FORTRAN programs with library calls. This is put through the regular FORTRAN compiler to be ready to run on TOP-1.

We have also created multiprocessor Common Lisp. We added parallel constructs such as FUTURE to Kyoto Common Lisp. The unique feature of this multiprocessor Common Lisp is that it has a real-time, multiprocessor garbage collector. It is real-time because the memory allocation terminates in short, bounded amount of time. It is parallel processing because the garbage collector runs on more than one processor. It is based on Minsky's parallel garbage collection algorithm, which spreads the tasks of mark and sweep garbage collection evenly over memory allocation operations.

6.3 Measurement

The unique point of TOP-1 over other shared-memory multiprocessors which are built using snoop cache is that is has measurement hardware built into the cache controller so that various cache and bus statistics can be obtained. These are now used to evaluate hardware design decisions. We believe it will be very useful to tune the application software in the future. We have built software monitor that runs on one dedicated processor in parallel to the application program. Hardware monitor consists of counters that can be configured to measure different parts of the multiprocessor by software control. When one of the counters overflow, an interrupt is raised and the software takes over to read the values of the counters.

One of the earliest measurement results were on the comparison of two snoop cache protocols. TOP-1 has an invalidate protocol and an update protocol. The invalidate protocol invalidates all the copies of the cache line in other cache when a write occurs to the shared cache line. The update protocol updates all the copies of the cache line in other cache. The results are in almost all the cases the invalidate protocol is superior. This is because the invalidate protocol eliminates unnecessary sharing.

7 Conclusion

We described unique hardware features and software systems of the multiprocessor workstation TOP-1. The design choices we made for TOP-1 were described and evaluated. The unique architectural features are the 2-way interleaved dual bus, the message broadcasting mechanisms for the effective asynchronous communication, the mechanism to allow several different snoop protocols to coexist at a time, and the efficient and fair arbitration mechanism. Especially the statistics unit is useful for evaluating the design precisely and for controlling various aspects of hardware mechanism dynamically for better preformance. It will be also valuable for developing highly paralell software. The hardware is now fully operational and several machines have been built.

We built a multiprocessor operating system based on the IBM AIX (TM) operating system, which is compatible with UNIX(TM). This operating system is also operational. Moreover, we are designing and implementing parallel processing languages and applications.

Acknowledgements

I am grateful to all the people who contributed to software and hardware projects of TOP-1.

In particular Shigenori Shimizu, Motokazu Hozumi, Toshiaki Kurokawa, Arch McKellar, and Tsutomu Kamimura had managing responsibilities.

The author also would like to thank Prof. Takayasu Ito for his recommendation and encouragement to write this paper.

References

[1] R. R. Atkinson and E. M. McCreight, *The Dragon Processor*, Proceedings of Second Int'l Conference on ASPLOS, pp. 65-69, 1987.

[2] C. P. Thacker and L. C. Stewart, *Firefly: a Multi-Processor Workstation*, Proceeding of Second Int'l Conference on ASPLOS, pp. 164-172,1987.

[3] R. Katz, et.al., *Implementing a Cache Consistency Protocol*, Proceedings of the 12th Int'l Symp. on Computer Architecture, IEEE, pp. 276-283,1985.

[4] J. R. Goodman, *Using Cache Memory to Reduce Processor-Memory Traffic*, Proceedings of the 10th Int'l Symp. on Computer Architecture, IEEE, p. 124-131,1983.

[5] J.Archiballd and J. L. Baer, *Cache Coherence Protoocos: Evaluation Using a Multiprocessor Simulation Model*, ACM Trans. on Computer Systems, Vol. 4, No. 4, pp. 273-298,1986.

[6] R. L. Lee, et.al., *Multiprocessor Cache Design Considerations*, Proceedings of the 14th Annual Int'l Symp. on Computer Architecture, pp. 253-262,1987.

[7] S. J. Eggers and R. H. Katz, *A Characterization of Sharing in Parallel Programs and Its Application to Coherency Protocol Evaluation*, Proceedings of the 15th Annual Int'l Symp. on Coomputer Architecture, pp. 373-382, 1988.

Figure 1. TOP-1 Workstation

Instruction Fetch Rate	0.38 word/cycle
Data Access Rate	0.35 word/cycle
Private Data : Shared Data	0.90 : 0.10
Clean Line : Dirty Line	0.70 : 0.30
80386 (20MHz no wait)	5MIPS

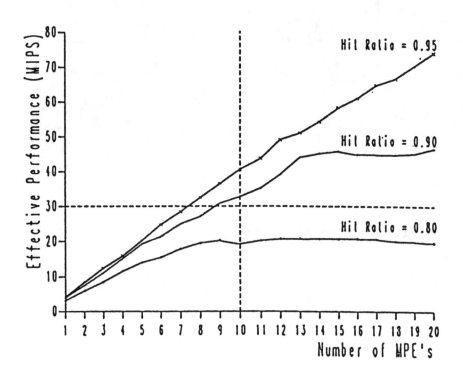

Figure 2. Effective Performance

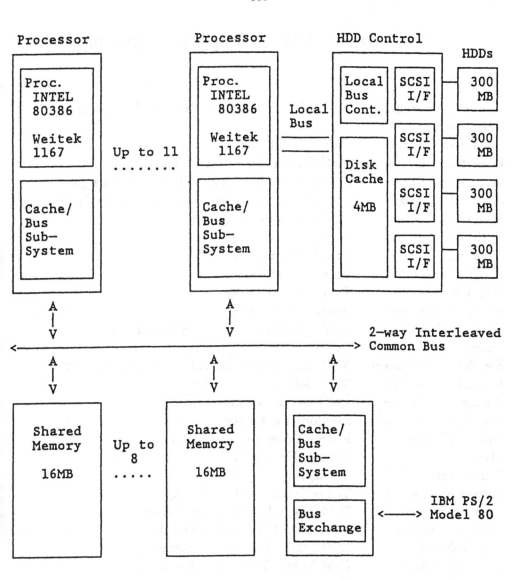

Figure 3. TOP—1 System

List of Workshop Participants

Zahira Ammarguellat	University of Illinois at Urbana-Champaign
Ron Goldman	Lucid, Inc.
Eiichi Goto	University of Tokyo
Robert H. Halstead	DEC Cambridge Research Lab
W. Ludwell Harrison	University of Illinois at Urbana-Champaign
Ryuzo Hasegawa	Institute for New Generation Computer Technology
Motokazu Hozumi	IBM Tokyo Research Laboratory
Norio Irie	Tohoku University
Takayasu Ito	Tohoku University
Hideya Iwasaki	University of Tokyo
Morry Katz	Stanford University
Robert R. Kessler	University of Utah
David A. Kranz	MIT Laboratory for Computer Science
James S. Miller	Brandeis University
Ken-ichiro Murakami	NTT Electrical Communications Laboratory
Hiroshi G. Okuno	NTT Software Laboratory
Randy B. Osborne	DEC Cambridge Research Lab
Joseph D. Pehoushek	Stanford University
Dan L. Pierson	Encore Computer Corporation
Masahiko Sato	Tohoku University
Carol Sexton	Lucid, Inc.
Etsuya Shibayama	Tokyo Institute of Technology
Norihisa Suzuki	IBM Tokyo Research Laboratory
Akikazu Takeuchi	Mitsubishi Central Research Lab
Ikuo Takeuchi	NTT Basic Research Laboratory
Tomoyuki Tanaka	IBM Tokyo Research Laboratory
Mario Tokoro	Keio University
Kazunori Ueda	Institute for New Generation Computer Technology
Akihiro Umemura	Tohoku University
Shigeru Uzuhara	IBM Tokyo Research Laboratory
Takuo Watanabe	Tokyo Institute of Technology
Joseph S. Weening	Stanford University
Hiroshi Yasui	Osaka University
Akinori Yonezawa	University of Tokyo
Taiichi Yuasa	Toyohashi University of Technology

Vol. 408: M. Leeser, G. Brown (Eds.),Hardware Specification, Verification and Synthesis: Mathematical Aspects. Proceedings, 1989. VI, 402 pages. 1990.

Vol. 409: A. Buchmann, O. Günther, T. R. Smith, Y.-F. Wang (Eds.), Design and Implementation of Large Spatial Databases. Proceedings, 1989. IX, 364 pages. 1990.

Vol. 410: F. Pichler, R. Moreno-Diaz (Eds.), Computer Aided Systems Theory – EUROCAST '89. Proceedings, 1989. VII, 427 pages. 1990.

Vol. 411: M. Nagl (Ed.), Graph-Theoretic Concepts in Computer Science. Proceedings, 1989. VII, 374 pages. 1990.

Vol. 412: L. B. Almeida, C. J. Wellekens (Eds.), Neural Networks. Proceedings, 1990. IX, 276 pages. 1990.

Vol. 413: R. Lenz, Group Theoretical Methods in Image Processing. VIII, 139 pages. 1990.

Vol. 414: A.Kreczmar, A. Salwicki, M. Warpechowski, LOGLAN '88 – Report on the Programming Language. X, 133 pages. 1990.

Vol. 415: C. Choffrut, T. Lengauer (Eds.), STACS 90. Proceedings, 1990. VI, 312 pages. 1990.

Vol. 416: F. Bancilhon, C. Thanos, D. Tsichritzis (Eds.), Advances in Database Technology – EDBT '90. Proceedings, 1990. IX, 452 pages. 1990.

Vol. 417: P. Martin-Löf, G. Mints (Eds.), COLOG-88. International Conference on Computer Logic. Proceedings, 1988. VI, 338 pages. 1990.

Vol. 418: K. H. Bläsius, U. Hedtstück, C.-R. Rollinger (Eds.), Sorts and Types in Artificial Intelligence. Proceedings, 1989. VIII, 307 pages. 1990. (Subseries LNAI).

Vol. 419: K. Weichselberger, S. Pöhlmann, A Methodology for Uncertainty in Knowledge-Based Systems. VIII, 136 pages. 1990 (Subseries LNAI).

Vol. 420: Z. Michalewicz (Ed.), Statistical and Scientific Database Management, V SSDBM. Proceedings, 1990. V, 256 pages. 1990.

Vol. 421: T. Onodera, S. Kawai, A Formal Model of Visualization in Computer Graphics Systems. X, 100 pages. 1990.

Vol. 422: B. Nebel, Reasoning and Revision in Hybrid Representation Systems. XII, 270 pages. 1990 (Subseries LNAI).

Vol. 423: L. E. Deimel (Ed.), Software Engineering Education. Proceedings, 1990. VI, 164 pages. 1990.

Vol. 424: G. Rozenberg (Ed.), Advances in Petri Nets 1989. VI, 524 pages. 1990.

Vol. 425: C.H. Bergman, R.D. Maddux, D.L. Pigozzi (Eds.), Algebraic Logic and Universal Algebra in Computer Science. Proceedings, 1988. XI, 292 pages. 1990.

Vol. 426: N. Houbak, SIL – a Simulation Language. VII, 192 pages. 1990.

Vol. 427: O. Faugeras (Ed.), Computer Vision – ECCV 90. Proceedings, 1990. XII, 619 pages. 1990.

Vol. 428: D. Bjørner, C. A. R. Hoare, H. Langmaack (Eds.), VDM '90. VDM and Z – Formal Methods in Software Development. Proceedings, 1990. XVII, 580 pages. 1990.

Vol. 429: A. Miola (Ed.), Design and Implementation of Symbolic Computation Systems. Proceedings, 1990. XII, 284 pages. 1990.

Vol. 430: J. W. de Bakker, W.-P. de Roever, G. Rozenberg (Eds.), Stepwise Refinement of Distributed Systems. Models, Formalisms, Correctness. Proceedings, 1989. X, 808 pages. 1990.

Vol. 431: A. Arnold (Ed.), CAAP '90. Proceedings, 1990. VI, 285 pages. 1990.

Vol. 432: N. Jones (Ed.), ESOP '90. Proceedings, 1990. IX, 436 pages. 1990.

Vol. 433: W. Schröder-Preikschat, W. Zimmer (Eds.), Progress in Distributed Operating Systems and Distributed Systems Management. Proceedings, 1989. V, 206 pages. 1990.

Vol. 435: G. Brassard (Ed.), Advances in Cryptology – CRYPTO '89. Proceedings, 1990. XIII, 634 pages. 1990.

Vol. 436: B. Steinholtz, A. Sølvberg, L. Bergman (Eds.), Advanced Information Systems Engineering. Proceedings, 1990. X, 392 pages. 1990.

Vol. 437: D. Kumar (Ed.), Current Trends in SNePS – Semantic Network Processing System. Proceedings, 1989. VII, 162 pages. 1990. (Subseries LNAI).

Vol. 438: D. H. Norrie, H.-W. Six (Eds.), Computer Assisted Learning – ICCAL '90. Proceedings, 1990. VII, 467 pages. 1990.

Vol. 439: P. Gorny, M. Tauber (Eds.), Visualization in Human-Computer Interaction. Proceedings, 1988. VI, 274 pages. 1990.

Vol. 440: E.Börger, H. Kleine Büning, M. M. Richter (Eds.), CSL '89. Proceedings, 1989. VI, 437 pages. 1990.

Vol. 441: T. Ito, R. H. Halstead, Jr. (Eds.), Parallel Lisp: Languages and Systems. Proceedings, 1989. XII, 364 pages. 1990.

This series reports new developments in computer science research and teaching – quickly, informally and at a high level. The type of material considered for publication includes preliminary drafts of original papers and monographs, technical reports of high quality and broad interest, advanced level lectures, reports of meetings, provided they are of exceptional interest and focused on a single topic. The timeliness of a manuscript is more important than its form which may be unfinished or tentative. If possible, a subject index should be included. Publication of Lecture Notes is intended as a service to the international computer science community, in that a commercial publisher, Springer-Verlag, can offer a wide distribution of documents which would otherwise have a restricted readership. Once published and copyrighted, they can be documented in the scientific literature.

Manuscripts

Manuscripts should be no less than 100 and preferably no more than 500 pages in length.
They are reproduced by a photographic process and therefore must be typed with extreme care. Symbols not on the typewriter should be inserted by hand in indelible black ink. Corrections to the typescript should be made by pasting in the new text or painting out errors with white correction fluid. Authors receive 75 free copies and are free to use the material in other publications. The typescript is reduced slightly in size during reproduction; best results will not be obtained unless the text on any one page is kept within the overall limit of 18 x 26.5 cm (7 x 10½ inches). On request, the publisher will supply special paper with the typing area outlined.
Manuscripts should be sent to Prof. G. Goos, GMD Forschungsstelle an der Universität Karlsruhe, Haid- und Neu-Str. 7, 7500 Karlsruhe 1, Germany, Prof. J. Hartmanis, Cornell University, Dept. of Computer Science, Ithaca, NY/USA 14853, or directly to Springer-Verlag Heidelberg.

Springer-Verlag, Heidelberger Platz 3, D-1000 Berlin 33
Springer-Verlag, Tiergartenstraße 17, D-6900 Heidelberg 1
Springer-Verlag, 175 Fifth Avenue, New York, NY 10010/USA
Springer-Verlag, 37-3, Hongo 3-chome, Bunkyo-ku, Tokyo 113, Japan

ISBN 3-540-52782-6
ISBN 0-387-52782-6